SHARON D. NELSON, DAVID G. RIE

LOCKED DOWN

2ND EDITION

PRACTICAL INFORMATION SECURITY FOR LAWYERS

ABALAW
PRACTICE
DIVISION
The Business of Practicing Law

Commitment to Quality: The Law Practice Division is committed to quality in our publications. Our authors are experienced practitioners in their fields. Prior to publication, the contents of all our books are rigorously reviewed by experts to ensure the highest quality product and presentation. Because we are committed to serving our readers' needs, we welcome your feedback on how we can improve future editions of this book.

Cover design by Kelly Book/ABA Design.

Printed in the United States of America.

20 19 18 17 16   5 4 3 2 1

Library of Congress Cataloging-in-Publication Data

Names: Nelson, Sharon D., author. | Ries, David G., 1949– author. | Simek, John W., author. | American Bar Association. Law Practice Division, sponsoring body.
Title: Locked down : Practical information security for lawyers / Sharon D. Nelson, David G. Ries, and John W. Simek.
Description: 2e. | Chicago, Illinois, : American Bar Association, 2016. | Includes index.
Identifiers: LCCN 2016001351 (print) | LCCN 2016001479 (ebook) | ISBN 9781634254144 (softcover : alk. paper) | ISBN 9781634254151 ()
Subjects: LCSH: Law offices—Computer networks—Security measures—United States. | Computer security—United States.
Classification: LCC KF320.A9 N45 2016 (print) | LCC KF320.A9 (ebook) | DDC 340.068/4—dc23
LC record available at http://lccn.loc.gov/2016001351

Dedication

AUTHORS NELSON AND SIMEK dedicate this book to our ever-growing family. We dedicate this book to Kelly and Jeff Ameen, JJ and Sarah Simek, Sara and Rob Singmaster, Jason and Natalia Simek, Kim and Chris Haught and Jamie and Lauren Simek as well as grandchildren Samantha, Tyler, Lilly, Henry, Jordan, Cash, Evan, and Parker. You all fill our lives with joy.

Author Dave Ries dedicates this book to his wife, Debbie, and to Dave Jr. and Jenelle Ries, grandchildren Ellie, Dave III and Lucy, Chris and Liz Ries and granddaughter Marah. Their love and support have made this book and much more possible.

Contents

About the Authors

Sharon D. Nelson, Esq.

Sharon D. Nelson is the president of Sensei Enterprises, Inc. Ms. Nelson graduated from Georgetown University Law Center in 1978 and has been in private practice ever since. She now focuses exclusively on electronic evidence and information security law.

Ms. Nelson, Mr. Simek and their Sensei colleague Maschke are the coauthors of the 2008–2016 editions of *The Solo and Small Firm Legal Technology Guide: Critical Decisions Made Simple*. Ms. Nelson and Mr. Simek are also coauthors of the previous edition of this book and *Encryption Made Simple for Lawyers* (American Bar Association 2015). Additionally, Ms. Nelson and Mr. Simek are coauthors of *The Electronic Evidence and Discovery Handbook: Forms, Checklists and Guidelines* (American Bar Association 2006). Ms. Nelson is a coauthor of *How Good Lawyers Survive Bad Times* (American Bar Association 2009). Their articles have appeared in numerous national publications, and they frequently lecture throughout the world on electronic evidence and legal technology subjects.

Ms. Nelson and Mr. Simek are the hosts of the Legal Talk Network's *Digital Detectives* podcast, and Ms. Nelson is a cohost of the Legal Talk Network's *The Digital Edge: Lawyers and Technology* podcast.

Ms. Nelson was the president of the Virginia State Bar June 2013–June 2014 and the president of the Fairfax Law Foundation July 2014–July 2015. She served as president of the Fairfax Bar Association 2004–2005. She has been the chair of the ABA's TECHSHOW Board and is a past chair of the ABA's Law Practice Management Publishing Board. She currently serves on the governing council of the ABA's Law Practice Management Division and as chair of its Professional Development Board.

She is a graduate of Leadership Fairfax and served on the governing council of the Virginia State Bar for nine years. She served as the chair of the VSB's Unauthorized Practice of Law Committee and on both its Technology Committee and its Standing Committee on Finance. She currently serves the Virginia State Bar as chair of its Future of Law Practice Committee, chair of its 2016 TECHSHOW, and chair of its Better Annual Meeting Committee. She is a member of the ABA, the Virginia State Bar, the Virginia Bar Association, the Virginia Trial Lawyers Association, the Virginia Women Attorneys Association, and the Fairfax Bar Association.

She has served as a court-appointed special advocate (CASA) for abused and neglected children for the past five years.

David G. Ries, Esq.

David G. Ries is of counsel in the Pittsburgh office of Clark Hill PLC, where he practices in the areas of environmental, technology, and data protection law and litigation. He has used computers in his practice since the early 1980s and since then has strongly encouraged attorneys to embrace technology—in appropriate and secure ways. He practiced with Thorp Reed & Armstrong, LLP from 1974 until the firm merged with Clark Hill in 2013. Mr. Ries served as chair of Thorp Reed's Technology Committee and E-Discovery and Records Management Group for over 10 years. He served two terms as a member and chair of a Hearing Committee for the Disciplinary Board of the Supreme Court of Pennsylvania. He received his JD from Boston College Law School in 1974 and his BA from Boston College in 1971.

Mr. Ries's technology practice has included a variety of litigation matters, including major systems implementation disputes, and advising clients on a number of technology law issues such as hardware, software, and cloud services agreements, information security and privacy compliance, information governance, e-discovery, and electronic contracting.

He has been a long-term active member of the ABA Law Practice Division and has served on Division Council, the Professional Development Board, the ABA TECHSHOW Planning Board, the Publishing Board, and the Ethics and Professionalism Committee. He is a member of the ABA Section of Science and Technology's Information Security Committee and the ABA Business Law Section's Cyberspace Law Committee. He is a member of the Board of Directors of InfraGard Pittsburgh and a member of the Information Systems Security Association and the ILTA LegalSEC Council.

Mr. Ries frequently speaks and writes on ethics, legal technology, and technology law topics for legal, academic and professional groups. He is a coauthor of *Encryption Made Simple for Lawyers* (American Bar Association 2015) and the first edition of *Locked Down: Information Security for Lawyers* (American Bar Association 2012) and a contributing author *to Information Security and Privacy: A Legal, Business and Technical Handbook,* Second Edition (American Bar Association 2011) and *Information Security for Lawyers and Law Firms* (American Bar Association 2006). He is the editor of *E-Discovery,* 3rd edition (Pennsylvania Bar Institute 2014) and earlier editions.

John W. Simek

Mr. Simek is the Vice President of Sensei Enterprises, Inc., an information technology, digital forensics and information security firm located in Fairfax, Virginia. Mr. Simek has a national reputation as a digital forensics technologist and has testified as an expert witness throughout the United States. He holds a degree in engineering from the United States Merchant Marine Academy and an MBA in finance from Saint Joseph's University.

Mr. Simek holds the prestigious CISSP (Certified Information Systems Security Professional) and EnCase Certified Examiner (EnCE) certifications. He is also a Certified Handheld Examiner, Certified Novell Engineer, Microsoft Certified Professional + Internet, Microsoft Certified Systems Engineer, NT Certified Independent Professional, and a Certified Internetwork Professional. Mr. Simek is also a member of the High Tech Crime Network as well as the American Bar Association and the Fairfax Bar Association.

He currently provides information technology support to over 200 area law firms, legal entities, and corporations. He is a cohost of the Legal Talk Network's *Digital Detectives* podcast and a coauthor of *Encryption Made Simple for Lawyers* (American Bar Association 2015), *Locked Down: Information Security for Lawyers* (American Bar Association 2012), *The Electronic Evidence and Discovery Handbook: Forms, Checklists and Guidelines* (American Bar Association 2006), *Information Security for Lawyers and Law Firms* (American Bar Association 2006), the 2008–2016 editions of *The Solo and Small Firm Legal Technology Guide: Critical Decisions Made Simple* (American Bar Association 2008–2016) and a contributing author of *E-Discovery,* 3rd edition (Pennsylvania Bar Institute 2014). He is a frequent author and speaker on information security, legal technology, and electronic evidence throughout the country.

Mr. Simek also serves on the 2016 ABA TECHSHOW Planning Board and blogs at **youritconsultant.senseient.com**. He is also a court-appointed special advocate (CASA) for abused and neglected children.

Acknowledgments

We EXPRESS OUR APPRECIATION to Chris Ries, an information security professional who currently focuses on software security. Chris has made numerous helpful suggestions for this book and shared his security insights with us over the years.

We thank Jeff Salyards, our editor, who survived the whirlwind of this new assignment with patience and good humor.

Thanks go to Allison Shields, the chair of the Law Practice Division's Publications Board, who has been encouraging and helpful throughout the publication process.

We are greatly appreciative of the efforts of JoAnn Hathaway, our project manager, who reviewed the book and made a number of helpful and insightful suggestions.

Sharon Nelson
Dave Ries
John Simek

Introduction

BE SURE AND CHECK *Appendix P (Updates) for late-breaking news that happened after the original manuscript was sent to our editor and before the final proof was due.*

What a difference four years makes! Since the first edition of this book was published in 2012, there has been a veritable revolution in information security. Four years ago, many lawyers were largely ignoring information security, content in general to delegate the responsibility for it to someone else.

No more. These days, lawyers are really running scared. So many law firms have been breached. And as the saying goes, there are two kinds of law firms; those who have been breached and those who will be breached.

Today, when we lecture on encryption, we have standing-room-only audiences. The people who come to our live sessions radiate a hunger for cybersecurity knowledge. They are genuinely scared—and perhaps more so because of the new versions of the ABA Rules of Professional Conduct 1.1 (Competence) and 1.6 (Confidentiality of Information), which together require competent and reasonable measures to safeguard information relating to clients. As we go to press, twenty states have adopted the changes to those rules—and it is clear that more states will be following suit soon.

This book, like its predecessor, sets out to make information security a little more approachable. There needs to be some technical explanations of course, but we've tried to keep the technical stuff to a minimum so that the average attorney can genuinely understand the security demons that are out there and how to defend against them. Forewarned really is forearmed.

Much of it is not a DIY sort of project, especially if you've suffered a security breach. We make no attempt in this book to document the myriad steps that a professional information security expert would take. Our objective is to teach the data security basics in language that can be readily understood by lawyers. If you're in over your head, you'll hear us advise you again and again to seek professional help. Even among those who call themselves experts, there is often a shocking knowledge shortfall or a failure to keep up with current developments, which happen with dizzying speed!

One of the greatest difficulties of information security is that it is a moving target and that target has been moving faster and faster in the last four years. The landscape of threats and defenses to those threats changes so quickly that last year's (and sometimes even yesterday's) knowledge is woefully inadequate to combat today's perils. "Eternal vigilance" is absolutely required for those of us who deal with data security issues.

Still, there are guiding principles that remain largely the same. We have tried to break information security down into digestible segments, knowing that some attorneys will pick up this book with concrete questions about specific security areas. Common questions we hear include:

1. How do I secure my computers and networks?
2. What constitutes a strong password today?
3. Are passwords dead?
4. What is multifactor authentication?
5. How do I secure my smartphone?
6. Do I need to encrypt all my devices?
7. Can I safely use my laptop at Starbucks?
8. And the big kahuna is the question about what is ethically required—and our answer to that has evolved.

We are now at the point where encryption should be deployed by all attorneys, where appropriate—and it is so cheap and simple to use these days—even to encrypt e-mail—that there is no longer any reason not to do so.

If your interests in cybersecurity are narrow, you should be able to find what you're looking for by scanning the Table of Contents. We would urge lawyers, however, to take a broad interest in the security of data because they have, unlike the general public, professional and ethical requirements to safeguard client data.

Although lawyers are all aware of ABA Model Rule 1.6 (and we have an entire chapter on an attorney's duties to safeguard confidential data), the challenge is how to keep client data secure in the digital era. It isn't easy and continues to become more difficult. The paper world was much simpler to lock down. The earlier days of information security, while challenging, were also simpler than today. It is much more difficult now that we have moved from individual computers and isolated networks, with limited connectivity, to the Internet, almost universal connectivity, and widespread mobility. The term du jour is now "cybersecurity"—focusing on cyberspace and connectivity. But cybersecurity is actually a subset of information security because individual computers, servers, and mobile devices need to be protected from threats like loss, theft, and unauthorized physical access—distinct from cyberspace. Information security can be expensive—and it takes time and effort to understand it—and you will never finish learning because threats, defenses and technology morph constantly.

Are lawyers doing enough to safeguard law firm and client information? Our opinion is that many are not. Here are a few reasons we hold that opinion.

- ◆ The FBI reported at a legal technology conference in 2013 that they are seeing hundreds of law firms being increasingly targeted by hackers.
- ◆ Mandiant, now part of InfoSec giant FireEye, reported that 7% of the breaches it investigated in 2014 involved law firms.
- ◆ Another report noted that 80% of the one hundred largest law firms, by revenue, had been hacked between 2011 and 2015.
- ◆ At a meeting of large firm information security experts from Washington, D.C., most admitted that they had been breached—and that they were aware from their colleagues that others had been breached as well.
- ◆ Even with the dismal record of reporting law firm data breaches, we still learn of them in the press and informally—and we will detail some of them for you.

While data breaches can happen despite reasonable (or even stronger) security, the frequency of law firm data breaches and reports on how some of them have occurred suggest that many attorneys have not been employing reasonable safeguards. Why do many otherwise competent lawyers fail so miserably in protecting firm and client data? Here are some of the reasons.

- Lack of knowledge—they simply need education—and many of them don't know they need education.

- The "it can't happen here" mentality is flatly wrong. Since the FBI issued an advisory in 2009 warning that law firms were specifically being targeted by identity thieves and by those performing business espionage, it has continued to meet with large firms to preach the gospel of information security. We were, in the earlier day, worried about cybercriminals, China, and other state-sponsored hackers, which continue to be major threats. Thanks to Edward Snowden, we now know that we also need to worry about surveillance by our own government.

- According to press reports, lawyers and law firms are considered "soft targets"; they have high-value information that's well organized and frequently have weak security—although we are happy to report that, at least at large firms, cybersecurity is now a very high priority.

- Though there are many low cost/free measures that solo and small-firm lawyers can take to protect sensitive data, true information security, including hardware, software, training, etc. is expensive. Protecting the security of client data can present a big burden for solos and small law firms. This does not take away a lawyer's ethical duty, however, and it is one reason the authors lecture so often on computer security. Once a lawyer sees the most common vulnerabilities, he or she can take remedial steps—or engage an IT (information technology) consultant to do those things that are beyond the lawyer's skill.

- The need for vigilance never stops. You cannot secure your data once and think you're finished; the rules of information security change on close to a daily basis. Certainly, someone in the firm needs to keep up with changes on a regular basis or the firm needs to engage a security consultant to do periodic reviews. While the necessary frequency of security assessments depends on the size of the firm, the sensitivity of the information, and identified threats, it is our judgment that mandatory assessments should be conducted at least annually. And clients are beginning to demand self-audits and third-party audits of law firm security. Sensei has never seen a client who passed such an audit on the first go-round. In fact, they don't even understand the audit questions, which doesn't bode well for the results.

In the paper world, keeping client data confidential was easy and cheap. In the digital era, abiding by this particular ethical rule is often hard and expensive, but it must be done. We hope this book takes some of the "hard" away and also helps lawyers understand how many inexpensive steps exist to protect data without breaking the bank.

Often, this subject seems so dense and unapproachable that lawyers have suffered the "ostrich effect" and simply bury their heads in the sand. Fortunately, as clients have woken up to the potential vulnerabilities of law firms, they are demanding much, much more in the way of security—it is clear that clients are leaving firms that don't meet their security expectations. Hence, the fairly sudden desire to get secure. In the AmLaw 200, firms are now reported to be spending an average of 1.9% of gross revenues on cybersecurity—and that can amount to as much as $7 million a year. That is an extraordinary change, to say the least.

In the American Bar Association's 2015 Legal Technology Survey Report, it was clear that data breaches continue to increase, especially at larger firms, which no doubt hold the most valuable information, although smaller firms handle valuable data too, such as those practicing family law. We'll go into more details from that survey later in this book.

We certainly are seeing an increasing focus on information security in large firms, but the trend as you go down the food chain is still too often to "hope for the best" after taking a minimum of security precautions. Smaller law firms are not used to budgeting for information security, and yet this is clearly mandated in a world where technology rules us all. The crown jewels of law firms are their electronic files, and yet many law firms guard them sloppily.

And if you think your insurance policy will protect you, think again. Be sure to read the chapter on cyberinsurance. We can just about guarantee that what you read in that chapter will make you go through your current policy with a fine-tooth comb and consider the need for additional coverage.

For years, we've been warning lawyers that it's not a question of whether law firms will become victims of successful hacking attacks; rather, it's a matter of when. We pointed to incidents of dishonest insiders and lost or stolen laptops and portable media. We've now reached the when—there have been numerous disclosed incidents of successful hacking attacks on law firms by cybercriminals and foreign governments and interests, and there is now a threat of NSA surveillance of law firms. The truth is that everyone is watching—governments (including our own), hackers, cybercriminals, competing businesses, etc.

We have even heard of two cases in 2015 where law firms allegedly hired hackers in order to glean information about their opponents in a case—

more on those later—and any like-minded lawyers need to read our ethics chapter!

We have included in this book security approaches, products, and solutions about which we have sufficient experience or information to include them. There are additional security approaches, products, and solutions that we could not cover in a book of this length. In addition, there will certainly be changes in technology, threats, and available safeguards, some rapidly evolving. Because of future developments and additional options, it is best to make sure that you have current information when selecting and implementing safeguards. Ask someone who stays current on information security or check reliable online resources. Chapter 27, Additional Information Resources, includes a comprehensive list of sources, starting with our Short List of Favorite Information Sources.

We have set out in this book to provide practical advice in a condensed format. We hope that sharing some of the InfoSec "war stories" by way of examples will serve to make a business case for genuinely focusing on information security on a regular basis and, depending on the size of your firm, the sensitivity of the information and your area of practice, making sure that sufficient funds, time, and attention are allocated to protecting your firm's data.

CHAPTER ONE

Current Developments Affecting Law Firm Information Security

What's New in the Data Breach World?

Sometimes recent statistics provide compelling reasons to take a hard look at your law firm security. So let's start there.

The 2015 Verizon Data Breach Investigations Report contained a wealth of information. A few of the highlights from the report:

- The year 2014 had 2,122 confirmed data breaches and 79,790 security incidents in which information was compromised.
- RAM scraping has become major—this kind of malware was present in many high-profile retail breaches.
- In 60% of the cases, attackers were able to compromise an organization within minutes.
- A hefty 23% of recipients open phishing messages and 11% click on attachments.
- An amazing 50% open e-mails and click on phishing links within the first hour after transmission.
- Out of tens of millions of mobile devices, the number of ones infected with truly malicious exploits was negligible, only 0.03%—that surprised a lot of folks.

One lesson gained from the report was crystal clear: Humans need to be trained—and trained again—in safe computing and social engineering!

The Symantec 2015 Internet Security Threat Report stated that ransomware that encrypts data (offering you the decryption key for a price) increased by a whopping 4000% in 2014. Law firms across the United States have been struck by variants of CryptoLocker and CryptoWall, the most common forms of ransomware. While not technically a data breach, there have been instances where data was sent out of servers before it was encrypted. And if your data is encrypted, you won't suffer much of a loss of business continuity, assuming you can restore from a nonimpacted backup or get the decryption key. For information about how to properly engineer your backups so they cannot be encrypted by ransomware, see the Backup and Business Continuity chapter.

A report issued by data protection firm SafeNet in 2014 looked at 237 data breaches worldwide—encryption was in place in just 10 of the 237 breaches. As you'll see later in this chapter and others, we are beginning a forced march toward encryption—forced in large part by our clients.

What New Developments Have Affected Law Firm Information Security?

The Legal Services Information Sharing and Analysis Organization (LS-ISAO) Services was launched in 2015 with the help of the financial services industry whose fifteen-year-old Financial Services Information Sharing and Analysis Center (FS-ISAC) is considered one of the most mature ISAC/ISAO groups today.

Applications to become members of the group were sent to about two hundred law firms (mostly large firms)—membership is $8000 per year. This is obviously a work in progress, and unlikely to help solo, small, and midsized law firms.

ISACs and ISAOs provide an official mechanism for sharing information about the latest cyberattacks and threats spotted targeting specific industries, for instance, and include databases of the threats and vulnerabilities for their members, as well as provide conferences and other ways for members to interact and share their experiences to better collaborate in fighting cybercrime and cyber espionage actors. Among the industries with ISACs and ISAOs are the aviation, the defense industrial base, emergency services, IT, maritime, nuclear energy, real estate, public transportation, retail, and water utilities.

Initially, the LS-ISAO will offer members access to intel-sharing list servers with threat information and advisories from vendors and government agencies as well as member-to-member threat sharing and other resources.

Ultimately, it will evolve to offer portal services for members to securely and anonymously share threat intelligence, as well as the Holy Grail of intel-sharing—automating the use of the information into the member's internal security tools and networks.

Also in 2015, the Federal Trade Commission (FTC) had its authority over corporate information security confirmed by the Third Circuit Court of Appeals. The court ruled that the FTC could proceed with a lawsuit alleging that hotel chain Wyndham Worldwide Corp. shoulders some of the responsibility for three breaches from 2008–2010 in which hackers allegedly stole more than 619,000 credit and debit card numbers.

Without a national data breach law, the FTC has stepped in, bringing more than fifty data-security cases based on its authority to take action against unfair and deceptive business practices. Most cases have settled, but not this one. The FTC alleged that Wyndham failed to implement reasonable safeguards, including leaving consumer data unprotected by firewalls and using outdated software that couldn't receive security updates (and how many law firms are currently running Microsoft XP, Office 2003, or Windows Server 2003?). Wyndham argued that the FTC was overreaching and trying to hold businesses, rather than hackers, responsible for cyber theft. The Third Circuit three-judge panel disagreed in a unanimous ruling. Given the number of attacks, the court found that it should have been painfully apparent to Wyndham that a court could find its conduct potentially problematic.

There is no reason that the FTC couldn't take similar action against law firms.

In 2014, the Federal Communications Commission (FCC) ventured into data security litigation levying a $10 million fine against two telecom companies that allegedly stored personally identifiable customer data online without firewalls, encryption, or password protection.

The two companies, YourTel America and TerraCom, share the same owners and management. From September 2012 to April 2013, according to the FCC, the companies collected information online from applicants to Lifeline, the government's telephone subsidy program for poor Americans. To prove their eligibility, potential customers are asked for personal information, including Social Security numbers, dates of birth, addresses, names, and drivers' license numbers.

The companies apparently didn't store the data securely or destroy it when users had proved their eligibility. Allegedly they kept the information on publicly accessible Internet servers. Reporters found the data with a Google search and notified the FCC. As many as 300,000 customers may have been affected by the unsecured data.

Travis LeBlanc, the FCC's top enforcement official said, "[T]his is the first data security action [by the FCC], but it will not be the last." Yet another federal agency is now policing the information security of businesses.

After we learned that the 2014 Target data breach came about because of access to the corporate network by an HVAC vendor whose network had been compromised, vendor management (investigating their security and severely restricting their level of access) has become a hot topic at all information security conferences. Law firms may have many third-party vendors (including cloud providers) and need to feel comfortable that they are managing the risk of any access to their networks carefully and ethically.

You might consider requiring in third-party contracts, employee security training, insurance coverage for data breaches, a warranty of performance up to "industry standards," a warranty about backups and data integrity, indemnification in the event of a breach, a duty to notify you and to investigate any suspected security incident, and a warranty to protect confidential information. The power to negotiate will be a major factor as the Davids of the world have little leverage against the Goliaths.

As we go to publication, the Cyber Information Sharing Act (CISA) has been signed by the President. Most of the privacy-related amendments were defeated.

The Electronic Freedom Foundation posted that the bill is "fundamentally flawed due to its broad immunity clauses, vague definitions, and aggressive spying authorities."

Although CISA has been promoted as a cybersecurity bill, it does nothing to actually improve the effectiveness of security systems. It's concerned instead with increasing the amount of information that corporations share with government and protecting those companies from liability for violating customers' privacy. Privacy advocates believe it makes it much easier for the U.S. government to spy on its own companies. Humorously or sadly, *Wired* magazine gave the bill "An F for Security But an A+ for Spying." Great recommendation, huh?

Even the Department of Homeland Security has said CISA is terrible, warning in a letter to Sen. Al Franken that it could harm privacy and increase "complexity and difficulty" in responding to cybersecurity threats. An amendment to narrow the definition of a "cyber threat indicator"—used by companies in deciding which data to pass to federal agencies—was also left out.

The final CISA language does not address problems that caused recent highly publicized computer data breaches, problems like unencrypted files, poor computer architecture, failure to update and patch servers and software, and poorly trained or untrained employees opening phishing e-mail and clicking on malware links. Computer security specialists opposed the bill as did academics, privacy organizations and major tech companies including Google, Microsoft, Apple, Twitter, Yahoo, Amazon, and Dropbox. The Business Software Alliance and the Computer & Communications Industry Association also opposed CISA.

The Rise of Spear Phishing

Spear phishing is targeted phishing. Phishing is a way of attempting to acquire information such as usernames, passwords, and credit card details by masquerading as a trustworthy entity in an electronic communication. It is more likely to succeed because it often appears to come from someone you trust and the subject line is designed to engage the recipient. For instance, it might say: "Check this out—you're quoted in this article." An appeal to ego is often successful. Once in, the perpetrators will look for administrator accounts and the accounts of managing or senior partners to allow them to move freely within the larger network.

In a smaller firm, the e-mail's subject line might well read "Referring a case to you"; that would certainly be appealing. Spear phishing is regarded as the most effective way to breach a law firm—and it has gotten much more sophisticated. An e-mail might be signed with a partner's nickname (advance reconnaissance is growing) or mention something personal about the sender or the recipient. The English is likely to be very good.

Since the first edition of this book was published, we have seen phishing e-mails appear to come from court or from large, well-known law firms such as Reed Smith, Baker & McKenzie, Sidley Austin and Skadden Arps.

What can stop people from clicking on attachments in a spear phishing e-mail? Training, of course. For all those law firms who decline to do regular training because of the loss of billable time, note the following story.

In 2010, the Los Angeles-based firm Gipson Hoffman & Pancione survived an attempted spear phishing attack. The firm had filed a $2.2 billion copyright infringement suit on behalf of CYBERsitter LLC. Shortly thereafter, the firm noted a dramatic increase in suspicious e-mails.

The e-mails appeared to be sent from lawyers at the firm and included a message requesting the recipients to open an attachment. The firm's internal investigation revealed that the attachment contained malware which appeared to come from China. We can never say enough about the value of training, and training saved the firm from making an error in this case.

Attorneys and support staff had been warned to be on the lookout for suspicious e-mails after the suit was filed because the suit accused the Chinese government and several companies of stealing code from CYBERsitter's Internet filtering program. No one clicked on the attachments, so no malware bomb was detonated.

If you need more convincing, the FBI warned in 2015 that 7,000 U.S. businesses have reported $747 million in losses from such attacks, with an average loss of $130,000 since October 2013. And imagine how many were not reported.

The Bad Rap Law Firms Get on Information Security Is Slowly Changing

Security consultants consistently report that law firms are "stingy" about spending money on data security and lag far behind their corporate counterparts. Only at the largest firms does one generally find security specialists. To be sure, certified IT consultants know a good deal about information security, but they are not certified in it—and it is a niche expertise. Basic IT best practices may not constitute adequate data security.

Laws firms in general, and small firms in particular, are not very likely to have vulnerability assessments done. If they do have an assessment done, they often don't follow the best practice of repeating the assessments at regular intervals. But since the first edition of this book, times have changed. Now we see clients requiring that law firms fill out security assessments—anywhere between 25–60 pages in length. Somewhat comically, the lawyers generally don't even understand the questions they are being asked and they often don't know how to answer them. Once they bring in experts to assist, they don't like the answers because they know they will be unsatisfactory to clients. So they crowbar their firm wallet open, bite the bullet, and spend considerable monies. If they don't, they are pretty sure the client or prospective client will go elsewhere.

Sometimes they don't answer the questions accurately or fully. This is always a bad idea that may come back to haunt you, for both ethical and legal reasons, in the event of a data breach.

Firm-wide encryption is almost unheard of. We forget how our mobility has opened up new vulnerabilities. Flash drives, tablets, smartphones—all are easily lost or stolen, yet most lawyers do not encrypt these mobile devices. Sadly, many do not even go to the trouble to have a password or PIN on their devices. Now we have an opinion (Opinion 648, issued in 2015) from the State Bar of Texas which identifies several instances where encryption or some other method of security may be appropriate, including:

♦ communicating highly sensitive or confidential information via e-mail or unencrypted e-mail connections;

♦ sending an e-mail to or from an account that the e-mail sender or recipient shares with others;

♦ sending an e-mail to a client when it is possible that a third person (such as a spouse in a divorce case) knows the password to the e-mail account, or to an individual client at that client's work e-mail account, especially if the e-mail relates to a client's employment dispute with his employer;

♦ sending an e-mail from a public computer or a borrowed computer or where the lawyer knows that the e-mails the lawyer sends are being read on a public or borrowed computer or on an unsecure network;

♦ sending an e-mail if the lawyer knows that the e-mail recipient is accessing the e-mail on devices that are potentially accessible to third persons or are not protected by a password; or

♦ sending an e-mail if the lawyer is concerned that the NSA or other law enforcement agency may read the lawyer's e-mail communication, with or without a warrant.

The drive toward encryption has been fast recently—encrypting e-mail is now so simple and inexpensive that it may be unethical NOT to use it in many instances. If you are not encrypting your e-mail where appropriate, you certainly are not managing risk well—and you may find yourself in ethical hot water sooner rather than later. The revised Rule 1.1 and Rule 1.6, which so far have been adopted by twenty states are enough to potentially sustain a finding of unethical conduct where encryption should have been used and was not.

Security firm Sophos has often opined: "Dance like no one's watching. Encrypt like everyone is." They even turned that excellent advice into a T-shirt and a video.

More sobering was an interview that e-discovery company Logikcull did with information security expert Bruce Schneier—here's a snippet:

Logikcull: So let us ask you this: If you're a major law firm, and you turn out to be the next Sony or Ashley Madison—a victim, as you've written about, of organizational doxing—what are you supposed to do? What are the next steps if your data is dumped indiscriminately over the Internet?

Schneier: That's a good question. You tell me! At that point, it's too late for anything someone like me could do. I mean, you lament is what you do. You apologize is what you do. You accept the lawsuits is what you do. You go out of business is what you do.

We suspect these are some of the nightmares that plague law firm partners.

The large firms have stepped up their game, now spending an average of 1.9% of their gross revenues (up to $9 million per year) on information security. We are also seeing law firms achieve the ISO 27001 certification in an attempt to assure nervous clients that they are indeed paying careful attention to securing their data.

Okay, You're Convinced: What's Next?

First, understand how data breaches happen. Here are the most common ways:

- ◆ Devices with unencrypted data are stolen or lost.
- ◆ Security patches (software fixes issued by manufacturers) are not installed.
- ◆ Lawyers and staff are not trained about social engineering. One example is when someone pretends to be your IT provider and needs an employee's ID and password to "fix something."
- ◆ Malware comes in via an attachment or through social media (this would include the previously referenced spear phishing).
- ◆ Hackers, cybercriminals, and even nations find vulnerabilities in your network.

Since the old, innocent days of script kiddies, youngsters who copied malicious code easily available on the Internet, we now have more sinister types trying to get your information, and their skill set has vastly improved along with the tools available. Also, our networks are becoming more interconnected and complex all the time. As Philip Reitinger, the director of the National Cybersecurity Center in the Department of Homeland Security, has said, "Complexity is the enemy of security." As he further pointed out, if someone really wants your data, they stand an excellent chance of getting it.

The Department of Defense reports that its computers are probed hundreds of thousands of times each day. Now, your law firm probably isn't probed that often, but rest assured that it is being probed. Even the power of the cloud can be used by hackers to automate the probes.

Here's another reason to be wary from Alan Paller, the director of research at the SANS Institute: "If I want to know about Boeing and I hack into Boeing, there are a billion files about Boeing. But if I go to Boeing's international law firm, they're perfect. They're like gold. They have exactly what I'm looking for. You reduce your effort."

When an incident is over, sit down and do some serious Monday morning quarterbacking. You may have policies, procedures, or technology to change. Whatever your incident response plan, it probably did not wholly survive first contact with the enemy.

Never think that you can handle a data breach without expert involvement. Only an information security specialist can truly do that, which is one reason that we haven't included a complicated set of technical instructions here. For one thing, they'd be obsolete as soon as written—and for another, they would constitute a book in and of themselves.

The real answer to the "What's Next" question posed above is to read this book cover to cover. Take notes. Highlight. Then talk to your information technology consultants/employees and your information security consultants/employees. In all likelihood, you will find in the chapters to come questions you need to ask and faulty security that needs to be addressed. Training your employees should be constantly on your to-do list—so should monitoring the security of any vendors that have access to your network.

In the last edition of this book, we featured a quote from Daniel Garrie, the founding editor of the *Journal of Law & Cyber Warfare*. He said, "Law firms have no incentive to protect themselves from being attacked because, to date, there has been no meaningful financial impact to the law firms' bottom line." It strikes us that this is no longer the case. Nervous clients today will storm the exit doors of even major law firms if they believe the firm is not properly securing confidential data. As mentioned above, these days you may face a cybersecurity questionnaire or a third-party audit required by your clients and prospective clients. Want to get or keep the client? You're going to have to play by their rules.

CHAPTER TWO

Real-Life Law Firm Data Breach Nightmares

Can Your Law Firm Be Breached?

The answer is clearly yes. And even worse, it may have been breached and you don't know it.

So now you've read in the introduction to this book and seen that the FBI has warned law firms that they are targets for hackers and that the security firm Mandiant spent 7% of its time investigating data breaches in law firms during 2014. You've read that the American Bar Association's 2015 Legal Technology Survey Report shows that data breaches continue to increase, especially at larger firms. Finally, you've read that the AmLaw 200 are ponying up 1.9% of their gross revenues—as much as $7 million annually to secure their data.

We can no longer say, as we once did, that law firms are taking the "ostrich" approach to securing their data. Most firms acknowledge the problem and are attempting to deal with it.

Even the smaller firms understand that they hold data of interest to cyber-criminals, including Social Security numbers, birth dates, and credit card and other detailed financial information. This is precisely the kind of data that identity thieves are looking for. They routinely scan for vulnerable systems seeking such data.

Business espionage is another motivation for breaking into law firms. Perhaps you represent a company and a foreign interest or a competitor wishes to acquire business intelligence from you.

There is also the press. In 2011, the *News of the World* notoriously hacked into cell phones to feed the public's insatiable appetite for gossip. Consider all the interest in a murder trial—is it conceivable that a reporter might seek private information to get a scoop? Of course.

The Nonlawyer Breaches

It is an open secret that law firms have played breaches very close to the vest and demand strict confidentiality agreements from information security vendors who investigate any compromise of their networks. This means, of course, that there may be law firms out there that have chosen not to comply with state data breach notification laws, which frankly doesn't surprise us.

But it isn't as easy for large companies.

In 2013, suspected Russian hackers breached Target through a third-party HVAC vendor (and how well do you control access to your network by third-party vendors?). Seventy million customers were affected.

Home Depot reported in September 2014 that hackers had used malware to break into the company's system and had exposed fifty-six million debit and credit cards.

JP Morgan, the largest bank in the nation, was the victim of a high-profile cyberattack during the summer of 2014. The breach compromised the data of seventy-six million households—more than half of all U.S. households—and 7 million small businesses.

Sony was breached in November 2014 by the "Guardians of Peace" which demanded the cancellation of the film *The Interview* about a plot to assassinate North Korean leader Kim Jong-un. The ploy by the alleged North Korean hackers failed and the fairly dismal comedy died a fairly quick death on its own merits. But it was a major breach.

In January 2015, health care insurer Anthem, the second largest in the country, was breached by hackers suspected to be Chinese. Names, addresses, Social Security numbers, birth dates, and other personal information belonging to eighty million customers and employees were compromised.

In April 2015, the Office of Personnel Management was breached in what is widely reported to be the largest breach of government data ever. The estimated number of records compromised was 21.5 million including Social Security numbers, names, dates and places of birth, and addresses. The breach also involved the theft of detailed security clearance information. Very significantly, 5.6 million fingerprints were compromised, which made us wonder about the future security of biometrics.

While no law firms were impacted in that breach, note that federal judges and judicial employees were notified that they may have had their data compromised. The Administrative Office of the U.S. Courts has been sending updates to those whose data may have been leaked and also established an internal website with current information about the situation.

After all these breaches, you'd think we would see a national data breach law—with teeth. But it appears as far away as ever after years of debate and likely some very successful lobbying by those who might suffer at the hands of a strong federal law. Even state attorneys general and privacy advocates oppose a national law if it includes preemption because they want to keep states in control of data breach laws.

Law Firm Data Breaches

You might wonder why there aren't more data breaches listed here. As we mentioned in the Introduction, a lot of law firm data breaches go unreported. In fact, the *New York Times* revealed in 2015 that a Citigroup report chided law firms for not disclosing data breaches. Privately, we have heard of many law firm breaches—but are not at liberty to discuss them. But there are good lessons to be learned from some of the breaches that have become public.

2015: Atkinson, Andelson, Loya, Ruud & Romo

SC Magazine reported in July 2015 that California-based law firm Atkinson, Andelson, Loya, Ruud & Romo was notifying an undisclosed number of people that an attorney's laptop was stolen and that their personal information may have been compromised. As an encrypted laptop would not have to be reported under the law (because the data would be safe), we are guessing the laptop was not encrypted.

The information on the laptop included names, addresses, telephone numbers, Social Security numbers, and possibly certain financial information or medical records. The theft occurred on April 23rd while a firm attorney was on the MTS Trolley in San Diego. It was reported to the police on April 24th. The laptop was not recovered.

The firm offered recipients of the notification letter a free year of identity theft protection and credit monitoring services. The notification letter states, "We have no reason to believe that the laptop was stolen for the information it contained." It also said, "We also have no information indicating that this information has been accessed or used in any way."

Most likely, that is true. But why are lawyers traveling anywhere with unencrypted mobile devices? It is a lesson we seem never to learn.

2015: An Alleged Data Breach

The *ABA Journal* carried a very disturbing story, whose ending we do not know. Understanding these are only allegations, note that two law firms allege that they suffered data breaches at the hands of another firm which, it is claimed in two pending lawsuits, resulted because the law firm allegedly conspired in hiring hackers to get opposing counsel's data. If there is any truth to the story, it is possible that we have to consider a new kind of threat—our opposing counsel and their clients.

The *ABA Journal* story involved a California law firm which said insurers hacked into tens of thousands of confidential client files as part of a nationwide scheme to get an advantage in worker's compensation cases.

The federal class action filed by Hector Casillas names as defendants not only the insurers allegedly involved but also law firm Knox Ricksen, four attorneys, and a claims service company, as well as two insurance company employees.

"Powerful insurance companies and their co-conspirators who, because of their immense wealth and power, acted as if they were above the law" hired investigators who hacked into and stole attorney-client files, the Los Angeles suit said. It alleges that the files in which unauthorized access occurred concerned worker's compensation cases where the defendant insurers were potentially liable for making payments. Knox Ricksen, the suit states, "willingly and knowingly participated."

Casillas, a client of the California firm Reyes & Barsoum, said his lawyers first suspected hacking at an April 20, 2014, hearing. At that hearing, opposing counsel from the Knox Ricksen firm turned up with an attorney-client privileged intake packet for Casillas's case. It listed Rony Barsoum's name and included the firm's retainer agreement. Asked by the judge at the hearing how they got the confidential file for Casillas, opposing counsel gave several explanations and finally said they didn't know, the suit alleges.

The suit asserts causes of action for alleged fraud, conversion and invasion of privacy, and violation of state and federal statutory law, among other claims. Remedies sought include injunctive relief, disgorgement, and exemplary damages.

Law360 (sub. req.) said a state court lawsuit making similar claims was filed by Reyes & Barsoum against Knox Ricksen in Los Angeles in February. That suit claims that 2,000 case materials were taken from Reyes & Barsoum. That suit also alleges that Knox Ricksen attorneys admitted that they had obtained more than 30,000 files and documents from a password-protected computer network operated by HQ Sign-Up Services Inc., which Reyes & Barsoum used to store privileged and confidential documents.

Please be mindful that we do not know the truth of the allegations, but it certainly widens the possible field of threats to law firm data.

Note that in 2015, the *New York Times* reported that a New York private investigator who hired hackers pled guilty to one charge of conspiracy— he said he had done work for about 20 law firms specializing in personal injury and medical malpractice litigation. Authorities reported at the time that they were increasingly worried that law firms might be directly or indirectly engaging hackers in support of litigation matters.

2014: Compromise of a Law Firm to Target Clients

At an information security conference in Washington, D.C., in October 2014, Mandiant gave a presentation called "Opening Acts: How Attackers Get Their Big Breaks." As its title suggests, it explored examples of how attackers first get into targeted networks—the initial vectors of compromise. The first case study in the presentation was a compromise of a law firm e-mail system that was used as a platform to attack biotechnology and pharmaceutical clients.

The attackers first sent spear-phishing e-mails (targeted, malicious e-mails) to law firm personnel. The e-mails contained malicious links to spoofed Outlook Web Access log-on pages and infected Microsoft Word attachments that, when opened, launched prompts for users to enter their e-mail credentials. The attackers then used e-mail credentials harvested from users who entered them to get access to the e-mail accounts in the law firm's network. They looked for past e-mails with attachments that the law firm had sent to individuals at the target companies and then sent e-mails with infected attachments to those individuals. When some of the recipients opened the malicious attachments, malware was installed on the target companies' networks. The malware set up communications channels with the attackers' servers to steal confidential information.

This was a particularly dangerous attack pattern because the malicious e-mails were actually sent from the law firm's e-mail system to individuals at target clients who had received e-mails with attachments in the past. Most, if not all clients, would routinely open e-mails and attachments from their attorneys.

2014: Imhoff and Associates

On August 27th, *SC Magazine* reported that law firm Imhoff and Associates, PC had notified on the previous day an undisclosed number of individuals that their personal information—including Social Security numbers— was on a backup hard drive that was stolen from the locked trunk of an employee's vehicle on June 27th. This was done in accordance with California's data breach notification law. The notification letter, which may be of interest to readers, can be found at **http://oag.ca.gov/system/files/ IMHOFF_Individual_Notification_0.pdf**

The compromised data included names, addresses, phone numbers, birth dates, e-mail addresses, driver's license numbers, and Social Security numbers.

Law enforcement was notified. The firm said it was strengthening internal processes regarding encryption, and enhancing policies, procedures, and staff education on the safeguarding of company property and information. All impacted individuals were notified and offered a free year of identity theft protection services.

The letter noted that "Imhoff has no reason to believe that the hard drive was stolen for the information it contained or that your information has been accessed or used in any way."

It is worth mentioning that, had the backup drive been encrypted, the data would have been safe and no notification would have been necessary, which is true under most state data breach notification laws.

2014: Wilson Sonsini Goodrich & Rosati

The *New York Times* reported on September 17th that federal authorities, for the second time in three years, charged an employee of Wilson Sonsini Goodrich & Rosati, a prominent law firm, with using confidential information about corporate deals to make illegal trades in stocks.

Dmitry Braverman, an information technology employee with Wilson Sonsini, was charged with generating about $297,000 in illegal profits from insider trading in eight stocks. What makes this a data breach? Here is a common definition: A data breach is an incident in which sensitive, protected, or confidential data has potentially been viewed, stolen, or used by an individual unauthorized to do so.

He traded on confidential information about corporate deals the law firm was working on during a three-year period, according to a criminal complaint filed in federal court in Manhattan. Mr. Braverman was charged with one count of securities fraud.

Mr. Braverman's arrest came more than three years after federal authorities charged Matthew Kluger, a former Wilson Sonsini lawyer, with taking part in a 17-year insider trading conspiracy that netted him and his associates more than $32 million in illegal profits. Mr. Kluger is serving a 12-year prison sentence after pleading guilty in December 2011 to stealing confidential information about corporate deals from Wilson Sonsini and three other law firms where he had worked.

The arrest of Mr. Kluger in April 2011 only stopped Mr. Braverman for a short time. Eighteen months later, he began resuming trading on confidential information about the firm's clients such as Dealertrack Technologies Inc. and Xyratex Ltd. Braverman was sentenced to two years in prison in 2015.

The criminal complaint filed by federal prosecutors in New York notes that after Mr. Kluger's arrest, the law firm sent an e-mail to all employees reminding them of their obligation to maintain client confidences and to not trade on inside information. While there is nothing wrong with such a letter, we certainly hope that the firm now has DLP (data loss prevention software) and access control measures in place.

2014: Snowden Revelation of NSA Surveillance

In 2014, we learned that an Australian ally of the National Security Agency spied on communications between a U.S. law firm and its client, the government of Indonesia, according to a top-secret document obtained by Edward Snowden.

The *New York Times* reported on the document and identified the law firm apparently subjected to the surveillance: Mayer Brown, which was representing Indonesia in trade disputes with the United States. According to the story, the NSA's Australian counterpart, the Australian Signals Directorate, notified the NSA of its surveillance of the talks and offered to share its findings. The Directorate said the surveillance might include information covered by attorney-client privilege and asked for guidance.

According to the document, the Australian agency received "clear guidance" from the NSA general counsel's office, and was able to continue to monitor the communications, providing "highly useful intelligence for interested U.S. customers." This certainly made us wonder what constituted "interested U.S. customers."

Mayer Brown issued a statement that stopped short of a full denial, saying "There is no indication, either in the media reports or from our internal systems and controls that the alleged surveillance occurred at the firm."

The *Chicago Tribune* also reported on Mayer Brown's statement. The newspaper asked a Mayer Brown spokesman whether the firm was saying that there was no evidence of spying at the firm, or that there was no evidence of spying of the firm. The spokesman replied "at the firm."

Many regarded the failure to completely deny the surveillance as an attempt to reassure Mayer Brown's many international clients.

Subsequently, then ABA President James R. Silkenat wrote a letter to the NSA about the incident. He requested clarification on the agency's current policies and practices designed to protect the attorney-client privileged information that it intercepts or receives and whether those directives were followed in connection with the alleged incident.

The NSA responded to the letter, saying it is "firmly committed to the rule of law and the bedrock legal principle of attorney-client privilege." It refused to comment on the reports that the Australian ally monitored communications between law firm Mayer Brown and its client, the government of Indonesia. NSA director Gen. Keith B. Alexander said his agency "absolutely" agrees that the attorney-client privilege "deserves the strong protections afforded by our legal system" and says it is "vital" to have in place policies and practices to prevent the erosion of the privilege.

"Let me be absolutely clear," Alexander continued. "NSA has afforded, and will continue to afford, appropriate protection to privileged attorney-client communications acquired during its lawful foreign intelligence mission in accordance with privacy procedures required by Congress, approved by the Attorney General, and, as appropriate, reviewed by the Foreign Intelligence Surveillance Court. Moreover, NSA cannot and does not ask its foreign partners to conduct any intelligence activity that it would be prohibited from conducting itself in accordance with U.S. law. This broad principle applies to all of our signals intelligence activities, including any activities that could implicate potentially privileged communications."

The word "appropriate" appeared multiple times in the letter, which seemed to muddy the waters a bit. The entire incident persuaded many, including the authors, that law firms, particularly those dealing with foreign governments, companies, and individuals, would be well-advised to regard surveillance by the NSA a potential threat even in matters that appear to be unrelated to antiterrorism activities.

2013: McKenna Long & Aldridge

The Office of Inadequate Security blog reported that the international law firm of McKenna Long & Aldridge notified the Maryland Attorney General's Office on February 26, 2014, that 441 current and former employees' W-2 information and other information had been compromised when a vendor's database was accessed by someone who was able to acquire a client's login credentials. The blog quoted from a notification the firm sent to current and former employees:

> *"As a result of that investigation and further information provided by the vendor, it appears that some information related to current and former employees was accessed on November 28, 2013 (Thanksgiving Day), December 11, 2013, and December 12, 2013 and that such access was obtained through the malicious and unauthorized access to the user identification and password of an account administrator. MLA has since reset all passwords for each user and asked all users to establish a new password. We are also working with our vendor to ensure that this does not occur again.*

> *Regrettably, our investigation appears to show that your personal information was accessed without authorization during this incident, including Federal Wage and Tax Statement Form W-2 name, address, wages, taxes and Social Security number information; date of birth, age, gender, ethnicity; and Visa, Passport or Federal Form I 9 documents numbers."*

Those affected were offered a year of free credit monitoring with Experian ProtectMyID.

2012: Unknown New York Law Firm

This story came to light through a guest post on *Forbes* by SANS research director Alan Paller. He said that two visitors from a large law firm in New York came to his home, the managing partner and IT partner of a large New York law firm.

They said that the FBI had come to the firm saying that their files had been found on a server in another country. The server was used as a way station for sending data to a large Asian country. Off the record they said it was China. The FBI agents showed them a listing of what the hackers had. It was all of the firm's client files.

Paller asked them, "What are you planning to tell your clients?"

The answer was "Are you crazy? Can you think of a better way to destroy their trust in us than letting them know we had lost every document they gave us under (attorney-client) privilege?"

This is the apocryphal story we often tell when seminar attendees doubt that some law firms don't disclosure data breaches, their ethical duties (and possible requirement under state law, depending on the language of the data breach notification law) notwithstanding.

2012: Puckett & Faraj

According to the *ABA Journal*, Neal Puckett was unaware of the existence of the hactivist group Anonymous until his firm was hacked. His Virginia-based law firm was offline for a while and returned under the stewardship of a new consultant.

The one who previously oversaw the firm's website, he says, had his servers wiped clean of all client e-mail, not simply the Puckett firm's material. So, after the consultant spent the weekend getting all his other clients relaunched with backup material, "I don't think he's all that eager to keep us as a client," Puckett said of his now-former website contractor.

The firm's Google e-mail passwords weren't secure enough to keep out hackers who may have been using equipment that can rapidly try multiple possible combinations, according to Puckett. So the firm changed all of its e-mail passwords and made them more complex. Fortunately, although the e-mail was copied by Anonymous hackers, it wasn't deleted.

The *Guardian* reported at the time that the hackers leaked a trove of e-mails from the law firm, angry because it represented Marine staff sergeant Frank Wuterich, accused of leading a group of Marines responsible for the deaths of twenty-four unarmed Iraqi civilians at Haditha. The files were published on Pirate Bay, a file-sharing site popular with hackers.

Wuterich pled guilty in a military court to dereliction of duty, telling the judge that he regretted ordering his men to "shoot first, ask questions later." He was demoted to private and technically sentenced to ninety days' confinement but, by the terms of the plea deal, he did not serve any time. The sentence meant none of the Marines accused in the incident faced time in prison.

Representing controversial clients, as you can see, may make your firm a target. We will be talking about the need for strong, complex passwords (and more) later in this book.

2011: Wiley Rein

Bloomberg reported in 2012 that Washington, D.C., law firm Wiley Rein LLC had been breached in 2011 by Chinese hackers. Byzantine Candor, the team of hackers responsible, is known in security circles as the Comment group for its trademark of infiltrating computers using hidden web page computer code known as "comments."

Thirty North American security researchers watched the hackers work and documented their findings. Twenty victims were identified, many of whom had data that could give China an advantage as it seeks to become the world's largest economy. The targets included lawyers pursuing trade claims against the country's exporters and an energy company getting ready to drill in waters claimed by China.

A former FBI official calls the hackers' activity "the biggest vacuuming up of U.S. proprietary data that we've ever seen. It's a machine."

Exploiting a hole in the hackers' own security, the researchers created a digital diary, logging the intruders' every move as they snuck into networks, shut off antivirus systems, camouflaged themselves as system administrators and covered their tracks, making them invisible to their victims. Sounds like a Hollywood movie, doesn't it?

Byzantine Candor was linked to China's military, the People's Liberation Army, by a 2008 diplomatic cable released by WikiLeaks. Two former intelligence officials verified the essence of the document. The hacking group has been active at least since 2002 and is thought to have penetrated more than one thousand entities.

Of the ten Comment group victims reached by *Bloomberg*, those who learned of the hacks chose not to disclose them publicly, and three said they were unaware they'd been hacked until contacted for this story.

Dale Hausman, Wiley Rein's general counsel, said he couldn't comment on how the breach affected the firm or its clients. He said Wiley Rein has strengthened its network security.

2011: Baxter, Baker, Sidle, Conn & Jones

On October 10, 2011, it was reported in the press that the Maryland law firm of Baxter, Baker, Sidle, Conn & Jones had lost the medical data of 161 patients in a malpractice suit.

So how did this one come to light? The *Baltimore Sun* obtained a copy of one of the notifications sent to the patients.

Here's what happened: One of the law firm's employees brought home a hard drive containing backup data, which was the firm's method of ensuring that it had an offsite backup. She took the Baltimore light rail system home and—you guessed it—left the drive on the train. Though she returned just a few minutes later, the drive was gone. And yes, the drive was unencrypted.

In any event, it should be clear that traveling with unencrypted backup data is a very bad idea. The firm began encrypting its data and was looking into offsite data storage.

2008: An Unknown Law Firm

In 2008, security firm Mandiant discovered that a law firm's network had been breached for more than a year after the law firm was tipped off to the breach by law enforcement. We don't know how law enforcement knew, but it is common for the FBI to advise law firms that they have been breached.

It is a very interesting question as to how the FBI knows about so many breaches.

The law firm could not be named due to Mandiant's confidentiality agreement, but Mandiant stated that the firm was involved in litigation involving China, common in many breaches in spite of the Chinese government's many protestations of innocence when the words "state-sponsored hacking" come up. The intruders at the law firm were able to obtain more than 30 sets of user credentials and harvested thousands of e-mails and attachments from mail servers; they also had full access to all servers and computers on the network for an extended time. The fact that this could happen to a law firm should give lawyers a serious case of the willies.

Conclusion

As you can see, law firm data breaches happen to both large and small firms. And some are never made public. Let's travel onward from the misfortunes of others to prevention (desirable but not always possible) and response to data breaches should that nightmare befall your firm.

CHAPTER THREE

Lawyers' Duty to Safeguard Information

Confidential data in computers and information systems, including those used by attorneys and law firms, faces greater security threats today than ever before. And they continue to grow! These threats are substantial and real. As discussed in our previous chapter on data breach nightmares, they have taken a variety of forms, ranging from phishing scams and social engineering attacks (e.g., using e-mail to trick attorneys to visit a malicious website or to be lured into fraudulent collection schemes for foreign "clients") to sophisticated technical exploits that result in long-term intrusions into a law firm's network to steal information. They also include inside threats—malicious, untrained, inattentive, and even bored personnel—and lost and stolen laptops and mobile devices.

Attorneys have ethical, common-law, and statutory obligations to protect information relating to clients. Many attorneys also have contractual obligations to protect data. Beyond these requirements, protection of confidential information is sound business and professional practice. It is critical for attorneys to understand and address these obligations and to exercise constant vigilance to protect client data and other confidential information.

Ethical Duties Generally

An attorney's use of technology presents special ethics challenges, particularly in the areas of competence and confidentiality. The duty of competence (ABA Model Rule 1.1) requires attorneys to know what technology is necessary and how to appropriately and securely use it. This duty also requires attorneys who lack the necessary technical competence to either learn what is necessary or consult with qualified people who have the requisite expertise. The duty of confidentiality (ABA Model Rule 1.6) is one of an attorney's most important ethical responsibilities. Together, these rules (included in Appendix B) require attorneys using technology to take competent and reasonable measures to safeguard information relating to clients. It is a continuing obligation as technology, threats, and available security measures evolve. This duty extends to all use of technology, including computers, portable devices, networks, technology outsourcing, and cloud computing. Effective information security is an ongoing process that requires constant vigilance.

Model Rule 1.1 covers the general duty of competence. It provides that "A lawyer shall provide competent representation to a client." This "requires the legal knowledge, skill, thoroughness and preparation reasonably necessary for the representation." It includes competence in selecting and using technology.

Model Rule 1.6 generally defines the duty of confidentiality. It begins as follows:

> A lawyer shall not reveal information relating to the representation of a client unless the client gives informed consent, the disclosure is impliedly authorized in order to carry out the representation or the disclosure is permitted by paragraph (b).

Rule 1.6 broadly requires protection of "information relating to the representation of a client"; it is not limited to confidential communications and privileged information. Disclosure of covered information generally requires express or implied client consent (in the absence of special circumstances such as misconduct by the client).

The Ethics 2000 revisions to the model rules (over ten years ago) added Comment 16 [now 18] to Rule 1.6. This comment requires reasonable precautions to safeguard and preserve confidential information.

Acting Competently to Preserve Confidentiality

[16] A lawyer must act competently to safeguard information relating to the representation of a client against inadvertent or unauthorized disclosure by the lawyer or other persons who are participating in the representation of the client or who are subject to the lawyer's supervision. See Rules 1.1, 5.1 and 5.3.

The ABA Commission on Ethics 20/20 conducted a review of the ABA Model Rules of Professional Conduct and the U.S. system of lawyer regulation in the context of advances in technology and global legal practice developments. One of its core areas of focus was technology and confidentiality. Its Revised Draft Resolutions in this area were adopted by the ABA at its Annual Meeting in August 2012.[1]

The amendments include addition of the following underlined language to the Comment to Model Rule 1.1 Competence:

> [8] To maintain the requisite knowledge and skill, a lawyer should keep abreast of changes in the law and its practice, including the benefits and risks associated with relevant technology . . .

The amendments also added the following new subsection (underlined) to Model Rule 1.6 Confidentiality of Information:

> (c) A lawyer shall make reasonable efforts to prevent the inadvertent or unauthorized disclosure of, or unauthorized access to, information relating to the representation of a client.

This requirement covers two areas—inadvertent disclosure and unauthorized access. Inadvertent disclosure includes threats like leaving a briefcase, laptop, or smartphone in a taxi or restaurant, sending a confidential e-mail to the wrong recipient, erroneously producing privileged documents or data, or exposing confidential metadata. Unauthorized access includes threats such as hackers, criminals, malware, and insider threats.

The amendments also include the following changes to Comment [18] to this rule:

> ### Acting Competently to Preserve Confidentiality
> [18] Paragraph (c) requires a A lawyer must to act competently to safeguard information relating to the representation of a client against unauthorized access by third parties and against inadvertent or unauthorized disclosure by the lawyer or other persons or entities who are participating in the representation of the client or who are subject to the lawyer's supervision or monitoring. See Rules 1.1, 5.1 and 5.3. The unauthorized access to, or the inadvertent or unauthorized disclosure of, confidential information does not constitute a violation of paragraph (c) if the lawyer has made

---

1. See, **www.americanbar.org/groups/professional_responsibility/aba_commission_on_ethics_20_20.html**.

reasonable efforts to prevent the access or disclosure. Factors to be considered in determining the reasonableness of the lawyer's efforts include the sensitivity of the information, the likelihood of disclosure if additional safeguards are not employed, the cost of employing additional safeguards, the difficulty of implementing the safeguards, and the extent to which the safeguards adversely affect the lawyer's ability to represent clients (e.g., by making a device or important piece of software excessively difficult to use). A client may require the lawyer to implement special security measures not required by this Rule or may give informed consent to forego security measures that would otherwise be required by this Rule. Whether a lawyer may be required to take additional steps to safeguard a client's information in order to comply with other law, such as state and federal laws that govern data privacy or that impose notification requirements upon the loss of, or unauthorized access to, electronic information, is beyond the scope of these Rules. For a lawyer's duties when sharing information with nonlawyers outside the lawyer's own firm, see Rule 5.3, comments [3]–[4].

Significantly, these revisions are clarifications rather than substantive changes. They add additional detail that is consistent with the then-existing rules and comments, ethics opinions, and generally accepted information security principles.[2]

Model Rule 1.4 also applies to attorneys' use of technology. It requires appropriate communications with clients "about the means by which the client's objectives are to be accomplished." It requires keeping the client informed and, depending on the circumstances, may require obtaining "informed consent." As stated in ABA Formal Ethics Opinion 95-398, "Access of Nonlawyers to a Lawyer's Database" (October 27, 1995), it may require notice to a client of compromise of confidential information relating to the client if the release of information "could reasonably be viewed as a significant factor in the representation."

---

2. ABA Commission on Ethics 20/20, *Report to Resolution 105A Revised* (2012): "The proposed amendment, which appears in a Comment, does not impose any new obligations on lawyers. Rather, the amendment is intended to serve as a reminder to lawyers that they should remain aware of technology, including the benefits and risks associated with it, as part of a lawyer's general ethical duty to remain competent." (Model Rule 1.1) "This duty is already described in several existing Comments, but the Commission concluded that, in light of the pervasive use of technology to store and transmit confidential client information, this existing obligation should be stated explicitly in the black letter of Model Rule 1.6."

The comment references Model Rule 5.1 (Responsibilities of Partners, Managers, and Supervisory Lawyers) and Model Rule 5.3 (Responsibilities Regarding Nonlawyer Assistants), which are also important in attorneys' use of technology. Partners and supervising attorneys (including junior attorneys supervising staff or service providers) are required to take reasonable actions to ensure that those under their supervision comply with these requirements.

Model Rule 5.3 (Responsibilities Regarding Nonlawyer Assistants) was amended to expand its scope. "Assistants" was expanded to "Assistance," extending its coverage to all levels of staff and outsourced services ranging from copying services to outsourced legal services. This requires attorneys to employ reasonable safeguards such as due diligence, contractual requirements, supervision, and monitoring to insure that nonlawyers, both inside and outside a law firm, provide services in compliance with an attorney's duty of confidentiality.

Attorneys must also take reasonable precautions to protect confidential information to which third parties, such as information systems consultants and litigation support service providers, are given access. ABA Formal Ethics Opinion 95-398, provides guidance in this area and concludes, "[a] lawyer who gives a computer maintenance company access to information in client files must make reasonable efforts to ensure that the company has in place, or will establish, reasonable procedures to protect the confidentiality of client information."

In August 2008, the ABA issued an ethics opinion that comprehensively addresses outsourcing by attorneys of both legal services and nonlegal support services. ABA Formal Ethics Opinion 08-451, "Lawyer's Obligations When Outsourcing Legal and Nonlegal Support Services" (August 2008). It includes requirements for protecting confidentiality.

A 2011 Pennsylvania opinion (included in Appendix C) analyzes ethics requirements for attorneys' use of cloud computing, a form of outsourcing. Formal Opinion 2011-200, "Ethical Obligations for Attorneys Using Cloud Computing/Software as a Service While Fulfilling the Duties of Confidentiality and Preservation of Client Property." It concludes:

> An attorney may ethically allow client confidential material to be stored in "the cloud" provided the attorney takes reasonable care to assure that (1) all such materials remain confidential, and (2) reasonable safeguards are employed to ensure that the data is protected from breaches, data loss and other risks.

These requirements are further discussed in our chapters on outsourcing and cloud computing.

A number of state ethics opinions have addressed professional responsibility issues related to attorneys' use of various technologies. Several examples are discussed in this chapter. It is important for attorneys to consult the rules, comments, and ethics opinions in the relevant jurisdiction(s).

An early ethics opinion on this subject, State Bar of Arizona, Opinion No. 05-04, "Formal Opinion of the Committee on the Rules of Professional Conduct" (July 2005), provides a well-reasoned explanation of these duties for electronic files and communications. It notes that "an attorney or law firm is obligated to take competent and reasonable steps to assure that the client's confidences are not disclosed to third parties through theft or inadvertence." The opinion also calls for "competent and reasonable measures to assure that the client's electronic information is not lost or destroyed." It further notes that "an attorney must either have the competence to evaluate the nature of the potential threat to the client's electronic files and to evaluate and deploy appropriate computer hardware and software to accomplish that end, or if the attorney lacks or cannot reasonably obtain that competence, to retain an expert consultant who does have such competence."

An April 2006 New Jersey ethics opinion takes a consistent approach in reviewing obligations in lawyers' use of electronic storage and access of client files. New Jersey Advisory Committee on Professional Ethics, Opinion 701, "Electronic Storage and Access of Client Files" (April 2006), observes:

> The obligation to preserve client confidences extends beyond merely prohibiting an attorney from himself making disclosure of confidential information without client consent (except under such circumstances described in RPC 1.6). It also requires that the attorney take reasonable affirmative steps to guard against the risk of inadvertent disclosure. . . .

> The critical requirement under RPC 1.6, therefore, is that the attorney "exercise reasonable care" against the possibility of unauthorized access to client information. A lawyer is required to exercise sound professional judgment on the steps necessary to secure client confidences against foreseeable attempts at unauthorized access. "Reasonable care," however, does not mean that the lawyer absolutely and strictly guarantees that the information will be utterly invulnerable against all unauthorized access. Such a guarantee is impossible, and a lawyer can no more guarantee against unauthorized access to electronic information than he

can guarantee that a burglar will not break into his file room or that someone will not illegally intercept his mail or steal a fax.

A later Arizona opinion contains a similar analysis, with emphasis on requirements of awareness of limitations of lawyers' knowledge of technology and periodic review of security measures. State Bar of Arizona, Opinion No. 09-04, "Confidentiality; Maintaining Client Files; Electronic Storage; Internet" (Formal Opinion of the Committee on the Rules of Professional Conduct) (December 2009), explains:

> Lawyers providing an online file storage and retrieval system for client access of documents must take **reasonable precautions** to protect the security and confidentiality of client documents and information. Lawyers should be **aware of limitations in their competence** regarding online security measures and take appropriate actions to ensure that a competent review of the proposed security measures is conducted. As technology advances over time, a **periodic review** of the reasonability of security precautions may be necessary.

> (Emphasis added.)

A recent California ethics opinion addresses the use of a laptop by an attorney, where the laptop may be monitored by the law firm, and use of the laptop in public and home wireless networks. The opinion concludes that such use may be proper under the ethics rules if an adequate evaluation is made and appropriate precautions are taken. State Bar of California, Formal Opinion No. 2010-179 (included in Appendix D).

The Digest to this opinion states:

> Whether an attorney violates his or her duties of confidentiality and competence when using technology to transmit or store confidential client information will depend on the particular technology being used and the circumstances surrounding such use. Before using a particular technology in the course of representing a client, an attorney must take appropriate steps to evaluate: 1) the level of security attendant to the use of that technology, including whether reasonable precautions may be taken when using the technology to increase the level of security; 2) the legal ramifications to a third party who intercepts, accesses or exceeds authorized use of the electronic information; 3) the degree of sensitivity of the information; 4) the possible impact on the client of an inadvertent disclosure of privileged or confidential information or work product; 5) the urgency of the situation; and 6) the

client's instructions and circumstances, such as access by others to the client's devices and communications.

The opinion contains a detailed analysis of the ethics requirements for attorneys' use of technology and their application to the technology covered in the opinion, including a detailed discussion of factors an attorney should consider before using a specific technology. Significantly, it includes the requirement of an evaluation **before** an attorney uses a particular technology. If an attorney cannot determine that the safeguards are adequate, he or she is required to obtain informed consent from clients before using it.

Attorneys need to stay up to date as technology changes and new threats are identified. For example, following news reports that confidential information had been found on digital copiers that were ready for resale,[3] the Florida Bar issued Professional Ethics of the Florida Bar Opinion 10-2 (September 2010) that addresses this risk. Its conclusion states:

> In conclusion, when a lawyer chooses to use Devices that contain Storage Media, the lawyer must take reasonable steps to ensure that client confidentiality is maintained and that the Device is sanitized before disposition. These reasonable steps include: (1) identification of the potential threat to confidentiality along with the development and implementation of policies to address the potential threat to confidentiality; (2) inventory of the Devices that contain Hard Drives or other Storage Media; (3) supervision of nonlawyers to obtain adequate assurances that confidentiality will be maintained; and (4) responsibility for sanitization of the Device by requiring meaningful assurances from the vendor at the intake of the Device and confirmation or certification of the sanitization at the disposition of the Device.

New York Opinion 1019, "Remote Access to Firm's Electronic Files" (August 2014), cautions attorneys to analyze necessary precautions in the context of current risks:

> Cybersecurity issues have continued to be a major concern for lawyers, as cybercriminals have begun to target lawyers to access client information, including trade secrets, business plans and personal data. Lawyers can no longer assume that their document systems are of no interest to cybercrooks. That is particularly true where there is outside access to the internal system by third parties, including law firm employees working at other firm offices, at

---

3. E.g., Armen Keteyian, "Digital Copiers Loaded with Secrets," *CBS Evening News* (April 19, 2010). **www.cbsnews.com/news/digital-photocopiers-loaded-with-secrets**.

home or when traveling, or clients who have been given access to the firm's document system.

It leaves it up to attorneys and law firms to determine the specific precautions that are necessary:

> Because of the fact-specific and evolving nature of both technology and cyber risks, we cannot recommend particular steps that would constitute reasonable precautions to prevent confidential information from coming into the hands of unintended recipients, including the degree of password protection to ensure that persons who access the system are authorized, the degree of security of the devices that firm lawyers use to gain access, whether encryption is required, and the security measures the firm must use to determine whether there has been any unauthorized access to client confidential information.

The opinion requires attorneys to either make a determination that the selected precautions provide reasonable protection, in light of the risks, or to obtain informed consent from clients after explaining the risks.

There are now multiple ethics opinions on attorneys' use of cloud computing services such as online file storage and software as a service (SaaS).[4] For example, New York Bar Association Committee on Professional Ethics Opinion 842 "Using an outside online storage provider to store client confidential information" (September 2010), consistent with the general requirements of the ethics opinions above, concludes:

> A lawyer may use an online data storage system to store and back up client confidential information provided that the lawyer takes reasonable care to ensure that confidentiality is maintained in a manner consistent with the lawyer's obligations under Rule 1.6. A lawyer using an online storage provider should take reasonable care to protect confidential information, and should exercise reasonable care to prevent others whose services are utilized by the lawyer from disclosing or using confidential information of a client. In addition, the lawyer should stay abreast of technological advances to ensure that the storage system remains sufficiently advanced to protect the client's information, and the lawyer should monitor the changing law of privilege to ensure that storing information in the "cloud" will not waive or jeopardize any privilege protecting the information.

---

4. The ABA Legal Technology Resource Center has published a summary with links, "Cloud Ethics Opinions around the U.S.," available at **www.americanbar.org/groups/departments_ offices/legal_technology_resources/resources/charts_fyis/cloud-ethics-chart.html**.

Additional examples of opinions covering cloud services are Pennsylvania Bar Association, Committee on Legal Ethics and Professional Responsibility, Formal Opinion 2011-200, "Ethical Obligations for Attorneys Using Cloud Computing/Software as a Service While Fulfilling the Duties of Confidentiality and Preservation of Client Property" (November 2011) and North Carolina State Bar 2011 Formal Ethics Opinion 6, "Subscribing to Software as a Service While Fulfilling the Duties of Confidentiality and Preservation of Client Property" (January 2012).

The key professional responsibility requirements from these various opinions on attorneys' use of technology are **competent and reasonable measures to safeguard client data**, including an understanding of limitations in attorneys' competence, obtaining appropriate assistance, continuing security awareness, appropriate supervision, and ongoing review as technology, threats, and available security evolve.

Ethical Duties: Electronic Communications

E-mail and electronic communications have become everyday communications forms for attorneys and other professionals. They are fast, convenient, and inexpensive, but also present serious risks. It is important for attorneys to understand and address these risks.

In addition to adding the requirement of reasonable safeguards to protect confidentiality, the Ethics 2000 revisions to the Model Rules, over ten years ago, also added Comment 17 [now 19] to Rule 1.6. This comment requires reasonable precautions to safeguard and preserve confidential information during electronic transmission. This Comment, as amended in accordance with the Ethics 20/20 recommendations (underlined), provides:

> [19] When transmitting a communication that includes information relating to the representation of a client, the lawyer must take reasonable precautions to prevent the information from coming into the hands of unintended recipients. This duty, however, does not require that the lawyer use special security measures if the method of communication affords a reasonable expectation of privacy. Special circumstances, however, may warrant special precautions. Factors to be considered in determining the reasonableness of the lawyer's expectation of confidentiality include the sensitivity of the information and the extent to which the privacy of the communication is protected by law or by a confidentiality agreement. A client may require the lawyer to implement special security measures not required by this Rule or may give informed consent to the use of a means of communication that would otherwise be prohibited by this Rule. Whether a lawyer may be

required to take additional steps in order to comply with other law, such as state and federal laws that govern data privacy, is beyond the scope of these Rules.

This Comment requires attorneys to take "reasonable precautions" to protect the confidentiality of electronic communications. Its language about "special security measures" has often been viewed by attorneys as providing that attorneys never need to use "special security measures" such as encryption.[5] While it does state that "special security measures" are not generally required, it contains qualifications and notes that "special circumstances" may warrant "special precautions." It includes the important qualification—"if the method of communication affords a reasonable expectation of privacy." There are, however, questions about whether unencrypted Internet e-mail affords a reasonable expectation of privacy.

Respected security professionals for years have compared e-mail to postcards or postcards written in pencil.[6] A June 2014 post by Google on the *Google Official Blog*[7] and a July 2014 *New York Times* article[8] use the same analogy—comparing unencrypted e-mails to postcards. Encryption is being increasingly required in areas such as banking and health care. Recent laws in Nevada[9] and Massachusetts[10] (which apply to attorneys as

---

5. Encryption is a process that translates a message into a protected electronic code. The recipient (or anyone intercepting the message) must have a key to decrypt it and make it readable. E-mail encryption has become easier to use over time. Transport layer security (TLS) encryption is available to automatically encrypt e-mail between two e-mail gateways. If a law firm and client each have their own e-mail gateways, TLS can be used to automatically encrypt all e-mails between them. A virtual private network is an arrangement in which all communications between two networks or between a computer and a network are automatically protected with encryption. See, David G. Ries and John W. Simek, "Encryption Made Simple for Lawyers," *GPSolo Magazine* (November/December 2012).

6. E.g., B. Schneier, *E-Mail Security—How to Keep Your Electronic Messages Private,* (John Wiley & Sons, Inc. 1995) p. 3; B. Schneier, *Secrets & Lies: Digital Security in a Networked Work,* (John Wiley & Sons, Inc. 2000) p. 200 ("The common metaphor for Internet e-mail is postcards: Anyone—letter carriers, mail sorters, nosy delivery truck drivers—who can touch the postcard can read what's on the back."); and Larry Rogers, *Email—A Postcard Written in Pencil*, Special Report (Software Engineering Institute, Carnegie Mellon University 2001).

7. "Transparency Report: Protecting Emails as They Travel Across the Web," *Google Official Blog* (June 3, 2014) (". . . we send important messages in sealed envelopes, rather than on postcards. . . . Email works in a similar way. Emails that are encrypted as they're routed from sender to receiver are like sealed envelopes, and less vulnerable to snooping—whether by bad actors or through government surveillance—than postcards.") **http://googleblog.blogspot.com/2014/06/transparency-report-protecting-emails.html**.

8. Molly Wood, "Easier Ways to Protect Email From Unwanted Prying Eyes," *New York Times* (July 16, 2014) ("Security experts say email is a lot more like a postcard than a letter inside an envelope, and almost anyone can read it while the note is in transit. The government can probably read your email, as can hackers and your employer.") **www.nytimes.com/2014/07/17/technology/personaltech/ways-to-protect-your-email-after-you-send-it.html?_r=0**.

9. Nev. Rev. Stat. 603A.010, et seq.

10. Mass. Gen. Laws Ch. 93H, regulations at 201 CMR 17.00.

well as others) require defined personal information to be encrypted when it is electronically transmitted. As the use of encryption grows in areas such as these, it will become more difficult for attorneys to demonstrate that confidential client data needs lesser protection.

Comment 19 also lists as a consideration "the extent to which the privacy of the communication is protected by law" as a factor to be considered. The federal Electronic Communications Privacy Act[11] and similar state laws make unauthorized interception of electronic communications a crime. Some observers have expressed the view that this should be determinative and attorneys are not required to use encryption. The better view is to treat legal protection as only one of the factors to be considered. As discussed above, some of the newer ethics opinions conclude that encryption may be a reasonable measure that should be used, particularly for highly sensitive information.

An ABA ethics opinion in 1999 and a number of state ethics opinions have concluded that special security measures such as encryption are not generally required for confidential attorney e-mail.[12] However, these opinions should be carefully reviewed because, like Comment 19, they contain qualifications that limit their general conclusions. In addition, more recent ethics opinions, discussed below, are increasingly recognizing that encryption may be a required safeguard, at least in some circumstances.

For example, New York Bar Association Committee on Professional Ethics Opinion 709 "Use of Internet to advertise and to conduct law practice focusing on trademarks; use of Internet e-mail; use of trade names" (September 1998) concludes:

> We therefore conclude that lawyers may in ordinary circumstances utilize unencrypted Internet e-mail to transmit confidential information without breaching their duties of confidentiality . . . to their clients, as the technology is in use today. Despite this

---

11. 18 U.S.C. §§ 2510 et seq.

12. E.g., ABA Formal Opinion No. 99-413, *Protecting the Confidentiality of Unencrypted E-Mail* (March 10, 1999) ("based upon current technology and law as we are informed of it . . . a lawyer sending confidential client information by unencrypted e-mail does not violate Model Rule 1.6(a). . . ." "[T]his opinion does not, however, diminish a lawyer's obligation to consider with her client the sensitivity of the communication, the costs of its disclosure, and the relative security of the contemplated medium of communication. Particularly strong protective measures are warranted to guard against the disclosure of highly sensitive matters.") and District of Columbia Bar Opinion 281, "Transmission of Confidential Information by Electronic Mail," (February 1998), ("In most circumstances, transmission of confidential information by unencrypted electronic mail does not per se violate the confidentiality rules of the legal profession. However, individual circumstances may require greater means of security.").

general conclusion, lawyers must always act reasonably in choosing to use e-mail for confidential communications, as with any other means of communication. Thus, in circumstances in which a lawyer is on notice for a specific reason that a particular e-mail transmission is at heightened risk of interception, or where the confidential information at issue is of such an extraordinarily sensitive nature that it is reasonable to use only a means of communication that is completely under the lawyer's control, the lawyer must select a more secure means of communication than unencrypted Internet e-mail.

A lawyer who uses Internet e-mail must also stay abreast of this evolving technology to assess any changes in the likelihood of interception as well as the availability of improved technologies that may reduce such risks at reasonable cost. It is also sensible for lawyers to discuss with clients the risks inherent in the use of Internet e-mail, and lawyers should abide by the clients' wishes as to its use.

Consistent with the questions about the security of e-mail, some ethics opinions express a stronger view that encryption may be required. For example, New Jersey Opinion 701 (April 2006), discussed above, notes at the end: "where a document is transmitted to [the attorney] . . . by email over the Internet, the lawyer should password a confidential document (as is now possible in all common electronic formats, including PDF), since it is not possible to secure the Internet itself against third party access."[13] This was over nine years ago.

California Formal Opinion No. 2010-179, also discussed above, notes that "encrypting email may be a reasonable step for an attorney in an effort to ensure the confidentiality of such communications remain so when circumstances call for it, particularly if the information at issue is highly sensitive and the use of encryption is not onerous."

An Iowa opinion on cloud computing suggests the following as one of a series of questions that attorneys should ask when determining appropriate protection: "Recognizing that some data will require a higher degree of protection than others, will I have the ability to encrypt certain data using higher level encryption tools of my choosing?" Iowa Ethics Opinion 11-01.

---

13. File password protection in some software, such as current versions of Microsoft Office, Adobe Acrobat, and WinZip, uses encryption to protect security. It is generally easier to use than encryption of e-mail and attachments. However, the protection can be limited by use of weak passwords that are easy to break or "crack." See chapter 24 for more details.

A Pennsylvania ethics opinion on cloud computing concludes that "attorneys may use email but must, under appropriate circumstances, take additional precautions to assure client confidentiality." It discusses encryption as an additional precaution that may be required when using services such as web mail. Pennsylvania Formal Opinion 2011-200.

Texas Ethics Opinion 648 (2015) takes the same approach:

> In general, considering the present state of technology and email usage, a lawyer may communicate confidential information by email. In some circumstances, however, a lawyer should consider whether the confidentiality of the information will be protected if communicated by email and whether it is prudent to use encrypted email or another form of communication.

The opinion includes examples of circumstances where encryption may be required.

Summarizing these more recent opinions, a July 2015 ABA article notes:[14]

> The potential for unauthorized receipt of electronic data has caused some experts to revisit the topic and issue [ethics] opinions suggesting that in some circumstances, encryption or other safeguards for certain email communications may be required.

In addition to complying with any applicable ethics and legal requirements, the most prudent approach to the ethical duty of protecting confidentiality of electronic communications is to have an express understanding with clients (preferably in an engagement letter or other writing) about the nature of communications that will be (and will not be) sent electronically and whether or not encryption and other security measures will be utilized.

It has now reached the point (or at least is reaching it) where all attorneys should have encryption available for use in appropriate circumstances.

Common-Law Duties

In addition to the duties arising from applicable rules of professional conduct, there are parallel common-law duties to protect confidentiality. These duties are defined by case law in the various states. The Restatement (Third) of the Law Governing Lawyers (2000) summarizes this area of the law. See Section 16(2) on competence and diligence, Section 16(3) on

---

14. Peter Geraghty and Susan Michmerhuizen, "Encryption Conniption," *Eye on Ethics, Your ABA* (July 2015) **www.americanbar.org/publications/youraba/2015/july-2015/encryption-conniption.html**.

complying with obligations concerning client's confidences, and Chapter 5, "Confidential Client Information." Breach of these common-law duties may result in malpractice liability.

There are also instances when lawyers have contractual duties to protect client data. This is particularly the case for clients in regulated industries, such as health care and financial services, that have regulatory requirements to protect privacy and security. Clients are recognizing that law firms may be the weak links in protecting their confidential information and are increasingly requiring specified safeguards, providing questionnaires about a law firm's security imposing security requirements, and even requiring security audits.[15]

Attorneys and law firms who accept credit cards are "merchants" that are required to comply with the Payment Security Industry Data Security Standard (PCI). It is generally required under the merchant processing agreement with a bank or processor.

Statutes and Regulations

In addition to the ethical and common-law duties to protect client information, various state and federal statutes and regulations require protection of defined categories of personal information. Some of them are likely to apply to lawyers who possess any covered personal information about their employees, clients, clients' employees or customers, opposing parties and their employees, or even witnesses.

At least twelve states now have general information security laws that require reasonable measures to protect defined categories of personal information (including Arkansas, California, Connecticut, Illinois, Maryland, Massachusetts, Nevada, New Jersey, Oregon, Rhode Island, Texas, and Utah). While the scope of coverage, the specificity of the requirements, and the definitions vary among these laws, "personal information" is usually defined to include general or specific facts about an identifiable individual. The exceptions tend to be information that is presumed public and does not have to be protected (e.g., a business address).

The most comprehensive law of this type to date is a Massachusetts law,[16] which applies to "persons who own, license, store or maintain personal

---

15. Kenneth N. Rashbaum, Jason M. Tenenbaum, and Liberty McAteer, "Cybersecurity: Business Imperative for Law Firms," *New York Law Journal* (December 10, 2014) **www.newyork lawjournal.com/id=1202678493487/Cybersecurity-Business-Imperative-for-Law-Firms?slreturn =20141127155939** and Sharon D. Nelson & John W. Simek, "Clients Demand Law Firm Cyber Audits," *Law Practice* (November/December 2013) **www.americanbar.org/publications/law_ practice_magazine/2013/november-december/hot-buttons.html**.

16. Mass. Gen. Laws Ch. 93H.

information about a resident of the Commonwealth of Massachusetts." Covered "personal information" includes Social Security numbers, driver's license numbers, state-issued identification card numbers, financial account numbers and credit card numbers. With its broad coverage of "persons," this law is likely to be applied to persons nationwide, including attorneys and law firms, when they have sufficient contacts with Massachusetts to satisfy personal jurisdiction requirements. It requires covered persons to "develop, implement, and maintain a comprehensive information security program that is written in one or more readily accessible parts and contains administrative, technical, and physical safeguards."

The implementing regulation, 201 CMR 17 (included in Appendix F), became effective on March 1, 2010. It requires covered persons to "develop, implement, and maintain a comprehensive information security program that is written in one or more readily accessible parts and contains administrative, technical, and physical safeguards." The regulation contains detailed requirements for the information security program, including a risk assessment, assigning responsibility for security, training requirements, and requiring security for third parties who are given access to protected information. It also includes detailed computer system security requirements. The requirements include the following, with subparts requiring additional details:

- Secure user authentication protocols.
- Secure access measures.
- Encryption of all transmitted records and files containing personal information that will travel across public networks, and encryption of all data containing personal information to be transmitted wirelessly.
- Reasonable monitoring of systems for unauthorized use of or access to personal information.
- Encryption of all personal information stored on laptops or other portable devices.
- For files containing personal information on a system that is connected to the Internet, there must be reasonably up-to-date firewall protection and operating system security patches (fixes issued by the manufacturer), reasonably designed to maintain the integrity of the personal information.
- Reasonably up-to-date versions of system security agent software which must include malware protection and reasonably up-to-date patches and virus definitions, or a version of such software that can

still be supported with up-to-date patches and virus definitions, and is set to receive the most current security updates on a regular basis.

♦ Education and training of employees on the proper use of the computer security system and the importance of personal information security.

Lawyers and law firms should understand the requirements of the Massachusetts law because they may directly apply, they are based on generally accepted security principles, and some observers believe that they will become a model for legal requirements for comprehensive protection of personal information.

Nevada also has laws that require "reasonable security measures" and encryption (NRS 603A.210 and NRS 597.970), although they are much less detailed than the Massachusetts law. In addition, encryption is already required for federal agencies that have information about individuals on laptops and portable media. As encryption becomes a security standard, it is likely to become the standard of what is reasonable for lawyers.

The legal obligations don't stop, however, at requiring these kinds of measures to protect the confidentiality of information. Forty-seven states and the District of Columbia and the Virgin Islands have laws that require notification concerning data breaches (all but Mississippi, New Mexico, and South Dakota). While there are differences in their scope and requirements, they generally require entities that own, license, or possess defined categories of personally identifiable information about consumers to notify affected consumers if there is a breach. Like the reasonable security laws, many of these laws apply to covered information "about" residents of the state. Some require notice to a state agency in addition to notice to consumers. Most of these laws have encryption safe harbors, which provide that notice is not required if the data is encrypted and the decryption key has not been compromised.

To add to the web of issues involved, at least nineteen states also now have laws that require secure disposal of paper and electronic records that contain defined personal information. The Federal Trade Commission's Disposal Rule[17] has similar requirements for consumer credit reports and information derived from them.

At the federal level, an attorney who receives protected personally identifiable health information (PHI) from a covered entity under the Health Insurance Portability & Accountability Act (HIPAA) will generally be a

---

17. 16 C.F.R. Part 682.

"business associate" and be required to comply with the HIPAA security requirements. The 2009 Healthcare Information Technology and Clinical Health (HITECH) Act enhanced HIPAA security requirements, extended them directly to business associates, and added a new breach notification requirement.

Standards for Competent and Reasonable Measures

The core challenge for lawyers and law firms in establishing information security programs is deciding what security measures are necessary and then implementing and maintaining them. Determining what constitutes "competent and reasonable measures" can be difficult. If attorneys are governed by legal requirements such as HIPAA or the new Massachusetts law, or by contractual requirements, they must comply with them. Consensus government and industry standards are now commonly used by law firms, as well as other businesses and enterprises, in determining what constitutes reasonable security. Legal standards that apply in other areas, such as health care and financial services, can also be helpful in providing a framework for security, even where they do not legally apply.

Consensus government and industry standards are discussed in the next chapter. Commonly used examples are those published by the National Institute for Standards and Technology (NIST), part of the U.S. Department of Commerce, such as its *Framework for Improving Critical Infrastructure Cybersecurity, Version 1.0* (February 2014) and its *Small Business Information Security: the Fundamentals, Draft NISTIR 7261, Rev. 1* (December 2014). Standards such as those published by the International Organization for Standardization (ISO) (available at **www.iso.org**) are also being commonly used, particularly by larger firms. They include ISO/IEC 27002:2013, "Information Technology—Code of Practice for Information Security Management," ISO/IEC 27001:2013, "Information Technology—Security Techniques— Information Security Management System—Requirements," and others.

The FTC's Safeguards Rule under the Gramm-Leach-Bliley Act (included in Appendix G) also provides a helpful basic framework that lawyers can use to assist in complying with their obligations to safeguard client data, even when it is not a legal requirement. The requirements in the rule, "Standards for Safeguarding Customer Information," 16 CFR, Part 314, are general and cover fewer than two pages in the *Federal Register*. It provides an overall process, but not all of the necessary details.

Legal groups, including the American Bar Association, state bars, and the International Legal Technology Association (ILTA) LegalSEC initiative have been working to tailor these kinds of standards for attorneys and law firms. Details are discussed in the information security overview chapter. In addition to considering frameworks and standards such as these, attorneys should also consider generally accepted security practices. For example, after the high-profile theft of a Department of Veterans Affairs laptop and portable drive containing personal information on more than twenty-eight million veterans in 2006, the Office of Management and Budget (OMB) issued new security guidelines for federal agencies. They require encryption of laptops and mobile devices. Both before this incident and increasingly since it, encryption of laptops and mobile devices containing confidential has become a standard security practice. This has become a standard security practice, not just a federal requirement.

Despite this standard practice, there have been a number of reported thefts and losses of unencrypted laptops and portable drives from law firms. There most likely have been many more that have not been disclosed. The *Verizon 2014 Data Breach Investigation Report*, which covers 2013, explains the risk of lost and stolen devices and a solution to it—encryption—this way: [18]

Physical Theft and Loss—Recommended Controls

The primary root cause of incidents in this pattern is carelessness of one degree or another. Accidents happen. People lose stuff. People steal stuff. And that's never going to change. But there are a few things you can do to mitigate that risk.

Encrypt Devices

Considering the high frequency of lost assets, **encryption is as close to a no-brainer solution as it gets for this incident pattern**. Sure, the asset is still missing, but at least it will save a lot of worry, embarrassment, and potential lawsuits by simply being able to say the information within it was protected. (Emphasis added.)

It's not just Verizon; this view is widely held by information security professionals and government agencies.[19] This raises the question: Are attorneys who are not using encryption for laptops and mobile devices taking competent and reasonable measures to protect them?

---

18. **www.verizonenterprise.com/DBIR/2014**.

19. E.g., US-CERT, the National Institute of Science and Technology (NIST), the Federal Communications Commission, and the Department of Health and Human Services have all recommended or required encryption on mobile devices to protect confidential information.

The Sedona Conference has recently published the *Sedona Conference Commentary on Privacy and Information Security: Principles and Guidelines for Lawyers, Law Firms, and Other Legal Service Providers* (November 2015) that summarizes requirements for attorneys.

Conclusion

Confidential data in attorneys' computers and information systems today faces substantial, real, and growing security risks. It is critical for attorneys to understand and address these risks to comply with their ethical, common-law, and regulatory obligations to safeguard confidential data. Fortunately, these duties do not require attorneys to become computer scientists or security specialists (the last thing that most attorneys want to do). They do require attorneys to be aware of the risks and security requirements and to ensure that security is adequately addressed, including the involvement of qualified professionals where necessary. Constant security awareness by attorneys and staff is key. Finally, information security is an ongoing duty as technology, risks and available security measures change over time.

Selected Ethics Opinions: Technology, the Internet, and Cloud Computing

ABA Formal Ethics Opinion 11-459, "Duty to Protect the Confidentiality of E-Mail Communications with One's Client," (August 2011)

ABA Formal Ethics Opinion 08-451, "Lawyer's Obligations When Outsourcing Legal and Nonlegal Support Services" (August 2008)

ABA Formal Ethics Opinion 99-413, "Protecting the Confidentiality of Unencrypted E-Mail" (March 1999)

ABA Formal Ethics Opinion 95-398, "Access of Nonlawyers to a Lawyer's Data Base" (October 1995)

Alabama Ethics Opinion 2010-02, "Retention, Storage, Ownership, Production and Destruction of Client Files" (includes cloud computing)

State Bar of Arizona, Opinion No. 09-04, "Confidentiality; Maintaining Client Files; Electronic Storage; Internet" (December 2009)

State Bar of Arizona, Opinion No. 05-04, "Electronic Storage; Confidentiality" (July 2005)

State Bar of California, Formal Opinion No. 2010-179, "Use of Technology to Transmit or Store Confidential Client Information, Including Public and Home Wireless Networks," (a copy is included in Appendix D)

Professional Ethics of the Florida Bar, Opinion 06-1, "Electronic File Storage" (April 2006)

Illinois State Bar Association, Opinion 10-01, "Law Firm Computer Network Managed by Offsite Third-Party Vendor" (July 2009)

Maine Professional Ethics Commission, Opinion #194, "Client Confidences: Confidential Firm Data Held Electronically and Handled by Technicians for Third-Party Vendors" (June 2008)

Massachusetts Bar Opinion 2005-04, "Third-Party Software Vendor Access to Confidential Client Information Stored on the Firm's Computer System for the Purpose of Allowing the Vendor to Support and Maintain a Computer Software Application Utilized by the Law Firm" (March 2005)

State Bar of Nevada, Formal Opinion No. 33, "Use of Outside Party to Store Electronic Client Information" (February 2006)

New Jersey Advisory Committee on Professional Ethics, Opinion 701, "Electronic Storage and Access of Client Files" (April 2006)

New York State Bar Association, Committee on Professional Ethics, Opinion 1020, "Confidentiality: Use of Cloud Storage for Purposes of a Transaction" (September 2014)

New York State Bar Association, Committee on Professional Ethics, Opinion 1019, "Remote Access to Firm's Electronic Files" (August 2014)

New York State Bar Association, Committee on Professional Ethics, Opinion 842, "Using an Outside Online Storage Provider to Store Client Confidential Information" (September 2010)

New York State Bar Association, Committee on Professional Ethics, Opinion 820, "Use of E-Mail Service Provider That Scans E-Mails for Advertising Purposes" (February 2008)

North Carolina State Bar 2015 Formal Ethics Opinion 6, "Lawyer's Professional Responsibility When Third Party Steals Funds from Trust Account" (October 2015)

North Carolina State Bar 2011 Formal Ethics Opinion 6, "Subscribing to Software as a Service While Fulfilling the Duties of Confidentiality and Preservation of Client Property" (January 2012)

Pennsylvania Bar Association, Committee on Legal Ethics and Professional Responsibility, Formal Opinion 2011-200, "Ethical Obligations for Attorneys Using Cloud Computing/Software as a Service While Fulfilling the Duties of Confidentiality and Preservation of Client Property" (November 2011) (a copy is included in Appendix C)

State Bar of Texas, Professional Ethics Committee, Opinion No. 648 (communicating confidential information by email) (April 2015)

Virginia Legal Ethics Opinion 1818, "Whether the Client's File May Contain Only Electronic Documents with No Paper Retention" (September 2005)

CHAPTER FOUR

Physical Security

Introduction

You get a call from your spouse, upset because the basement is flooded. You leave work quickly and rush home to assist. Not only do you leave your computer on, but you have no screen saver password required—and you were reconciling the law firm's trust account at the time. Overnight, $100,000 is removed from that account. Taken by someone in your firm or the cleaning service? You've got a major league problem because you left your computer wide open for anyone to wander by and access the trust account. It is not going to be a good day.

Physical security is the protection of equipment, software, information, materials, and documents from damage, theft, and vandalism. It is the task of ensuring that only authorized people have access to your systems. Physical security protects your people, your devices and infrastructure, your paper, and your electronic data. In these hypersecurity days, a data center might even be protected by concrete or landscaped bunkers.

Where Is Your Server and Who Has Access to It?

The funniest "server room" we ever saw was a bathroom (not a functional one). This tiny old bathroom held the server and a monitor. To work on the server, you had to sit on the toilet. The door was (of course) unlocked, and the temperature was far from ideal.

Happily, we've only seen that sort of server room once. Unhappily, we see servers located in lot of law firms with inadequate ventilation and little or no security.

So where is your server? Ideally, you have given your server or servers a well-ventilated home where the temperature does not rise precariously and endanger sensitive equipment. But for the sake of security, whether your server is in an oversized closet or an actual room, it should be, at a minimum, under lock and key.

Who needs access to the server? Our own preference would be not to give the key to an outside IT provider. Who knows how many copies of the key might be made and who might have them? Perhaps one partner and one trusted employee? Servers can also be installed in locked cabinets if the actual room cannot be physically locked.

How much security to provide will vary on a case-by-case basis, but using a proximity card and biometrics (most often, a fingerprint reader) to get into server rooms is common in these security-conscious days.

What you certainly do not want to do is leave your server(s) completely exposed to a fired employee with a grudge and a truncheon—or even to someone who wants to "help fix" the server.

Alarm Systems, UPS, and Paper

Alarm systems are now installed in many law firms, and access is often granted by keycards. You may install motion detectors as well; we've actually seen a firm breached by someone who came through the drop ceiling, installed spyware and left undetected. If it sounds like a Tom Cruise escapade, just remember that it happened in real life, collecting the firm's data and shooting it off to the intruder. Surveillance cameras may also be installed to record comings and goings. Smoke detectors and fire alarms are mandatory.

All of your network devices should be attached to an uninterruptable power supply (UPS) in case there is a power surge or power is lost. When attached to a server, the UPS should be large enough to supply the server with enough time to allow the operating system to shut down safely. This prevents damage to the operating system and the data on the hard disks.

American Power Conversion Corporation (APC) produces many UPS devices used in network environments, though of course there are many other manufacturers. Prices range from $200 or so up to several thousand dollars. In a small office, you may spend $400–$500 for a device that will protect multiple computers. At a bare minimum, make sure all computers are plugged into a surge protector, but remember that they can only protect against surges; they do not supply power to the computers in the event of a "hard shutdown."

Sounds like a lot of money for a small firm, doesn't it? Not to mention effort. What is "reasonable" is going to vary from law firm to law firm, but every lawyer needs to consider sources of potential threats and then determine which measures will best mitigate any risks.

Not all our data is electronic, of course. And yes, Dumpster diving is still common by identity thieves or those seeking business intelligence. We used to recommend good quality crosscut shredders, but here as elsewhere, times have changed. Now you should have a good quality microcut shredder—HIPAA compliant of course. Are they costly? Yes. Large firms should have very high-grade shredders (often seen in the $2000–$4000 range). Smaller firms can get away with a smaller and less expensive unit.

Larger firms may opt to have a shredding company dispose of documents, and they often recycle the shredded paper. No worries, pulp is unreadable—so go green.

Security Assessments

If you do a security assessment, problems with physical security will be addressed along with recommendations for remediation. You need an independent third-party information security firm to do such an assessment. Never entrust such an assessment to your IT provider who has a vested interest in making the assessment look good—and who may not have adequate security credentials.

The law has something to say about physical security. HIPAA, PCI ,and various state privacy laws explicitly mandate that physical security measures be in place.

The ABA's Commission on Ethics 20/20 gave us this advice: "Always restrict access to the data room. It should remain locked with access limited to authorized parties only." Very good advice.

Let's talk about your office building for a moment.

- How secure is your building?
- Are the doors locked after hours?
- How is after-hours access handled?
- Does the cleaning crew have access?
- Are background checks run on the cleaning personnel?
- Are the communications closets locked?
- Do visitors have ready access to the building and can they simply roam around?

♦ Is there a camera security system in place internally and externally?

♦ Is there an alarm system to notify police of an intrusion?

♦ Do police regularly patrol the surrounding area?

If the answers don't give you a warm and fuzzy feeling, you may need to talk with your landlord about enhancing security measures.

Laptops

We've talked about servers, but what about laptops, which are so frequently stolen from airports, hotels, and other locations? It is now very common for lawyers to use a laptop to "carry their office anywhere." When they return to the office, they insert their laptop in a docking station, and they are on the firm's network.

The desire to be mobile, to work from anywhere, is understandable as we all tend to work from home and while traveling. But there is a concomitant risk as these mobile devices present an attractive target to thieves whether we are at the airport or just leave the laptops in our cars.

Airports are dangerous places for laptops. If you go to the bathroom, you should bring the laptop. If you are traveling with children, make sure they are old enough that their attention won't wander when they are supposed to be minding the laptop.

One simple protection: Have a strong (fourteen alphanumeric characters and a special character) password to log in, and make sure to require that the password be used to unlock the computer after the screen saver engages. Whole disk encryption is mandatory these days.

Many security measures are expensive but not so the keyed cable lock, which is a rubber-coated steel cable that inserts into the Kensington Security slot that is found in almost all of today's laptop and notebook computers. It is a tiny metal-reinforced hole designed to secure the computer, with the other end being secured around a permanent object (think about a mattress frame in a hotel). It is very unlikely that a hotel thief will walk off with your laptop and the mattress frame.

Keyed cable locks are made by many companies, but Kensington Security slots are so-called because Kensington set the standard. They are not only inexpensive but simple and easy to use—a major benefit for often-technophobic lawyers. Most of the time, when we're staying at a hotel, the desk has a pass-through hole for computer, electrical, and phone cables; you can simply thread the cable lock through the pass-through hole and wrap it around the back of the desk. Now you can go out on the town and feel secure. In an airport, you can wrap the cable around the bolted-down seats in the waiting area.

Want to leave your laptop in the car? Wrap the cable through the steering wheel or through the baby seat hook above the backseat. If you leave your laptop at work, install the cable lock to the desk to prevent the cleaning crew from walking out with a nice prize.

Keyed cable locks are not only cheap, but they have low administrative overhead. A lock is good through any number of hardware upgrades and can be reprovisioned if an employee leaves the law firm.

If you have a number of employees, they can each have their own unique keys, and there can also be a master key that opens all locks. Note that there are now ultrathin notebook locks as well as "twin" locks that enable you to protect two devices, such as a laptop and an external hard drive.

Lost and Stolen Devices

If you think all this is overkill, just browse the instances of data loss resulting from lost or stolen computers. According to the technology research firm Gartner, a laptop is stolen every fifty-three seconds. Yikes. You will have noticed in the chapter on real-life data breaches that stolen laptops made several appearances.

The year 2014 showed a sharp rise in health information data breaches involving stolen or lost devices. Almost 79% of the reported breaches were due to stolen or lost computers or data storage devices (flash drives primarily) where the electronic protected health information was stored unencrypted. We are sure the figures for law firm breaches would look much the same.

Tracking services like Prey, LoJack, and LockItTight all provide a range of features allowing you to trace mobile devices and secure or delete data. It's also possible to discover the IP address of the thief if he or she tries to log in to various sites and services. If you have an up-to-date Apple Macbook, you can switch on the Find My Mac option in the iCloud settings, then track it and delete the hard drive via your iPhone or another browser.

Training

We can never talk about training enough, but it is as important here as in other areas of security. Your employees should be trained about social engineering, become wary of suspicious persons, and provided with enough information to recognize dangerous situations and respond appropriately.

They should be aware of their surroundings and conscious of any threats to their devices, primarily the threat of theft. They need to be careful not to let someone into an area that requires, for instance, a swipe card. Our tendency, being nice folks, is to allow someone else in behind us when we should be deaf to protestations that they forgot their card unless the person is well known to us.

In 2015, an office "creeper" got into a Norfolk law firm—among many other places. Ameenah Franks has been called an "office creeper" in crime alerts. She represents an aspect of security that many law firms ignore. The thirty-year-old has already served time for stealing from businesses.

How did she get into all these businesses? She had an extensive jailhouse interview about that with the *Virginian-Pilot*. Dressing and speaking well helped her gain access to offices, as did subterfuges such as presenting fake credentials; tailgating legitimate employees as they entered; and standing outside a door, with cigarette in hand, ready to walk in after what appeared to be a smoke break.

Gaining workplace access allowed her to steal money and electronic devices. But it also gave her a sense of belonging from people who mistakenly thought she was a fellow employee, Franks said. Sometimes she took nothing.

She's been linked to "creeping" into the Nuclear Regulatory Commission, the Federal Aviation Administration, the Department of the Treasury, the Government Accountability Office, the Department of Housing and Urban Development, the Environmental Protection Agency and others. It's more than a little scary that she could get into places which should be ultra-secure.

In the case of the Norfolk law firm, she tried to persuade a security guard she was an employee there, then pried open a locked door after staff had gone home. She took money, laptops, and more.

Obviously, the security guard did a good job. But a door that can be pried open probably isn't adequately defending a law office from a physical security standpoint. Franks got into at least two law firms. We sure hope the devices she took in Norfolk were encrypted!

Guests

All law firms have lots of guests, but guests present a danger. Guests should not be left to wander around at will. They should not be given direct access to firm computers any more than they should be left alone in a lawyer's office or in a room where case files are stored. A "guest" wireless ID, properly secured, is fine, but we've seen too many examples of clients left by themselves in a room where paper or electronic data was not secured. Remember, even the names of your clients are confidential. In the average lawyer's office, there are piles of client files that contain names and much more. As elementary as this seems, lawyers fail to protect the physical security of these files on a regular basis.

Incident Response Plans and Disaster Recovery Plans

What if, in spite of your best efforts, something goes wrong? Now you need an incident response plan to determine the steps to be taken. You must have someone, or a team, ready to investigate the incident and figure out how to remedy the problem for the future.

If you experience a true disaster—an earthquake, flooding, act of terrorism, or something similar—you must make sure you have a disaster recovery plan that will ensure that physical security is restored at the earliest possible opportunity.

Physical Security Assessments

This is pretty new, but law firms are beginning to have physical (as well as cybersecurity) assessments. A physical security assessment is a method of testing the security of a business using social engineering techniques which are realistic, but designed in a way that don't disrupt the client's business. Independence from the company providing the on-site security services or suppliers of security equipment is vital to ensure there are no conflicts of interest.

Businesses are often at their most vulnerable during out-of-office hours. Computers are left on and papers are spread across desks. But social engineering during office hours works frequently too. You may want to consider such an assessment to see how well your employees perform.

Just like "pen testing" of networks, there are physical penetration tests as well—testing the security of the building as well as of your office. There is sometimes a bonus in the engagement agreement if the company gains access to confidential data.

The testers will often engage in surveillance of the building—as a real intruder might—to see if they come to someone's attention and are questioned. After the assessment is over, there is generally a report with a list of vulnerabilities and remediation recommendations.

If you think your physical security is pretty good, having one of these assessments just might change your mind.

CHAPTER FIVE

Information Security Overview

Information security is a process to protect the confidentiality, integrity, and availability of information. Comprehensive security must address people, policies and procedures, and technology. Technology is a critical component of effective security, but the other aspects must also be addressed. As explained by Bruce Schneier, a highly respected security professional, "[i]f you think technology can solve your security problems, then you don't understand the problems and you don't understand the technology."[1] The best technical security is likely to fail without adequate attention to people and policies and procedures. An equally important concept is that security requires ongoing vigilance and awareness. It must go beyond a one-time "set it and forget it" approach.

As discussed in the first chapter, the current approach to the security process includes the following functions: **identify, protect, detect, respond, and recover**. It starts with an inventory of information assets to determine what needs to be protected and a risk assessment to identify anticipated threats to the assets, including external and internal threats. The next step is development and implementation of a comprehensive information security program to employ reasonable physical, administrative, and technical safeguards to protect against identified risks. This is generally the most difficult part of the process. It must address people, policies and procedures and technology. It needs to include assignment of responsibility, training, monitoring for compliance, and periodic review and updating. The program should also include appropriate measures to detect security incidents and breaches, to respond to them, and to recover from them.

---

1. Bruce Schneier, *Secrets and Lies—Digital Security in a Networked World* (Wiley 2000) at p. xii.

There is no such thing as absolute or perfect security. Gene Spafford, an information security pioneer with Purdue University, put it this way:

> The only truly secure system is one that is powered off, cast in a block of concrete and sealed in a lead-lined room with armed guards—and even then I have my doubts.[2]

This observation was made over twenty-five years ago, before the subsequent explosive growth in technology, before the Internet, and before today's almost universal connectivity and mobility. The threats and security challenges are much greater today.

The requirement for lawyers is reasonable security, not absolute security, although attorneys should strive to provide stronger protection than this minimum requirement. As discussed earlier, New Jersey Ethics Opinion 701 states "'[r]easonable care,' however, does not mean that the lawyer absolutely and strictly guarantees that the information will be utterly invulnerable against all unauthorized access. Such a guarantee is impossible." The amended Comment to Model Rule 1.6 also recognizes that "[t]he unauthorized access to, or the inadvertent or unauthorized disclosure of, confidential information does not constitute a violation of paragraph (c) if the lawyer has made reasonable efforts to prevent the access or disclosure."

Security sometimes involves balancing and trade-offs to determine what risks and safeguards are reasonable under the circumstances. The analysis includes the sensitivity of the information, the risks and available safeguards (including their cost, difficulty of implementation, and effect on usability of the technology). There is frequently a trade-off between security and usability.

Strong security often makes technology more difficult to use, but easy-to-use technology is frequently insecure. The challenge is striking the correct balance among all of these often-competing factors.

Security Frameworks and Standards

As discussed in the duty to safeguard chapter, the core challenge for lawyers in establishing information security programs is deciding what security measures are necessary and then implementing them.

This requires determining what constitutes "competent and reasonable measures" and then implementing those, or stronger, measures. The eth-

---

2. Quoted by A. K. Dewdney in "Computer Recreations: Of Worms, Viruses and Core War," *Scientific American* (March 1989), p. 110.

ics requirements are the floor—anything less is a violation of attorneys' professional responsibility obligations. Attorneys should aim for stronger safeguards to protect their clients and themselves. They must meet legal requirements like HIPAA or the new Massachusetts law, if they apply, and any requirements to which attorneys have agreed by contract. In determining what is reasonable, attorneys can look to guidance from bar groups, legal standards in other areas, government publications, and consensus security standards.

The American Bar Association regularly publishes materials and provides educational programs on information security. Examples include the Law Practice Division (**www.lawpractice.org**) (including resources such as this book, the Legal Technology Resource Center (LTRC), ABA TECHSHOW, and articles in *Law Practice* magazine and *Law Practice Today* webzine), the Cybersecurity Legal Taskforce, the Standing Committee on Law and National Security, the Business Law Section's Cyberspace Law Committee, and the Section of Science and Technology's Information Security Committee. Many state bar associations provide similar materials and programs. This kind of information is particularly helpful to attorneys because it is tailored to the practice of law.

The International Legal Technology Association (ILTA) (**www.iltanet.org**), a professional organization devoted to technology for law firms and law departments, regularly provides security education and materials and has peer groups that regularly exchange information. ILTA has established the LegalSEC initiative that has been working for several years to provide the legal community with tailored guidelines for risk-based information security programs. It conducts an annual LegalSEC summit and provides additional educational programs and resources.

The ABA LTRC conducts an annual survey and publishes an annual Legal Technology Survey Report—covering a broad range of legal technology topics. It reports on law firm security staffing, policies, controls, and incidents (excerpt is included in Appendix A). It is based on survey responses by attorneys. ILTA's LegalSEC publishes an Annual Study of the Legal Industry's Information Security Assessment Practices—covering current and future security practices of legal organizations in North America. It is based on responses by technology and security staff in law firms and legal offices.

There are numerous security frameworks, standards, and guidance documents that can be used for implementing law firm information security programs. It is important to select and use one or more that fit the size of the firm and the sensitivity of the information to use as a framework. This can be a daunting task with the alphabet soup of available resources: NIST, ISO, FTC, SANS, CERT, ILTA, and more.

The National Institute of Standards and Technology (NIST) (**http://csrc .nist.gov**) has published numerous security standards and guidance documents and periodically updates them. While many of them are very technical and more appropriate for government agencies and large companies (and large law firms), some are basic and tailored for small and midsized businesses. Of particular importance is the NIST Framework for Improving Critical Infrastructure, Version 1.0 (February 12, 2014). While the Framework is aimed at security of critical infrastructure, it is based on generally accepted security principles that can apply to all kinds of businesses and enterprises, including law firms. NIST Special Publication 800-53, Revision 4, Security and Privacy Controls for Federal Information Systems and Organizations (April 2013) and standards referenced in it provide a comprehensive catalog of controls and a process for selection and implementation of them through a risk management process.

NIST's Small Business Information Security: The Fundamentals, Draft NISTR 7621, Revision 1 (December 2014) presents an overview of security requirements for small businesses in light of the Framework. For larger firms, consensus security standards such as those published by the International Organization for Standardization (ISO; available at **www.iso.org**) provide a good framework. They include the ISO/IEC 27000 series of standards, which define and include comprehensive requirements, processes, and controls for Information Security Management Systems. The Federal Trade Commission's (FTC) Safeguards Rule under the Gramm-Leach-Bliley Act (included in Appendix G) provides a helpful framework for lawyers in smaller firms, although it does not generally apply to lawyers (unless they have agreed by contract to do so). The requirements in the rule, "Standards for Safeguarding Customer Information," 16 CFR, Part 314, are general and cover fewer than two pages in the *Federal Register*. The Massachusetts regulation, 201 CMR 17, and guidance under it can also be a helpful framework, even where it does not legally apply. Although it has been criticized as onerous, most or all of its requirements are standard information security measures.

In addition to these frameworks and standards, there are also various published sets of controls that focus on parts of comprehensive security programs. Some of the more common ones are discussed below. They range from complete sets of controls to cover most types of common attacks to short lists that suggest the best starting points.

The NIST Cybersecurity Framework

In February 2014, NIST released the Framework for Improving Critical Infrastructure Cybersecurity Version 1.0, which uses a risk-based approach to managing cybersecurity risk. A copy of the Framework (without appendices) is included in Appendix H of this book. While it is aimed at security of critical infrastructure, it is based on generally accepted security principles that can apply to all kinds of businesses and enterprises, including law firms. It provides a structure that organizations, regulators and customers can use to create, guide, assess, or improve comprehensive cybersecurity programs. The Framework, "created through public-private collaboration, provides a common language to address and manage cyber risk in a cost-effective way based on business needs, without placing additional regulatory requirements on businesses."

"The Framework enables organizations—regardless of size, degree of cyber risk or cybersecurity sophistication—to apply the principles and best practices of risk management to improving the security and resilience of critical infrastructure" as well as other information systems. It is called "Version 1.0" because it is supposed to be a "living" document that will be updated to reflect new technology and new threats—and to incorporate "lessons learned."

The core of the Framework, its magic words, are **"identify, protect, detect, respond** and **recover,"** the core security functions that should shape any law firm's cybersecurity program. It explains them this way:

- ♦ **Identify**—Develop the organizational understanding to manage cybersecurity risk to systems, assets, data, and capabilities.

  The activities in the Identify Function are foundational for effective use of the Framework. Understanding the business context, the resources that support critical functions, and the related cybersecurity risks enables an organization to focus and prioritize its efforts, consistent with its risk management strategy and business needs. Examples of outcome Categories within this Function include: Asset Management; Business Environment; Governance; Risk Assessment; and Risk Management Strategy.

- ♦ **Protect**—Develop and implement the appropriate safeguards to ensure delivery of critical infrastructure services.

  The Protect Function supports the ability to limit or contain the impact of a potential cybersecurity event. Examples of outcome

Categories within this Function include: Access Control; Awareness and Training; Data Security; Information Protection Processes and Procedures; Maintenance; and Protective Technology.

+ **Detect**—Develop and implement the appropriate activities to identify the occurrence of a cybersecurity event.

  The Detect Function enables timely discovery of cybersecurity events. Examples of outcome Categories within this Function include: Anomalies and Events; Security Continuous Monitoring; and Detection Processes.

+ **Respond**—Develop and implement the appropriate activities to take action regarding a detected cybersecurity event.

The Framework includes three parts: the Framework Core, the Framework Profile, and the Framework Implementation Tiers, as follows:

> The Core is "a set of cybersecurity activities, outcomes, and informative references that are common across critical infrastructure sectors, providing the detailed guidance for developing individual organizational Profiles. Through use of the Profiles, the Framework will help the organization align its cybersecurity activities with its business requirements, risk tolerances, and resources. The Tiers provide a mechanism for organizations to view and understand the characteristics of their approach to managing cybersecurity risk."

It provides a common classification scheme and mechanism for businesses and enterprises to:

1. Describe their current cybersecurity posture;
2. Describe their target state for cybersecurity;
3. Identify and prioritize opportunities for improvement within the context of a continuous and repeatable process;
4. Assess progress toward the target state; and
5. Communicate among internal and external stakeholders about cybersecurity risk.

The Framework follows an evolving approach to security that recognizes the increasing importance of detection and response. For years, the major emphasis was on protection. While detection and incident response have long been necessary parts of comprehensive information security, they have taken a back seat to protection. Their increasing importance is now being recognized. Gartner, a leading technology consulting firm, has predicted that by 2020, 75% of enterprises' information security budgets will be allocated for rapid detection and response approaches, up from less than 10% in 2012.

The Framework includes, in Table 2 to Appendix A, cross-references to controls to the ISO and NIST standards discussed below.

For law firms that do not have a security program, the Framework can be used as a reference for establishing a program. For firms that already have programs, it can be used to review and potentially strengthen them.

The FTC Safeguards Rule

As discussed above, the FTC Safeguards Rule can provide a helpful basic framework for a law firm information security program for small firms if it is expanded beyond financial information to cover client and law firm information. The rule was adopted by the FTC under Section 501(b) of the Gramm-Leach-Bliley Act, which requires the FTC (and other agencies) to "establish appropriate standards for the financial institutions subject to their jurisdiction relating to administrative, technical, and physical safeguards" to protect consumer financial information. The requirements under the rule include security programs that (1) ensure the security and confidentiality of customer records and information; (2) protect against any anticipated threats or hazards to the security or integrity of such records; and (3) protect against unauthorized access to or use of such records or information that could result in substantial harm or inconvenience to any customer.

The requirements in the rule are general and brief. The FTC explained in its press release, when the rule was issued, that it sought to strike "an appropriate balance between allowing flexibility . . . and establishing standards." In accordance with this approach, the rule provides only general requirements, with considerable flexibility in their application. Many of the entities regulated by the FTC under the act are small and midsized businesses, so the FTC adopted a streamlined approach that can be scaled to smaller businesses.

The rule requires a formal information security program for paper and electronic records, reasonably designed to meet stated objectives and including specific elements. Covered institutions are required to develop, implement, and maintain a comprehensive information security program that is written and contains administrative, technical, and physical safeguards appropriate to the institution's size and complexity, the nature and size of its activities, and the sensitivity of any customer information at issue.

The information security program must be reasonably designed to meet the three objectives just listed, which are taken directly from the statutory language.

The required elements for an information security program include:

- Designation of an employee or employees to coordinate the information security program.

- Reasonable identification of foreseeable internal and external risks to the security, confidentiality and integrity of customer information that could result in the unauthorized disclosure, misuse, alteration, destruction, or other compromise of information, and an assessment of the sufficiency of any safeguards in place to control the risks.

- Design and implementation of information safeguards to control risks identified through risk assessment and monitoring of the effectiveness of the safeguards.

- Assurance that contractors or service providers are capable of maintaining appropriate safeguards for the customer information and requiring them, by contract, to implement and maintain such safeguards.

- Evaluation and adjustment of the information security program in light of developments that may materially affect the entity's safeguards.

The rule requires a formal program, with flexibility, designed to meet the stated objectives, including, at a minimum, these elements. Again, it can be a good framework for small law firms if it is expanded beyond consumer financial information.

ISO 27000 Standards

The ISO 27000 series of standards are consensus international standards for a comprehensive Information Security Management System (ISMS), including its elements, processes, and controls, published by the International Organization for Standardization (ISO; available at **www.iso.org**). The systems are described in ISO/IEC 27000:2014. There are various additional standards in the series that provide additional details. Together, they provide the framework and details for establishing, implementing, monitoring, and continually improving an ISMS.

The core standards include:

- ISO/IEC 27001:2013—Information Security Management Systems—Requirements
- ISO/IEC 27002:2013—Code of Practice for Information Security Management Controls
- ISO/IEC 27005:2011—Information Security Risk Management

ISO 27002 includes 14 security domains, as follows:

1. Information Security Policies
2. Organization of Information Security
3. Human Resource Security
4. Asset Management
5. Access Control
6. Cryptography
7. Physical and environmental security
8. Operation Security—procedures and responsibilities, Protection from malware, Backup, Logging and monitoring, Control of operational software, Technical vulnerability management and Information systems audit coordination
9. Communication security—Network security management and Information transfer
10. System acquisition, development, and maintenance—Security requirements of information systems, Security in development and support processes and Test data
11. Supplier relationships—Information security in supplier relationships and Supplier service delivery management
12. Information security incident management—Management of information security incidents and improvements
13. Information security aspects of business continuity management—Information security continuity and Redundancies
14. Compliance—Compliance with legal and contractual requirements and Information security reviews

For these 14 domains, there are 35 main security categories (each with a control objective to be achieved and controls to achieve it) with a total of 114 controls.

Other standards in the 27000 family provide additional details and guidance. A law firm or other enterprise can be certified under ISO/IEC 27001. Certification is done by an authorized third party. Certification can cover all of an enterprise's information technology or specified systems such as e-mail, document management systems, remote access, litigation support, and device management. Certification by a third party demonstrates to clients and prospective clients a law firm's commitment to security and its implementation in accordance with a consensus standard. While a limited, but slowly growing, number of law firms report having or seeking formal certification under the ISO 27000 standards, a greater number report using these standards, or parts of them, as guides. ILTA's LegalSEC initiative has been focusing on aligning the legal community with the 27000 standards.

NIST Standards

In addition to the Framework, NIST has published numerous standards and guidance documents on information security. Many of them have been published for implementation of information security requirements for covered federal agencies and information systems supporting them. The core document in this area is NIST Special Publication 800-53, Revision 4, Security and Privacy Controls for Federal Information Systems and Organizations (April 2013). SP 800-53 and the standards referenced in it provide for categorizing information, risk assessment, selection and implementation of security controls, and monitoring of security. It includes 18 families of security controls that include 260 controls.

While designed for federal agencies, the NIST process and various NIST standards can be used by law firms or businesses as guides. There is no formal process for certification under NIST like there is under ISO 27001. Some law firms have reported that they are aligning their security programs with NIST standards.

The NIST Small Business Guide

NIST's Small Business Information Security: The Fundamentals, Draft NISTR 7621, Revision 1 (December 2014) provides NIST's recommendations for small businesses to establish reasonably effective cybersecurity programs. It defines typical small businesses as ones with up to 500 employees but recognizes that it may vary with the type of business. It provides three classifications of security practices: absolutely necessary, highly recommended, and more advanced:

The "absolutely necessary" cybersecurity actions that a small business should take to protect its information, systems, and networks

1. Manage risk.
2. Protect information/systems/networks from damage by viruses, spyware, and other malicious code.
3. Protect your Internet connection.
4. Install and activate software firewalls on all your business systems.
5. Patch your operating systems and applications.
6. Make backup copies of important business data/information.
7. Control physical access to your computers and network components.
8. Secure your wireless access point and networks.
9. Train your employees in basic security principles.
10. Require all individual user accounts for each employee on business computers and for business applications.
11. Limit employee access to data and information, and limit authority to install software.

Highly Recommended Cybersecurity Practices

1. Be careful with e-mail attachments and e-mails requesting sensitive information.
2. Be careful with web links in e-mail, instant messages, social media, or other mediums.
3. Watch for harmful popup windows and other hacker tricks.
4. Do online business or banking more securely.
5. Exercise due diligence in hiring employees.
6. Be careful when surfing the Web.
7. Be concerned when downloading software from the Internet.
8. Get help with information security when you need it.
9. Dispose of those old computers and media safely.
10. Protect against social engineering.
11. Perform an asset inventory (and identify sensitive business information).
12. Implement encryption to protect your business information.

More Advanced Cybersecurity Practices

1. Plan for contingency and disaster recovery.
2. Identify cost-avoidance considerations in information security.

Significantly, the guide is addressed to typical small businesses and does not consider in its categorization of practices the more stringent requirements that generally apply to law firms. While it provides a good list of security practices, it is our view that law firms should implement all of the absolutely necessary and highly recommended practices as soon as practicable, if they do not already employ them, and we would put encryption and contingency and disaster recovery in the absolutely necessary category for law firms. And of course, cost avoidance is always a consideration for law firms of all sizes.

US-CERT Resources for Small and Midsized Businesses

US-CERT, a part of the U.S. Department of Homeland Security, has published a list of cybersecurity resources for small and midsized businesses (available at **www.us-cert.gov/ccubedvp/getting-started-business**). They include resources such as a "Toolkit for Small and Midsize Businesses" and "Why Every Small Business Should Use the NIST Cybersecurity Framework."

The Critical Security Controls

The *Critical Security Controls for Effective Cyber Defense: Consensus Audit Guidelines,* first published in 2008, were developed as "an approach to prioritizing a list of the controls that would have the greatest impact in improving risk posture against real-world threats." They were coordinated by the SANS Institute, a leading information research and education provider, and were agreed upon by a consortium including the National Security Agency, U.S.-CERT, the Department of Defense, Joint Task Force Global Network Operations (JTF-GNO) Command, the Department of Energy Nuclear Laboratories, the Department of State, the Department of Defense Cyber Crime Center, the Federal Bureau of Investigation, leading commercial forensics consultants and pen testers, and others. In 2013, coordination of the project was transferred to the Council on Cyber-Security and they are now called the *Critical Security Controls*, currently in version 5.1. (**www.counciloncybersecurity.org/critical-controls**). They have evolved over time and it is important to consult the Council or SANS website for the current version.

The current *Critical Security Controls* include:

1. Inventory of Authorized & Unauthorized Devices
2. Inventory of Authorized & Unauthorized Software
3. Secure Configurations for Hardware and Software on Mobile Devices, Laptops, Workstations, and Servers
4. Continuous Vulnerability Assessment & Remediation
5. Malware Defenses
6. Application Software Security
7. Wireless Access Control
8. Data Recovery Capability
9. Security Skills Assessment & Appropriate Training to Fill Gaps
10. Secure Configurations for Network Devices such as Firewalls, Routers, and Switches
11. Limitation and Control of Network Ports, Protocols, and Services
12. Controlled Use of Administration Privileges
13. Boundary Defense
14. Maintenance, Monitoring & Analysis of Audit Logs
15. Controlled Access Based on the Need to Know
16. Account Monitoring & Control
17. Data Protection
18. Incident Response and Management
19. Secure Network Engineering
20. Penetration Tests and Red Team Exercises[3]

SANS has identified a *First Five Quick Wins*—subcontrols of the *Critical Security Controls* "that have the most immediate impact on preventing the advanced targeted attacks that have penetrated existing controls and compromised critical systems at thousands of organizations." They include:

1. Application whitelisting
2. Using common, secure configurations
3. Patch application software within 48 hours

---

3. A Red Team Exercise is a comprehensive attempt to gain access to a system by any means necessary, and usually includes cyber penetration testing, physical breach, testing all wireless systems present for potential wireless access, and also testing employees through social engineering and phishing tests. These are real-life exercises performed by a skilled small team of security professionals. Other controls are discussed below and in later chapters.

4. Patch systems software within 48 hours

5. Reduce the number of users with administrative privileges

These *Quick Wins* are listed in the Critical Controls and on a SANS poster that lists and explains the *Critical Security Controls*. (**https://www.sans.org/media/critical-security-controls/spring-2013-poster.pdf**) Details of various controls are covered in later chapters. Here are brief descriptions:

Application whitelisting is a security tool that controls the applications and services that can run on a computer or network. Permitted apps and services are entered on a whitelist and all others are blocked by default. Unauthorized or malicious apps and services are blocked since they are not included in the authorized list. It is a strong control, but not foolproof, and can be difficult to administer.

Common, secure configurations are secure settings on a computer, device, or network, such as setting a secure password or passphrase, setting browser security controls, and turning off unneeded services.

A patch is an update to software to fix or improve it—often to address a security vulnerability. Patches should be promptly applied when they are released. This *Quick Win* recommends that they should be applied within 48 hours. They should be applied to the operating system and all programs and applications—including browser plug-ins.

Both Windows and OS X have multiple kinds of accounts for users. They include standard user accounts and administrator accounts. The standard user accounts have limited privileges. Administrator accounts have more privileges and can, accordingly, do more, such as installing new software and devices. For routine use, computers should be operated in standard user account mode. Administrator accounts should be used only when necessary to perform functions that are limited to them. Operating in a standard user account provides better protection because some (but not all) malware and attacks need administrator access to be successful.

The *Critical Security Controls* do not define the requirements for a comprehensive information security program, but instead, "prioritize and focus on a smaller number of actionable controls with high-payoff, aiming for a 'must do first philosophy.'" For law firms starting information security programs, the *Controls* can be used for setting priorities and making sure that the key controls are covered. For those with established programs, they can be used as part of the auditing and updating process.

Strategies to Mitigate Targeted Cyber Intrusions

The Australian Signals Directorate, an intelligence agency in the Australian Government Department of Defence, publishes a set of *Strategies to Mitigate Targeted Cyber Intrusions*. (**www.asd.gov.au/publications/Mitigation_Strategies_2014.pdf**). The current version (February 2014) lists thirty-five measures and provides details about them. The *Strategies* take an approach similar to the *Critical Security Controls*. Significantly, the Signals Directorate reports that four of the measures, as a package, would have mitigated at least 85% of the incidents to which it responded.

Its *Top 4 Mitigation Strategies* are:

1. Application whitelisting
2. Patching systems
3. Restricting administrative privileges
4. Creating a defence in depth system

The *Strategies*, like the *Critical Security Controls,* are not themselves a comprehensive security strategy—they identify a detailed set of measures that can have a great return in stronger security. The *Top 4*, like the *First Five Quick Wins*, are subsets of larger sets of controls that can have significant protective impacts. For the most part, *Top 4* and the *First Five Quick Wins* overlap. *The Top 4* adds defence in depth, while the *Quick Wins* adds secure configuration.

The LegalSEC Top 10

At the ILTA LegalSEC Summit 2013, one of the sessions presented the "LegalSEC Top 10," tailoring the kinds of short lists of security measures discussed above to the legal profession:

1. Patch Management
2. Elevated Privilege
3. Multi-Factor Authentication
4. Leverage Your Entire Security Suite
5. Application Whitelisting

6. Security Web/Email Gateways

7. Utilize Peer Networks [for sharing information on threats and security measures]

8. Intrusion Detection/Prevention

9. Clean up your Policies

10. Security Awareness

This is a particularly helpful list for law firms because it focuses on their profession. As with the other short lists, it covers measures that can have a high return on greater security, but does not include everything necessary for a comprehensive security program.

Five Common Failures in Network Security

Dell SecureWorks, a leading security consulting and incident response service provider, recently posted "Incident Response Teams Find Common Pitfalls in Network Security" on its Security and Compliance blog (**www.secureworks.com/resources/blog/incident-response-teams-find-common-pitfalls-in-network-security**). It reports that its teams have found the following common shortfalls that have aggravated the compromise of networks for which it has investigated intrusions:

♦ The network architecture is designed for delivery, not security. Networks are usually flat allowing any user to access files that have nothing to do with their duties. This increases the ease of administration, but certainly doesn't help security.

♦ Companies don't know what hardware and software they have, nor do they know all the cloud services their organizations are using and how they connect to the corporate network. They don't know who is authorized to access these systems.

♦ Organizations purchase and deploy security devices but don't have the skill sets to manage and monitor them.

♦ Companies are not monitoring endpoints (workstations, laptops, and servers).

♦ Organizations lack a structured approach to responding to security incidents.

The post suggests that organizations should do the opposite of these common pitfalls to prevent or limit compromises and provides details on the recommended opposites.

The 80-20 Rule

For a preliminary step in the evaluation of technical controls, Symantec's 80-20 Rule of Information Security, published years ago, is helpful:

> This rule states that 80% of security risk is effectively managed by implementing the most important 20% of available technical security controls, which are removing unneeded services, keeping service patches current, and enforcing strong passwords. (**http://securityresponse.symantec.com/avcenter/security/ Content/security.articles/fundamentals.of.info.security.html**)

Although the rule does not have mathematical certainty, as its name may suggest, it does identify what many consider to be the first things that should be addressed in technology, with a high return in security. A computer or system that does not utilize these controls would generally be considered to have deficient security. This is a starting point; it should not be a substitute for a complete risk-based security program (covering people, processes and procedures, and technology) and should not be taken as a justification for failure to address additional technical safeguards.

Security Programs and Policies

An information security program implements a process to protect the confidentiality, integrity, and availability of information. It must address people, policies and procedures, and technology. The terms "security program" and "security policy" are sometimes used to mean the same thing. Other times, "program" is used broadly to describe the entire process and "policy" more narrowly to describe the document that implements it.

Although there are numerous descriptions of what should be included in an information security program, the following are generally accepted elements:

- An inventory of information assets
- A risk assessment
- Assignment of duties and responsibilities
- Physical security
- Networks and network devices (wired and wireless networks)
- Servers
- Access control-including multifactor authentication where appropriate

- Application security
- Endpoints—desktops and laptops
- Portable and mobile devices
- Electronic communications
- Encryption of data in storage and data in transit
- External connections, including the Internet
- Remote access
- Backup and business continuity
- Secure disposal
- Security of service providers (including cloud services)
- Training and enforcement
- Security awareness
- An incident response plan
- Monitoring, auditing, and updating

All of these areas need to be addressed for an effective information security program. Several of the areas are discussed in this chapter. The rest are covered in the remaining chapters of this book. Law Firm security policies are discussed more fully in chapter 6. A checklist for an information security program prepared by the authors is included in Appendix J.

Inventory and Risk Assessment

The first step in developing and implementing an information security program is an inventory. It should include all information assets: data, software, hardware, appliances, and infrastructure. You can't protect it if you don't know you have it. Next is a risk assessment, a structured process to identify, evaluate, and prioritize threats to a law firm's information assets and operations. The results are used to develop an information security program.

For the risk assessment function, it is best to use a framework or outline to make sure that everything is covered. The National Institute for Standards and Technology (NIST) has developed the *Federal IT Security Assessment Framework* for government agencies. It is also available for businesses and is an appropriate tool for large law firms. A complete, formal approach is CERT's OCTAVE (Operationally Critical Threat, Asset, and Vulnerability Evaluation[SM]). It is a good framework for large law firms and companies. OCTAVE-S is a version of OCTAVE that is tailored for smaller organizations with one hundred or fewer people. OCTAVE materials, including worksheets, are available without charge. For small law firms, even the

OCTAVE-S framework can be scaled down. SearchMidmarketSecurity has published a step-by-step security risk assessment for small and midsized businesses (available at **http://searchmidmarketsecurity.techtarget.com**). Many IT consultants and security professionals have their own checklists. All of these documents can be found on the Internet, but frankly, these are technical documents; just make sure anyone doing a risk assessment is familiar with them!

People

The statement about the environment by the cartoon character Pogo, "We have met the enemy and he is us," applies equally to attorneys and staff using technology. Many breakdowns in security are caused or facilitated by the users of technology. Internal threats can come from insiders who are dishonest, disgruntled, bored, careless, or untrained. As discussed earlier, the people element of security is critical. Supervising attorneys have a professional responsibility to ensure that they and those they supervise take reasonable measures to safeguard confidential information. This duty applies as well to junior attorneys who supervise staff and service providers.

The people element starts at the top. Management, whether a solo practitioner or a managing partner of a large firm, must take ownership of the information security program. Time and time again, it has been demonstrated that a "top-down" approach is necessary.

Another important people consideration is assignment of responsibility. Management should appoint a person to be in charge of the security program. Depending on the size of the firm, that may be the sole function of a chief security officer or one of multiple duties of a lawyer or administrator. Someone must be in charge. The program should define security roles and responsibilities of everyone, from the highest executive to the most basic user.

Security must be a major consideration in the hiring of new employees. A thorough background check and review of references are necessary for law firm employees. They will have access to all kinds of client and firm information, and it is critical that they can be trusted.

The example of Kevin Mitnick should be enough to teach all attorneys about the need to be thorough in this area. He was a legendary hacker on the FBI's Ten Most Wanted list. As the FBI was closing in on him, he fled and moved to Denver, where he took on a new identity—Eric Weiss (Harry Houdini's real name). He needed a job, so he applied for one as a systems administrator in the Denver office of a major law firm. He used the name Eric Weiss. For a reference, he made up a fake IT company, rented a mailbox in its name, and opened an account with a telephone answering service. He returned a call from the law firm, gave himself a glowing recommendation, and got the job. The law firm then had a most wanted fugitive as a systems administrator. The law firm dodged a bullet only because Mitnick was laying low while the feds were pursuing him.

Although he was a capable hacker, Mitnick was more successful in social engineering—the art of tricking people to voluntarily give up information (user IDs, passwords, etc.), access to systems, copies of software and much more. Social engineers prey on the tendency of people to be trusting and helpful, exploiting people rather than technology. It is critical for security programs to address this risk—either don't trust until proven, or trust, but verify. Social engineering can take place in person, over the phone, by e-mail and on websites.

Phishing is a form of social engineering that uses e-mail to try to trick recipients into giving up confidential information or installing malware by opening a file or clicking on a link to a malicious website. That "client" in Nigeria is really not going to pay you thousands of dollars for depositing a check and forwarding most of the proceeds to the client. Your bank or Internet service provider is really not going to cancel your account if you don't immediately give it your login credentials or Social Security number. It's amazing how many people, including attorneys and law firm personnel, fall prey to these kinds of schemes. Employees must be trained about this risk, be periodically reminded, and exercise constant vigilance. The Anti-Phishing Working Group (**www.antiphishing.org**) is a good information source in this area.

Training is a core part of security. Everyone with access to technology should be thoroughly trained in safe computing, both initially and periodically thereafter. Beyond formal training, there should be constant security awareness, with everyone considering security as a part of everything they do with computers, mobile devices, and data—every day, every time they use technology. The SANS Institute publishes a Security Awareness Tip of the Day that is a great tool for maintaining awareness (**www.sans.org/tip_of_the_day.php**). SANS also publishes *OUCH!*—a monthly security awareness newsletter that is targeted to end users. It is available for free distribution (**http://www.securingthehuman.org/ resources/newsletters/ouch/2015**).

Policies and Procedures

As discussed above, an information security policy is a formal writing that defines the assets that are covered, threats to them, and protective measures. It also assigns responsibility for security functions and defines the acceptable and unacceptable use of information systems. It defines potential security incidents and breaches and provides for incident response when they occur. The policy should address the different classifications of data in the system and define the appropriate levels of access and security for them.

Whether there is an overall technology policy that includes security or a series of coordinated policies, the following should be covered: information security, physical security, acceptable use of technology, Internet use, and e-mail and electronic communications. In larger organizations, more complex policies are generally needed, and policies may need to be supplemented with written procedures that provide more detail.

To be effective, the entire policy must be understood, monitored, and enforced. A policy that stays on a shelf or buried deep in a network may be worse than no policy at all because it may be constantly violated. Additional details are covered in our chapter on policies and plans.

Technology

The technology element of security is complex and involves numerous details, even in a small firm. It includes a number of areas such as consideration of security in selecting technology (such as buying business grade laptops with a business version of Windows that support stronger security than consumer versions), secure configuration of computers, devices, and networks (such as enabling encryption, automatic logoff after inactivity, and setting secure passwords or passphrases), and security software and appliances (such as firewalls, malware protection, and enterprise mobility management). They are discussed throughout this book.

Third Parties and Outsourcing

Protection of information to which third parties are given access is an important part of information security. Appropriate due diligence, legally binding requirements to protect security, and monitoring are necessary. This area of security is discussed in detail in our outsourcing and cloud computing chapters.

Incident Response

An incident response plan is a critical part of a security program. Procedures and responsibilities should be defined in advance for response to security incidents and breaches. This can help to limit the impact, preserve evidence, and correlate data from all sources. It will also identify external resources, such as forensics experts and law enforcement, which may be necessary to address a breach. Potential public relations issues should also be addressed. Incident response is discussed in more detail in the Polices and Plans chapter.

Threat Intelligence and Information Sharing

A critical part of security is understanding the threats: "Know your enemy!" There are several excellent threat reports that provide information in this area. Some of the ones that we regularly consult are the Verizon Data Breach Investigations Report, Mandiant's M-Trends, Symantec's Internet Security Threat Reports, and HP's Cyber Risk Reports. They are issued quarterly or annually and provide valuable information because many threats and mitigation measures continue from year to year. But threats often evolve much more quickly, so it is also important to understand what has happened more recently, sometimes in past days or hours. Two approaches that provide this kind of current threat information are threat intelligence and information sharing. They are currently getting a lot of attention in the security community.

A recent Ponemon Institute survey reported that 65% of those surveyed that had a breach in the last twenty-four months believed that threat intelligence could have prevented the breach or minimized the consequences.

While there is no uniform definition, threat intelligence involves collecting information about threats from a variety of sources, internal and external, and analyzing it to create actionable information for the relevant system or systems. Information comes from sources such as data feeds (free and subscription), research networks, honeypots (systems set up to analyze malicious traffic), commercial sources, data from internal networks, and shared data from external networks.

Large enterprises often rely on internal staff to analyze and apply threat intelligence on their own or with outside resources. Smaller and midsized enterprises generally rely on service providers. Enterprises of all sizes get the benefit of some threat intelligence because it is used by security vendors to update security software on endpoints (desktops and laptops), servers, firewalls, and intrusion detection/prevention systems. Threat intelligence providers generally provide a higher level of intelligence and more quickly, but for a subscription price. Some of the leading threat intelligence service providers are Dell SecureWorks, Cyveillance, FireEye, IID, LogRythm, RSA, and iDefense. Most offer multiple levels of service for different prices.

Information sharing is a related area that covers both formal and informal sharing of threat and mitigation information between or among different enterprises, including law firms. It can be as simple as two security professionals in different companies communicating wither each other. It can also include communications through a security or industry discussion list. For example, in legal technology these kinds of discussions take place in the International Legal Technology Association's (ILTA) Server Operations and Security peer group and LegalSEC.

It can also take place through formal Information Sharing & Analysis Centers (ISACs), which have been established with US-CERT to address the information sharing process for specific sectors of critical infrastructure, such as communications, energy, financial services, and transportation. As discussed in Chapter 1, the fifteen-year-old Financial Services Information Sharing and Analysis Center (FS-ISAC) is considered one of the most mature ISACs today. The Legal Services Information Sharing and Analysis Organization (LS-ISAO) Services was launched in 2015 with the help of the FS-ISAC. Because of its current dues structure, it is likely to be limited to large law firms, at least for now.

Intelligence and information also takes place through sources such as US-CERT (**www.us-cert.gov**), the SANS Internet Storm Center (**https://isc.sans.edu/dashboard.html**), and the FBI's InfraGard program (**https://www.infragard.org**).

Defense in Depth

Defense (or defence as the Aussies say) in depth is a core information security principle. It is the approach of protecting computers and networks with a series of layered defenses, so that if one defense fails, another will already be in place to stop or limit an attack. For example, if malware gets through an access control, it may be stopped by security software, or if not by the software, by limitations on a user account. The concept of defense in depth comes from the military and multiple defenses behind the front lines. It is well suited to protecting networks and information systems. As data moves outside the fortress of a network (e.g., on laptops and mobile devices), it is important to protect the data as well as the information systems. The recommendations in this book follow this principle. While there may appear to be some redundancy in the recommendations that we make, they are redundant to apply this principle.

Conclusion

A comprehensive information security program that addresses people, policies and procedures, and technology is a must for all attorneys and law firms today. It should cover all of the core security functions: identify, protect, detect, respond, and recover, as explained in the NIST Framework. It should also include a comprehensive set of security controls based on one or more of the generally accepted standards. The program should be appropriately tailored to the size of the firm, the sensitivity of the information, and anticipated threats. It should promote constant security awareness by all users and provide for review and updating. This chapter explored the key concepts, frameworks, and sets of security controls. Details of applying them are provided throughout the rest of the book.

CHAPTER SIX

Law Firm Security
Policies and Plans

Technology Users Run Amok

They can be rogues, far more apt to do what they please than what their employers dictate. Sometimes law firms try to control their employees with technology. At this point, some employees will end run the technology, with their own devices or networks. Technology is forever limping far behind the wiles of employees who are determined to do what they want—they are tech anarchists. Policies that have a dose of common sense and are well explained can often accomplish more than technology. Accompanied by periodic training, monitoring, and (we can't stress this enough) discipline for noncompliance, policies work hand in hand with technology to secure your confidential data.

Law firms also need plans. In terms of security, the most important plan is an incident response plan, which you hope to high heaven you never have to implement. In a modern-day nightmare, what happens if you find out that someone has hacked into your law firm servers? What's the plan, Stan?

As we discussed in our security overview chapter, policies and plans are an important part of a comprehensive information security program. Policies and plans should be appropriately scaled to the size of the firm, the sensitivity of the information, and identified threats. We could write a complete book on the policies and plans listed below, but we are just giving you an overview of the basics here—there are a lot of resources available (some in the appendices to this book) that will give you more specifics. This is a condensed version to get you thinking about whether you should be developing policies and plans you don't have or reviewing those you do have to see if they need updating. Remember, there are many more policies and plans that law firms should have, but these are some that are specifically related to securing your data.

And for heaven's sake, train, train, train at least once a year, or preferably more often. No one remembers the fine points of plans and policies without at least annual memory refreshers. At a minimum, technology updates will necessitate minor and sometimes major changes, which will need to be learned.

Electronic Communications and Internet Use Policy

There is a lot that can go into this sort of policy, but you certainly want to forbid downloading applications or other executables without the consent of your IT folks. You want to mention drive-by-downloads of malware and explain how pornography and many other forms of websites (screen savers and free utilities are notorious) can get malware onto the network just by visiting the sites. Stress known and trusted sites as the only places to visit. Using a secure and properly configured browser (e.g., Chrome) can help as well.

Phishing is the bane of our time and targeted phishing, as we've mentioned, is the most successful way to get into firms. Explain it in your policy and training and give them clues to look for evidence that an e-mail may be a phishing expedition and that no hyperlinks or attachments should be opened.

If you allow the use of social media sites, you'll need to stress the dangers they present, both in the policy and in your training. See more on this in our Social Media chapter.

A toothless policy won't work. If you are going to make rules, you need to be able to monitor conduct, at least periodically, and to enforce them through retraining or discipline. This is true for all policies, so be prepared to police your policies once they are implemented.

Social Media Policy

Many law firms do not include their social media policy in their Internet usage policy. They make it separate, perhaps because it is such a pervasive problem with unique characteristics. In the social media world, the Indians run the reservation while the chiefs are left helplessly wringing their hands.

Forbidding the use of social media doesn't work for most law firms. It not only irks employees, but they ignore the prohibition. If you have technology enforcing the prohibition, they will use their smartphones or other personal communication devices. Stress that social media is often the source of grief with frequent leakages of confidential data.

By way of contrast, large firms generally embrace social media, though we have heard of a few that prohibit its usage. At one general counsels meeting in New York, we heard the general counsels of Sprint and Coca-Cola happily laud their employees as "social media ninjas." They go out and spread the gospel on behalf of the companies. Of course, in law firms, we have to be mindful of our ethical rules, but within those rules, one can do a lot of good for the firm.

So, follow the KISS principle and keep the policy simple. No obscenities, no discriminatory postings, no angry postings, no confidential information, don't speak on behalf of the firm unless authorized, don't give legal advice, remember that social media lives forever, speak politely to everyone you interact with, proof before you post, and report problems to a supervisor. Think **before** you post!

Document Retention Policy

If only law firms would learn to take out the digital trash. Instead, they tend to move all their data when they do a technology upgrade because storage is so cheap. What is not cheap is searching through all sorts of useless data, either when looking for client documents or in response to a discovery request in a lawsuit.

Moreover, if we don't take out the trash, we end up with a lot of "dark data"—data we don't even know we have. We can't tell you how many times we've seen evidence in a case on a flash drive or hard drive—and no one knew it was there. Law firms need to manage all their data, securely destroy it when it is no longer needed (if not under a litigation hold or required to retain it because of compliance with laws and regulations) and not left lying fallow somewhere where someone might find and expose it, however inadvertently. These devices are ripe for being stolen—and often unencrypted.

Physical Security Policy

You wouldn't, in the paper world, allow files to be scattered around conference room tables when the office is closed for the night and the cleaners arrived. Likewise, you need a policy that might involve alarm systems, prox cards, biometrics, video surveillance, and the physical security of your server, including a locked room with restricted access—or at least a server in a locked rack. You'll find more information that you would want to put in a physical security policy in the Physical Security chapter of this book.

Secure Password Policy

We are still seeing lots of firms without password policies, which is unforgiveable after all this time. Using passwords alone may be a thing of the past before long, but right now most law firms use them. We know we're not going to be very popular with our recommendations.

- ◆ Employees must have alphanumeric—with special characters—passwords of 14 or more characters.
- ◆ They must change their passwords at least every 30 days and cannot repeat them for a given period of time, often two or three years.
- ◆ Suggest the use of passphrases (IclimbedEVEREST2016!) and prohibit storing passwords on computers or on sticky notes (though storing them on an encrypted flash drive or in a password manager where you have the encryption key is permissible).
- ◆ Don't reuse the password elsewhere.
- ◆ Have both a login and screensaver password.

Most of the above steps can be enforced through technology. A typical Windows Group Policy can assure that the passwords are a certain length, change frequently, are not repeated at a certain interval, and are properly applied.

BYOD, BYON, and BYOC

Yes, we know it's an alphabet soup. But the truth is that you need to understand the dangers of having employees getting around security by those acronyms above: Bring Your Own Device (which can be Bring Your Own Disaster), Bring Your Own Network (which can be Bring Your Own Nightmare), and Bring Your Own Cloud (which can be Bring Your Own Catastrophe). Elsewhere in this book, we discuss each of these things. If you are going to allow these things, you are going to have to manage them by both policy and technology.

Disaster Recovery Plan

By now, most lawyers understand what a disaster recovery plan is. Your server has had a meltdown, your building is engulfed in flames, or your office is under water. Catastrophes take many forms and many of them impact your data security. We would stress that the No. 1 problem in disaster situations is communication. Make sure your plan identifies who is in charge of what and gives alternative ways to communicate with those who have specific job functions.

Protecting lives is the first goal, but then restoring business continuity is key. If your confidential data has been impacted (as happened during Hurricane Katrina and during 9/11), you have to make one component of your business continuity planning, thus ensuring that your sensitive data remains protected. There are so many factors to consider that it boggles the mind. As we learned when two of the authors had a fire and had no access to our office for a week, no disaster recovery plan survives first contact with the enemy. Once the disaster is over, you will no doubt find that you need to revisit and revise your plan.

Mobile Security Policies

Lawyer mobility has expanded so much in the last ten years that most can now work from anywhere and have access to our office documents as long as we have an Internet connection. But all this connectivity means we have serious security concerns as we connect with laptops, tablets, and smartphones, not to mention the networks that many lawyers connect to when on the road.

If you are traveling, say to China, you might want to take special precautions. A lot of large firms send lawyers with "clean laptops," "throw-away cell phones" and "clean flash drives" so that no confidential data travels to China with the lawyer.

It is critical that our remote connections are secure and that we transport and store confidential data in a secure manner. Would it take an epic novel to tell you how? Yes. But we do include a lot of tips in our Mobile Security chapter.

Equipment Disposal Policy

It can't leave "home" with data on it. So you can't junk your devices or donate them to charity without doing a secure wipe of the data. We recommend a free product called Darik's Boot and Nuke, although it will not work on solid state drives. Just make sure you have a policy explaining what must be done and it should be on a checklist for equipment disposal just so you don't forget. See our chapter on secure disposal for details.

Though we can't delve extensively into the components of all of these policies, we have tried to provide a snapshot of the most common policies and plans. These policies and plans are an integral part of risk management and ensuring business continuity, two things near and dear to the heart of all lawyers.

Incident Response Plans

This core of the response function is advanced planning. This means attorneys and law firms need a plan, usually called an Incident Response Plan (IRP), which is often focused on data breaches, but "incidents" can refer to responding to ransomware, fighting attempted hacks, an insider accessing data without authorization, or a lost or stolen laptop or mobile device.

Most large firms now have these plans in place, but many smaller firms do not. More and more, clients and insurance companies are asking to review law firms' IRPs. In the face of ever-escalating data breaches, now is a good time to develop and implement a plan or to update an existing one. After all, football teams don't get the playbook on game day!

The problem with all plans is that they may not survive first contact with the enemy. That's OK. Far worse is having no plan at all and reacting in panic with no structure to guide your actions. The first hour that a security consultant or law enforcement spends with a business or law firm after a data breach has been discovered is a very unpleasant time. Kevin Mandia, the founder of Mandiant, a leading security firm, has called it "the upchuck hour." It is not a happy time.

Don't rely on a template IRP. While templates may be a starting point, no two law firms are identical and all have different business processes, network infrastructures, and types of data. An IRP must be customized to fit the firm—the smaller the firm, the shorter the plan is likely to be. For a solo practice, it may just be a series of checklists, with who to call for what. Books and standards have been written about IRPs. They can be reviewed and qualified professionals can be consulted for more details. The following is a condensed and, hopefully, digestible overview.

The Elements of an IRP

- Identify the **internal personnel** responsible for each of the functions listed in the IRP. Identify them by position titles rather than by name, since people come and go. It will require a broad-based team for a firm of any size—management, IT, information security, human resources, compliance, marketing, etc. Have a conference call bridge line identified in case a breach happens at night or on a weekend and include home/cell phone numbers and personal as well as work e-mail addresses. This list will need to be updated regularly as people join or leave the firm.

- Identify the contact information for an experienced **data breach lawyer**—many large firms now have departments that focus on security and data breach response and some smaller firms have a focus on the area. Don't think you can handle this without an attorney who is experienced in data breaches. Your data breach lawyer (if you selected a good one) will be an invaluable quarterback for your IRP team—and he or she may be able to preserve under attorney/client privilege much of the information related to the breach investigation.

- Identify the location of your **insurance policy** (which darn well better cover data breaches). You need to make sure you are covered before you start and list the insurer's contact information because you are going to need to call your insurer as soon as you are aware of a possible breach.

- Identify the contact information for **law enforcement**—perhaps your local FBI office—often the first folks called in.

- Identify the contact information for the **digital forensics consultant** you would want to investigate and remediate the cause of the breach. Often, a firm has been breached for seven months or more before the breach is discovered—it will take time to unravel what went on.

- Include in the IRP **containment and recovery** from a breach. A law firm that has been breached has an increased risk of a subsequent (or continuing) breach—either because the breach has not been fully contained or because the attacker has discovered vulnerabilities that it can exploit in the future.

- Determine the **data that has been compromised** or potentially compromised. You'll want to know if all data that should have been encrypted was indeed encrypted in transmission and in storage. If it was, this may lessen the notification burden. Identify any PII (Personally Identifiable Information) that may have been compromised.

- Identify and preserve **systems logs** for your information systems. If logging functions are not turned on or logs are not retained, start maintaining them before a breach.

- If you have **intrusion detection or data loss prevention** software, logs from them should be preserved and provided to your investigators immediately. If you don't, you may want to think about implementing such software.

- Identify the contact information for **your bank** in case your banking credentials have been compromised.

- (Optional but often useful) Identify the contact information for a good **public relations firm**. If you are not required to make the breach public, you may not need one, but if it does go public, you may need to do some quick damage control. Your insurance coverage may provide for this, in which case the insurance company will put you in contact with the appropriate firm.

- How will you handle any **contact with clients and third parties**, remembering that you may wish not to "reveal all" (if notice is not required) and yet need to achieve some level of transparency? Be forewarned that this is a difficult balance. You will feel like the victim of a data breach, but your clients will feel as though you have breached their trust in you. A data breach that becomes public can cause a mass exodus of clients, so work through your notification planning with great care. Be wary of speaking too fast before facts are fully vetted—this is a common mistake, trying to limit the damage and actually increasing it as the scope of the breach turns out to be far greater or different than first known.

- How will you handle **informing employees** about the incident? How will you ensure that the law firm speaks with one voice and that employees do not spread information about the breach in person or online? How will your social media cover the breach, if at all?

- If you have a **data breach notification law** in your state (and almost all do), put it right in the plan along with compliance guidelines. You may be required to contact your state Attorney General. These laws vary widely, so be familiar with your own state law. Also, determine whether other states' breach notice laws may apply—residences of employees or clients, location of remote offices, etc. Make sure that the relevant data breach regulations are referenced in the plan and attached to it.

- Identify any **impacted data that is covered by other legal obligations** such as HIPAA or client contractual requirements and comply with notice requirements.

- Conduct **training on the plan**. Make sure that everyone understands the plan and their role under it.

- **Test the plan**. This can range from a quick walk through of hypothetical incidents to a full tabletop exercise. Include contacts with external resources to make sure that everything is up to date. This will help to make everyone familiar with the plan and to identify areas that should be revised.

- Does the breach require that IT and **information security controls and policies** be updated or changed? Does what you learned from the breach require that the IRP itself be revised? The IRP should mandate at least an annual review even without an incident.

Prepare now! The new mantra in security is that businesses (including law firms) should prepare for *when* they will suffer a data breach, not for *if* they may suffer a breach. This requires security programs that include detection, response, and recovery, along with identification and protection of data and information assets. Successful response requires an effective Incident Response Plan. Attorneys who are prepared for a breach are more likely to survive and limit damage. Those who are unprepared are likely to spend more money, lose more time, and suffer more client and public relations problems.

CHAPTER SEVEN

Authentication and Authorization[1]

Authentication and authorization are steps in access control for computers, devices, networks, websites, and cloud services. **Authentication** establishes the identity of a user (or device). **Authorization** controls what the identified user (or device) is permitted to access and do. Together, they manage the keys to the data kingdom—a critical line of defense.

Passwords have been the primary method of authenticating users for as long as computers have been in use. They continue today to be the most common form of authentication for computers, smartphones, tablets, networks, websites, and cloud services. Strong passwords are difficult to remember, particularly when a user needs multiple passwords, so they frequently select weak ones and use the same passwords for multiple computers, devices, networks, and websites. Weak passwords can be broken and a compromise of one can then be a compromise of all. Passwords can also be compromised by users or by data breaches that expose databases of passwords, particularly those stored in clear text or utilizing weak hashing.

There have been a number of recent high-profile data breaches involving compromised passwords—the iCloud leak of sensitive photos of celebrities in 2014, a Russian hacker gang stealing 1.2 billion usernames and passwords in 2014, the hack and posting of 5 million Gmail account passwords in 2014, the Adobe breach in 2013 that exposed at least 150 million passwords, the 32 million exposed Ashley Madison passwords in 2015 and many more.

---

1. This chapter is adapted from Ivan Hemmans and Dave Ries, "Two-Factor Authentication: Another Reasonable Step to Secure the Information Entrusted to You," course materials, ABA TECHSHOW 2015.

Leading technology and security professionals from tech companies such as Microsoft and Google have proclaimed that "Passwords are dead!" This raises the question, "Is there a better way?" The answer is a resounding "Yes!" It's multifactor authentication—using additional authentication factors like one-time passwords, security tokens, digital certificates, fingerprints, facial recognition, and other developing technologies. There are now options that are readily available, reasonably priced, and easy to use.

This chapter explores multifactor authentication—what it does, how to implement it effectively, the tools you need, and the common challenges involved with this important security approach.

"Why a String of Characters Can't Protect Us Anymore"

Wired magazine published a cover story in November 2012, "Kill the Password: Why a String of Characters Can't Protect Us Anymore." It was written by senior writer Mat Hohan, whose online accounts were compromised by hackers.[2] He reported:

> This summer, hackers destroyed my entire digital life in the span of an hour. My Apple, Twitter, and Gmail passwords were all robust—seven, 10, and 19 characters, respectively, all alphanumeric, some with symbols thrown in as well—but the three accounts were linked, so once the hackers had conned their way into one, they had them all. They really just wanted my Twitter handle: @mat. As a three-letter username, it's considered prestigious. And to delay me from getting it back, they used my Apple account to wipe every one of my devices, my iPhone and iPad and MacBook, deleting all my messages and documents and every picture I'd ever taken of my 18-month-old daughter.
>
> THE AGE OF THE PASSWORD IS OVER. WE JUST HAVEN'T REALIZED IT YET.

He goes on to explain:

> **How do our** online passwords fall? In every imaginable way: They're guessed, lifted from a password dump, cracked by brute force, stolen with a keylogger, or reset completely by conning a company's customer support department.

***

---

2. Mat Hohan, "Kill the Password: Why a String of Characters Can't Protect Us Anymore," *Wired* (November 15, 2012), **www.wired.com/2012/11/ff-mat-honan-password-hacker.**

Hackers also get our passwords through trickery. The most well-known technique is phishing, which involves mimicking a familiar site and asking users to enter their login information.

This kind of hijacking of online accounts is consistent with breaches generally—most have involved compromised credentials. Mandiant has reported that 100% of security breaches it has studied involved the use of stolen credentials.[3] Where compromised credentials have not been the initial attack vector, they have been used to keep and expand the unauthorized access.

The *Verizon 2013 Data Breach Investigation Report* reported that about 76% of network intrusions involved weak credentials. Attacks on authentication (guessing passwords, using cracking tools, trying passwords from other sites, etc.) were factors in four of every five hacking incidents. Stolen passwords were a factor in 48% of breaches classified as hacking, including stolen passwords from other breaches, keyloggers, and phishing. Significantly, Verizon estimated that 80% of data breaches would have been prevented, or at least made more difficult, if a "suitable replacement" for passwords, such as multifactor authentication, had been used.

The *Verizon 2014 Data Breach Investigation Report* used a different reporting format, but also stressed the importance of strong authentication. Its recommended controls for protection against web-based attacks and crimeware included authentication beyond passwords:

Web Based Attacks
Single-password fail
The writing's on the wall for single-factor, password-based authentication on anything internet-facing. Even though it may draw you out of a known comfort zone, if you're defending a web application seek out alternatives to this method of identity verification. If you're a vendor in the web application space, also consider mandating alternative authentication mechanism for your customers.

***

Crimeware
Use two-factor authentication
Our results link crimeware to stolen credentials more often than any other type of data. This points to the key role of crimeware when the attack objective is to gain access to user accounts. Two-

---

3. Its experience is reported in its *M-Trends* and *APT1* Reports, **available at www.mandiant.com**.

factor authentication won't prevent the theft of credentials, but it will go a long way toward preventing the fraudulent re-use of those credentials. (Pages 22 and 34.)

Authentication

Passwords, passphrases, and PINs (personal information numbers) all use something that a user (and hopefully only the user) knows. **Something the user knows** is the first factor that can be used for authentication. There are two other factors—**something the user has** and **something the user is**. The following table summarizes authentication factors commonly used for access control:

Factor	Only the User:	Examples
Knowledge	**Knows**	username/password, passphrase, PIN, answer to challenge question
Possession	**Has**	smart cards, digital tokens, USB keys
Inherence	**Is**	fingerprint, palm print, eye (iris), face

Authentication that is stronger than a password can be implemented by using one of the other authentication factors or by using two or more authentication factors in combination (or multifactor authentication). The term two-factor authentication is often used when two of the three factors are used.

Something the user has and something the user is are generally considered to provide stronger authentication methods than something the user knows, **if** they are properly implemented and protected. For example, properly implemented fingerprint authentication is generally considered to be stronger than a password. Fingerprint-based authentication may not be stronger on consumer devices, such as smartphones, that do not have enterprise level hardware to implement them. If a fingerprint is the only form of authentication, as it is on many laptops and mobile devices, it's still single-factor authentication, because it uses only one factor—something the user is. But it is generally more secure than a password.

Multifactor authentication uses two or more factors, in combination. A common, everyday example is debit cards when they are used in card-present transactions. They require the card (something the user has) and a PIN (something the user knows). Another example is a security token, such as the RSA SecureID that is discussed below. It is a separate device that generates a new number every minute (a one-time password) that must be entered for access to a computer, network, or website. If an attacker intercepts the number, it will not work after a couple of minutes. SecureID's are commonly used with a password or PIN for two-factor authentication (something the user has plus something the user knows).

Something the User Knows

Despite pronouncements that "passwords are dead," something the user knows is still the most commonly used method of authentication today. A password (or personal information number—PIN), sometimes with a username, is the most frequent form of authentication for access to devices (smartphones, tablets, laptops, desktops, and servers), networks, websites, and cloud services. They are frequently used as the sole authentication factor and are also commonly used as one of the factors in multifactor authentication.

Security depends on using a password or PIN that cannot be easily guessed or broken thereby protecting its confidentiality. In theory, only the user knows his or her password or PIN and entry of it establishes the user's identity. For this reason, it is critical to protect the confidentiality of a password or PIN. If a user has to write it down, it should be kept in a secure location, such as a wallet, and certainly not kept on a sticky note on a laptop or monitor.

Passwords and PINs should be changed periodically. Recommendations by security professionals generally range from changing every thirty days, sixty days, or ninety days, depending on the sensitivity of the information being protected.

Because passwords are still commonly used, and will most likely continue to be used for the foreseeable future, it is important for users to understand how to create strong passwords and for enterprises such as law firms to enforce strong passwords through security policies and network management tools such as Microsoft Group Policy.

Stronger access control can be implemented for a device, network, website, or cloud service by limiting the number of unsuccessful log-on attempts that are permitted before a user is locked out—requiring a time delay or a reset by an administrator before additional log-on attempts can be made.

One of the major shortfalls of passwords is that users frequently select weak passwords and reuse them for multiple accounts. Studies repeatedly find that users choose and reuse weak passwords. For example, a recent study by Splash Data reported that the following were the most frequently used passwords found in 2014:[4]

---

4. Thomas Clabunh, "Password Fail: Are Your Workers Using 123456?" *InformationWeek* (January 20, 2015).

1. 123456
2. password
3. 12345
4. 12345678
5. Qwerty (moving across the top line of letters on a standard keyboard)
6. 123456789
7. 1234
8. baseball
9. dragon
10. football

The strength of a password depends on its length and complexity. The longer and more complex a password is, the greater protection it provides against attacks by guessing, automated brute force, and dictionary attacks. The strength of various passwords can be measured mathematically by a calculation called entropy. The challenge is creating a password that is strong, but one that can be remembered by a user.

As this chart shows, a passphrase is one way to achieve both of these goals.

Secure Passwords and Passphrases

Current recommendations for strong passwords or passphrases include the following:

- Minimum length of fourteen characters.*
- Contain lower and upper case letters
- Include numbers
- Include a symbol or symbols
- Avoid dictionary words

* For years, the recommended length of passwords and passphrases was eight characters. Recent research has shown that they can be easily defeated with the use of today's computing power, including use of video cards to use brute force attacks to guess passwords. This has led to recommendations of minimums of twelve characters and now, fourteen characters. Requirement of a twelve- or fourteen-character minimum is not yet common in businesses and law firms, but many are moving toward it. Configuration of a computer or network to reset or lock after a set number of failed log-on attempts (such as five or ten) makes a successful brute force attack much more difficult.

A passphrase uses words that are easier to remember than a random password. Here's an example:

Iluvmy2005BMW!

This one meets all of the recommendations. It can be made even stronger by inserting some random letters, numbers, or symbols.

IluvmXy2005BXMW!

Bruce Schneier recommends the approach to passwords demonstrated in the following box, based on combining "a personally memorable sentence with some personally memorable tricks to modify that sentence into a password to create a lengthy password."[5] He uses a default minimum length of twelve characters.

- WIw7,mstmsritt... = When I was seven, my sister threw my stuffed rabbit in the toilet.
- Wow...doestcst = Wow, does that couch smell terrible

He recommends the use of two-factor authentication when it's available. He also suggests the use of password tools such as Password Safe that generate and store "random unmemorable alphanumeric passwords (with symbols, if the site will allow them)."

A password manager or locker stores passwords, so the user just has to remember one strong password or passphrase to access the manager and it contains the unique password for each network, website, and cloud service. They can also generate strong, random passwords for each of them. In addition to Password Safe, some common password managers/generators are LastPass, Roboform, Norton Identity Safe, SplashID, and 1 Password. The user of a computer or mobile device then needs only a strong password or passphrase for the computer or device and one for the password manager.

Along with strong passwords or passphrases, security experts also recommend using false answers to security challenge questions. Much of the information requested by them can be obtained by an online search by the

---

5. *Schneier on Security* blog, "Choosing Secure Passwords" (posted March 3, 2014), **https://www. schneier.com/blog/archives/2014/03/choosing_secure_1.html**.

user. For questions such as city of birth, city of marriage, mother-in-law's name, first car, etc., make up a fictitious answer that you'll remember.[6]

Until stronger authentication methods replace passwords, users should keep up with developments on password security and apply them where they have to use this form of authentication. They should also consider the use of stronger authentication and multifactor authentication. This is particularly important for attorneys and law firms in addressing their duty to safeguard information relating to clients.

Something the User Has

People have used "possession-based authentication" for many years. Today, virtually every car and home in the world use keys and locks to prevent unauthorized individuals from gaining access to and using the possessions of others. Many companies distribute security cards to employees so that they may gain access to parking garages, buildings, or even secure areas within the organization. Some computers use smart cards or USB keys before allowing access to stored content. And certain web-based applications require a digital token be supplied before unlocking. It is clear that authentication based on something that only a specific person has is very effective.

The following figures illustrate some of the common applications of something the user has:

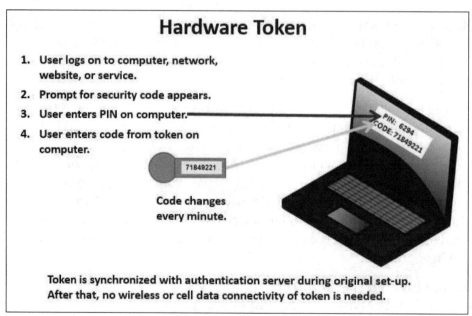

Figure 7-1

---

6. Jon Brodkin, "The secret to online safety: Lies, random characters, *and* a password manager," *Ars Technia* (June 3, 2013), **http://arstechnica.com/information-technology/2013/06/the-secret-to-online-safety-lies-random-characters-and-a-password-manager/3/**.

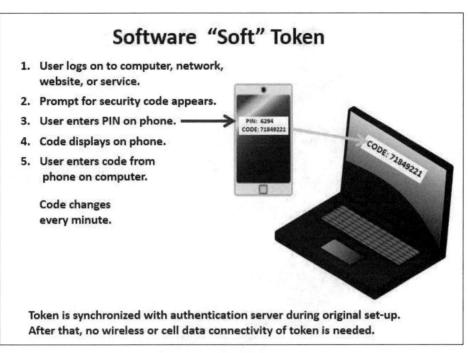

Software "Soft" Token

1. User logs on to computer, network, website, or service.
2. Prompt for security code appears.
3. User enters PIN on phone.
4. Code displays on phone.
5. User enters code from phone on computer.

   Code changes every minute.

PIN: 6294
CODE: 71849221

CODE: 71849221

Token is synchronized with authentication server during original set-up. After that, no wireless or cell data connectivity of token is needed.

Figure 7-2

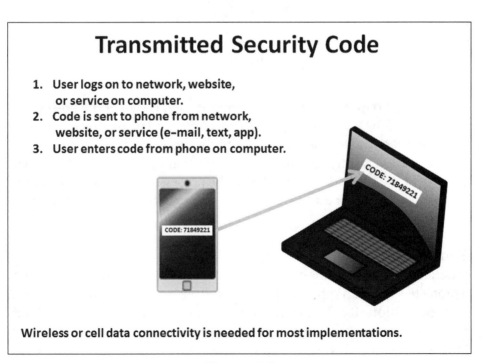

Transmitted Security Code

1. User logs on to network, website, or service on computer.
2. Code is sent to phone from network, website, or service (e-mail, text, app).
3. User enters code from phone on computer.

CODE: 71849221

CODE: 71849221

Wireless or cell data connectivity is needed for most implementations.

Figure 7-3

Figure 7-4

The weakness of possession-based authentication is that of the possession, itself. If the user loses their key or security card or an attacker steals or
copies it, then the attacker gains unrestricted access to all of the areas the
authentication token granted. This method of authentication relies on the
security of the key and the integrity of the possessor of the key. Although
replacing a lost key or token is a lot more practical than trying to replace
biometrics.

Something the User Is

Inherence factors rely upon something the user is before granting access to
a protected system. Voiceprints, fingerprints, iris and retina scanning, and
face recognition all fall under what many call "biometric authentication."
In general, inherence factors can provide reasonable certainty that a given
individual is the only one who can gain access to a protected system. Each
voice, finger, retina, and face is different.

Current examples of inherence authentication are fingerprint readers available on many laptops, Apple's iPhone's Touch ID (using a fingerprint reader built into the Home button), and Google's Android Face Unlock (using facial recognition with the user facing camera).

Laptop Fingerprint Reader
Figure 7-5

As discussed above, biometric authentication on consumer devices is often equivalent to or weaker than a password or passcode. One potential problem with biometric authentication is artificial copies of biometric data. For example, could a system that relies on facial recognition be fooled by a mechanical duplicate, such as a photo? If so, there would be no easy way for the true face to be changed. In 2011, CNET ran an article detailing how such a system was fooled.[7] Shortly after the iPhone 5s (with the TouchID fingerprint reader) was released, a security researcher demonstrated that it could be fooled with a copy of the user's fingerprint. However, it required a difficult technique and the researcher still called the TouchID "awesome."[8]

7. Elinor Mills, "Digital image can dupe Android face-based lock," *c|net* (November 11, 2011), **http://www.cnet.com/news/digital-image-can-dupe-android-face-based-lock**.

8. Marc Rogers, "Why I Hacked Apple's TouchID, and Still Think It Is Awesome," *Lookout Blog* (September 23, 2013), **https://blog.lookout.com/blog/2013/09/23/why-i-hacked-apples-touchid-and-still-think-it-is-awesome** and David Pogue, "The iPhone 5's Fingerprint Scanner Was Hacked, But I'm Not Worried," *New York Times* (September 26, 2013), http://pogue.blogs.nytimes.com/2013/09/26/the-iphone-5ss-fingerprint-scanner-was-hacked-but-im-not-worried/?_r=1.

Windows 10 includes *Windows Hello*, which is support for strong biometric authentication built into the operating system. It works with enterprise-level fingerprint readers and infrared readers for facial recognition. They are generally considered to be stronger than the ones on consumer devices such as smartphones. It integrates with Active Directory, a network directory that is part of Windows Server.

The Need for Multiple Factors

Over the past thirty years, the Internet has become an integral part of the way that individuals and institutions conduct business every day. And, where most computers from thirty years ago were only accessible to authorized people with physical access to them, today Internet-connected computers are potentially accessible to anyone online, regardless of where they are in the world. This ever-connected world has led to an increase in cyberattacks online.[9] The primary goal of cyber attackers is to steal money or information, including user names and passwords. Different authentication factors have different weaknesses, so combining different factors can protect against these weaknesses. Requiring multifactor authentication also is more secure because an unauthorized person is less likely to have access to more than one. Additional authentication factors can help to safeguard computers, devices, or online accounts against unauthorized access by third parties.

Multifactor authentication is becoming a security standard for highly sensitive data, remote access, and administrator access.

As discussed above, federal agencies have been required for years to use multifactor authentication for their own remote access to their databases, and President Obama has issued an executive order requiring agencies to develop plans for multifactor authentication for citizen remote access involving sensitive information. In October 2015, as part of National Cyber Security Awareness month, the FBI encouraged all Internet users, including small, midsized and large businesses to use two-factor authentication.[10]

The FIDO (Fast Identity Online) Alliance, an industry group including a number of major technology companies, is working to develop and implement "technical specifications that define an open, scalable, interoperable set of mechanisms that reduce the reliance on passwords to authenticate users."[11]

---

9. http://www.pewinternet.org/2014/10/29/cyber-attacks-likely-to-increase.
10. https://www.fbi.gov/news/news_blog/cyber-tip-protect-yourself-with-two-factor-authentication.
11. https://fidoalliance.org/about.

In February 2015, Microsoft announced that Windows 10 will support the FIDO standard to enable password-free sign-on for a number of supported applications, listing Office 365 Exchange Online, Salesforce, Citrix, Box, and Concur as examples.[12] This feature in Windows 10 is called *Microsoft Passport*. It uses a digital certificate that complies with the FIDO standard for sign-on to websites and services that support it, including most Microsoft sites and services. With Windows Hello (using a fingerprint or facial recognition) and Microsoft Passport, a user can log on to the computer and access supported sites and services without using a password. These Windows features and the FIDO Alliance are major steps toward replacing passwords.

Multifactor Authentication—Some Examples

Because of the growing recognition of the limitations and weaknesses of passwords, alternate authentication methods and multifactor authentication options are rapidly developing and their use is growing. Law firms and businesses are more frequently implementing solutions such as RSA SecureID, SecureAuth, and Authentify. Many online service providers now offer multifactor authentication as a safeguard users can enable with just a few clicks. Google, Dropbox, and Apple each refer to their security setting as two-step verification and provide detailed instructions for how to turn it on.

We can't cover all the options in a book of this length. In addition to the examples that we discuss, some of the leading service providers in this area include CA Technologies, Duo Security, Entrust, SafeNet, Secure Access Technologies, Yubico, and VASCO Data Security. There is an online chart, Two Factor Auth (2FA) Providers, which lists service providers and the authentication methods they offer, including SMS, phone call, hardware token, and software implementation.[13] When selecting multifactor authentication solutions, it is important to consult current reviews, get input from knowledgeable technology professionals, and check with users who have implemented the technology.

RSA SecureID

RSA Security produces and sells SecureID authentication that many companies use to grant their office workers access to sensitive company data. For years, the use of RSA SecureID tokens has been virtually ubiquitous

---

12. **http://blogs.windows.com/business/2015/02/13/microsoft-announces-fido-support-coming-to-windows-10**.

13. **https://twofactorauth.org/providers**.

among banks, government agencies, many large companies, and a number of law firms. Microsoft, Facebook, Amazon, and IBM are just a few that reportedly depend on this technology for access by their employees.

The SecureID tokens use two-factor authentication to verify that a user has rights to access certain company systems. During a login attempt, the system prompts the user for a PIN and an authentication code. The SecureID token displays the code, which the user enters to access the system. As part of the process, the PIN and code are sent to a server running the RSA Authentication Manager, where they are verified. A newer alternative, called a soft token, displays the code on a smartphone or mobile device. If found to be valid, the user is granted access to the protected system. They use the process displayed in Figures 1 and 2 above.

SecureAuth and Authentify, Multifactor Authentication Solutions

SecureAuth[14] and Authentify[15] are solutions that companies and law firms can use to add multifactor authentication to their existing remote access tools. They can be configured to intercept the standard login process and provide an extra layer of authentication for VPN, OWA (Outlook Web Access), mobile devices, or applications on the Web. SecureAuth and Authentify also include adaptive authentication methods that can inspect device fingerprints, validate geolocation, and more. Firms that have remote access, but have not yet implemented multifactor authentication, will find both SecureAuth and Authentify to be cost-effective solutions for securing access to sensitive data.

Google Two-Step Verification

Google developed a learning portal[16] to educate its users on the importance of two-step verification. The portal answers three basic questions about this security feature: 1) why people need it, 2) how it works, and 3) how the protection works. "With 2-Step Verification, you'll protect your account with both your password and your phone."

To enable this extra safeguard, visit Google's learning portal, then click **Get Started**. A person who enables two-step verification is prompted to enter a primary phone number where he or she will receive text messages or phone calls that deliver a one-time-use verification code. These codes are sent to the designated number whenever anyone attempts to log in to the Google account with a correct password from an untrusted device. After entering the verification code successfully, the person can choose to

---

14. **http://secureauth.gscadmin.com/Product.aspx**.
15. **http://www.authentify.com**.
16. **https://www.google.com/landing/2step**.

tell Google that the device is trusted. Trusted devices do not require verification codes at login as a second factor, but still require a password.

Backup Phones and Codes

In the event that the primary phone is lost or otherwise unavailable, Google provides a couple of backup options for logging in. A person can specify backup phones where verification codes can be delivered. "A good backup phone might be your home, office, or family member's phone." In addition to backup phones, a person can specify "backup codes," which can prove useful when a person is traveling and is unable to receive text messages or phone calls at either the primary or backup phones. Backup codes can be downloaded or printed, but should be kept in a safe place.

Google Authenticator App

For smartphone users, Google Authenticator is an app that can be used instead of a phone for receiving verification codes. It is available for both Android and iOS.

Dropbox Two-Step Verification

Dropbox has instructions that describe all the steps required to enable two-step verification on its service.[17] To enable it, sign into the Dropbox website and then click the account name in the upper, right-hand corner, then click **Settings**. Upon enabling two-step verification, a person is prompted to re-enter the account password. The subsequent prompt allows the person to choose how to receive verification codes, by text message or with a smartphone mobile app. Selecting **Use text messages** will display a box that allows a phone number to be entered.

Mobile Authenticator Apps

Dropbox is compatible with several smartphone mobile apps that work across a variety of mobile platforms. Google Authenticator, Duo Mobile, Amazon AWS MFA, and Authenticator for Windows Phone 7. If the **Use a mobile app** option is selected in the Dropbox's security settings window, then a person can scan a QR code with the smartphone or manually enter a provided secret key to configure the mobile app to receive Dropbox verification codes for the account.

Emergency Backup Code

Before enabling two-step verification with Dropbox, the service delivers a special sixteen-digit backup code. The user should print or write down the

---

17. **https://www.dropbox.com/en/help/363**.

retrieval key and store it somewhere safe. It will be required to access the account in the event the phone or mobile app is unavailable to retrieve verification codes.

Apple's iCloud Two-Step Verification

Apple has instructions that describe how its two-step verification system works,[18] as well as a list that answers frequently asked questions.[19] The overall process is similar to that of Google and Dropbox.

To enable Apple's iCloud two-step verification, log into **http://appleid .apple.com** with an Apple or iCloud account from a computer. Click **Password and Security** and then answer security questions, if prompted. Then, in the **Two-Step Verification** section, click **Get Started**. After continuing, a person will be prompted to log into their Apple ID account. Apple will send a verification code to one of the person's Apple devices. Then, upon successful entry of the code, the device will be set to receive future one-time verification codes whenever someone logs into iCloud or makes an iTunes or App Store purchase from an untrusted device.

It is important to note that Apple's two-step verification system protects only iCloud account information accessible at **iCloud.com**, plus iTunes and App Store purchases. At present, it does not protect FaceTime, Messages, Photo Streams, or iCloud backup data. A recent TechCrunch article[20] describes how some of Apple's systems fall outside of what two-step verification protects.

Recovery Key

As part of the two-step verification activation process, Apple provides a recovery key. "Once enabled, the **only** way to make changes to your account will be to sign in with two-step verification."

- There will be no security questions for you to remember or for other people to guess.
- Only you will be able to reset your password.
- If you forget your password, you can reset it with a trusted device and your Recovery Key.

Be sure to make a note of the recovery key and keep it in a safe place.

---

18. **http://support.apple.com/kb/PH14668?viewlocale=en_US**.
19. **http://support.apple.com/en-us/HT204152**.
20. **http://techcrunch.com/2014/09/02/apples-two-factor-authentication-doesnt-protect-icloud-backups-or-photo-streams**.

Multifactor Authentication for Office 365

Adding multifactor authentication to an organization using Office 365, to a subset of an organization, or to a subset of apps for a subset of users in an organization is easy to do. Microsoft hosts a collection of pages on its Microsoft Developer Network[21] in a section titled *Multifactor Authentication*. These pages provide a simple overview of what multifactor authentication is and how to enable it in Office 365.

Unlike consumer-facing services such as Google's Gmail or Apple's iCloud, the user doesn't specify whether multifactor authentication is enabled for an account. That decision falls to the people who manage Office 365 for the organization. The administrators can choose to enable the feature in one of a few ways; however, the end-user experience is virtually identical, regardless of the method administrators choose to employ. Once enabled, each user will be prompted to configure a secure second factor, such as a cellphone number or mobile authenticator app. Then the user will be prompted to verify possession of the cellphone or app by entering a code during the Office 365 login process. Each login attempt from a new device will trigger the verification code check via the second factor.

In the event the user loses their second factor device, an Office 365 admin can help them to gain access to the account once more.

Other Services with Two-Factor Authentication

The services mentioned above are but a few of the many that supply some form of multifactor authentication to users. The list of providers is constantly growing and changing. However, there is a site that attempts to track these changes as they happen, Two Factor Auth (2FA).[22] It contains a list of websites and services, shows whether they support two-factor authentication, links to available documentation, and delineates the available verification code delivery methods.

Conclusion

Despite proclamations that "passwords are dead," or dying, something a user knows is likely to be an authentication method for the foreseeable future—either as a single authentication method or as a factor in multifactor authentication. It is, accordingly, important for attorneys and law firms to understand password security and to implement secure passwords or

---

21. **https://msdn.microsoft.com/en-us/library/azure/dn249471.aspx**.
22. **www.twofactorauth.org**.

passphrases. Multifactor authentication and factors stronger than passwords are particularly appropriate for highly sensitive data, remote access, and administrator access. As multifactor authentication becomes a more generally accepted security approach, including recommendations for its use in the legal profession, attorneys and law firms should consider it in their analysis of the reasonable measures that they should take to safeguard information relating to clients and their own information.

CHAPTER EIGHT

Encryption:
Its Time Is Here

Encryption is a topic that most attorneys don't want to touch with a ten-foot pole, but it is becoming a more and more important part of security. Encryption is an electronic process to protect the security and confidentiality of data. While an increasing number of attorneys are using encryption, many attorneys use excuses such as "I don't need encryption," "it's too difficult," and "it's too expensive." These excuses are misplaced: attorneys need encryption, and easy-to-use (after setup) and inexpensive (sometimes free) encryption solutions are now available today. While attorneys will often need technical assistance to install and set up encryption, it's generally easy from there. It has now reached the point where all attorneys should generally understand encryption, have it available for use when appropriate, and make informed decisions about when encryption should be used and when it is acceptable to avoid it. As discussed in the chapter on attorneys' duty to safeguard, some ethics opinions are now concluding that encryption may be a necessary safeguard in appropriate circumstances.

Why Attorneys Need Encryption

Encryption can provide strong protection for stored data (on servers, desktops, laptops, tablets, smartphones, portable devices, etc.) and transmitted data (over wired and wireless networks, including the Internet and e-mail).

For example, a joint US/UK research team has written that full disk encryption is so effective that law enforcement and federal agencies are complaining that they are unable to retrieve encrypted data in criminal investigations. Federal courts are struggling with the issue of whether compelled disclosure of passwords and passphrases for decryption is prohibited by the Fifth Amendment. Recently, British Prime Minister David Cameron, FBI Director James Comey, an Assistant Attorney General in the U.S. Department of Justice, and a group of state attorneys general have called for legally required backdoors to encryption available to the U.S. government for national security and law enforcement. They have complained that Apple and Google cannot provide access to encrypted iPhones, iPads, and Android devices because they no longer store decryption keys, leaving them with users.

There has been enhanced attention to encryption since the disclosure of widespread surveillance by the NSA and advocacy by tech companies, privacy advocates, security professionals, and Edward Snowden that encryption should be used to protect against this surveillance. They have strongly opposed encryption backdoors, arguing that hackers and oppressive governments could also use them. In October 2015, the Obama administration announced that it will no longer pursue a legally required backdoor in the United States.

After the high-profile theft from an employee's home of a Department of Veterans Affairs laptop and external hard drive containing personal information of more than 28 million veterans in 2006, security guidelines for federal agencies added the requirement of encryption of all data on laptops and portable devices, unless it is classified as "non-sensitive." That was almost ten years ago.

In January 2007, eighteen laptops were stolen from the offices of a law firm in Orlando, Florida. The laptops were reportedly protected by encryption, and the incident received very little publicity. In discussing this incident, the SANS Institute, a leading information security organization, noted, "[l]aptop thefts aren't going away, but by this time next year, this type of item (laptop stolen, but the data was protected) shouldn't be newsworthy." That was more than nine years ago.

In one data breach report in 2011, a Maryland law firm lost an unencrypted portable hard drive that contained medical records of patients in a lawsuit against its client hospital. One of the law firm's employees took the hard drive containing backup data home with her. This was the firm's method of ensuring that it had an off-site backup. She took the light rail system home and left the drive on the train. When she came back a few minutes later, it was gone. Backup is a good practice, but not if it's done in a way that exposes confidential data. If the drive had been encrypted, it would have had a strong level of protection. As it was, it had little or none. It is not uncommon for backup software to have built-in ability to encrypt the backed-up information. Generally, it is just a simple matter to check an option for the backup to be encrypted.

In another example in 2014, an external hard drive was stolen from the trunk of the car of an employee of a law firm with an operations base in Atlanta. It contained confidential information about clients. It was not encrypted. It happened again in April 2015, when an attorney's laptop was stolen on a trolley in San Diego. These examples are almost certainly the tip of the iceberg. We have informally heard of numerous additional instances where law firm laptops, smartphones, tablets, and portable devices have been lost or stolen.

As these examples demonstrate, encryption is particularly important for laptops and portable media. A lost or stolen laptop or portable device that is encrypted is protected unless the decryption key has been compromised. As discussed in our Duty to Safeguard Chapter, Verizon has called encryption a security no-brainer.

Attorneys also need encryption because electronic communications can be intercepted (during transmission and storage) and wired and wireless networks can be intercepted or accessed. Cyberspace is a dangerous place!

Encryption Overview

Encryption is the conversion of data from a readable form, called plaintext, into a form, called ciphertext that cannot be easily understood by unauthorized people.

Decryption is the process of converting encrypted data back into its original form (plaintext), so it can be understood.

Encryption uses a mathematical formula to convert the readable plaintext into unreadable ciphertext. The mathematical formula is an **algorithm** (called a cipher). Decryption is the reverse process that uses the same algorithm to transform the unreadable ciphertext back to readable plaintext. The algorithms are built into encryption programs—users don't have to deal with them when they are using encryption (except for sometimes having to choose an algorithm from a list when encryption is originally set up).

This graphic shows the basic steps:

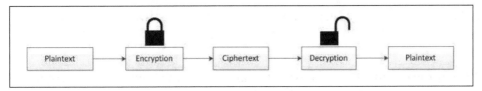

Figure 8-1

Encryption keys are used to implement encryption for a specific user or users. A key generator that works with the selected encryption algorithm is used to generate a unique key or key pair for the user(s). A key is just a line or set of data that is used with the algorithm to encrypt and decrypt the data. Protection is provided by use of the algorithm with the unique key or keys.

The process is called **secret key** or **symmetric key encryption** where the same key is used with an algorithm to both encrypt and decrypt the data. With secret key encryption, it is critical to protect the security of the key because it can be used by anyone with access to it to decrypt the data.

Here is an example of a secret key for a commonly used algorithm called the Advanced Encryption Standard-256 (AES-256) algorithm. The same key is used to both encrypt and decrypt the data.

+30NbBBMy7+1BumpfmN8QPHrwQr36/vBvaFLgQM561Q=

Example AES-256 Key

Where a **key pair** is used, one to encrypt the data and a second one to decrypt the data, the process is called **asymmetric encryption**. For this kind of encryption, a key generator is used to generate a unique key pair, one for encryption (a public key) and the other for decryption (a private key). With key pairs, it is critical to protect the private decryption key since anyone with access to it can decrypt the data. The public key can be distributed to anyone because it can be used only to encrypt.

Let's look at a simple example of its application. A short line of readable plaintext, "This is an encryption demo," becomes unreadable ciphertext when this key is used with the algorithm in an encryption program.

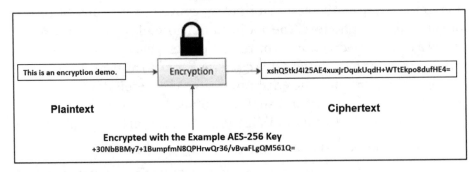

Simple Example of Encryption
Figure 8-2

The same key must be used with the algorithm in an encryption program to convert the ciphertext back to readable plaintext.

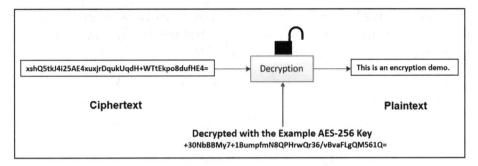

Simple Example of Decryption
Figure 8-3

Symmetric key encryption is frequently used to protect data stored on servers, laptops, portable media, etc. The key is frequently used and stored on a single computer or mobile device where providing the key to someone at a remote location is not necessary. It is difficult to use symmetric key encryption for communications because it is a challenge to securely share the key with the recipient.

The following illustration provides a simplified analogy to show how the encryption process works. The lock is like an encryption program, the internal mechanism is like the encryption algorithm, and the encryption key or keys are like a physical key or keys.

A Simplified Overview
Figure 8-4

Fortunately, users don't have to deal with keys during everyday use of encryption. When they log on with the correct password or passphrase, the program automatically accesses the key to decrypt the data. When they log off or shut down, the data is automatically encrypted.

The following is a longer example—a draft of an article written by two of the authors. A single key is used to encrypt the article. The same key is necessary to convert it back to plaintext.

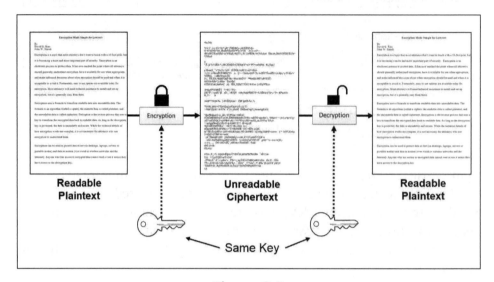

Figure 8-5

Here's an enlarged view of the plaintext and ciphertext:

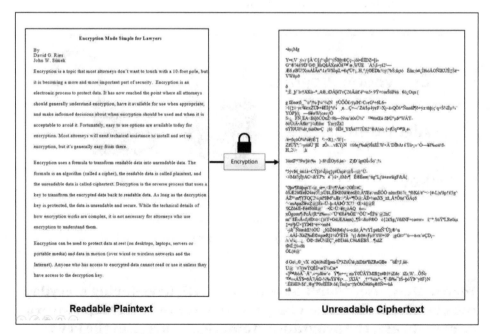

Enlarged Example: Symmetric Key Encryption
Figure 8-6

Asymmetric encryption uses a key pair instead of a single key—one key (a public key) is used to encrypt the data and a second one (a private key) is used to decrypt the data. Key pairs are frequently used for encrypted communications. The sender uses the recipient's public encryption key to encrypt the communication. The public key cannot decrypt it; only the decryption key can do that. The recipient uses the decryption (private key) to decrypt the data.

Graphically, the process works this way:

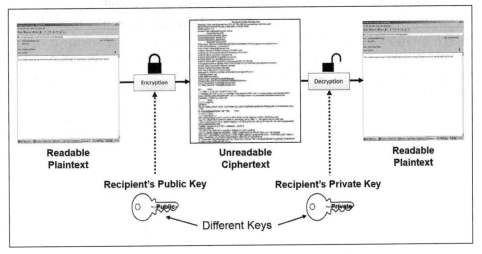

Example of Public Key Encryption
Figure 8-7

This is a brief overview of symmetric and asymmetric encryption and how it works. Attorneys do not have to understand the details or the involved mathematics. As noted above, encryption can protect both data at rest and data in motion. After encryption has been set up, it's generally automatic or point and click. Specific applications of encryption are discussed in the remaining chapters of this book.

Encryption can be inexpensive—even free. Apple's iPhones and iPads and Google's Android smartphones and tablets include encryption capability. Current versions of Windows (business versions) and Apple's OS X have built-in encryption. All of them are free with the respective operating systems.

Conclusion

Attorneys have ethical and common-law duties to protect information relating to clients and often also have contractual and regulatory duties.

The Ethics 20/20 updates to ABA Model Rules 1.1 and 1.6 made explicit attorneys' duty to take competent and reasonable measures to safeguard information relating to clients. Encryption is an important consideration in addressing these duties.

Encryption is now a generally accepted practice in information security for protection of confidential data. Attorneys should understand encryption and have it available for use it in appropriate situations. All attorneys should use encryption on laptops, portable storage media, smartphones, and tablets that contain information relating to clients. They should make sure that transmissions over wired and wireless networks are secure. Attorneys should have encryption available for e-mail or secure file transfer and use it when appropriate. Although attorneys will often need technical assistance to install and set up encryption, use of encryption after that is generally easy.

CHAPTER NINE

Security Tools
and Services

We couldn't write a book about securing your information without discussing some tools and services to validate if you really are secure. There are free tools and some that could cost you tens of thousands of dollars. We can't possibly cover all of your options, but we'll mention a few of our favorites just to wet your whistle. We previously discussed some tools to check endpoints for current patches and secure configuration and explore some more here. If you want to embark upon a more intensive security assessment, it is generally best to hire a third party that does it for a living. After all, you went to law school to practice law and not to concentrate on penetration testing.

Managed Security

A growing trend in security is the outsourcing of part of the security process to managed security service providers (MSSPs). They provide services such as remote management and updating of security appliances, such as firewalls, remote updating of security software, and 24 x 7 x 365 monitoring of network security. For a long time, these kinds of services focused on larger enterprises. More recently, they have been expanding their offerings to small and midsized businesses, as security compliance requirements have grown in this sector. Like many forms of outsourcing, MSSPs enable small and midsized businesses to obtain security services, such as 24 x 7 x 365 monitoring, that they could not afford on their own. Some of the leading MSSPs are BT Counterpane Internet Security, Dell SecureWorks, IBM Internet Security Services, Solutionary, Symantec, and Verizon. There are also regional MSSPs in various parts of the country. MSSPs also offer security consulting services. It is important for law firms using managed security to understand that the law firm retains responsibility for many parts of the information security process—particularly the people part. The complete security process cannot be outsourced.

Incident Management

Law firms need both proactive and reactive processes to deal with incident management. Proactive measures are to actually detect when an incident occurs, whereas the reactive measures make sure those incidents are properly dealt with. Most firms only have an incident response plan, which deals with how the incident should be handled. A better approach is to have technology in place that monitors what is going on in your network and triggers actions should an incident actually occur. This commonly involves aggregating logs of system information and event management systems (SIEM) and user education. SIEM systems gather logs from various devices (e.g., routers, firewalls, servers, switches, etc.) and attempt to provide an analysis from correlating the log data. There is so much data that flows over a network that it is impossible for a human to analyze it all. A SIEM system can quickly identify an incident in a near real-time fashion.

Spam Filtering

Spam (unsolicited e-mail messages) has been around for a while and will continue to hound us into the future. Not to worry. There are a lot of choices and ways to deal with spam. One of the most common methods is to invest in a software solution. They are not that expensive and typically cost from $20—$50 per computer. The good news is that you may not have to spend any money at all. You may have antispam capability provided by your antivirus security software.

The spam filtering works by scanning the message contents for words or items that are typically associated with spam transmissions. In other words, there are specific rules within the software that control whether a message is determined to be spam. A single word could identify an e-mail as spam or it could be the collective score after all the spam "words" were counted. Normally, a system administrator would "tune" the spam filter rules. This may mean adding additional spam words to the rating logic or removing certain criteria. Once a message has been classified as spam, what do you do with it? Should the message be deleted, quarantined, or perhaps the spam designation ignored and the message delivered to the user's inbox? Most spam filters will deliver the message to a quarantine area for the user to review at a future time.

The challenge with spam filters is to minimize the amount of spam messages that are delivered to your inbox and to also minimize false positives (nonspam messages that get quarantined). It may take some time to get the logic tuned for your environment. Rather than deal with the maintenance of spam filters, many firms use an outsourced service.

Using a service provider makes a lot of sense and adds additional benefits such as e-mail continuity and virus scanning. The outsourced spam services normally cost a few dollars per month per mailbox. They work by configuring all mail flow to go through the service provider. The provider then scans for any virus or malware attachments. It also analyzes the e-mail message and makes a determination whether it is spam or not. If not, then the message is sent on its way to the user's inbox or local mail server. Spam messages are typically held in quarantine for subsequent review by the user. Typically, the user gets a periodic "report" of the messages quarantined as spam. The authors use service providers and have their spam notices sent once a day for review.

Another advantage to using a service provider is the sharing of information about spam messages. Users have the ability to flag a message as spam, which is then sent back to the service provider. If enough people tag particular messages as spam, the provider changes its rules to immediately block the messages for all of its customers. In other words, all the service provider customers benefit. This helps stop those spam campaigns that are constantly changing.

Part of the spam solution can also provide business continuity for your e-mail. The service two of the authors use will spool and hold e-mail messages if their local e-mail server or Internet connection goes down. During the failure period, e-mail can still be reviewed and replied to by using a secure web portal. Once the Internet connection is restored or the e-mail server brought back online, the service provider then delivers all of the held messages. With this type of business continuity capability, the sending party doesn't even know there was a problem on the recipient's end.

Another alternative is to purchase a hardware appliance to filter for spam. Larger firms may opt for the hardware solution to avoid routing e-mail through a third party. Instead of purchasing of a dedicated hardware appliance, the antispam features are now added to your firewall. Products such as the Cisco ASA-55XX series firewalls and Cyberoam Technologies CR1000iNG-XP are examples of firewalls that can have antispam capabilities added as an option. Typically, when adding spam filtering to your firewall, the option will include a subscription to the vendor's update service. In this way, the firewall will receive periodic updates for such things as virus definitions and known spam senders and message characteristics. The updates constantly improve the accuracy of the spam filtration without burdening a systems administrator with managing the device.

Blacklists and Whitelists

Blacklists are used to permanently flag the sender's e-mail address as spam. Therefore, all messages sent from the address will immediately be deleted or quarantined without further analysis. Whitelist addresses are just the opposite. A message from an e-mail address on the whitelist is always delivered without analyzing it for spam content. A practice point is to whitelist the domain name for any courts where you practice. That way, you won't risk getting any e-mail messages from the courts getting stuck in the spam quarantine. There is a downside to whitelisting a domain or single e-mail address. If someone spoofs the sender's e-mail address, which is extremely easy to do, the message will get delivered to the recipient's inbox, since no spam processing is performed.

Web Filtering

Another tool or service to consider is web filtering. Why would you even considering filtering Web URLs or block access to particular websites? The short answer is accessing a website could infect your computer with malware. Just visiting a web page could begin a "drive-by" download to your computer without you knowing it or requesting the download.

Just like spam filtering, you can purchase specific software designed to block access to unwanted and dangerous websites such as known malware distribution, pornography, shopping, and even fantasy sports sites. The software is configured to block access to categories of websites. Just like your current antivirus solution, the web filtering software gets periodic updates to keep the database current as more websites are discovered.

Web filtering services are also available to block access to harmful, inappropriate, or dangerous websites. The service can be configured to block specific sites, categories, or even provide granular blocking down to a specific web page. Like spam filtering, you can add the web filtering feature to your firewall and purchase a subscription for the database updates.

Wireshark

One of the most valuable tools you can have in your arsenal is one that can monitor network traffic. You may have heard the term "sniffer," which is another name for something that monitors (sniffs) network traffic. It is available as a free download from **https://www.wireshark.org/**. Wireshark has been around since 1998 and is described as "the world's foremost network protocol analyzer. It lets you see what's happening on your network at a microscopic level. It is the de facto (and often de jure) standard across many industries and educational institutions." It captures and analyzes network traffic in wired and wireless networks. Some of the included features are:

- Deep inspection of hundreds of protocols, with more being added all the time
- Live capture and offline analysis
- Standard three-pane packet browser
- Multiplatform: Runs on Windows, Linux, OS X, Solaris, FreeBSD, NetBSD, and many others
- Captured network data can be browsed via a GUI, or via the TTY-mode TShark utility
- The most powerful display filters in the industry
- Rich VoIP analysis
- Read/write many different capture file formats: tcpdump (libpcap), Pcap NG, Catapult DCT2000, Cisco Secure IDS iplog, Microsoft Network Monitor, Network General Sniffer® (compressed and uncompressed), Sniffer® Pro, and NetXray®, Network Instruments Observer, NetScreen snoop, Novell LANalyzer, RADCOM WAN/LAN Analyzer, Shomiti/Finisar Surveyor, Tektronix K12xx, Visual Networks Visual UpTime, WildPackets EtherPeek/TokenPeek/AiroPeek, and many others
- Capture files compressed with gzip can be decompressed on the fly
- Live data can be read from Ethernet, IEEE 802.11, PPP/HDLC, ATM, Bluetooth, USB, Token Ring, Frame Relay, FDDI, and others (depending on your platform)
- Decryption support for many protocols, including IPsec, ISAKMP, Kerberos, SNMPv3, SSL/TLS, WEP, and WPA/WPA2
- Coloring rules can be applied to the packet list for quick, intuitive analysis
- Output can be exported to XML, PostScript®, CSV, or plain text

Notice that Wireshark can even reveal the contents of some encrypted data streams. When capturing network traffic, you must consider where to insert your tool into the data transmission. Network switches move traffic between the source and destination. They "see" what device(s) are attached to which port and move traffic accordingly. The purpose of the switch is to preserve bandwidth and not expose devices to traffic that isn't intended for it. If you connect a sniffer tool to a switch port, make sure that you are "spanning" the port(s) so that you can capture the appropriate traffic. Wireshark is the analysis engine and doesn't do the actual capture. The data capture is accomplished using WinPcap, which is included with the Wireshark download.

Nmap

Another free tool is the Nmap ("Network Mapper") security scanner. Nmap is used to scan a network to determine what hosts and services exist. Nmap works by sending specially crafted IP data packets to the targeted hosts and analyzing the resulting response. Not only can Nmap determine if a host exists at particular IP address, but it can also determine what services may be available and what operating system may be running on the device.

According to the website (**https://nmap.org/**) for Nmap, it is described as:

- **Flexible:** Supports dozens of advanced techniques for mapping out networks filled with IP filters, firewalls, routers, and other obstacles. This includes many port scanning mechanisms (both TCP & UDP), OS detection, version detection, ping sweeps, and more. See the documentation page.

- **Powerful:** Nmap has been used to scan huge networks of literally hundreds of thousands of machines.

- **Portable:** Most operating systems are supported, including Linux, Microsoft Windows, FreeBSD, OpenBSD, Solaris, IRIX, Mac OS X, HP-UX, NetBSD, Sun OS, Amiga, and more.

- **Easy:** While Nmap offers a rich set of advanced features for power users, you can start out as simply as "nmap -v -A targethost." Both traditional command line and graphical (GUI) versions are available to suit your preference. Binaries are available for those who do not wish to compile Nmap from source.

- **Free:** The primary goals of the Nmap Project is to help make the Internet a little more secure and to provide administrators/auditors/ hackers with an advanced tool for exploring their networks. Nmap is available for free download, and it also comes with full source code that you may modify and redistribute under the terms of the license.

- **Well documented:** Significant effort has been put into comprehensive and up-to-date map pages, whitepapers, tutorials, and even a whole book! Find them in multiple languages here.

- **Supported:** While Nmap comes with no warranty, it is well supported by a vibrant community of developers and users. Most of this interaction occurs on the Nmap mailing lists. Most bug reports and questions should be sent to the Nmap-dev list, but only after you read the guidelines. We recommend that all users subscribe to the low-traffic Nmap-hackers announcement list. You can also find Nmap on Facebook and Twitter. For real-time chat, join the #nmap channel on Freenode or EFNet.

- **Acclaimed:** Nmap has won numerous awards, including "Information Security Product of the Year" by Linux Journal, Info World, and Codetalker Digest. It has been featured in hundreds of magazine articles, several movies, dozens of books, and one comic book series. Visit the press page for further details.

- **Popular:** Thousands of people download Nmap every day, and it is included with many operating systems (Redhat Linux, Debian Linux, Gentoo, FreeBSD, OpenBSD, etc.). It is among the top ten (out of 30,000) programs at the Freshmeat.Net repository. This is important because it lends Nmap its vibrant development and user support communities.

Nmap is a very valuable tool to help assess the security of your network. Typically, professionals use Nmap as a port scanning tool. In other words, you can use Nmap to see what ports may be open on a particular computer. Many times, law firms are unaware of what ports may be open on a particular computer, making them a potential target for attack. Another common use is to test firewalls to make sure that only desired traffic is allowed to pass through. Some firms will even use Nmap as an inventory-type tool. They configure Nmap to scan every IP address in their network to find all the hosts that may exist. In this way, they can also determine if someone has placed an unauthorized device on the network. Nmap can also be used to find and exploit vulnerabilities in a network.

Penetration Testing Tools

What Is Penetration Testing?

There are many different approaches to evaluating an organization's information security. Penetration testing, or pen-testing, is an evaluation method that utilizes the same techniques that real-world attackers use to compromise organizations. Penetration tests can be performed from various perspectives, such as a hacker targeting the organization over the Internet, a malicious insider, or even someone attempting to compromise the physical security of an organization.

Penetration tests are used to accomplish a variety of different goals. Since the assessment utilizes the same techniques as real-world attacks, the results can be used to give organizations an idea of where their security is the weakest, and what types of common attacks are most likely to compromise them. Additionally, penetration tests offer good opportunities to evaluate the effectiveness of security monitoring capabilities.

At a higher level, penetration tests can allow an organization to determine whether they are allocating sufficient resources to information security. For example, a penetration test may find that an organization is susceptible to common real-world attacks. By showing that attackers can gain access to an organization's most valuable resources and data using common techniques, a penetration test may convince the organization to make a greater investment in security.

Lastly, penetration tests are often required to meet standards or certifications, or to fulfill contractual agreements. For example, the Payment Card Industry's (PCI) Data Security Standard (DSS) requires periodic penetration tests. In the case of PCI, penetration tests are used to assess how well the organization has implemented the DSS requirements. Most law firms that process credit card transactions will obtain their PCI penetration testing through the provider of their merchant account. Typically, the penetration testing is done on a monthly basis and a report is prepared for each test. Be sure to retain these reports as proof of PCI compliance.

NIST SP 800-53A, Rev.1 "Guide for Assessing Security Controls in Federal Information Systems and Organizations" (June 2010) covers detailed security assessment requirements for federal agencies and some federal contractors.[1] Appendix E of the NIST publication contains a good, brief overview of penetration testing.

There are many exploitation tools and frameworks with hundreds or even thousands of built-in exploits and payloads. For example, the freely available **Metasploit** tool allows a pen tester to select one or more targets, choose an exploit, and then attack the targets. If successful, the pen tester can choose from a variety of payloads to run on the target, such as arbitrary system commands, adding accounts, or obtaining remote access to

---

1. http://csrc.nist.gov/publications/nistpubs/800-53A-rev1/sp800-53A-rev1-final.pdf.

the machine via a shell or remote desktop. Other commercial tools, such as **Core Impact**[2] and **Immunity CANVAS**,[3] offer similar functionality. These tools make it incredibly easy to carry out sophisticated attacks. Just plug in a few values and go, and you've owned the machine.

Metasploit

The Metasploit framework is a very popular free open-source project used for penetration testing and is available at **http://www.rapid7.com/ products/metasploit/**. As the saying goes, you can't fix it if you don't know it's broken. That's where Metasploit comes in. You point Metasploit at your target host and test for vulnerabilities. It simulates real world attacks just as a malicious attacker would.

Pineapple Mark V

One of our favorite tools is the Pineapple Mark V from Hak5. The Pineapple is a device used to test wireless networks. There have been several versions of the product with the Mark V being the latest. Essentially, the Pineapple masquerades as a wireless access point and "inserts" itself between the target and a destination to perform a man-in-the-middle attack.

To appreciate how simple the Pineapple is, it is important to understand how wireless connections are made. When a device goes to connect to a wireless network, it "walks down" all of the known networks that may have been "remembered" in the past. If you select the "connect automatically" option with a Windows computer, you have elected to remember what that network is. As the computer searches for available networks, it looks to see if a remembered network exists. If so, the computer connects. Essentially, the Pineapple answers as if it is the desired wireless network.

In other words, if your computer wants to connect to the Starbucks network, the Pineapple will answer as if it is the real Starbucks Wi-Fi network. The connected computer does not know it is not connected to the real Starbucks network. Once the computer is connected to the Pineapple, the attacker can "sniff" the data stream using a tool such as Wireshark. There are additional functions that can be performed with the Pineapple. The included penetration testing packages contain aircracking, dsniff, easy-creds, ettercap, hping3, httptunnel, karma, kismet, macchanger, mdk3, ngrep, nmap, nodogsplash captive portal, privoxy, ptunnel, snort, sslsniff, sslstrip, ssltunnel, stunnel, tcpdump, tor, and reaver.

---

2. http://www.coresecurity.com/core-impact-pro.
3. https://www.immunityinc.com/products/canvas/.

Other Types of Security Assessments

In addition to penetration testing, there are a variety of other types of security assessments. Each approach varies slightly in goals, scope, and resources required. Companies that perform these assessments may have different names for these assessments and may offer different subsets of them under the same assessment, but the following are some other common approaches:

- *Vulnerability Assessments* typically involve running automated scanners against the organization's network. Aside from analyzing the results and eliminating false positives, this approach usually requires minimal resources and is therefore often performed more frequently than other approaches. Vulnerability assessments may also be a good starting point to eliminate the "low-hanging fruit" for organizations just getting started with information security. However, given their automated nature and the focus on breadth versus depth, vulnerability assessments often do not uncover all of the security issues on an organization's network.

- *Application Assessments* typically focus on a single application (or small set of applications). These are useful when securing a new application, or when verifying that a new release of an application does not introduce security issues. Application assessments may involve a number of different techniques, such as automated web application scans, manual testing, or possibly code reviews. These assessments are more narrowly focused than most other approaches, but usually go into greater depth.

- *Information Security Audits* typically go into much greater depth than other approaches. They typically include the techniques used for some of the other assessments but also look at the organization's information security from the inside. This may include reviewing configurations and documentation, interviewing staff, performing various types of scans, and reviewing the organization's security policies and procedures. These audits may be scoped to a subset of the organization or may aim to assess the entire organization's security program. They can be performed internally, if qualified personnel are available, or externally by a service provider.

Client Security Assessments

We are increasingly seeing information security assessments being requested of law firms. Clients want to know how secure their law firms are, especially since they are entrusting their data to the firm. They range from questionnaires to thorough onsite audits by the client or a service provider retained by the client. While some law firms are well-prepared to respond to them, others have no clue how to respond. Smaller firms tend to turn to their IT support companies to complete the multipage audit questionnaires. Larger firms are now used to seeing the audit requests and respond accordingly. Some firms have even taken proactive steps and have obtained ISO 27001 certification, a standard for information security management.

CHAPTER TEN

Desktops, Laptops, and Servers

Desktop and laptop computers are still the workhorses for virtually all attorneys today, although there has been some movement to tablets as "PC replacements." Windows is the dominant operating system for lawyers, but Apple's OS X has been gaining, particularly in the last few years. This chapter explores security basics for desktops and laptops. It also includes tablets with the Windows operating systems because they are similar to Windows laptops. While setup, configuration, and administration of servers is almost always done by IT professionals, this chapter includes some basic security considerations for servers.

The basic steps for securing personal computers, whether at home, in a law office, or on the road are:

1. Use strong passwords, passphrases, or other strong authentication (such as biometrics).
2. Operate in a standard user account without administrator access for routine use.
3. Configure the operating system, Internet browser, and other software in a secure manner.
4. Install and use security software, including malware protection and a software firewall—keep them current with updates.
5. As patches (software fixes) are released, apply them—to the operating system and all programs and applications—including browser plug-ins.
6. Install and use a hardware firewall for the local network.

7. Enable full disk encryption on laptops—hardware, in the operating system, or with an encryption program.

8. Backup important files and folders—or the complete drive.

9. Use care when downloading and installing programs.

10. Be careful when browsing the Internet.

11. Use care with e-mail attachments and embedded links.

For more details on authentication and authorization and encryption, see the chapters on these topics.

Authentication

Authentication and authorization form the first line of defense for desktops, laptops, and servers. Desktops, laptops, and servers should, at a minimum, be protected with a password or passphrase. Major laptop manufacturers offer fingerprint readers as an option. More advanced authentication and multifactor authentication should be considered for laptops and servers, particularly for remote access. With the strong support for fingerprint authentication and facial recognition in Windows 10, laptops with hardware to support these authentication methods is likely to become more common.

Strong passphrases, such as the following, are recommended:

IloveABATECHSHOW2016! and IluvmXy2005BXMW!

User Accounts

Both Windows and OS X have multiple kinds of accounts for users. They include standard user accounts and administrator accounts. The standard user accounts have limited privileges. Administrator accounts have more privileges and can, accordingly, do more, such as installing new software and devices. For routine use, computers should be operated in standard user account mode. Administrator accounts should be used only when necessary to perform functions that are limited to them. Operating in a standard user account provides better protection because some (but not all) malware and attacks need administrator access to be successful. When operating in an administrator account, it is particularly important to pay attention to dialogue boxes and warnings.

In Windows, local user accounts are typically managed in the control panel. In OS X, user accounts are typically managed in System Preferences.

In network environments, passwords are often managed centrally with tools such as Microsoft's Group Policy in a Windows environment.

Secure Configuration

Secure configuration or "hardening" is the process of setting up or adjusting the operating system, Internet browser and all applications in ways that maximize security and minimize the potential for compromise. The approach should use the highest security settings that will allow the computer to perform necessary functions. In addition, services and functions that are not necessary should be disabled or blocked.

Current versions of operating systems and application software should be used because they are generally more secure than older versions. For example, the current versions of Windows and OS X have more security functionality than older versions. Microsoft Office 2016, Microsoft's Edge browser, and Adobe Acrobat DC and Reader DC all have much stronger security than older versions. Unless there are compatibility issues with other applications, upgrades should be promptly made.

During installation, the user is prompted for various security settings and enabling of various services. When in doubt, choose the higher security settings and do not enable services that you do not need. For questions, check the installation instructions and help files or consult someone with technical knowledge.

The following services should be disabled if you don't need them: print sharing, file sharing, window sharing, and remote log-in. They present unnecessary security exposure if they are not being used. If you use them, you will need to enable them and manage the risks. For example, remote log-in should be set to require strong authentication—multifactor authentication is best.

The first step is setting up user accounts, as discussed earlier. Security software (including a firewall), patching, and browser configuration, all important parts of hardening, are discussed below.

While the technical details of secure configurations are beyond the scope of this book, they are available on Microsoft's website (**www.microsoft.com/security/default.aspx**) (for nontechnical users) and (**http://technet.microsoft.com/en-us/security/bb291012**) (for technical users). Series of articles on secure configuration of Windows are available at **https://technet.microsoft.com/en-us/windows/security-and-control.aspx** and **https://technet.microsoft.com/en-us/library/mt601297(v=vs.85).aspx**.

Apple has Security Configuration Guides for the various versions of OS X in the Support section of its website at **www.apple.com/support/security/guides/**.

For those with technical ability, there are various tools to assist with secure configuration. Microsoft has tools such as the Microsoft Security Compliance Manager, Microsoft Baseline Security Analyzer (a tool that allows users to scan one or more Windows-based computer for common security mis-configurations) and the Security Configuration Wizard (to assist in creating, editing, applying, or rolling back security policies with Windows Server). The National Institute for Science and Technology (NIST) has published security configurations for various operating systems and software as part of the U.S. Government Configuration Baseline and the Federal Desktop Core Configuration. Compliance with them is generally required for federal agencies, and they can be used as guidance for others. The Center for Internet Security (CIS) Security Benchmarks Division publishes consensus security configuration standards for operating systems, browsers, servers, network devices, and mobile devices. (**https://benchmarks.cisecurity.org**) Automated tools are available to test computers for compliance with these standards, including tools published by CIS.

Another publisher of these kinds of tools is Belarc (**www.belarc.com**). Its Belarc Advisor builds a detailed security profile, including missing Windows patches and security configuration. It is only available as a free download for personal use and not for commercial or government purposes. Belarc does make products for commercial usage such as BelSecure and BelManage. Additional tools are discussed in the Patching section below.

Security Software

Security software should be used on all desktops, laptops, and servers. While there has been much debate about the need for security software on Macs, let it end here. Macs are vulnerable as has been demonstrated many, many times over the years. There is no reason to take a chance in light of the ready availability of security software and its low cost. The malware targeted at Macs is increasing as Apple's market share has grown. In Macs running both OS X and Windows, both operating systems should be protected. In recent years, the major security software vendors have moved from individual products, such as antivirus and firewalls, to security suites that integrate multiple security functionality, such as malware protection, software firewalls, web browsing protection, and spam filters. Some of them include advanced features such as rootkit protection and basic intrusion protection. We're beginning to see encryption capabilities available as well. They offer the advantage of being a single integrated product, which is easier to install, configure, manage, and keep up to date.

Various publications, such as *SC Magazine, CSO, PC Magazine, CNET,* and even *Consumer Reports,* rate security software from time to time. It is a good idea to look at current reviews before selecting a new product. Although opinions vary on which product is best at any given time, it is clear that any of the major security vendors' current security suites, with up-to-date definitions, will make a desktop, laptop, or server significantly more secure than one that is not protected. Some leading vendors include Symantec, McAfee (Intel), F-Secure, Sophos, Trend Micro, and Kaspersky. Vendors are now offering multidevice packages that provide protection for up to three or five devices—desktops, laptops, and smartphones—for both PCs and Macs. A list of security software for Macs can be found at **http://mac-antivirus-software-review.toptenreviews.com**. The authors have had good experience with Kaspersky, F-Secure, Sophos, and Symantec products.

One of the ways that security software detects malware is through the use of signatures. A signature looks for a specific known pattern of code that has been found in the malware. In addition to specific malware signatures, some of the newer security software also reviews more general patterns of behavior to attempt to detect malware for which there are not yet signatures. Some security software for desktops, laptops, and servers also includes basic intrusion protection. Security software that is out of date is only marginally better than no security software at all.

In addition to security suites, there are software host intrusion prevention systems (IPS) that provide a more advanced level of protection to laptops and desktops. They have stronger capability to protect against unknown threats. They are generally centrally administered in networks rather than used as stand-alone solutions on individual computers or in small networks. Some examples are IBM EPP, Symantec Endpoint Protection, and McAfee Host Intrusion Prevention for Desktop. At the network level, host IPS is often used to protect servers.

There is an ongoing arms race between security vendors and malware authors. Signatures are written to detect known malware, and then malware writers change their code to avoid detection. Because of this, it is critical to keep the security software up to date with new definitions, which are often available multiple times a day. Security software should generally be set to automatically receive updates.

A firewall is software or a device that controls the flow of data to or from a computer or network. It helps protect against attacks from the outside. Some firewalls also block or alert to outbound traffic. Both Windows and

OS X now include built-in software firewalls. Many consider the firewalls in the security suites to provide better protection than the built-in ones. One or the other should definitely be used. In a law firm, firewalls in security suites should generally be used in addition to a hardware firewall for the entire network.

Patching

A vulnerability is a flaw in software. An exploit is code that takes advantage of a vulnerability to cause unintended or unanticipated behavior in the software. It can range from causing the software to crash to giving an attacker complete control of the computer. Software vendors prepare and distribute patches to address vulnerabilities. Patches frequently address security issues.

It is critical to apply security patches promptly. Until they are applied, a computer is exposed to the vulnerability. Where available, it is generally best to allow automatic downloads of updates. This feature is available from Microsoft and Apple. One caveat is that, in a network environment, it is sometimes necessary to test patches before they are applied. Although they have been tested for the vendor's products, they may cause problems with other vendors' products, including legal applications such as case management and document assembly products.

With Microsoft products, the patching process is not difficult because Microsoft issues patches each month on "Patch Tuesday," including patches for Windows, Internet Explorer, and Microsoft Office. Apple issues patches less frequently, and OS X can be set for automatic download when they are issued.

The significant challenge is making sure that everything else is patched: applications, media players, browser plug-ins, and on and on. Security studies frequently report that they find exploits that target vulnerabilities for which patches have been available for a long time. One reported that the most commonly blocked attack was for a vulnerability for which a patch was available for months and the second was one for which a patch had been available for almost three years.

A zero-day attack, under varying definitions, is one that attempts to exploit a vulnerability not known to the software developer or to the security industry or for which a patch is not yet available. For this reason, they are particularly dangerous. Some of the zero-day attacks in the past year have exploited vulnerabilities in Microsoft Windows, Microsoft Office, Apple OS X, Adobe Acrobat and Reader, Adobe Flash, and Java—

all programs regularly used by attorneys. Zero-day attacks are most frequently used in targeted attacks (against a specific victim or group of victims) but are sometimes used in more widespread attacks.

There are software tools available from major security vendors to search computers for vulnerabilities from missing patches. Secunia (recently acquired by Flexera) has a Personal Software Inspector (PSI) that is free for personal use. It scans the computer and reports on programs that are security threats because they are missing patches or are end of life and no longer supported. When this program was first released, a lot of security professionals were surprised when they ran it on their home computers that they incorrectly thought were up to date. The commercial version of this program, Corporate Software Inspector (CSI), is available for business use, including law firms. Other examples of enterprise vulnerability managers are tools by Symantec, McAfee, and Qualys. Without a tool like these, it can be necessary to manually check everything for current updates. Patch management functionality is also bundled with some endpoint management software, which can be used to patch, configure, and manage all desktops and laptops in an organization. Examples are IBM's Tivoli Endpoint Manager and Dell KASE and LanDESK. These kinds of tools are used on networks, particularly larger ones, and require IT professionals to install and use them. Attorneys should be aware that these kinds of tools are available and consult with qualified experts about the need for them.

Because every installed program can be a target for attack, only necessary programs should be installed on computers used for the practice of law. The more software that is installed, the more that needs to be kept up to date.

Hardware Firewall

A hardware firewall is a network device that controls the flow of traffic. It helps block unauthorized access from the outside and unauthorized outbound traffic and can hide the identity of individual computers from outside the network. Whenever possible, a desktop or laptop should be used in a network protected by a hardware firewall.

Encryption

Encryption is becoming more important to protect data on desktops and laptops. Most security professionals consider encryption to be a security no-brainer for laptops and portable devices. While not commonly in use, some law firms are also starting to encrypt desktops and servers—some driven by client requirements.

To avoid the loss of data, it is important to understand how the encryption works, to back up data that is encrypted, and to keep a copy of the recovery key in a secure place. Enterprise controls are available to centrally manage encryption.

Disk Encryption Basics

There are two basic approaches to encrypting data on hard drives: full disk encryption and limited encryption. As its name suggests, full disk encryption protects the entire hard drive. It automatically encrypts everything and provides decrypted access when an authorized user properly logs in. Limited encryption protects only specified files or folders or a part of the drive. With limited encryption, the user has to elect to encrypt the specific data by saving it in an encrypted partition or folder. Because it can be easy to forget to put confidential data in an encrypted partition or file, full disk encryption is usually more secure and therefore recommended.

There are three options for protecting laptops and portable devices with encryption: hardware encryption, operating system encryption (such as Windows and Apple OS X), and encryption software.

All hard drive manufacturers now offer drives with hardware full disk encryption, called Self-Encrypting Drives (SED). There are encrypted options available for both traditional hard drives and newer solid state drives. The major laptop manufacturers all offer models with hardware encryption. Hardware encryption is generally easier to use and administer than encryption software. Some examples of drives with hardware encryption are Seagate Secure and Momentus (**www.seagate.com**), Hitachi Self-Encrypting Drives (**www.hgst.com**), Western Digital (**www.wdc.com**), CMS Products (**www.cesecure.com**), SanDisk (solid state) (**www.sandisk.com**), and Imation (**www.imation.com**). Secure use simply requires enabling encryption and setting a strong password or passphrase. The contents of the drive are automatically decrypted when an authorized user logs in. It is automatically encrypted when the user logs off or the laptop is turned off.

Some IT professionals have recommended avoiding SED encryption because of concerns that data may be more difficult or impossible to recover in the event of a drive failure. They recommend encryption using one of the other options. With SEDs, backup of the data is particularly important.

Dell and Hewlett-Packard (HP) offer security suites that provide encryption, strong authentication, and additional security features. Dell's security package is called Dell Data Protection. It includes a number of separate options, ranging from strong authentication and encryption for a single desktop or laptop, to enterprise and cloud management tools (**http://software.dell .com/solutions/data-protection/**). HP's suite is called ProtectTools. It also offers a number of options, from protection of an individual desktop or laptop, to central enterprise management (**http://h20331.www2.hp.com/ hpsub/cache/281822-0-0-225-121.html**).

Encryption in Operating Systems

Current business versions of Windows and current versions of Apple OS X have built-in encryption capability.

Windows

Windows Vista Enterprise and Ultimate and Windows 7 Enterprise and Ultimate, Windows 8 and 8.1 Professional and Enterprise, and Windows 10 Professional and Enterprise include an encryption feature called BitLocker. BitLocker works below the Windows operating system and encrypts an entire volume on the hard drive. This means that when the drive is encrypted, the encryption protects the operating system, as well as all software and data on the drive. For versions of Windows that do not support BitLocker, software encryption, discussed below, can be used.

On versions before Windows 8.1, BitLocker required either a computer that is equipped with a Trusted Platform Module (TPM) chip or use of an external USB drive to hold the decryption key. A TPM module is a security chip on the computer's motherboard that supports encryption. If a user plans to use BitLocker on a computer, it is important to select one that has a TPM chip that meets the current specification. Check the hardware requirements for the version of Windows that you are using and compare it with the specifications for the desktop or laptop. Or ask someone for advice—the major PC manufacturers have chat features on their websites to answer questions about their products. Use of a key on a USB drive is less secure because encryption can be defeated if an intruder gains access to the USB key. With Windows 8.1 and Windows 10, there's another alternative for BitLocker with computers that don't have a TPM chip. It can be set up directly on the computer, but it requires a pre-boot passphrase that accesses the decryption key. This means that a user has to enter a pre-boot passphrase, then log into Windows. A user can set up the same passphrase for both, but it has to be entered twice, once for pre-boot and once for logging in.

The business versions of Windows also include an encryption function called Encrypting File System (EFS). It allows encryption of files and folders. An authorized user who is logged in has access to decrypted data. It is encrypted and unreadable to anyone else (unless they can defeat the login process). EFS is considered a fairly weak encryption method that is easily cracked using forensic tools. You are better off using BitLocker or one of the other third-party encryption products discussed below.

Setup of BitLocker is fairly technical. For many attorneys, it will be necessary to obtain technical assistance to implement it. There are instructions on Microsoft's website. During setup, there is a set of dialog boxes that take a user through the process. The instructions are available at:

♦ Windows 10:
   http://windows10-update.blogspot.com/2014/11/how-to-turn-on-bitlocker-in-windows-10.html

♦ Windows 8.1:
   http://windows.microsoft.com/en-us/windows-8/bitlocker-drive-encryption

♦ Windows 7:
   http://windows.microsoft.com/en-us/windows/protect-files-bitlocker-drive-encryption#1TC=windows-7

♦ Vista:
   http://windows.microsoft.com/en-us/windows/protect-files-bitlocker-drive-encryption#1TC=windows-vista

The BitLocker setup instructions include the following warning:

> "**Warning:** When you turn on BitLocker for the first time, make sure you create a recovery key. Otherwise, you could permanently lose access to your files."

A Bitlocker recovery key is a line or set of data that can be backed up to a Microsoft account, a law firm network, or another computer. It can also be printed on paper. Make sure that the backup location is secure or the recovery key could be used to compromise the encryption. A BitLocker recovery key looks like this:

609430-136796-639472-379917-216106-640223-465533-702097

When backing up the recovery key, the drive identifier will be saved in the text file along with the actual BitLocker recovery key. If you have multiple partitions on the hard disk or multiple drives, you need to back up the key for each partition and drive. When utilizing the recovery key, you will need to match the appropriate identifier code to the correct drive.

Windows 8.1 and 10 have an additional encryption option called Device Encryption. It's included in all versions of Windows 8.1 and 10, not just the business ones. It has very specific hardware requirements that most current PCs do not meet. It also requires InstantGo, a feature that allows a PC to instantly wake up. For information about these requirements and whether a PC meets them, compare the requirements on Microsoft's website with the manufacturer's specifications for the PC or ask someone for help.

Device Encryption is automatically enabled when a user with an administrator account logs on to a Microsoft account. The recovery key is automatically backed up to the Microsoft account. While this option provides strong security for a PC, there is a risk that an unauthorized person can defeat it by getting access to a user's Microsoft account and the recovery key.

Device Encryption can also be turned on manually and the recovery key backed up to a network with Active Directory (a special-purpose database for Windows networks used for authentication and authorization). There does not currently appear to be an option for enabling Device Encryption without a Microsoft account or network with Active Directory (**http://windows .microsoft.com/en-us/windows-8/using-device-encryption**).

Apple OS X

Older versions of Apple OS X have built-in file encryption in FileVault. Newer versions, starting with Lion, have full disk encryption available in FileVault 2. Follow Apple's instructions for turning it on. After a password is set, it just requires turning on the FileVault button in System Preferences. Instructions are available at **http://support.apple.com/kb/ht4790**. FileVault 2 also generates a recovery key that it prompts the user to store. It provides an option for storing it with Apple.

Recent advances have attacked Apple's encryption scheme, and the Passware software suite claims to be able to defeat FileVault 2 in less than an hour.[1] Even with the availability of forensic tools, a laptop encrypted with FileVault is still far more secure than one without encryption.

Encryption Software

The third option for disk encryption (in addition to self-encrypting drives and operating system encryption) is encryption software. Some commonly used third-party encryption software products for hard drives include those offered by Symantec (PGP and Endpoint; **www.symantec. com**), McAfee (Endpoint Encryption; **www.mcafee.com**), Check Point (ZoneAlarm DataLock; **www.zonealarm.com**), WinMagic (SecureDoc; **www.winmagic.com**), and Sophos (SafeGuard; **www.sophos.com**). These vendors all have options available for Macs.

---

1. However, in order to use this tool, you must have a physical memory image file (acquired while the encrypted volume was mounted). Unless you're a forensic technologist, you won't even know how to create the physical memory image file, which is a forensic image of the memory contents of a running computer.

Most encryption solutions have single sign-on options, where entry of the logon credentials automatically enters them for both encryption and Windows or OS X.

An open-source encryption program that was formerly widely used is TrueCrypt (**www.truecrypt.org**). However, it has been discontinued and should no longer be relied upon. Its developers have posted the following on the TrueCrypt website: "WARNING: Using TrueCrypt is not secure as it may contain unfixed security issues."

Laptops

Of the computers covered in this chapter, laptops present the greatest threat of loss, theft, and unauthorized access, because they are compact and portable. They can easily be lost or stolen outside the office. They also present the greatest risk inside an office because they are small, portable, and expensive, so they present an attractive target if physical security fails. This section covers laptops. Encryption of smartphones and tablets is included in the next chapter.

Many laptop vendors offer biometric access (fingerprint reader) to facilitate encryption of the hard disk. This avoids the use of passwords or passphrases at boot-up because the fingerprint is used in lieu of a password. You should configure as least two fingerprints (one from each hand) in addition to a backup boot password or passphrase should the fingerprint reader fail. A best practice would be to register two fingers from each hand (four total fingerprints).

The major laptop vendors all offer models with self-encrypting drives and with the business versions of Windows that include BitLocker. Apple's current OS X on Mac laptops includes FileVault 2. The easiest way to protect laptops is generally with hardware level encryption or BitLocker or FileVault. The third-party encryption software products, discussed earlier in this chapter, are also options for encrypting laptops.

Except for solos and small firms, enterprise management of encrypted devices, including laptops, is highly recommended.

Desktops

Some law firms that are at the leading edge of security are encrypting desktops, going beyond encryption of laptops. While not yet a standard practice, it provides for strong security. There is a much greater risk of loss or theft with devices that are regularly used outside of offices, but there have been incidents of burglaries and insider thefts that have involved desktop computers. The risk of stolen desktops have increased as they have become more compact, including all-in-one models.

Desktops can be encrypted with all three options discussed above: self-encrypting drives, operating system encryption, or encryption software.

Servers

Encryption is a security measure that is increasingly being employed to protect confidential data on servers. They often process and store very high volumes of sensitive data. While a discussion of server security is beyond the scope of this book, it is a safeguard that attorneys should explore with their IT staff and consultants.

Backup

Backup and disaster recovery are critical steps to protect data on any computer, network, or portable media. These topics are discussed in this book's backup chapter.

Installing Programs

It is important to exercise care in selecting and installing programs.

In a law firm, only necessary programs should be used. Every installed program increases the surface for potential attack and must be managed and kept up to date.

When downloading programs from the Internet, use only trusted sources and pay attention to warnings about website certificates.

For software, code signing with certificates verifies the source of the code and shows that it has not been tampered with. If a warning pops up that the certificate is invalid, don't install the program.

Peer-to-peer file sharing should not be used on law firm or business computers. It has the potential to expose all files on the computer and potentially other data on a network.

Safe Browsing

Internet browsers, such as Microsoft Edge (new with Windows 10), Internet Explorer, Chrome, Safari, and Firefox, are great productivity tools for attorneys because they are the gateway to the vast information resources of the Internet and serve as the interface to access cloud resources such as software as a service. Unfortunately, they also are the gateway to the dark side of the Internet where criminals are trying to do nefarious things such as stealing information or taking over vulnerable computers.

Just visiting a malicious website or a compromised legitimate site may be enough to compromise a computer (called "drive-by malware"). A scary example is that the *New York Times* website was reportedly infected through the compromise of a third-party service that fed ads to the site. Just a visit to the site was enough to expose a computer to malware.

Be very careful about visiting websites with which you are not familiar. Malicious sites have frequently appeared high in search engine results. Some security products provide warnings about known malicious and suspicious sites.

Fortunately, the security of browsers has improved greatly over the years, and today's browsers are more secure than older ones. For this reason, it is important to use the latest version of the browser, to configure it securely, and to stay current with patches.

If the security software or browser provides a warning, pay attention to it. Don't blindly click OK. Some of the newer browsers include features called "sandboxes" that isolate the browser from the operating system. They provide warnings if a website tries to install a program or to access the operating system. But they can be defeated if a user blindly clicks OK and ignores their warnings.

As mentioned above, routine operation of a computer should be in a standard user account and not an administrator account. This is particularly important when surfing the web. Secure configuration of the browser is also a key step. In Internet Explorer, this is controlled by clicking on Internet Options, under Tools, and then clicking on Security. It should be set to Medium-High or greater. Custom levels may also be set, but this is better left to someone with technical knowledge. Disabling of functions like ActiveX, Flash, Java, and JavaScript provides greater security but also affects functionality. Do not install or enable browser plug-ins unless you need them. Use current versions and keep them patched.

Some browsers, such as Chrome, let users limit the websites that can use plug-ins, such as Flash. Some plug-ins, such as Java, let users define which websites can use it.

A vulnerability in a plug-in still leaves you exposed even if the browser itself is up to date.

Some businesses are putting the browser in a sandbox that isolates it and helps protect against attacks. If the browser is partitioned off, data elsewhere remains safe.

When you visit a site where you have to enter a username and password or provide any confidential information, make sure that the displayed Web address starts with "https." In Internet Explorer, a picture of a lock is also displayed. The "s" means that it should be a secure connection. It's not an absolutely sure thing, though, because websites can be spoofed, and you may have a secure connection to a malicious website. So also, look at the Web address (URL) displayed in the browser and make sure that the one displayed is for the site you want to go to—without misspellings or strange characters. Use of multifactor authentication and approaches such as the digital certificates used by Windows 10 Passport protects against interception or compromise of usernames and passwords.

Attachments and Embedded Links

E-mail attachments are frequently used to install malware. Embedded links in e-mails are often used to take the user to an infected website. Don't open attachments from unknown sources and scan attachments for malware before you open them. Be very careful of clicking on links unless you are sure of the sender and are familiar with the site. Phishing (falsified e-mails purporting to be from banks, PayPal, eBay, and other legitimate sites) is now a very common form of attack. It attempts to steal information, often logon credentials, either by trying to trick people into providing them or by planting malware that steals them. Some malware can be installed by opening an infected attachment or just visiting an infected website. E-mails from legitimate sources may also contain malware. Spear phishing (e-mails targeted to specific recipients) are particularly dangerous. The Anti-Phishing Working Group is a helpful source of information in this area (**www.antiphishing.org**). Attorneys and law firm staff should be periodically trained about this risk.

Laptops

As discussed in our chapter on encryption, security of laptops is a particular area of current concern. There have been a number of recent high-profile incidents in which confidential data has been compromised by theft or loss of laptops from businesses, accounting firms, nonprofits, and government agencies. As previously noted, one survey reports that 70% of data breaches have been from the loss or theft of laptops and other mobile devices and media.

As a starting point, laptops should be protected by the basic security measures, discussed above, which apply to all computers. Some additional recommendations for protecting laptops include:

1. Don't store unnecessary confidential information on a laptop.
2. Use strong authentication.
3. Encrypt your data—full disk.
4. Never leave access numbers, passwords, or security devices in your carrying case.
5. Back up important data.
6. Consider using a laptop tracking and wiping program.
7. Provide for physical security of the laptop, including:
   - Carry your laptop with you.
   - Keep your eye on your laptop.
   - Avoid setting your laptop on the floor where you might forget about it.
   - Use a laptop security device.
   - Use engraving or an asset tag to identify the owner.
   - Use a screen guard.
   - Avoid using traditional computer bags—they make their contents obvious.
   - Watch your laptop when going through airport security.
   - Avoid leaving a laptop in view in a parked car.
   - Try not to leave your laptop in your hotel room without proper use of a laptop lock or with the front desk. If your hotel room has a safe, use it.

As discussed in our chapter on the subject, encryption is particularly important for laptops and portable media because of the high risk of loss or theft. As discussed above, there have been a number of law firm data breaches involving lost laptops and portable drives. Encryption of laptops and portable media is now a standard security measure that should be used by attorneys—a security no-brainer.

Tracking programs are available to report the location of lost or stolen laptops to security centers when the laptops are connected to the Internet. A commonly used example is Absolute Data and Device Security (consumer and small business version: LoJack for Laptops) for PCs and Macs (**https://www.absolute.com/en**) and zTrace (**www.ztrace.com**). Some of these programs include remote wiping of the data on a laptop if it is reported as lost or stolen. Orbicule (**www.orbicule.com**) has a product for Macs which repeatedly transmits network information, screenshots, and photos from the laptop's built-in camera after a laptop is stolen. It then makes the laptop malfunction and displays a message that it has been stolen when it is connected to a different network.

Physical security is important because laptops are portable. They are frequently stolen from cars and airport security checkpoints. New laptop bags, called "checkpoint friendly," are available for use in air travel. They allow the laptop to remain in the bag during screening. You can find them at vendors such as Targus, Aerovation, Eagle Creek, and MobilEdge.

CHAPTER ELEVEN

Mobile Devices: Smartphones and Tablets

Businesses, including law firms, are well into the era of consumerization of enterprise technology, with employees and managers either using their own technology for work or insisting that businesses provide what has previously been viewed as consumer technology. Smartphones and tablets have led the way. Bring Your Own Technology (BYOT) or Bring Your Own Device (BYOD) are currently hot topics in most IT departments. Articles on consumerization and mobility are included in virtually every edition of online and print IT publications.

This growing phenomenon has created challenges to law firms and businesses and enterprises of all kinds. Devices that were designed as consumer products must now be managed and secured in an enterprise environment. Unfortunately, smartphone and tablet users can be exposing their employers to security threats in major ways, and faster than anyone imagined, which has grave implications for law firms as well as other enterprises. Wearable technology presents new challenges. This chapter explores the things that you and your firm should know and do. The time has come for all attorneys and law firms to address these thorny issues.

There is a growing consensus that the use of smartphones and tablets, if done the right way, can be accomplished safely and will greatly benefit businesses and professionals. However, it is important to understand and address the risks—including measures to secure and manage smartphones and tablets. This is critical for attorneys and law firms because of their duty to safeguard information relating to clients.

Some Statistics

According to an August 2015 ComScore survey, 191 million people in the United States own smartphones (77% of mobile users). Smartphone use appears to be one area of technology where attorneys are ahead of the curve. The 2015 *American Bar Association Legal Technology Survey Report* states that 90% of responding attorneys report that they use smartphones for law-related tasks. Almost 50% report that they use tablets.

The ABA survey contains additional information about attorneys' use of smartphones and tablets, including how they are used and the security measures employed. The International Legal Technology Association (ILTA) also publishes an annual survey of legal technology. Like the ABA survey, ILTA's 2015 survey also shows a substantial and growing use of smartphones and tablets by lawyers.

Attorneys' Duty to Safeguard Client Information

Attorneys have ethical and legal duties to take competent and reasonable measures to safeguard information relating to clients. These obligations arise from the rules of professional conduct and common law; they may also arise from contracts and laws and regulations. They apply to attorneys' use of smartphones and tablets as well as other types of technology. Details are discussed in our chapter on attorneys' duties to safeguard. Two ethics opinions highlight attorneys' duties with respect to mobile devices, as follows:

A California opinion in 2010 applies these duties to the use of technology to transmit or store confidential client information, including the use of public and home wireless networks. State Bar of California, Formal Opinion No. 2010-179. Its conclusions include:

> **Before using a particular technology** in the course of representing a client, an attorney must take appropriate steps to evaluate: 1) the level of security attendant to the use of that technology, including whether reasonable precautions may be taken when using the technology to increase the level of security.

(Emphasis added.)

Pennsylvania Formal Opinion 2011-200 on cloud computing addresses attorneys' use of phones in that context. It notes that:

The advent of "cloud computing," as well as the use of electronic devices such as cell phones that take advantage of cloud services, has raised serious questions concerning the manner in which lawyers and law firms handle client information. . . .

Compounding the general security concerns for e-mail is that users increasingly access webmail using unsecure or vulnerable methods such as cell phones or laptops with public wireless internet connections. Reasonable precautions are necessary to minimize the risk of unauthorized access to sensitive client information when using these devices and services, possibly including precautions such as encryption and strong password protection in the event of lost or stolen devices, or hacking.

This kind of evaluation should be made for attorneys' selection and use of smartphones and mobile devices. It appears that many attorneys have joined the wave of smartphone and tablet users without evaluating the risks and without addressing security measures.

Mobile Security Basics

An important starting point in the security of mobile devices is focusing on and understanding the security issues and ways to mitigate them. Many security breakdowns are caused by lack of attention to the risks and security. When buying a new smartphone, tablet, laptop, or other mobile device, attorneys should consider security (both native and available add-ons) in making a selection. They should always make sure that all mobile devices are securely configured and used. *Constant security awareness is also essential—every day, every time mobile technology is being used.*

The attributes that make smartphones and tablets great personal and productivity tools also present high risk. They are mobile, compact, and powerful, with high storage capacity. But they can be lost or stolen and communications to and from them can be intercepted.

Mobile security is part of the overall information security, which is a process to protect the confidentiality, integrity, and availability of information. Comprehensive security must address people, policies and procedures, and technology. Details are covered in our security overview and policies chapters.

The following sections outline the basic steps for secure setup and use of mobile technology.

Smartphones and Tablets

Basic security setup for smartphones and tablets includes:

1. **Review and follow the security instructions of the device manufacturer and carrier.**

   This is an important step that is often forgotten or ignored. Most manufacturers' Quick Start Guides do not adequately address security.

   For Apple devices, User Guides for iPhones and iPads are available at **http://support.apple.com/manuals**. See also, Apple, *iOS Security* (iOS 9.0 or later) (September 2015), **https://www.apple.com/business/docs/iOS_Security_Guide.pdf** and iOS Security (iOS 8.3 or later) (June 2015), **https://www.apple.com/ca/ipad/business/docs/iOS_8.3_Security_Guide_EN.pdf**.

   For Android devices, see the device manufacturer's and carrier's security instructions. See also, *TechRepublic*, "10 Things You Can Do to Make Android More Secure," (June 17, 2014), **www.techrepublic.com/blog/10-things/10-things-you-can-do-to-make-android-more-secure**; Google Android Official Blog, "A Sweet Lollipop, with a Kevlar Wrapping: New Security Features in Android 5.0," (October 28, 2014), **http://officialandroid.blogspot.com/2014/10/a-sweet-lollipop-with-kevlar-wrapping.html**; and *Techworld*, "Android Marshmallow's 10 Most Important Security Features," (September 30, 2015), **http://www.techworld.com/picture-gallery/security/android-marshmallows-10-most-important-security-features-3626468/#3**.

   For Windows devices, consult the Microsoft instructions for the operating system and version and the device manufacturer's instructions. See also, Microsoft, "Get Smart about Mobile Phone Security," **www.microsoft.com/security/online-privacy/mobile-phone-safety.aspx**.

   For BlackBerry devices, consult BlackBerry's instructions for setup of the specific model of phone.

2. **Maintain physical control of the device.**

3. **Set a strong password, passphrase, or personal identification number (PIN).**

4. **Set locking after a set number of failed log-on attempts.**

5. **Set automatic logoff after a defined time of inactivity.**

6. **Encrypt confidential data on the device and any storage cards.** Encryption is automatic on iPhones and iPads when a per-

sonal identification number or password is set. It has to be enabled on current Androids and BlackBerrys by checking a box or boxes. Google has announced that encryption would be automatically enabled with a PIN, password, or swipe pattern, starting with Lollipop (although automatic encryption was enabled only on selected devices). Google has recently announced that it will require automatically enabling encryption on devices shipped with its newest version, Marshmallow.

7. **Provide for protection of data in transit, including secure, wired, and wireless connections.** (See Chapter 16.)

8. **Disable interfaces that are not being used, e.g., Bluetooth, Wi-Fi, etc.**

9. **Enable remote location, locking, and wiping of a lost device.**

10. **Consider using third-party security applications, e.g., antivirus, encryption, remote locating, and wiping, etc.**

11. **Back up important data.**

12. **Do not "jailbreak" or "root" a smartphone. These unlock a device, including its security controls.**

13. **Promptly apply updates to the operating system and apps—they often address security issues.**

In addition to secure setup for smartphones and tablets, there are several recommended measures for **secure use**:

1. **Limit confidential data on the phone or tablet to what is necessary. Don't put it on your phone or any mobile device just because you can.** Remember that some data may be written to a device without you knowing—if you are reading a client document from an e-mail attachment in your iPhone and you then press the "Home" button, the document will be saved to the phone.

2. **Be careful in selecting and installing applications. This is particularly important with Android for apps obtained from sources other than Google Play.**

3. **Pay careful attention to *permissions* given to apps, i.e., what the app can access, and the *terms of service*, i.e., what the app or service may do with data it accesses, including sharing it with third parties.**

4. **Configure Web accounts and remote access to use secure connections—https or virtual private networks (VPN).**

5. **Don't use public wireless clouds for confidential use or, at a minimum, take appropriate precautions.** Communications through cell carriers' networks are more secure. While some observers have expressed the view that public wireless clouds may be used if sufficient safeguards are employed, US-CERT's recommended precautions for mobile phones include the following: "Avoid joining unknown Wi-Fi networks and using public Wi-Fi hotspots."

6. **Don't open suspicious e-mails or follow suspicious links in e-mails and text messages.**

7. **Be careful with attachments—they sometimes contain malware.**

Encryption: A Security No-Brainer

Encryption is particularly important for smartphones, tablets, laptops, and portable media because of the risk of loss or theft. As discussed in the chapter on encryption, Verizon and other information security professionals and government agencies have strongly advocated its use—a security no-brainer.

On mobile devices, encryption is tied to an authorized user's logon credentials (username, plus password, passphrase, or other authentication, such as a fingerprint). When the user logs on with the correct credentials, the program automatically decrypts the data. When he or she logs off or shuts down, the data is automatically encrypted. Because of this feature, it's important to use a strong password or passphrase or enterprise grade biometrics with encryption to protect the data. See our chapter on authentication and authorization.

Additional Security Considerations

In addition to secure setup and use, including encryption, there are several other security considerations that are important.

BlackBerry (**us.blackberry.com**) was long considered to be the gold standard in mobile device management and security. However, it did not keep up with the market transition to smartphones and its market share rapidly declined. *The 2015 ABA Legal Technology Survey Report* states that only 8.2% of attorneys report that they use BlackBerry. In May 2011, BlackBerry (previously known as RIM) purchased ubitexx, a German provider of mobile device management software. After the acquisition, BlackBerry announced that it would use the ubitexx technology to support management of iPhones and Android phones through BlackBerry Enterprise Server. This service is now available through BlackBerry's BES12. It provides a common management platform for iPhones, iPads, and Androids, with secure delivery of e-mail and personal information management. BlackBerry also acquired Good Technology, a leading MDM (Mobile Device Manager) provider. Then BlackBerry announced the PRIV—its first smartphone using the Android operating system.

There has been considerable discussion about which platform, iOS or Android, is the "more secure" of the newer operating systems and there have been comparisons of both of them to the BlackBerry OS. While much of this discussion has been based on facts and technical information, some of it has been based on unsupported opinions and emotion. The relevant question for attorneys should not be which mobile OS is, in theory, "more secure." It instead should be whether the OS that they are considering or using, as configured, with any additional security and mobile management apps, is reasonably secure (or preferably stronger), considering the threats and sensitivity of information that may be at risk. This will require ongoing attention as circumstances change.

Two considerations in these comparisons have been vulnerabilities and the prevalence of malware. A vulnerability is a flaw in a system, OS, or software that can leave it open to attack. Security updates or patches are developed and distributed to provide protection against them. One report stated that in 2014 there were (1) 127 total vulnerabilities in iOS, 32 of them of high severity and (2) 6 total vulnerabilities in Android, 4 of them of high severity. These are the totals; it would take additional analysis, like actual exploits and time for patches for a full comparison. The numbers for Android do not include any vulnerabilities in the device manufacturer's code. The vulnerabilities for both are in the OS, not in third-party apps.

There is an advantage for iOS in security updates because Apple distributes them directly to end users. With Android, Google prepares the updates, but they are distributed through device manufacturers that provide them to users through the cell carriers. This can take time, sometimes the delay is very substantial. The exception is Google Nexis devices that get updates directly from Google. Google announced in October 2014 that it will start providing monthly updates and Samsung, LG, and BlackBerry (for its Android products) announced that they will distribute them monthly. Other manufacturers have not yet announced their plans.

There has been malware for both iOS and Android. The number of malicious apps for Android has been much greater over the years, but malicious apps for iOS have recently increased. All apps for iOS are distributed through Apple's App Store that has tight security controls, but they are not foolproof. Recently, Apple removed over 300 apps from the App Store that were infected with malware XCodeGhost that was introduced by compromised app developer tools. Apps for Android are distributed through

Google Play and a number of other sources. In response to malicious apps, Google added a feature to Google Play in 2012 called Bouncer that runs apps and tests them for malware. Shortly after that, Google added a feature called Verify App to Android devices. When used, it checks for known malicious apps. They are not foolproof, but they represent significantly improved Android security.

The prevalence of malware by itself does not tell the full story. The greatest volume of Android malware, by far, has been in Asia and spread through apps from sources other than mainstream. In the United States, the malware found on Android devices has been reported to be comparable or lower than that found on PCs. Added security can be provided by (1) downloading apps only from Google Play and other established providers such as Amazon and the major cell carriers and (2) using a security app.

A law firm should have a policy that governs acceptable use of mobile devices, including secure configuration and use. It can either be a part of a comprehensive security policy or a separate policy, coordinated with other policies. It should include coverage of bring your own device (BYOD), where personally owned mobile devices are used for the practice of law—including areas such as reporting loss or theft and procedures for securing firm data if an employee leaves.

Additional important considerations are securely getting data on and off mobile devices, secure remote access, and secure connectivity. These topics are discussed in separate chapters.

The NSA has developed a high-security version of Android called Security Enhanced (SE) Android. Some of its features are being incorporated by Google into the Android operating system. Android devices using Android SE and strong controls are reportedly being produced for the federal government for military and national security use.

Silent Circle (**www.silentcircle.com**) produces the Blackphone 2, a highly secure Android smartphone that includes peer-to-peer encrypted audio, video calling, and secure messaging. The secure audio, video calling, and secure messaging are also available as apps for iPhones and Android phones.

Open Whisper Systems (**https://whispersystems.org**) offers a free app/service that provides, for iPhones and Androids, encrypted voice and text communications, using their Signal product. It has been endorsed by Bruce Schneier, a leading security and cryptography expert, and Edward Snowden. We have heard that a number of attorneys are using its service.

In an enterprise environment such as a law firm, some form of mobile device management (MDM) is frequently used in addition to the security measures applied to each device. MDM is a set of controls that provides for enterprise control (by IT staff or a service provider) of secure setup and use of mobile devices. MDM can implement settings or force users to employ security requirements, such as complexity and age of passwords and encryption. MDM can also be used to locate and wipe lost or stolen devices. The tools can be used for storing encryption recovery keys and providing alternative administrator access to encrypted mobile devices. MDM has been evolving into Enterprise Mobility Management (EMM), which adds features like data protection and application control.

A number of service providers have products and services in this area, either as a tool for the enterprise to install and operate or as hosted services. Examples of leading MDM service providers include AirWatch, Citrix (Xenmobile), Good Technology (recently acquired by BlackBerry), IBM Mobile First Protect (MaaS360), and MobilIron. Microsoft is now offering Microsoft Intune, a cloud-based service for managing mobile devices and applications.

A "compartment," or sandbox, on a smartphone or tablet is a configuration of the device that puts enterprise (law firm) apps and data in a separate partition of the device from personal apps or data. The compartment is encrypted and isolated from the rest of the device to protect the enterprise apps and data.

Good Technology has offered, for a number of years, a secure compartment that separates enterprise applications and data from personal ones, encrypts it, and requires a password for access to the enterprise compartment. It can remotely wipe the contents of the compartment or all data on the device. It has been certified for certain uses under the security requirements of the Federal Information Processing Standard (FIPS) for federal agencies. Other MDM providers have been adding this capability.

BlackBerry 10 operating system and Samsung's Knox security feature have the built-in capability to separate business and personal apps and data. Business apps and data are contained in a secure partition that is isolated from the rest of the phone, similar to Good Technology's add-on. Samsung devices require a compatible MDM to enable the secure compartment. Google now offers Android for Work, a feature for use with MDMs to separate business and personal data.

Additional Information

Sources of additional information generally are included in the chapter on Additional Information Resources.

CHAPTER TWELVE

Portable Storage Devices

One survey reported that 70% of data breaches resulted from the loss or theft of off-network equipment (laptops, PDAs, and USB drives). As we previously discussed, there have been several recent reported incidents of law firms experiencing lost or stolen laptops or portable storage media. There most likely have been many more. Strong security is a must.

As in other areas of technology, attorneys must consider all of their duties to safeguard confidential data in this area, starting with their ethical duties. Encryption is viewed as a "no-brainer" security measure that provides strong protection in the event of loss or theft of portable devices and there are requirements, like those in the Nevada statute and Massachusetts regulation, that require encryption of covered data on portable devices.

In one data breach report, as we described in the Real-Life Data Breaches chapter, a Maryland law firm lost an unencrypted portable hard drive that contained medical records of patients in a lawsuit against its client hospital. One of the law firm's employees took home the hard drive containing backup data. This was the firm's method of ensuring that it had an offsite backup. She took the light rail system home and left the drive on the train. When she came back a few minutes later, it was gone. Backup is a good practice, but not if it exposes confidential data. If the drive had been encrypted, it would have had a strong level of protection. As it was, it had little or none.

USB flash drives now come in capacities as large as 1 TB and capacities just keep growing. External hard drives now equal capacities of internal hard drives in computers, as high as 4 TB, and also keep growing. They can store huge volumes of data that needs to be protected. A massive amount of data, in compact media, can be easily lost or stolen. With these devices, an attorney or employee can lose or steal the equivalent of a truckload of information.

The security considerations for laptops have been discussed previously and apply equally to portable devices. But portable devices present a greater risk because of their size; they can be more easily lost or stolen.

For portable media, the following security measures should be used:

1. Don't store unnecessary confidential information on portable media.
2. Use strong authentication—a complex password or passphrase.
3. Encrypt the data.
4. Never leave the password or passphrase with the portable device.
5. Back up important data.
6. Provide for physical security of the portable media, including:
   ♦ Keep it with you.
   ♦ When it's not with you, keep it in a locked place.
   ♦ Don't keep it connected to a desktop or laptop when it's not in use.
   ♦ Use a lanyard or case.
   ♦ Use engraving or an asset tag to identify the owner.

After the high-profile theft of a Department of Veterans Affairs laptop and external hard drive containing personal information on more than 28 million veterans in 2006, the Office of Management and Budget issued security guidelines for federal agencies, including the requirement of encryption of all data on laptops and portable devices, unless it is classified as "non-sensitive." This is now a standard for information security that should be employed by attorneys.

Like hard drives in computers, portable drives, both USB flash drives and external hard drives, can be protected by built-in hardware encryption or software encryption. Software encryption can be preinstalled on the drive or added by Windows (BitLocker to Go), Apple's OS X (FileVault 2) or by third-party encryption products.

Encrypted USB Flash Drives

Individual USB drives are available with built-in encryption. Examples include the CMS Secure Vault (**www.cesecure.com**), IronKey (**www.imation.com**), Kanguru Micro (**www.kanguru.com**), Kingston

Data Traveler (**www.kingston.com**), and SanDisk Cruzer Professional and Cruzer Enterprise (**www.sandisk.com**). Available products keep changing. They are readily available from office supply stores and online. Check the reviews for others' experience with the current options.

Thumb drives with encryption look no different from unencrypted ones. The difference is "under the hood":

CMS Products CE Vault Flash Drive
Figure 12-1

To enable encryption, follow the manufacturer's instructions and remember to back up the encryption key by saving it in a safe location off the device. After that, it's just a matter of using a password or passphrase to open the device. Here's an example:

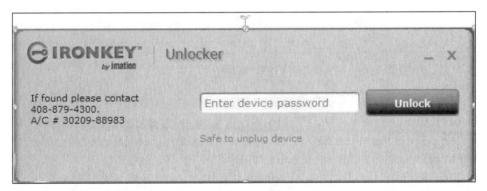

Figure 12-2

The drive is decrypted when the password or passphrase is entered. It is encrypted when it is removed from a computer, it is closed, or the computer is shut down.

A note of caution: Some drives that use encryption software, rather than hardware, are fully encrypted after encryption has been enabled. Others have an encrypted portion, with the rest of the drive unencrypted. When you connect the drive to a computer, it may show up as two drives—one encrypted and the other not encrypted. Make sure that you understand and follow the directions.

Here's an example—a screenshot of the files on a SanDisk Cruzer Blade flash drive. It uses SanDisk SecureAccess encryption that is included with the drive. Files and data that are saved in the Vault are protected with AES-128 encryption. Files and data on the rest of the drive are not encrypted. (**http://www.sandisk.com/products/usb/drives/cruzer-blade**) The Cruzer Blade comes in sizes from 4 GB to 64 GB and works with Windows and Macs.

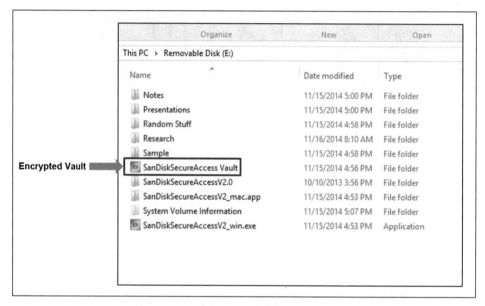

Figure 12-3

On any device that is not fully encrypted, it is critical to store confidential information in the encrypted part. Otherwise, it is not protected. Fully encrypted devices eliminate the risk of storing confidential data outside the encrypted part leaving it vulnerable.

The IronKey, by Imation, is a favorite of the authors. It includes strong encryption, wiping if the wrong credentials are entered too many times, and strong physical construction. As an added bonus, several of the models contain a secure password management application called Identity Manager. Be aware, the Identity Manager only works with older versions of Internet Explorer or the included Firefox browser. IronKey devices have a custom version of the Mozilla Firefox Internet browser installed on them. When it is connected to a computer and the Internet accessed through it, all of the browsing activity occurs on the IronKey instead of the computer. That is very secure browsing!

Some models of the IronKey (the W300, W500, and W700) support Windows to Go (part of Windows 8.1 and 10 Enterprise) (**www.microsoft .com/en-us/windows/enterprise/products-and-technologies/devices/ windowstogo.aspx**). Windows to Go allows the IronKey to work as an image of a law firm or enterprise computer. When it is plugged into a supporting computer, such as a home computer, all of the computing activity is securely done on the IronKey, basically using the computer as a terminal.

The Kingston Traveler Workspace (**www.kingston.com/us/usb/bootable# DTWS**) and several drives by Spyrus (**http://www.spyrus.com/windows-to-go-live-drives/**) also support Windows to Go. This is a new feature of Windows that has the potential for providing high security when away from the office—at home or on the road. It was new with Windows 8.1, so it is important to watch for reports about its utility and security.

The drive displayed in Figure 12-1 is a CMS Products CE Secure Vault Flash Drive. It has hardware encryption, using AES-256, which encrypts all data on the device. These drives range in capacity from 8 GB to 32 GB and work on PCs and Macs. One of the authors has used CMS Products encrypted drives and secure backup products and has had good experience with them (**http://www.cmsproducts.com/ce-secure-vault-hardware-encrypted-flash-drive**).

Encrypted External Hard Drives

External hard drives with built-in hardware encryption (self-encrypting drives) are similar to encrypted internal drives for laptops.

An example of an external hard drive with hardware encryption is the CMS Products CE-Secure DiskVault. It uses AES-256 encryption and is available in capacities from 120 GB to 960 GB. This model works only with Windows (**www.cesecure.com**).

There are a number of available options. See the discussion in our chapter on desktops and laptops.

Operating System Encryption of Portable Drives

Software encryption can be installed on compatible USB flash drives and external hard drives by using Windows BitLocker to Go or Apple's FileVault 2. BitLocker is available on Windows Vista and 7 (Ultimate and Enterprise) and Windows 8, 8.1, and 10 (Professional and Enterprise).

Encryption Software

Another option for encrypting portable devices is encryption software available from major security vendors. Some examples include McAfee Endpoint Encryption (**www.mcafee.com**), Sophos SafeGuard Easy (**www.sophos.com**), Symantec Endpoint Encryption and Whole Disk Encryption (**www.symantec.com**), and WinMagic Removable Media Encryption (**www.winmagic.com**).

Enterprise Management

As with laptops and desktops, it is best in an enterprise setting such as a law firm to actively manage encryption for portable drives centrally on firm servers.

Portable storage devices present a high-security risk that must be managed when they are used by attorneys.

CHAPTER THIRTEEN

The Internet of Everything

It was once called The Internet of Things, but is now more commonly called The Internet of Everything (IoE). So what is it exactly?

It was explained in a *Wired* article this way:

> "IoE expands on the concept of the "Internet of Things" in that it connects not just physical devices but quite literally everything by getting them all on the network. It moves beyond being a major buzzword and technology trend by connecting devices to one another and the Internet, and offers higher computing power. This connection goes beyond basic M2M communications, and it is the interconnection of devices that leads to automation and advanced "smart" applications. IoE works to connect more devices onto the network, stretching out the edges of the network and expanding the roster of what can be connected. IoE has a major play in all industries, from retail to telecommunications to banking and financial services."

We would certain add the legal industry to the list.

In September 2015, cybersecurity expert Bruce Schneier said in an interview: "The Internet of Things moves computers into every aspect of our lives. It will bring about profound changes in ways we don't understand."

Lawyers and IoE

What does it mean for lawyers and their security? Oh, so many possible things. We have already seen law firms ban Google Glass because of the fear that it could be recording/transmitting images or conversations that might compromise security.

We will no doubt soon see clients wanting to pay legal fees with their smartphones or smartwatches. After all, we are seeing a small but growing number of law firms accepting bitcoins in payment. In England, in 2014, we saw a law firm with 520 lawyers pilot an experiment wearing a bracelet that connected wirelessly with their time capture and case management systems.

As IoE advances, law firm video surveillance systems may be connected to the Internet. Even the appliances in the firm kitchen may be Internet connected. A coffee machine could well lead to the leakage of the passwords to the law firm's wireless network. Smartphones will be connected to lawyers' cars which will be connected to the Internet. Your car may alert your office when you are on the way in. Will someone be able to hack into your car to see where you are or into your smartphone to hear your conversations? With your car and Bluetooth, you can do a little billing by talking to clients about case strategy while you sit in traffic. How are you going to protect the privacy of those conversations?

Law firm heating and cooling systems may be connected to the Internet so you can adjust and monitor them remotely. Remember the Target breach? The bad guys got in because Target's HVAC contractor was compromised and had more access to their network than was warranted, causing the breach of Target's system.

You may use your video conferencing system (somewhat enhanced) to make remote appearances in court—that may more be the rule than the exception one day, with real-time recording of proceedings and real-time machine-assisted translation where needed. And of course, proceedings may be webcast by default. You may connect to the court's network which may connect to a broadcasting system's network. Any of these interconnections is only as secure as its weakest link.

Many law firms have Smart TVs in their lobbies—perhaps in their conference rooms or kitchens. Some of those TVs are capable of using a camera to watch you or, if they are configured to accept verbal commands from you, they could also be listening to what's going on in the room—and where is that data going? Perhaps not to the manufacturer, but to some third party for storage and indexing.

VoIP phone systems in a law firm may be hackable, along with security systems. Even IoE lightbulbs can add to the enormous risk of possible IoE usage in the future.

On the road? Your smartphone or smartwatch, both of which have access to your calendar, will softly ping you from time to time so you don't forget to call a client or attend a meeting—they will know how long it will take you to get to the airport and remind you when it is time to leave. Even while clearing security, you'll be able to keep up with your e-mails and texts while standing in line thanks to your smartwatch or smartphone. And if you don't mind people thinking you're talking to yourself, you can inquire from either device about the weather at your destination. Hungry? Stop and grab a burger—and pay with your iPhone via ApplePay. All the time, your location is being recorded and your voice may also be recorded depending on the technology you use. If you're talking to Siri, your conversation is running through Apple servers.

Come home and talk to your Amazon Echo and if you forget to turn it off, it will be listening to you and transferring what it hears to Amazon. Better not talk about anything sensitive to your spouse or to anyone on your smartphone.

All of this is only the tip of the iceberg.

IoE Devices: Their Rise and Their Shortcomings

Bruce Schneier has said, "These are devices that are made cheaply with very low margins, and the companies that make them don't have the expertise to secure them." While that may not be universally true, it is worrisome.

Schneier also warned about employees bringing their IoE devices to work in an interview with *Computer World*, "Will employees bring their IoT devices to work, thereby presenting another point of vulnerability? Sure."

More vintage Schneier: "They no longer say you can't bring in your own tablet. People would just quit. I think you'll have a hard time enforcing any of those rules because [IoT] is so powerful. If the CEO says, "We're saving 20% of our energy bill," and the security guy says, "But it's insecure," the CEO will say, "Shut up. We're saving 20% on our energy bill. Go away.""

After the crash, does he believe it will be better? Yes. "It's going to be solved by weird stuff, like there'll be security within the (network) because the endpoints are all crap." No one can say Mr. Schneier doesn't speak plainly.

Research firm Gartner anticipates that revenues from wearable tech will more than triple by 2016, going from $1.6 billion to $5 billion. It is no wonder that companies are rushing to board that train. When we saw Google purchase Nest (which makes Internet connected thermostats among other things), we knew that IoE was going to be BIG. Apple has obviously seen the inevitability of IoE. Many businesses are now seeing the world through the prism of endless interconnection possibilities.

We live in a world where cars drive themselves, health monitors can interact with medical staff, and refrigerators can order food for you (they can also send out spam if compromised—yes, this has really happened). We can make sure our elderly parents take their medications and even watch or listen to them to make sure they haven't fallen. We can watch our kids at school and our dogs at the doggie day care center. It is getting to the point where we almost lose track of all the ways in which we are connected to the Internet.

This is largely the point. When Apple representatives talk about the "Apple ecosystem," they refer to having interconnected computers everywhere in our lives—and all Apple products of course.

Privacy

How safe is our data in such an interconnected world? Which laws apply to protect it? Can the United States protect information which will likely be scattered across the globe with domestic laws alone? Is there any realistic way for international law to govern and to be adequately enforced?

From a government snooping point of view, the IoE is a Christmas gift many times over. Data, data everywhere. The more IoE you have, the more you can analyze the resulting "big data" and even anonymized information might lead to identifying individuals and their activities. It is simply a complicated mosaic which the supercomputers can figure out—far better and faster than the humans.

Needless to say, from the point of view of commercial vendors, all the data about us will be collected, analyzed, and sold. As it is often wryly observed, "If something online appears to be free, you are the product."

Security

While we used the word "privacy" as a subheader, we might just as well have used the word "security" since the two are so closely intertwined. The greater the volume of data kept on all of us, the less likely it is to be adequately secured. And we guarantee, much of the time, we will be so busy living our lives connected to the Net or functioning via the Net (sometimes without any real thought on our part) that we will be clueless about all the "evidence" we leave documenting where we are, what we are doing, thinking, buying, etc. Lawyers will not be immune to that reality.

While the greatest threat from IoE devices such as the Apple Watch, Android watches, and Google Glass appears to be to personal privacy, from the collection, storage, and potential sharing of personal information, they also present threats to law firm and enterprise security. Depending on the device and its features, they can intercept and store or transmit voice communications, take digital photos and videos, including photos of confidential documents, and potentially place malware on a network to which they are connected.

We have already seen (many times over) how easy it is to hack a car to cause an accident or how simple it might be to hack a medical device such as (yikes!) a pacemaker. Former Vice President Dick Cheney was so concerned about this that he deactivated the Wi-Fi function on his pacemaker.

A July 2014 HP study revealed that 70% of IoE devices use unencrypted network services and 80% of devices did not require passwords of sufficient length and complexity. Why? Because the majority of IoE devices are targeted to the consumer, where convenience and ease of use are far more important than security. Adding security, authentication, and logging functions will also add additional cost. Hence, the resistance to go down that road.

There is even an Internet of Things Security Foundation whose mission is to make the IoT secure. It has this to say about the IoT: "The resultant benefits of a connected society are significant, disruptive and transformational. Yet, along with the opportunity, there are fears and concerns about the security of IoT systems."

The Open Web Application Security Project lists the top ten IoT vulnerabilities which are:

1. Insecure Web Interface
2. Insufficient Authentication/Authorization
3. Insecure Network Services
4. Lack of Transport Encryption
5. Privacy Concerns
6. Insecure Cloud Interface
7. Insecure Mobile Interface

8. Insufficient Security Configurability

9. Insecure Software/Firmware

10. Poor Physical Security

Certainly, it is a list which would make a law firm CIO pause before investing in IoT devices.

A 2015 study of 7,000 IT and cybersecurity professionals by ISACA found that 78% of professionals believe IoT security standards are insufficient. If the professionals believe that, lawyers should be listening attentively.

Security Tips in an IoE World

As ever, encryption is your friend, and you should encrypt your data wherever possible, but sometimes the protection of your data, including your law firm data, is managed (or mismanaged) by a third party over whom you have no control. Make sure all devices are configured correctly from a security standpoint. Change any default ID/password. Monitor and install promptly all security updates. Be wary of unknown data usage.

Keep educated on the security risks of IoE. State-sponsored hackers, cyber-criminals, and those engaged in business espionage will all take up residence in the IoE world. They may use information there to attack utilities and military targets, or to discredit people. A *Corporate Counsel* article in 2015 predicted that IoE will exponentially increase the number of data breaches. We agree.

Apparently, the Federal Trade Commission (FTC) agrees too. It has made IoE a priority and is going after companies who fail to secure their products adequately. It issued a report in January 2015, warning that IoT devices present huge risks and urging companies to follow "security by design"(not as an afterthought), to disassociate data with actual users, and to be transparent with data collection and use.

The FTC has encouraged companies to use encryption where sensitive information is involved (law firms come to mind) and even to employ "smart defaults" which would require owners of IoT devices to change the default authentication settings during the setup process. It also advised data minimization, collecting only information that is specifically needed. In a world where data is gold and readily saleable, we doubt anyone will listen minus a law with teeth. While a number of experts have suggested stronger privacy laws to guard against the dangers of the IoE world, the reality is that they are unlikely to be enacted in a Republican-controlled Congress.

The Future of IoE

While no one can predict the future of IoE with any certainty, the vast monies invested in it indicate that widespread adoption is inevitable. Our guess is that no more than five to ten years will be required before IoE is the rule rather than the exception for all except the poor.

We can pretty well guarantee that the law will lag far behind the technology as it always has. Law firms, many of which don't even have "bring your own device" (BYOD) policies, will fail to adopt policies or controls governing IoE in the workplace. Privacy will continue to diminish and governments and cybercriminals will increasingly snoop on all of us, each for their own reasons.

The IoE is unstoppable. Like a global earthquake, it is sure to rattle (and open) windows into all our lives. Lawyers will need to be vigilant that their personal and professional use of the IoE doesn't result in the compromise of client data. The line between personal and professional use may blur beyond recognition in an always-connected world—and the crossover is dangerous.

Another danger? IoE may become invisible to us. Will we know/remember all the ways in which we are connected? Probably not. Will we know how to protect our data? Will we know if our devices have back doors? The legal world will be walking on security quicksand even more than it is today.

CHAPTER FOURTEEN

Secure Disposal

Confidential information, including law firm data, has been found too frequently on discarded computers, on hard drives at used computer stores and even on eBay. Secure removal of data from computer hard drives and portable media before discarding or reuse, called disk sanitization, is an important information security measure for everyone. It is a critical security measure for lawyers and law firms because of the requirement to protect information relating to clients. Like shredding, which is now a generally accepted security measure before disposal of confidential paper records, sanitizing hard drives and portable media before disposal or reuse is now a generally accepted safeguard to protect confidential data.

Safe disposal of computer media presents a challenge because many attorneys do not fully understand the technical issues or the risks. Most important, many computer users incorrectly believe that the Delete key or command securely removes data. "Delete" does not mean that the data is permanently gone. Many also believe that reformatting a hard drive securely removes the data on it. This is also incorrect. "Reformat" does not ensure that data has been securely removed.

As discussed below, the only currently accepted methods for secure removal of data are (1) physically destroying the drive or portable media, (2) degaussing (a magnetic process), and (3) overwriting the drive with effective disk-wiping software. Solid state drives, which do not use magnetic storage, present different considerations.

As a preliminary point, deletion, reformatting and secure wiping should never be used on data that is covered by a litigation hold. Severe sanctions for spoliation have been imposed when data has been wiped under those circumstances.

The Issues

As discussed above, confidential information, including law firm data, has been found on hard drives at used computer stores and even on eBay. The classic study in this area, conducted by two graduate students at Massachusetts Institute of Technology, is reported in S. Garfinkel and Abhi Shelat, "Remembrance of Data Passed: A Study of Disk Sanitization Practices," *IEEE Privacy and Security* (January/February 2003), at 17–27. The authors purchased 158 hard drives from used computer stores and on eBay. Of the 129 drives on which they could read data, only 12 (9%) had been properly sanitized. They found numerous hard drives containing files that had never been deleted or had been deleted but were recoverable. The files contained such confidential information as corporate personnel records, medical records, and financial records. Significantly, one drive they purchased at a used computer store had been in a law firm file server and contained privileged information. Later studies have reported similar findings.

Readable or recoverable data remains on hard drives like those in the studies, either because they were not sanitized at all or were ineffectively cleaned. Again, "delete" or "erase" in most cases does not mean that the data is securely gone. The Delete command in Windows only marks the file index with a notation that the disk space is available for reuse. The contents of the file remain intact and can be recovered, becoming very difficult or impossible to recover only if and when the file is later actually overwritten with new data. Even then, only part of a file may be overwritten, and remnants of the file may remain in other locations. Likewise, the Format command does not safely sanitize data. One study, for example, reported that Format overwrites slightly more than 0.1% of a disk's data. Until they have been overwritten with new data, deleted files can generally be recovered with utilities or forensics software.

There are differences of course in forensics with Mac OS X, but not as many as you'd think. The biggest difference is that the user is able to select the option to securely erase data. If the user does this, the data will not be recoverable.

These studies and the technical information they report make it clear that disposal or reuse of hard drives without proper sanitization presents a major security threat. This threat is present when computers or hard drives are sold, given away, discarded, or returned at the end of a lease. It also arises when defective hard drives are discarded or returned to vendors. The same risk is present with portable media such as CDs, DVDs, USB (thumb) drives, portable hard drives, and backup tapes.

Solutions

The need to sanitize or destroy old hard drives and other media is important for any computer user who must protect confidentiality. It is critical for lawyers and law firms because they are required to protect confidential information.

Until recently, courts and bar associations had not expressly analyzed this aspect of the duty of confidentiality. However, it should be clear that the general ethical and legal duties to safeguard client data apply equally in this area.

In early 2010, CBS News did a feature report on confidential data that it found on digital copiers that were available for resale, including shipment overseas. It found highly confidential information, including police files, employee records, and health records. This risk took many attorneys and others by surprise. A Florida ethics opinion, adopted later that year, found that there is a duty to securely dispose of electronic data in storage devices. Professional Ethics of the Florida Bar, Opinion 10-2 (September 24, 2010), concludes that "[a] lawyer who chooses to use Devices that contain Storage Media such as printers, copiers, scanners, and facsimile machines must take reasonable steps to ensure that client confidentiality is maintained and that the Device is sanitized before disposition."

In related fields, rules for secure disposal have been developing. As discussed in our chapter on the lawyer's duty to secure data, there has been a growing legal duty to securely dispose of protected information. For example, the Federal Trade Commission adopted a final rule under the Fair Credit Reporting Act for "Disposal of Consumer Report Information and Records," 16 C.F.R. Part 682 (2004) (included in the Appendix N). The rule requires proper disposal of covered information "by taking reasonable measures to protect against unauthorized access to or use of the information," including "[i]mplementing and monitoring compliance with policies and procedures that require the destruction or erasure of electronic media containing consumer information so that the information cannot practically be read or reconstructed." This rule requires that hard drives and other media be sanitized so that the information on them "cannot practically be read or reconstructed" but leaves the details of how to sanitize to regulated persons. There are now laws in at least 19 states with similar secure disposal requirements. Confidential information relating to clients should receive at least the same level of protection as consumer information.

The current generally accepted methods for secure removal of data are (1) physically destroying the drive or portable media, (2) degaussing (a magnetic process), and (3) overwriting the drive with effective disk-wiping software.

Destruction can be accomplished in various ways. Hard drives may be physically destroyed by disintegrating, incinerating, pulverizing, shredding, or smelting. Various articles and online instructions and videos include descriptions of methods such as drilling multiple holes, smashing with a sledge hammer, and grinding the surface of the disk, which are all time-consuming manual processes. An example of an automatic mechanical shredder for destroying hard drives is the Disintegrator by SEM (**http:// www.semshred.com/disintegrators**). There are also vendors such as Liquid Technology (**www.liquidtechnology.net/hard-drive-shredding.php**), Shred-it (**http://www.shredit.com/en-us/secure-hard-drive-destruction-service**) and Back Thru the Future Recycling (**www.backthruthefuture .com**) that provide hard drive shredding services. Don't forget about your backup tapes, either. In most cases, encryption was not enabled for the data on backup tapes, so physical destruction would be the best method to securely destroy the data. Besides using a service provider as mentioned, reasonably priced shredders are now available for portable media such as CDs and DVDs.

Degaussing is the second generally accepted secure disposal method. Degaussing is a magnetic process by which magnetic media are erased (returned to zero) by applying a reverse magnetic field using a degausser. Degaussing generally makes hard drives unusable. Examples of degaussers are ones offered by Garner Products (**www.garnerproducts.com**). An example of a service provider is Securis (**www.securis.com/data-destruction/degaussing**) and Data Devices International (**http://www .datadev.com/datagauss.html**). Because degaussing is a magnetic process, it works only on magnetic storage media, not on solid state drives.

The third generally accepted method to sanitize hard drives is overwriting with an effective disk-wiping program. Generally, this is done with software that overwrites every sector on the disk several times with random passes. Examples of disk-wiping programs include:

- Darik's Boot And Nuke (DBAN) (a free program, available at **www.dban.org**)
- Secure Erase (available for free download from the University of California, San Diego [UCSD], CMRR site, **http://cmrr.ucsd.edu/people/ Hughes/secure-erase.html**)

- Cyber Scrub (**www.cyberscrub.com**) (a commercial program)
- OnTrack Data Erasure Solutions (**http://www.krollontrack.com/ information-management/data-erasure-solutions/**) (a commercial offering)
- WipeDrive (**www.whitecanyon.com**) (a commercial program)
- The Mac's Disk Utility will show you all the drives mounted on the system, and you can choose to securely erase the entire disk.

Most ATA disk drives manufactured after 2001 (over 15 GB) have a Secure Erase feature included in their firmware (the software built into the device). However, it is often disabled in the BIOS of motherboards.

It is important to follow instructions carefully and verify that the data has been removed. The commercial programs generally have better instructions and support for nontechnical users.

There is also one other option, but it requires that steps be taken while the drive or portable medium is in use. Encryption, which protects data on a drive when it is in use, can also protect data when the drive or medium is no longer in use. If data is encrypted with strong encryption, it will be very difficult or impossible to read without the password or key. Unless the password or key is available, the data is protected if the drive is discarded, even without being sanitized. As discussed in our chapter on computers, laptops, and tablets, hard drives in laptops and portable media should be protected by encryption during use. Although protection by encryption should not be a reason for neglecting secure removal of data, it does provide a strong level of protection. If this method of sanitizing is used, it is critical that there be a way to verify that the decryption key has been removed or destroyed. Otherwise, secure deletion cannot be confirmed.

There has been recent concern about secure wiping of flash-based solid state drives (a newer type of drive). Although the built-in secure erase feature is generally effective, it has been reported that it has sometimes been implemented incorrectly by manufacturers. Degaussing and secure deletion tools written for magnetic media are not effective on these kinds of drives. For flash-based solid state drives, it is best to physically destroy the drive or consult a qualified professional.

CDs and DVDs should be physically destroyed. USB (thumb) drives should be wiped with a program such as Secure Erase or physically destroyed.

In addition to methods for sanitizing complete drives before they are discarded or reused, there are tools for securely deleting folders and files and data in unused disk space, slack space, and recycling bins. For Windows, examples include Eraser (**www.heidi.ie/eraser**), CCleaner (**www.piriform .com**), and Norton Utilities. In Mac OS X, files can be securely deleted by using the Secure Empty Trash command.

A government standard that is regularly cited on secure removal of data is NIST Special Publication 800-88 Rev. 1, "Guidelines for Media Sanitization" (December 2014). It discusses three levels of sanitization:

1. Clearing: a level of media sanitization that would protect the confidentiality of information against a robust keyboard attack (includes overwriting software or hardware products to overwrite storage space on the media with nonsensitive data).
2. Purging: a media sanitization process that protects the confidentiality of information against a laboratory attack.
3. Destroying: physical destruction of the media—the ultimate form of sanitization.

This publication includes, in Appendix A, "Minimum Sanitization Recommendation for Media Containing Data," a matrix covering sanitization methods for cell phones, PDAs, hard drives, portable drives, and other media. Most attorneys will not want to delve into these kinds of technical details, but they should be aware of the issues, ensure that someone with technical expertise sanitizes the data, and ask questions to make sure that it has been done.

The National Association for Information Destruction (NAID, **www.naid online.org**) is a trade association for companies offering data destruction services. It offers certification of service providers and its website has information about data destruction processes.

There are service providers that offer secure deletion and destruction of computer media. Examples include Iron Mountain (**www.ironmountain. com/Services/Data-Management/Secure-IT-Asset-Disposition.aspx**) and Shred-it (**www.shredit.com/en-us/home**). Before using a service, check reviews and references and be sure to get documentation of both receipt and secure deletion or destruction.

Computer security experts have debated whether overwriting is adequate to securely remove data and whether one overwrite or multiple overwrites are necessary. There is some consensus among researchers that, for many applications, overwriting a disk with a few random passes will sufficiently sanitize it. Given that many believe overwriting is acceptable for all but the most sensitive data, and based on presently available information, overwriting with effective sanitization software, plus verification, should be adequate for most legal data. The Department of Defense recognizes this method for all but classified data. If information is so sensitive that greater certainty is necessary, one of the other methods should be employed. Destruction or degaussing is also necessary if the hard drive is malfunctioning so that wiping software cannot be run.

Conclusion

Secure removal of data from hard drives and portable media before discarding or reuse should be a major concern for lawyers and law firms. The first step in addressing this issue is awareness—making sure that all involved personnel understand the problem. Next, firms should put in place policies and procedures to ensure that data security is maintained whenever computers or media are discarded or reused. Destruction, degaussing, or secure wiping should be employed, either by staff or a service provider, whenever disposal or redeployment occurs. Service providers should be carefully selected and audited. Finally, records should be prepared to document the sanitization or destruction.

CHAPTER FIFTEEN

Digital Copiers

We can't remember the last time we set foot into a law firm and didn't see a digital copier. We're sure someone out there still has an old clunker analog copy machine, but the modern day office is surely equipped with a digital one. Digital copiers are also called MFP for multifunction peripheral. The digital copier is a multifunction device and can act as a copier, scanner, printer and fax machine.

Acquiring a digital copier goes something like this. A salesperson discusses how many copies you typically need to make in a month. Do you need the ability to copy and or print in color? What about stapling, hole punching, and collation? Will you lease (typical) or purchase (not as common) the digital copier? Once all the options are determined, the device is delivered to your office and a technician installs it on your network. The good news is that you have a brand new machine to help make your practice more efficient. The bad news is that you have a brand new machine that can be a huge security risk. Not to worry. We'll help identify some of the risks and solutions to make your copier more secure.

Administration

The first area to deal with is the administration of the copier. This is the place where you configure the various features and access to functions. We're sure that someone in the office was given a little training about how to use and configure some of the copier features. We're also pretty sure that nobody at the firm knows what the administrative password is to gain access to additional configuration options. The administrative password is what the technician uses to initially set up the device. The problem with the administrative password is that it is left at a default value that every technician knows. Default values are not a good thing. You can find out what the default administrative passwords are by doing a Google search. As an example, just do a Google search for "administrative password for Canon copier." You see that the default password is "canon" or the device serial number. You may want to consider changing the default password.

You can also remotely manage the copier using a web browser. That means that the copier is actually hosting a specialized website on your network. You need to protect the copier's remote access just as you would any other website. Make sure the firewall is configured to prevent any outside access to the digital copier.

Scanner

Besides using the digital copier as a device to make copies, most law firms will heavily utilize the scanning function. When using the copier as a scanner, typically the scanned images are delivered as a PDF file. You may have other options to save the image as a TIFF or JPG file, but normally the default is to save as a PDF. The file format isn't that important. What's more important is how you deliver the file. One option is to deliver the scan to a "box" on the copier. You then access the scan box from your computer and download the file. You can have a single common box that everyone accesses, which isn't very secure or one for each individual. Having individual boxes is better than having a common one, but you still have to remember to download the file from your computer.

Another option is to configure the copier so that it uses FTP (File Transfer Protocol) to a place on the firm's server. This would mean that you need the FTP service running on your server. You can configure your FTP server to accept anonymous connections, which isn't very secure. If you don't allow anonymous connections, you'll need to configure a user ID and password in the copier. That's probably not a good alternative either since the ID and password would be exposed if someone were able to access the embedded website that is running on the copier.

A third and more desirable option is to deliver the file directly to a user's inbox via e-mail. Most copiers don't have an SMTP engine to deliver e-mail, which means you have to allow the copier the ability to relay messages through your current e-mail server. That's not a problem as long as you configure it properly. Most technicians will want to know the domain administrator user name and password for your network. They want the most powerful logon credential to make sure there are no problems with delivery of the scanned information. Don't do it. The technician will program the copier with the domain administrator credentials, which is a huge security risk. The best solution is to program your e-mail server to only allow relayed mail originating from a specific IP address (the IP address of the copier). If you are not sure how to configure the IP restriction, contact your IT provider.

Finally, don't configure the copier to allow direct user input of an e-mail address for delivery of the scanned document. In other words, the e-mail address destination should be preprogrammed by an administrator. If you allow the user to enter an e-mail address (perhaps for a client or expert), there will be no log of the transmissions and the recipient won't know who sent it. Normally, the copier sends the scanned file as originating from something like **copier@lawfirm.com**. Make the user scan the document and deliver it to their own inbox. They can forward the file or attach it to a new message.

Fax

The digital copier can also act as a facsimile machine. Receiving faxes to your copier may sound like a good thing and save you another piece of equipment. You have similar issues in delivering faxes as you do with scanned documents. Are you just going to print the fax as received? Will they get delivered to a common box or should they go as an attachment to an e-mail message? The difference between using your copier as a fax machine and a stand-alone fax is knowing that the copier is connected to your network. If you configure the copier to be used as an outbound fax, you may want to configure additional safeguards to try and minimize any confidential data being sent to the wrong destination.

Disposal

Whether you lease or purchase your digital copier, make sure you securely dispose of any client data that may exist. A digital copier has a hard disk that is used to store the images prior to printing or sending as scanned images. The hard disk has the same concerns that any computer hard drive would have. Deleted doesn't mean deleted and the data can potentially be recovered unless it is wiped. Some digital copiers have a secure deletion feature where the hard disk area is wiped after each printing or copy is made.

Even if your copier does not have a secure delete feature, make you that you wipe the hard drive prior to turning the copier in or selling it. Most modern-day digital copiers have a wipe disk feature that is accessible using the administrator ID and password. Perhaps accessing the advanced features is one reason why the technicians tend not to advise customers of the capability. If you don't know how to access the wiping routine or it doesn't exist for your particular copier model, just remove the hard drive and wipe it using wiping software such as DBAN, which you can find through a Google search. Remember that DBAN does not work with solid state drives, but we have yet to see any SSDs being used in a digital copier.

Other Considerations

No matter what other capabilities your copier has, think of the security implications if you enable a feature. Perhaps you don't want to enable a feature because it exposes potential access to data. Remember that the copier is connected to your network, so it potentially has access to all of your client data. If the copier is compromised, it may be the entry point to your network. And that's a very bad thing—so go back and re-read this chapter if needed to make sure you aren't making it easy for the bad guys to invade your network!

CHAPTER SIXTEEN

Networks: Wired and Wireless

There are a lot of pieces and parts when dealing with information networks. We'll try to dissect some of the components and identify some best practices for maintaining security. Network security needs to consider external and internal access. Certainly, you don't want any outsiders accessing the data flowing over your network, but you may also wish to restrict data access for your own employees and those folks internal to your network. Passwords and IDs are one way to limit data access, but we can also segregate access at the network level. Let's start with a brief description of a computer network and take it from there.

Essentially, computer networks are the technology used to provision the communications among different devices. This could be as simple as two computers sharing information between them or as complex as having hundreds of machines accessing several dozen servers and printers. Data can flow through physical wire (fiber optics as well) or through the air wirelessly. No matter what type of network you have, there are many considerations for securing it.

Authentication and Access Control

Strong authentication and access control should be implemented for both wired and wireless networks. You want to let authorized users in and keep intruders out. This requirement is discussed in the Information Security Overview, Authentication and Authorization, and Desktops, Laptops, and Servers chapters.

Wired Networks

Wired networks are just that—devices interconnected via physical wires. Security in this type of environment is pretty straightforward since you have control and access to physical wiring and where it gets connected. The wiring should be routed through spaces that you control and have access to. As an example, you wouldn't want to run any wiring through the ceiling of the office next door. If you do that, there is a potential for someone to "eavesdrop" on the communication by tapping into the line. So step one is to know where the wires are running. This sounds like a simple step, but you would be surprised how many firms have absolutely no documentation concerning their network and no clue how the wires are routed through the building.

Besides the physical wiring, there may be intermediate equipment such as a patch panel to centralize the connections. This patch panel area should also be physically secured to prevent anyone from accessing the network ports. This may not be possible for small offices where space is at a premium. Normally, you would have some device that is placed on the wall near the telephone and data equipment. This may be in a separate communications closet or in plain view in some corner of the office. The wires would run from the device to each network outlet throughout the office. Each network outlet would then be connected to a computer, printer, digital copier or some other data processing device. The network termination device may be a small (perhaps five-port) plastic mount that is about the size of a pack of cigarettes. Larger installations will have a multiport patch panel mounted to the wall or inserted in a 19-inch rack unit.

It is not an absolute requirement that the patch panels be physically secured, especially if your firm is the only one that occupies the office space. If you share office space with other tenants, then securing the patch panel behind some locked cabinet or in a locked room is highly recommended. Securing access to the physical connections at the patch panel helps prevent someone from tapping into the communication stream.

Wireless Networks

In a solo or small firm, if the investment cost to wire an office space with data cables is too expensive, a wireless solution may be the answer. Plus, who wants networking cables all over the place? This is particularly true in older properties—and may be aesthetically desirable in historic premises. A wireless network is extremely convenient for lawyers who use laptops, smartphones, or tablets because they can move from their office to the conference room with these devices and still stay connected to the local network and Internet. The cost to purchase a wireless networking device is extremely low, and the benefits gained are worth the small investment. However, do not implement a wireless network without taking the proper security precautions. In some sense, wireless networks are harder to secure because you can't see the other "end" of the communication connection. By default, most wireless routers and access points are preconfigured without enabling encryption on wireless connections. Thus, all communications between computers and the wireless device are unencrypted and are not secure. How many people have connected their laptop to an unencrypted wireless network so that they could check their e-mail or perform online banking? We see this all the time—even at legal technology conferences! Without an encrypted wireless connection, your data travels through the air in clear text just waiting for someone to "sniff" it down to their own computer.

Don't think that's possible? Perhaps you should do a Google search for "Firesheep." Firesheep is a plug-in for the Firefox browser that allows you to hijack session credentials from other users on the same network. Stealing the session is also called sidejacking. It is typically done with a wireless connection since all of the data is exposed in the wireless cloud. So how do you protect yourself from having your session hijacked? Blacksheep is also a Firefox plug-in that combats Firesheep. Blacksheep inserts "fake" session ID information and also monitors for the existence of Firesheep. Blacksheep sounds like a good tool to combat having your session hijacked, but the approach has some weaknesses and is specifically designed to combat Firesheep. A better Firefox plug-in to prevent sidejacking is available from the Electronic Frontier Foundation and is called HTTPS Everywhere. It is available for Firefox, Chrome, and Opera. It is available for download at **https://www.eff.org/https-everywhere**.

One year at the ABA TECHSHOW, author Simek demonstrated how easy it was to "sniff" data from the wireless cloud. Some lawyer was accessing his e-mail from the firm's server using an insecure method of communications (no encryption). It was a trivial process to show the audience the lawyer's user ID, the name of the firm's server, and potentially his password. The demonstration did not reveal his password, but it was in clear text on the next line of the sniffer trace.

Wireless networks should be set up with the proper security. First and foremost, encryption should be enabled on the wireless device. Most wireless devices come preconfigured with either an unencrypted network or a network encrypted using the wired equivalent privacy (WEP) 64- or 128-bit algorithm. Ultimately, neither of these solutions is adequate. WEP is a weak encryption algorithm and can be cracked in a matter of minutes using open-source software. Do not use WEP! To further support our recommendation not to use WEP, the Federal Trade Commission and the Canadian Privacy Commissioner have both found WEP encryption insufficient to secure credit card information. This followed a recommendation in 2004 by the Institute of Electrical and Electronics Engineers (which publishes the wireless standards) that WEP's security had been compromised. Some time back, Wi-Fi Protected Access (WPA) using the temporal key integrity protocol (TKIP) algorithm was cracked by a group of Japanese scientists in about a minute. So WPA encryption isn't safe either. This means that you should be encrypting using WPA2 only. If your wireless access device does not support WPA2, it's time to buy a new one. Second, if the wireless network is for the firm only, enable media access control (MAC) filtering on the wireless device. MAC filtering essentially limits the devices that may communicate with the wireless device. If the MAC address of a computer's wireless network card does not match an authorized MAC address, then the wireless device will not be allowed to communicate with the unauthorized computer. This is an added layer of security.

Next, the wireless access device should be securely configured. Most commonly, wireless routers and access points ship with default network names such as LINKSYS or NETGEAR. While in operation, these devices will broadcast their names so that wireless clients can locate the wireless networks. It is strongly recommended, for security reasons, that the default name of the wireless network be changed and that broadcasting the service set identifier (SSID), which is essentially the network name, be disabled. Transmitting the SSID is like erecting a billboard that everyone can see and sending the message "Connect to Me!" If you must broadcast the name of the network, change it to something that does not identify it as a law firm wireless network. The name should be nondescript enough to help prevent any targeted attacks. Imagine if you are an IP firm or one that handles mergers and acquisitions. If someone was trying to get information about a matter your firm was involved in, naming the wireless network to something such as "Hamilton_Law_Firm" makes you an easy target.

In addition, change the default password for configuring the wireless network. Outsiders can "sniff" wireless networks and determine the type of wireless device in use. Default passwords are freely available on the Internet.

To summarize the steps for setting up a secure wireless network:

1. Use WPA2 encryption. Do not use WEP or WPA.
2. Enable media access control (MAC) filtering.

3. Change the default network name.

4. Turn off broadcasting of the network name.

5. Change the default configuration password for the network.

There are many stories where the "bad guys" used an insecure wireless network to do bad things. You probably don't even know if someone is using your bandwidth if your wireless has not been secured. Imagine when the FBI comes knocking on your door because they have traced the downloading of child pornography to your IP address. We have had several cases involving exactly that scenario.

If the router that connects to the Internet doesn't come equipped with built-in wireless support, there are other wireless solutions available for your firm that provide reliable and secure network connections.

In the "old" days, AirCards (dedicated cellular data devices) were used to connect to the data network of your cellular carrier. We no longer see those devices being used today. Instead, users are investing in something such as the Verizon Ellipsis Jetpack or other MiFi (brand name used to describe mobile wireless hotspot) device. These devices create a local wireless network that can provide Internet access (over the cellular network) to up to ten devices. Verizon offers the Ellipsis Jetpack for $19.99 with a two-year commitment. It connects to the cellular carrier's 3G/4G data network. Each unit is registered to the carrier's network and creates an encrypted communication link to protect the data transmission. This means it is a secure connection and appropriate for the transmission of confidential information. Frankly, you should be using the "hot spot" capability that is built into your smartphone, which also encrypts the information over the 3G/4G data connection. That means you don't have to carry around or pay for another piece of equipment.

So can you securely communicate using a wireless network? Of course you can. Be wary of any "open" wireless clouds such as those at Starbucks, a public library, an airport, an Internet cafe, and the like. These wireless "hot spots" are typically unsecured and do not encrypt the communications. There is no problem using one of these hot spots, but make sure you are using a VPN client (encrypts the data stream) or are using SSL in your browser. Websites that have a URL that begins with https:// are using encrypted communications. There have been instances where the SSL certificates (those that drive the encryption) have been compromised, so there is no 100% guarantee that https:// connections are totally secure. Don't enter any identifiable or important information (e.g., passwords, credit card numbers, etc.) until you have an https:// URL. Using cell carriers' data networks, as describes above, is more secure. If you see a list of available networks and one of them says, for instance, "free downtown access," be careful. Hackers will often name their networks something that might attract you—sure you can use their bandwidth, but they'll be stealing your data while you're doing so.

In addition, it is important to have a firewall enabled on the laptop or other device used to access the wireless network and to disable file sharing on it. The other steps for secure configuration of laptops, discussed in the Desktops, Laptops, and Servers chapter, should also be followed.

Firewalls/IDS/IPS Devices

An intrusion detection system (IDS) is used to detect many types of malicious network traffic and computer usage that can't be detected by a conventional firewall or router. These attacks include network attacks against vulnerable services (web hosting, e-mail, databases), data-driven attacks on applications, host-based attacks such as privilege escalation, unauthorized logins, and access to sensitive files. Privilege escalation is the act of exploiting a known vulnerability in an application to gain access to resources that would have otherwise been protected from being accessed. When an IDS is used in combination with an intrusion prevention system (IPS), they also can detect and prevent malware such as viruses, Trojan horses, and worms from entering the network.

An IDS/IPS device is commonly placed at the gateway of the computer network so that all incoming and outgoing network traffic passes through the device. This allows the device to scan all incoming traffic before it is passed on to the destination located on the local computer network, denying any malicious traffic the ability to enter the local network. A firewall has the ability to permit or deny data traffic based on port number, originating or receiving Internet Protocol (IP) address and protocol type, to name just a few capabilities, and it is usually based on rules that are set up and configured by an administrator. An IP address is a unique address or identifier assigned to a networked device, such as a computer, that allows the device to communicate with other networked devices. Just think of an IP address as being the same as a home address, which is a unique way to identify your home's physical location.

A firewall device with these capabilities is critical for the protection and security of your firm's computer equipment and information systems. For those users who have a broadband Internet connection at home, a firewall should also be used to protect your home computer network from outside attacks. This is especially important for lawyers who work from home because you do not want your client's data to become compromised while working offsite. According to the Internet Storm Center, which is part of the SANS Institute, it only takes up to twenty minutes for an unprotected and unpatched computer connected to the Internet to become compromised. Imagine if that computer were yours and it contained confidential client data. This is the stuff nightmares are made of.

If you are wondering what firewall we would recommend, it would be the Cisco ASA 5500-X Series Adaptive-Security Appliance, which provides a good solution for solo and small firms looking to secure their local computer network from outside attacks. This appliance integrates firewall function, unified communications (voice/video) security, SSL (Secure Sockets Layer) and IPSec (Internet protocol security) VPN, intrusion prevention, and content security services into a single piece of hardware. These devices offer advanced security features such as granular control of applications and microapplications with behavior-based controls, highly secure remote access, and near-real-time protection against Internet threats. Combining all of the functionality into one piece of network hardware eliminates the need to purchase a single device for each function. Using a single piece of hardware saves time in setup and configuration, eliminates complexity, and tremendously reduces the cost to adequately secure your business computer network.

The Cisco ASA 5500-X Series provides intelligent threat defense and secure communications services that stop attacks before they affect your firm's business operations. The firewall technology is built on the proven capabilities of the Cisco PIX family of security appliances, allowing valid traffic to flow into and out of the local network while keeping out unwelcome visitors. The URL and content-filtering technologies implemented by the device protect the business as well as the employees from the theft of confidential and proprietary information and help the business comply with federal regulations, such as HIPAA and the Gramm-Leach-Bliley Act. The application control capabilities can limit peer-to-peer and instant-messaging traffic, which often leads to security vulnerabilities and can introduce viruses and threats to the network. The implementation of a Cisco ASA 5500-X Series device will deliver comprehensive, multilayer security to your computer network and will help you to sleep better at night knowing your electronic data and equipment are protected.

The cost of the Cisco ASA 5500-X Series device can range in the thousands of dollars, depending on the number of licenses, features, warranty, and support purchased with the product. When purchasing this device, we absolutely recommend that you get SmartNet maintenance. SmartNet allows you access to the excellent technical support personnel of Cisco, hardware replacement for failures, and upgrades to the device operating system.

One other Cisco IDS/IPS that is worth mentioning is the Cisco Meraki MX80. This security device, while not as robust as the ASA 5500-X series, is popular with small law firms. The device is configured, monitored, and receives its updates via the Cloud. The device, along with the required Advanced Security License (we recommend the three-year version) costs about $700.

The recommendation of these Cisco products is based on two of the authors' experience with small and midsized firms. There are a number of other available options. Other highly rated firewalls are available from other companies such as Palo Alto Networks and Juniper Networks. Some professionals prefer the user interface and configuration of Juniper products over Cisco's interface. Check reviews in information security publications and with IT and security professionals when making selections.

Data Loss Prevention

Data Loss Prevention (DLP) is a technology that protects against unauthorized downloading or transmission of data by insiders, whether deliberate or inadvertent. It is a new technology that has evolved over the last ten years and is now commonly used in law firms and other enterprises, particularly larger ones. While tools such as firewalls and IDS/IPS monitor and protect against threats, DLP protects sensitive data and user actions relating to it.

DLP can monitor points of egress from networks, such as Internet connections. It can also monitor servers, such as e-mail servers and endpoints, as well as desktops and laptops. DLP uses rules that are set to identify authorized access by users or groups of users to various classifications of data and what they are permitted to do with it. If there is an attempt to get unauthorized access or to make an unauthorized download or transfer, it is blocked or an alert is issued, depending on how it is set.

For example, if an employee tries to forward a firm e-mail outside the law firm network or to upload a law firm file to a consumer cloud storage service such as Dropbox, the upload could be blocked or an alert issued. If an employee sends an unencrypted e-mail containing a social security number, the e-mail could be blocked. If an employee tries to download data of a defined kind or a triggered amount of data to a USB thumb drive or to download it through remote access, the activity could be blocked or an alert issued. Some more advanced DLP solutions also look for anomalies in data access, transfer, and downloads on a per user basis.

DLP can provide a strong level of protection, to compliment the more traditional solutions, in protecting against inside threats.

Routers

A router is a computer-networking device that connects two or more independent networks together (e.g., your firm's local network to your Internet provider's network). A router's job is to determine the proper path for data to travel between the networks and to forward data packets to the next device along the path. Routers come in all shapes and sizes and with different features. For a solo or small firm, a basic router will be sufficient to connect the local network to the Internet, as well as to protect computers and other hardware devices on the local network from outside attacks. A basic router will require some configuration from the default values to get it configured and communicating with the ISP's network, as well as to strengthen the security and protection it provides to your information systems. Most basic routers are only capable of handling broadband Internet connections such as cable or DSL. If your firm has a T-1 or any variant of this Internet connection, you will most likely be provided with a router by your ISP. Whether you acquire the router from the ISP or purchase one yourself, make sure that it is properly configured and includes a firewall and logging capability. As with firewalls, there are also routers designed to handle much higher connection speeds and data throughputs as required by larger law firms.

Any router you implement should provide stateful packet inspection (SPI) of the traffic. Stateful packet inspection is where the firewall is programmed to distinguish legitimate packets for different types of connections such as web surfing, e-mail transmission, file transfers, etc. Only packets that match a known active connection will be allowed. Intrusion detection is another desired feature. Intrusion detection systems (IDS) monitor network traffic for any malicious activity or policy violations. They typically will alert the network administrator should such activity be observed. Content filtering capability can also help reduce the possibility of malware infection. Content filtering inspects the payload of each data packet to restrict unwanted content.

Today, the "bad guys" have gotten so good at breaking into law firms that it's becoming increasingly hard to keep them out. Hence, as we mention elsewhere in this book, the mantra has become "detect and respond." When they do get in, most law firms don't realize that they've been compromised until it's too late. Because of this, there isn't an entry-level routing solution that we can recommend with confidence anymore. You firm's data is just too valuable.

Given the types of information that your firm stores, such as social security numbers, credit cards and possibly patient records, the only way to combat a hacker's attack and to have a reasonable chance of keeping them out is through the implementation of a defense-in-depth security strategy. This type of information security strategy provides security at all levels of your computer network, including the point at which your local network interfaces with the public Internet. For this reason, even for a solo attorney, we recommend the Cisco Small Business RV Series line of routers.

The Cisco Small Business RV Series routers provide high-performance connectivity for small businesses and have built-in threat defense, including a proven stateful packet inspection firewall, intrusion detection system, and an optional content filtering subscription package to restrict a user's access to undesirable websites that may contain malware and phishing attacks. The Cisco RV130W router offers a wireless option for those firms that require it. The Cisco Small Business RV Series routers start at around $150. As with firewalls, Cisco has router models that will scale to the medium- and large-firm needs. The 800 series is an excellent choice for small to midsized firms. The Cisco 4000 series routers will scale to large-firm needs and are designed to meet Gigabit forwarding speeds enhancing network performance.

A Cisco device is a little more complicated to configure from the command line, although a graphical user interface (GUI) is available to assist those less familiar with the Cisco configuration syntax. Unless you are comfortable with the syntax of Cisco's IOS (yes, Apple used iOS after Cisco), we recommend that you not attempt to configure the device yourself. Seek the expertise of your IT professional or another resource that "speaks" Cisco's IOS language.

Switches

A switch is a piece of networking hardware that connects network segments (discrete sections of the network), allowing multiple devices to communicate with one another. For example, if two or more computers are connected into the same switch and are located within the same defined (IP, IPX, AppleTalk, etc.) network, the switch will allow these devices to communicate. Switches inspect data packets as they are received and, based on the source and destination hardware addresses, will forward the data packet appropriately. By delivering the packet of information only to the device it was intended for, network bandwidth is preserved, as well as confidentiality, and the information is delivered in a much quicker manner. As a comparison, network hubs send the traffic to all ports irrespective of the destination device and are rarely seen in production environments anymore. It is unlikely that you would be able to purchase a hub from any source other than eBay. Unlike network hubs, switches are "intelligent" devices that can operate on more than one layer of the Open Systems

Interconnection (OSI) model, such as a multilayer switch. Switches allow traffic to pass through them at speeds of 10 Mbps, 100 Mbps, 1 Gbps, or 10 Gbps, depending on the speeds of the ports.

The OSI model was created by the International Organization for Standardization as a way of subdividing a communications system into seven layers: Physical, Data Link, Network, Transport, Session, Presentation, and Application. We could write a whole book on the OSI model, but others already have.

For law firms that require or desire tighter security controls over their computer systems and users, a managed switch may be the solution to your firm needs. A managed switch, unlike an unmanaged switch, is a device that can be administered or controlled. Such advanced features include the ability to limit what computer systems can "talk" with one another at the physical level (private virtual-LANs), advanced performance monitoring, and increased bandwidth control. These switches also support Quality of Service (QoS), which can be used to prioritize certain network traffic over another, such as if your firm is using VoIP phones.

A managed switch would be used to segregate and secure specific network connections within your local environment. Virtual Local Area Networks (VLANs) are used to define which switch ports are included within each internal network. As an example, you should define a network just for the attorneys/staff and a separate one for visitors to your office. The network traffic for each would be separated through the use of VLANs. VLANs are then interconnected via a router, which has the intelligence to move appropriate traffic between the networks. An even more complex subject is VLAN tagging, which allows multiple VLANs to exist on a single network port. VLAN tagging is not for the faint of heart and is normally only found in large enterprise situations.

Servers and Network Devices

Servers and network devices, just as desktops and laptops, should be securely configured or hardened. Networks also need to be managed. These areas are beyond the technical ability (and interest) of most attorneys, but attorneys need to make sure that these issues are addressed by qualified experts.

For example, servers running Windows Server can use Group Policy for centralized configuration management. It can be set to control what users can and cannot do and to manage secure configuration of computers connected to the network. Group Policy can enforce security requirements such as complexity, length, and change period of passwords. The latest version of the server operating system (e.g., Windows Server 2012 R2) is almost always the most secure. There are, however, other considerations in upgrading, such as compatibility of hardware and application software. Whatever version is in use, the latest patches should be applied.

As another example, network firewalls should be set to control outbound traffic as well as inbound traffic. Control of outbound traffic can be set to enforce policies (e.g., blocking connection to peer-to-peer networks) and to limit the effect of an attack (e.g., blocking connection to an attacker's command and control server). Current versions of firmware (the software embedded in network devices) should be used and patches should be promptly applied. The National Institute for Standards and Technology (NIST), the Center for Internet Security, and network vendors such as Cisco and Juniper Networks publish secure configuration standards and guides.

As discussed in the Desktops, Laptops, and Servers chapter, there are security tools for testing secure configuration, managing patches, and locating vulnerabilities such as missing patches. These tools are generally used in a network setting.

Again, the details of hardening and network management are very technical. Attorneys should be generally aware of the concepts and make sure that these issues are addressed by qualified professionals.

Other Considerations

Besides the items already mentioned, you should only connect (patch) in those wired network ports that will have devices physically attached at all times. In other words, only the active connections should be terminated to a switch port and made part of your LAN. Why is this important from a security perspective? You don't want someone plugging a computer into an unused port and being able to access your network. Kevin Mitnick, a notorious hacker who was the first hacker to make the FBI's Ten Most Wanted list, tells a story in his book, *The Art of Deception*, where he walked into a conference room of an office and connected his laptop to the Ethernet wall jack.

He was immediately on the company network and began hacking the various servers. He would have never been able to attack the servers if the network connection was not "hot" and connected to a switch port. As a best practice, do not patch in unused (idle) network ports. Only connect them when they are needed.

CHAPTER SEVENTEEN

Remote Access

Most lawyers are road warriors today. If their entire office is not on their laptop, a large chunk of it is—and the rest is accessible through remote access. Whether in court, on vacation, traveling, or in a meeting, lawyers need access to their e-mail, calendar, appointments, and files.

Some lawyers have discarded workstations entirely, using only their laptops and a docking station at work and tablets while on the move. Others have both a workstation and a laptop. The popularity of laptops has zoomed in the last decade to the point where the lawyer without a laptop is a relative rarity. However, we are beginning to see a surge in tablet usage, especially with products such as the Surface Pro 3 and 4, which for many truly are laptop replacements. Our new mobile lawyers are now equipped with technologies that allow them to be as productive when on the road as they are in the office, minimizing downtime and maximizing billable hours (or productivity hours in the case of the alternative billers). There is a strong expectation by many clients and colleagues that lawyers will be constantly accessible via e-mail even, sadly, while on vacation. We privately joke (and lament) that vacations are times when our laptops get a nice view. So how do we stay in touch with the office?

We'll discuss some of the options for securely accessing your data remotely. The main consideration is to make sure that your data communication channel is secure (e.g., encrypted) and that you are not using any device that can potentially capture your information. This means you should not use any public computer such as those in a library or Internet café. It has been documented that most public computers are already infected with at least seven different types of malware, including keystroke loggers. In fact, in 2014 the Secret Service issued a warning to users of hotel business center computers. They said that crooks are targeting hotel business center computers and infecting them with keystroke loggers to steal personal and financial data from guests.

As discussed in the Duty to Safeguard chapter, New York Opinion 1019, "Remote Access to Firm's Electronic Files" (August 2014), concludes that "a law firm may use a system that allows its lawyers to access the firm's document system remotely, as long as it takes reasonable steps to ensure that confidentiality of information is maintained." This should be reviewed before remote access is provided and on an ongoing basis thereafter.

Virtual Private Networking

A virtual private network (VPN) connection is a secure communications network tunneled through another network, such as the Internet. The VPN connection allows a network user to connect to the office when working remotely. The communications tunnel encrypts the data traffic between the remote user and the office network, maintaining the security of the information as it is passed back and forth. This is extremely important for law firms when their lawyers are working on client files while traveling or away from the office. Best of all, the VPN server software is included with Microsoft's server operating systems, and the VPN client software is included with modern-day versions of Microsoft Windows.

The average lawyer is likely to be dumbfounded when confronted with setting up a VPN, so this is best left to your IT consultant. However, it is not terribly expensive, and it offers terrific security for your data. One of the key configuration settings is to make sure that all DNS requests are routed through the VPN tunnel and not to the local network connection. Not routing the requests through the VPN would make you subject to a process called DNS hijacking. DNS hijacking is where the traffic is rerouted to an alternate location. As an example, you may be making a request to access **facebook.com**, but the hijacked DNS resolution sends you to an alternate site, where malicious code is downloaded to your device. Having traffic routed through two different "interfaces" is known as split-VPN. Split-VPNs leave you subject to compromise by such as the DNS hijacking described above and is an insecure way to configure a VPN. Make sure whoever sets up the VPN has it configured so that ALL traffic (including DNS requests) are routed through the VPN tunnel as you connect to your law firm's network.

Attorneys should have VPN access available to them while traveling, but it also needs to be properly configured. Once configured, VPNs are very easy to use. The greatest advantage of VPNs is that they are multiuser, whereas other methods are one-on-one solutions.

Higher-end solutions add an additional security layer through the use of digital certificates. It is not uncommon to configure a Cisco VPN to require a digital certificate for authentication in order to create the secure VPN tunnel.

iTwin Connect

There is an interesting product that allows you to set up a public and a private VPN. It is a hardware-based solution that is quick and easy to implement. You first insert one of the iTwin devices into a computer on the network. Whenever you travel, you insert the other half of the iTwin into the device that will connect back. You can then use a private VPN to "teleport" to the other computer. You then use your office or home computer to access the Internet. If you prefer not to access the Internet via your home or office computer, you can use iTwin's public VPN to "teleport" through iTwin's servers located in the United States, Europe, or Asia. When you use the private VPN option, it's just like running a remote control application where you have access to all of the resources on the host computer. The best part is that you can set up the connection in less than a minute. No configuration of IP addresses, DNS, routers, or NATs is necessary.

Figure 17-1

Remote Control

There are several secure solutions available for any attorney to access their firm's information. Products like GoToMyPC and LogMeIn are remote control solutions. The services allow you to remotely connect to the computer in your office via an encrypted connection. The downside is that the computer in your office must always be turned on, and nobody else should be using it at the time you make the connection; if this occurs, you'll both be fighting for control. A remote control solution merely transmits keyboard, mouse, and video display. The actual computing is done on the host computer. The solutions mentioned even work with an Internet connection that has a dynamic IP address and do not require any modifications to the firm's firewall configuration. The other requirement is that the software must be installed on the host and guest computers prior to connecting. If you need to use remote control solutions, make sure you have a screen saver password enabled.

Some remote control solutions have limited functionality. Make sure that the product you select can perform all the tasks that you need. As an example, some products may not support file transfers or remote printing. The good news is you are no longer restricted to a computer-to-computer connection. Many of the solutions will allow you to use a smartphone or tablet device such as an iPad to remotely control the host computer. There was a time when you could make a one-time purchase of the software and install it on each device. Those days appear to be gone. The remote control solutions are moving to a subscription model, where you commit to a monthly or annual charge.

Remote Node

Another method of remote access allows multiple users to connect simultaneously to a single device. Microsoft Terminal Server and Citrix solutions are examples of this. Like the remote control methods, the remote node solution encrypts the data being transmitted between your computer and the receiving computer. Windows has a built-in client for connecting to another computer or Terminal Server. Typically, a user would use Remote Desktop Protocol (RDP) to the remote resource. The RDP client allows the user to have a "virtual desktop" displayed in a window on his or her computer. It acts just as if you were sitting at another computer, although you are not taking direct control as you would in a remote control situation.

Remote Authentication

No matter what method of remote access you use, there should always be some form of authentication. This is typically done with a user ID and password. An even tighter security control would be to use multifactor authentication, which is covered in the authentication and authorization chapter of this book. Multifactor authentication is highly recommended for remote access for law firms.

However you achieve remote access, please be wary of your risks and take the time to understand how your data is being protected. This is the minimum requirement to fulfill your ethical obligation to keep client data confidential.

CHAPTER EIGHTEEN

E-Mail Security

E-mail has become an everyday communication form for attorneys and other professionals. It is fast, convenient and inexpensive, but it also presents serious risks, particularly in the area of security—confidentiality, integrity and availability.

As with other areas of security, the starting point is the various duties that attorneys have to safeguard information, as discussed in our chapter on duty to safeguard. Attorneys have an ethical obligation to safeguard information relating to clients. Comment 19 to Model Rule 1.6 states that attorneys must take "reasonable precautions" to protect electronic communications. Although it states that "special security measures" are not generally required, it contains qualifications and notes that "special circumstances" may warrant "special precautions." Several older ethics opinions concluded that encryption is not generally required for attorney e-mail. However, these opinions should be carefully reviewed because they contain qualifications that limit their general pronouncements. More recent ethics opinions, including ones in California, Pennsylvania and Texas, have concluded that encryption of e-mail may be required in certain circumstances. Attorneys also have common law, contractual and regulatory duties to safeguard information. All of these duties are important in attorneys' use of e-mail.

There are nine areas of risk in the use of e-mail by attorneys (and others):

1. *Lack of confidentiality.* There is a risk of interception or unauthorized access on the sender's and recipient's computers and networks (particularly on mail servers), on the Internet service provider's systems at the sender's and recipient's end and in transit over the Internet. This risk is compounded by potential access during storage of electronic communications at these locations, which can continue long after an e-mail has been sent.

2. *Authenticity*. General absence of definite source identification. Risk of forgery or "spoofing."

3. *Integrity*. Risk of tampering and alteration.

4. *Nonrepudiation*. General inability to establish that the sender sent the communication and that the recipient received it.

5. *Misdirection or forwarding*. It's relatively easy for the wrong person to get a message because of misdirection or unexpected forwarding by the recipient, particularly with computer address books, distribution lists and the autocomplete function.

6. *Informality*. Tendency to treat e-mail communications as informal and casual and to include in an e-mail content which the sender would not otherwise put "in writing."

7. *Permanence*. A double risk. You can't depend on e-mail to be a permanent record if you need it unless you make sure that it is retained either on paper or electronically. You also can't be sure you can get rid of e-mail which you no longer want because of retention of deleted files, electronic copies, backups, printouts and copies made and forwarded by others. Deleting an e-mail or computer file does not mean that it's gone. You may not be able to retrieve it, but there is a strong likelihood, depending on the age of the document, that a computer forensics technologist will be able to recover it. It may also exist on backup media until overwritten by other data.

8. *Malware, such as Viruses, Worms and Spyware*. Often distributed in e-mails or e-mail attachments. Some malicious code can breach confidentiality by providing unauthorized access or by forwarding communications or data from a computer which it attacks.

9. *Inappropriate instant responses*. There is a temptation to immediately respond to e-mail even when research, deliberation or consultation is appropriate.

Some of these risks can be limited or even eliminated through proper practices and procedures and attention to the risks, and through technology (like encryption and authentication), but the risks are real.

Particularly important to attorneys is the confidentiality and integrity of e-mails. As discussed in several other chapters, respected security professionals have for years compared e-mail to postcards or postcards written in pencil. State ethics opinions continue to stress the requirement of reasonable and competent safeguards, including California Formal Opinion No. 2010-179 (see Appendix D) that states "encrypting email may be a reasonable step for an attorney in an effort to ensure the confidentiality of such communications remain so when circumstances call for it, particularly if the information at issue is highly sensitive and the use of encryption is not onerous." Encryption is increasingly required in areas like banking and health care and by new state laws. Attorneys today need to understand encryption. It has now reached the point (or at least is reaching it) where most attorneys should have encryption available for use in appropriate circumstances.

The term encryption is generally used to mean both the encryption and the authentication process that are used, in combination, to protect e-mail. Encryption protects the confidentiality of e-mail. Authentication (signing) identifies the sender of an e-mail and verifies its integrity.

Encryption is a process that translates a message into protected electronic code. The recipient (or anyone intercepting the message) must have a key to decrypt it and make it readable. While it still takes some technical knowledge to set up, e-mail encryption has become easier to use over time. Some implementations make encryption as easy as clicking a button labeled "Encrypt and Send."

Encryption generally uses a pair of keys to encrypt the e-mail. The sender uses the recipient's public key to encrypt the e-mail and any attachments. Since the public key only encrypts the message, it does not matter that it is available to the public or to various senders. The recipient then uses his or her private key to decrypt the e-mail. It needs to be safe-guarded because anyone who has access to the private key can use it for decryption.

The process is easy to use once the keys are set up in an e-mail program like Outlook. The most difficult process is getting the keys (digital IDs) and making the public key available to senders. Once it is set up in Outlook 2013 and 2016, the sender would select File then Properties in the message they are composing. Clicking on the Security Settings button will bring up the Security Properties dialog box as shown in Figure 18-1 with the option to encrypt being identified by the check mark. See **https://support.office .com/en-us/article/Encrypt-email-messages-8D6BF544-EC91-41EA-9E65-2C362F6A3F7F**. At the recipient's end, the message will automatically be decrypted if his or her private key has been installed. You can also increase the security level by requiring that an unlock password be entered whenever the key is accessed. Requiring a password to access the key would prevent someone from decrypting messages if they had physical access to your machine. When you import your digital ID you have the option to set the security level to "high," which would require that you enter a password whenever your key is accessed.

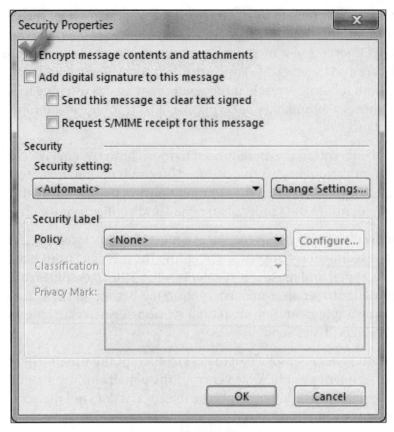

Figure 18-1

As an alternative, you would select the Encrypt icon in the Permission section of the Options tab as shown by the arrow in Figure 18-2. If you do not see the Encrypt and Sign icons in the Permission section, it means that you have not installed your digital ID.

Figure 18-2

Digital authentication of e-mail also generally uses a key pair. The sender uses his or her private key to digitally sign the e-mail. The recipient then uses the sender's public key to verify the sender and integrity of the message. In Outlook 2013 and 2016, after installation of the private key, the sender clicks the Sign icon in the Permission group of the Options tab.

Instructions on digital authentication are available at **https://support
.office.com/en-us/article/Secure-email-messages-by-using-a-digital-
signature-3167E2C6-8065-4090-AAF9-1BBC534F4ACE**. After the sender's
public key has been installed in the recipient's compatible e-mail program,
the recipient will receive an automatic notice of verification of the sender
and integrity.

For protection of confidentiality and authentication, the sender's and
recipient's key pairs are used in combination. The sender uses both the
Encrypt Message and Attachments command button (that uses the recipient's public key) and the Sign Message command (that uses the sender's
private key). At the receiving end, the e-mail program automatically uses
the recipient's private key to decrypt the messages and automatically uses
the sender's public key to verify authenticity and integrity.

Again the challenging part is obtaining key pairs, exchanging public keys
and setting them up in the e-mail program for encryption. The management and exchange of keys is the major reason why most users are reluc-
tant to employ encryption.

Keys are available from commercial public key authorities like Symantec
(**https://www.symantec.com/digital-id/**) and Comodo (**https://ssl
.comodo.com/personal-authentication.php**). Public key authorities
have online directories where their customers' public keys are available at **http://keyserver.pgp.com/**. Instructions for obtaining and
installing a digital ID (private/public key) to Outlook 2013 and 2016 are
available at **https://support.office.com/en-us/article/Get-a-digital-ID-
4e43fcd7-8705-489c-bf6d-2852b4bf0baf**. The URL also has instructions
for adding a recipient's public key to the Outlook contact record.

Another form of e-mail encryption is Transport Layer Security (TLS)
encryption that protects e-mail in transit. It automatically encrypts e-mail
between two e-mail gateways. By default, Microsoft's Exchange e-mail
server automatically utilizes TLS encryption if the recipient server also
supports it. If a law firm and client each have their own e-mail gateways,
TLS can be used to automatically encrypt all e-mails between them. TLS
encryption protects e-mails between e-mail gateways only. It does not
protect e-mails within the sender's and recipient's networks and does not
protect e-mail that is misaddressed or forwarded through other e-mail
gateways. If you use Outlook as your e-mail client, you have the option of
encrypting the data between Outlook and the Exchange server. The selection is available in the Encryption Section of the Security tab. For Outlook
2013 and 2016, you get there by selecting File and then the Account Settings button and Account Settings. Select the E-mail Account and the

Change icon. Clicking on the More Settings button will bring up the Microsoft Exchange dialog box where you can select the Security tab. Encrypting the communications between Outlook and the Exchange server has been the default setting ever since Outlook 2007.

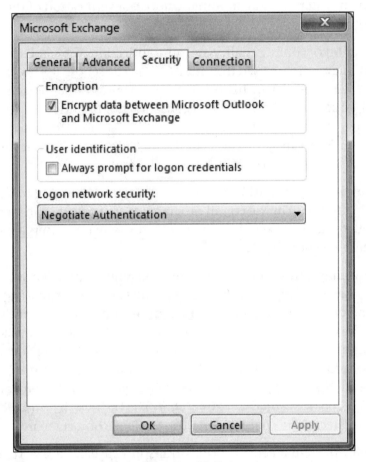

Figure 18-3

Secure e-mail is also available from managed messaging service providers like DataMotion, Mimecast, HP Voltage and Zix Corp. They are inexpensive and very easy to use, but you will likely need help with the initial installation and configuration. We are seeing more and more firms turn to this kind of encryption solution because of the ease of use and the low cost.

As an alternative to encryption, confidential information can be protected by putting it in a password-protected attachment rather than in the body of the e-mail. New Jersey Opinion 701 notes at the end: "where a document is transmitted to [an attorney] by email over the Internet, the lawyer should password a confidential document (as is now possible in all common electronic formats, including PDF), since it is not possible to secure the Internet itself against third party access." File password protection in some software, like current versions of Microsoft Office, Adobe Acrobat and WinZip uses encryption to protect security. It encrypts only the document and not the e-mail, so the confidential information should be limited to the attachment. It is generally easier to use than complete encryption of e-mail and attachments. However, the protection can be limited by the use of weak passwords that are easy to break or "crack."

In addition to complying with any legal requirements that apply, the most prudent approach to the ethical duty of protecting confidentiality is to have an express understanding with clients about the nature of communications that will be (and will not be) sent by e-mail and whether or not encryption and other security measures will be utilized. It has now reached the point (or at least is reaching it) where most attorneys should have encryption available for use in appropriate circumstances.

CHAPTER NINETEEN

Voice
Communications

You are probably wondering why there is a chapter on voice communications in a security book. There are a lot of areas to address security in voice communications, most of which are ignored or left at defaults. In addition, technology advances have changed the way we use voice systems and even the way we communicate. Text messaging has all but taken over the traditional phone call among the younger generation. We'll hit some of the highlights in securing voice communications.

You may be aware of some, and there are others we're sure you've never considered.

Traditional Telephone Systems

Many firms are still running a traditional telephone system or PBX (Private Branch Exchange). You'll have some piece of hardware that connects to the phone lines provided by your communications company and interfaces with the phones on everyone's desk and throughout the office. The PBX adds features to the telephones such as call forwarding, call park, do not disturb, distinctive ring, conference calling and so on. The PBX can be thought of as a specialized computer system. As such, you have the same considerations that you would have for any computer system. Access to the programming should be secured. The default user ID and password must be changed. If there is remote access (e.g., modem or via a network) to the PBX, secure the connection as mentioned in the remote access chapter of this book. Finally, the system itself should be physically secured or at least secured within your own office. All too often, we see telephone systems installed in a communications closet in a common hallway of the building. This means the equipment is out of sight and control. Any telephone technician or person with access to the communications closet could tap into the lines or damage the equipment. Now you know why your phone lines went down when a new tenant moved into the building.

Voice over Internet Protocol (VoIP) Systems

As a basic definition, Voice over Internet Protocol (VoIP) is a family of technologies for delivery of voice communications over Internet protocol networks, such as the Internet. VoIP systems are digital and can run both voice and data systems over the same network, reducing the investment on infrastructure costs. Corporate usage of VoIP phone systems has increased dramatically over the past decade, replacing the traditional copper-wire telephone systems that we all used in the past.

VoIP systems are primarily aimed at providing users with unified communications, delivering all services to a single location, regardless of the type, including voice, fax, voice mails and e-mail. VoIP systems are generally more flexible and less costly to implement than your standard copper-wire systems, and they can integrate easily with most existing data network infrastructures.

Security used to be a major concern for VoIP systems. That concern has been greatly reduced. It appears that vendors have finally overcome the performance hit associated with encrypting the voice traffic. You would be hard pressed to find a current vendor that sends voice traffic in an unencrypted stream. This means you'll sleep a little better knowing that your voice traffic travels in secure encrypted channels. That doesn't mean that your VoIP traffic isn't subject to hacking. In fact, security guru Bruce Schneier has published several blog posts describing how to hack a VoIP data stream. One of his posts discusses how it is possible to even "identify the phrases spoken within encrypted VoIP calls when the audio is encoded using variable bit rate codecs." Sound scary? The reality is that your calls probably aren't subject to intentional interception, especially if you take prudent steps to control access to the VoIP network and equipment. That's not to say the data stream won't get collected if a state-sponsored entity is engaged in bulk collection, which we are seeing more and more these days.

Voice Mail

Voice mail systems need passwords or access codes to gain access to the individual voice mailboxes. It should also be understood that access to the system itself (for administrative purposes) should be protected with a user ID and password just like any other computer system. Obviously, none of the password values should be left at the default settings. Most voice mail systems will have a default retention period of 7 to 30 days. This means that the message will automatically get deleted if it isn't manually deleted by the end of the configured retention period. Another feature to disable is the ability to perform outbound dialing. This means that you should never be able to make a phone call once logged into a voice mailbox. Believe it or not, most systems have this feature enabled by default, which means that, if a voice mailbox gets compromised, outbound calls can be made, perhaps to foreign countries. Many years ago, this happened to authors Nelson and Simek with an old telephone system in their conference room. So take heart, even experts get bitten.

Unified messaging systems will take the voice message, convert it to a sound file and send it to an e-mail address. This is how many of us get voice messages on our smartphones. It is another reason your smartphone should be secured as well. And bear in mind that voicemail which is on your smartphones or computers is discoverable in the event of a litigation hold. Many firms have a rigid disposal policy for voice mails, and with good reason!

CHAPTER TWENTY

Backup and Business Continuity

If you haven't realized it yet, your data is the most important item in your practice. Client information, deadlines, legal documents and many more bits of information are key to your continued success and longevity as a law firm. So where do you start with all this data and how do you protect it? The first place is data backup. Determine where your critical data resides and how long it should be retained. This is where you may need a little expert help, especially if some of the data may be subject to specific legal or regulatory retention periods.

Besides backing up your data, you will need to determine how long your systems can be down before it critically impacts your operation. We call this your "threshold for pain." You will need to take different steps if you can only stand to be "out of business" for four hours versus two days. Obviously, the shorter your outage window, the more expensive are the systems required to keep you operational.

Backup Job Types

There are three primary types of backup practices that you can implement. First, you need to decide what data you intend to back up.

If you want to ensure a complete system recovery, then you will need to back up the entire machine. This would include the operating system, application programs and any data that reside on the computer. Should the hardware fail, a complete backup can be restored to a new or repaired piece of hardware. Restoration and backup are a little different when you are dealing with virtualized servers and workstations.

Full

Full backups are just that—a complete backup of the targeted information. Normally, you would execute a full backup on a periodic basis such as weekly. Most firms run this type of backup on a Friday evening because it takes the longest time to run; thus, it would not significantly impact the firm's operation since it has the weekend to complete the backup job. More modern backup designs may only require one full backup as the originating "seed" set. Subsequent data changes are then built upon the original image.

Differential

A differential backup would back up any changed data from the last full backup. This type of backup is typically scheduled for each evening during the week. As an example, if you run a full backup on Friday, then the differential jobs would run on Monday through Thursday night. Each job would capture the data that had changed since the last full backup so the Thursday night job would back up the most data since it would include four days' worth of changes.

Incremental

This is the smallest of the data backup sets. An incremental backup only includes data that has changed from the last backup. Recovering your environment takes the longest time if you implement an incremental backup schedule. This is because you would have to restore the latest full backup and then apply each and every incremental backup set since the last full backup. In contrast, you would only need to restore from the last full backup and the latest differential backup set if you followed the differential backup schedule described above.

Backup Media

Tape is so yesterday. Seriously. Why we still see it is a mystery to us. All of the modern-day backup systems use hard drives since the cost of storage has come down so much. Even solid state drives are very affordable, but still a bit pricey to be used in a backup system. Backing up to tape is much slower than using hard drives (or a backup appliance with hard disks) and is also slower to recover. Mounting a tape and then seeking through it in a linear fashion could take several hours depending on the tape capacity.

Hard drive systems are much faster for backing up and restoring, not to mention that capacities are greater in a smaller form factor. Law firms will typically have one of two types of hard drive backup systems. Solo lawyers may use external USB hard drives to backup their data. This is the simplest and cheapest backup solution. Larger firms will use a backup appliance that contains multiple hard drives.

As with all backup solutions, you need to transfer your data to an offsite location to protect against destruction should something happen to your office area such as a fire or flood. In addition, the backup data should be encrypted on the media whether it is tape or hard disk. Encrypting the data will protect it should you happen to leave a backup hard disk on the light rail train (as previously noted, one law firm employee did this) or misplace one of your backup tapes. By default, the backup software does not encrypt the data. There may be a slight performance hit when encrypting, but not encrypting will cause you even more headaches if you have to report the loss of the data.

Backup Solutions

There are many options for backing up your environment. There may be an option contained within the operating system itself. Windows has a basic backup mechanism, and Apple provides software called Time Machine. Using the included backup software may be sufficient for your needs, but it generally lacks important features such as the ability to encrypt the backup data. As a result, many law firms use third-party products to get the additional functionality and technical support.

Backup Exec is a very popular, robust and powerful backup option. Backup Exec was part of the Symantec family, but it has recently spun off as a separate company. It's reverted back to the days of Veritas Backup Exec prior to being acquired by Symantec. You can purchase additional modules if you need to back up open files, Exchange databases, SQL databases, and so forth. The cost can be pretty expensive depending on the number of devices to back up and the features required. It would not be unreasonable to spend upward of a thousand dollars to back up several servers. You'll also need to purchase an annual maintenance agreement to obtain technical support and updates. We're not seeing many firms using Backup Exec anymore and have migrated to backup appliances where the vendor provides the application software.

One of our favorite backup solutions for a single user's computer or laptop is BounceBack Ultimate by CMS. You install the BounceBack software to your computer and connect an external USB hard disk as the target for the backup data. BounceBack will automatically back up your data in the background to the USB drive. You also have the option to encrypt the data, which we highly recommend. One of the nicest features of the software is the ability to continue operation if the hard disk in your computer crashes. The BounceBack drive will take over and keep you operational until you can replace the failed hard disk in your computer.

BounceBack will synchronize back to your computer all of the data, applications, operating system and so on. Essentially, BounceBack gives you a disaster recovery solution for your computer.

Another alternative is to use a third-party provider. Cloud services such as Carbonite, Mozy and EVault are just some of the many options. The third-party cloud solution is a good alternative for protecting your data, but it's not very practical for business continuity. This is primarily because the amount of data needed to recover from a disaster is very large, and it would take too long to download it from the provider site via the Internet. Some providers will put all of your data onto a hard disk and ship it overnight should you have a complete system failure. Make sure you understand the capabilities of the third-party provider should you need to use them as a disaster recovery solution. Also, make sure that you can encrypt the data before you transmit it offsite to their facilities and that they let you choose the encryption passphrase. Do not let the vendor select the passphrase for you because you do not want them to have the ability to decrypt your data. Be sure you read the terms of service, too, to make sure they don't have the ability to decrypt your data via some master administrator sort of access.

Business Continuity

No matter what data backup solution you select, the intent is to keep your firm operational and minimize any downtime or disruption to your practice. As already mentioned, one step is to make sure that you have backup data offsite in case something happens to your physical office space.

There is currently a move away from the legacy backup solutions and toward backup appliances. These appliances are hard drive based with specialized software to facilitate rapid recovery and restoration of function in the shortest period of time. Typically, the appliance backs up the selected computers (servers and/or workstations) in a near real-time fashion. Taking snapshots every 15 minutes is not an unusual schedule. This means you are no more than 15 minutes away from your current data. In addition to backing up the data, there is a mechanism to send the data offsite should some disaster strike the appliance itself. The other added feature is the ability to virtualize any computer that is being backed up. As an example, if your Exchange server had a severe hardware malfunction, a virtualized instance of the server can be "spun up" on the backup appliance. The virtual server would be an identical match for the failed server complete with current data. Spinning up the virtual instance should take no more than an hour or two to accomplish the various tasks needed to get the server in an operational state. Should a disaster strike the entire office and render the backup appliance unusable as well, the vendor can ship a replacement unit overnight already loaded with the data that has been collected from the offsite transmissions.

The other advantage with backup appliances is the protection from malware infections such as the various strains of ransomware (and there are many variants of the popular CryptoLocker and CryptoWall). Ransomware attacks data that is presented as a drive letter to the computer. If you use an external hard disk for backup, it is assigned a drive letter. If your computer gets infected with ransomware, the ransomware searches out data on all disk drives (including your external backup) and encrypts the files. Backup appliances typically use backup agents to facilitate the data transfer between the protected device (e.g. server, desktop, tablet, etc.) and the backup appliance. This means that there is no drive letter assignment that would make the backup vulnerable to a ransomware infection. Having seen four Northern Virginia law firms struck by ransomware in a two-week period, we can tell you that the two firms who had properly engineered backup had a much happier result than the two firms that did not. Even when you pay to get the decryption key (and they did), you have to wait for the files to decrypt, which can take days.

As you can see, implementing a backup appliance is an excellent way to securely back up your data and provide a business continuity solution to minimize any downtime for the firm. So figure out your threshold for pain and determine which backup solution is right for you.

CHAPTER TWENTY-ONE

Outsourcing and Service Providers

Outsourcing and use of service providers by attorneys is very common and increasing. In fact, attorneys and law firms could not practice today without it. It can take many forms, ranging from sending documents to a copy service across the street, to giving a technology consultant access to a law firm network, to using a hosted e-discovery service in another state, or to use of attorneys in a foreign country for legal services. Cloud computing, covered in the next chapter, is a form of outsourcing.

Vulnerability of service providers is a high profile concern in information security today. Federal and state regulators in areas like healthcare and financial services have been stressing the need for security in vendor management for a number of years. Assessment of security management of service providers is now a standard part of security audits. Its importance was highlighted by the report that the Target data breach in 2014 was caused by access to Target's corporate network through an HVAC vendor whose network had been compromised.

It's an issue for law firms too. The law firm data breach nightmare chapter includes an example in which a major law firm had current and former employees' W-2 data and other information compromised when a vendor's database was accessed by someone who was able to acquire a client's login credentials.

In another example, a college student who worked for a service provider at a major international law firm pled guilty to federal charges for theft of intellectual property. The student was brought into the firm's offices by his uncle, an employee of the service provider, because they were behind on the job of copying paper and electronic data for production in litigation. The firm represented DirecTV in litigation with one of its security vendors. The student worked in a secure area in the law firm's offices, where he worked on the copying project. He found the technology that controlled access by customers to DirecTV, copied it to a CD, and posted it on a hacker bulletin board.

Outsourcing and use of service providers presents a number of professional responsibility considerations that will vary with the services involved. As a starting point, attorneys must take reasonable precautions to protect confidential information to which third parties, like information systems consultants and litigation support service providers, are given access. ABA Formal Opinion 95-398, *Access of Nonlawyers to a Lawyer's Database* (October 27, 1995), provides guidance in this area and concludes, "[a] lawyer who gives a computer maintenance company access to information in client files must make reasonable efforts to ensure that the company has in place, or will establish, reasonable procedures to protect the confidentiality of the client information."

In August, 2008, the ABA issued an ethics opinion that comprehensively covered outsourcing by attorneys of both legal services and nonlegal support services. ABA Formal Ethics Opinion 08-451, *"Lawyer's Obligations When Outsourcing Legal and Nonlegal Support Services"* (August, 2008).

The headnote to the opinion summarizes its detailed analysis:

> *A lawyer may outsource legal or nonlegal support services provided the lawyer remains ultimately responsible for rendering competent legal services to the client under Model Rule 1.1. In complying with her Rule 1.1 obligations, a lawyer who engages lawyers or nonlawyers to provide outsourced legal or nonlegal services is required to comply with Rules 5.1 and 5.3. She should make reasonable efforts to ensure that the conduct of the lawyers or nonlawyers to whom tasks are outsourced is compatible with her own professional obligations as a lawyer with "direct supervisory authority" over them.*
>
> *In addition, appropriate disclosures should be made to the client regarding the use of lawyers or nonlawyers outside of the lawyer's firm, and client consent should be obtained if those lawyers or nonlawyers will be receiving information protected by Rule 1.6. The fees charged must be reasonable and otherwise in compliance with Rule 1.5, and the outsourcing lawyer must avoid assisting the unauthorized practice of law under Rule 5.5.*

As discussed in the duty to safeguard chapter, Model Rule 5.3 (Responsibilities Regarding Nonlawyer Assistants) was amended in 2012 to expand its scope. "Assistants" was expanded to "Assistance," extending its coverage to all levels of staff and outsourced services. The amended comments provide:

> [3] A lawyer may use nonlawyers outside the firm to assist the lawyer in rendering legal services to the client. Examples include the retention of an investigative or paraprofessional service, hiring a document management company to create and maintain a database for complex litigation, sending client documents to a third party for printing or scanning, and using an Internet-based service to store client information. **When using such services outside the firm, a lawyer must make reasonable efforts to ensure that the services are provided in a manner that is compatible with the lawyer's professional obligations.** The extent of this obligation will depend upon the circumstances, including the education, experience and reputation of the nonlawyer; the nature of the services involved; the terms of any arrangements concerning the protection of client information; and the legal and ethical environments of the jurisdictions in which the services will be performed, particularly with regard to confidentiality. See also Rules 1.1 (competence), 1.2 (allocation of authority), 1.4 (communication with client), 1.6 (confidentiality), 5.4(a) (professional independence of the lawyer), and 5.5(a) (unauthorized practice of law). When retaining or directing a nonlawyer outside the firm, a lawyer should communicate directions appropriate under the circumstances to give reasonable assurance that the nonlawyer's conduct is compatible with the professional obligations of the lawyer.

> [Emphasis added.]

The ethics considerations in outsourcing accordingly include competence, due diligence, confidentiality, supervision, appropriate disclosure and client consent, reasonable charges to clients, and not assisting in the unauthorized practice of law. An important part of this obligation is informed consent. As the Opinion 08-451 notes, "client consent should be obtained if those lawyers or nonlawyers will be receiving information protected by Rule 1.6."

While the necessary due diligence and contractual requirements will depend on the nature of the services and the sensitivity of the information, the following are considerations, where appropriate, for compliance with ethical duties and generally accepted security practices:

- ◆ Due diligence (including checking references)
- ◆ Contractual obligations
  - ◆ Confidentiality and security requirements
  - ◆ Policies
  - ◆ Certifications and audits
  - ◆ Security incident response
  - ◆ Breach notice
  - ◆ Cyber liability insurance
  - ◆ Employee background checks
  - ◆ Employee confidentiality agreements
  - ◆ Restrictions on outsourcing and subcontracting
  - ◆ Termination
  - ◆ Return of property and data
- ◆ Ongoing oversight or monitoring
- ◆ Contingency planning

The appropriate considerations for various kinds of outsourcing and use of service providers depend upon the sensitivity of the information, the risks to security, the nature and duration of the services and available protective measures. As an example, there are major differences between having a local copy shop print and bind a brief to be filed in court and outsourcing law firm office services to a provider that will work inside the firm's offices on a continuing basis.

The core duties in the rules and ethics opinions include conducting appropriate due diligence, taking competent and reasonable measures to protect the confidentiality and availability of client data, making sure there are appropriate, enforceable requirements for security, and conducting appropriate supervision or monitoring. Notice to clients and informed consent may sometimes be required. Additional details are covered in the next chapter on cloud computing, which is a form of outsourcing.

CHAPTER TWENTY-TWO

Cloud Computing

Definition

Cloud computing is currently one of the hottest topics of discussion in legal technology, perhaps second only to mobility (smartphones, tablets and bring-your-own-device to work). Cloud computing is really another way of saying that your data is stored and processed on resources that are not physically at your office. Instead, the data is stored, processed or both at a data center and delivered to you over the Internet.

The National Institute of Standards and Technology (NIST) defines cloud computing as a "model for enabling ubiquitous, convenient, on-demand network access to a shared pool of configurable computing resources (e.g., networks, servers, storage, applications, and services) that can be rapidly provisioned and released with minimal management effort or service provider interaction." It notes that "cloud computing is still an evolving paradigm." The NIST Definition of Cloud Computing, SP 800-145 (September 2011), is available at **http://csrc.nist.gov/publications/nistpubs/800-145/ SP800-145.pdf**.

The following are the recognized categories of cloud computing, with examples:

- Software as a Service (SaaS)—(Microsoft Office 365, Google Docs, **Salesforce.com**, Clio, Rocket Matter)
- Infrastructure as a Service (IaaS)—(Amazon Web Service, GoGrid)
- Platform as a Service (PaaS)—(Google App Engine, **Force.com**)

Many (if not most) attorneys today need to have at least a general understanding of cloud computing both because they may use it in their practice and because they may be asked to advise clients on the legal aspects of cloud computing. For a basic understanding, without technical detail,

US-CERT, *"The Basics of Cloud Computing"* (2011) and Grace Lewis, *"Basics about Cloud Computing"* are good starting points. For those looking for more technical detail, NIST has several helpful publications, including the NIST Definition and *"NIST Cloud Computing Synopsis and Recommendations,"* SP 800-146 (May 2012).

The Ethical Side of the Cloud

The ethics opinions that have generally addressed attorneys' use of technology have focused primarily on the duties of competence and confidentiality. Some have also addressed the duty to supervise and a duty to notify clients and obtain informed consent in some circumstances. The ABA Commission Ethics 20/20 and ethics opinions that expressly address cloud computing have the same focus. Additional areas of concern in cloud computing, along with competence and confidentiality include:

- ♦ Inability to provide timely legal services because of lost access to data or computing services (temporary or permanent)
- ♦ Loss of control over data, particularly where it may be hosted in foreign countries
- ♦ Obligations to communicate with clients about the use of cloud computing
- ♦ The potential need for informed client consent
- ♦ Fair billing practices when clients are billed for cloud services

The ABA Legal Technology Resource Center maintains a database, with links, of Cloud Ethics Opinions around the U.S. (**www.americanbar.org/ groups/departments_offices/legal_technology_resources/resources/ charts_fyis/cloud-ethics-chart.html**)

The Ethics 20/20's Commission's Working Group on the Implications of New Technologies published an *"Issues Paper Concerning Client Confidentiality and Lawyers' Use of Technology"* on September 20, 2010. It listed for discussion issues concerning confidentiality and technology and sought comments on them, including cloud computing. The paper raised issues for discussion; it did not provide answers. Comments on the subject have been solicited and received, and a hearing has been held.

The Working Group listed the following issues and concerns with lawyers' use of cloud computing:

- ♦ unauthorized access to confidential client information by a vendor's employees (or subcontractors) or by outside parties (e.g., hackers) via the Internet

- the storage of information on servers in countries with fewer legal protections for electronically stored information

- a vendor's failure to back up data adequately

- unclear policies regarding ownership of stored data

- the ability to access the data using easily accessible software in the event that the lawyer terminates the relationship with the cloud computing provider or the provider changes businesses or goes out of business

- the provider's procedures for responding to (or when appropriate, resisting) government requests for access to information

- policies for notifying customers of security breaches

- policies for data destruction when a lawyer no longer wants the relevant data available or transferring the data if a client switches law firms

- insufficient data encryption

- the extent to which lawyers need to obtain client consent before using cloud computing services to store or transmit the client's confidential information

In September 2011, the Commission released revised proposals for amendments to the ABA Model Rules, including ones on Outsourcing and Technology and Confidentiality. They were accepted by the ABA, resulting in the amendments to Model Rules 1.1, 1.6 and 5.3 (included as Appendix B). In addition to requiring competent and reasonable measures to safeguard information relating to clients, they also require appropriate due diligence in supervising or monitoring subordinates and service providers. The amended comments to Rule 5.3 include:

> [3] A lawyer may use nonlawyers outside the firm to assist the lawyer in rendering legal services to the client. Examples include the retention of an investigative or paraprofessional service, hiring a document management company to create and maintain a database for complex litigation, sending client documents to a third party for printing or scanning, and using an Internet-based service to store client information. **When using such services outside the firm, a lawyer must make reasonable efforts to ensure that the services are provided in a manner that is compatible with the lawyer's professional obligations.** The extent of this obligation will depend upon the circumstances, including the education, experience and reputation of the nonlawyer; the nature of the services involved; the terms of any arrangements concerning the protection of client information; and the legal and

ethical environments of the jurisdictions in which the services will be performed, particularly with regard to confidentiality. See also Rules 1.1 (competence), 1.2 (allocation of authority), 1.4 (communication with client), 1.6 (confidentiality), 5.4(a) (professional independence of the lawyer), and 5.5(a) (unauthorized practice of law). When retaining or directing a nonlawyer outside the firm, a lawyer should communicate directions appropriate under the circumstances to give reasonable assurance that the nonlawyer's conduct is compatible with the professional obligations of the lawyer.

(Emphasis added.)

In September 2010, the same month as publication of the Ethics 20/20's Commission's Working Group report, the New York State Bar published an ethics opinion that addresses use of an outside online storage provider to store electronic client confidential information. It notes that "various companies offer online computer data storage systems that are maintained on an array of Internet servers located around the world. (The array of Internet servers that store the data is often called the 'cloud.')"

This opinion concludes that "a lawyer may use an online 'cloud' computer data backup system to store client files provided that the lawyer takes reasonable care to ensure that the system is secure and that client confidentiality will be maintained." It notes that the "reasonable care" standard requires a lawyer to "stay abreast of technology advances to ensure that the storage system remains sufficiently advanced to protect the client's information."

The opinion states that "reasonable care" to protect a client's confidential information against unauthorized disclosure may include the following:

♦ Ensure that the online data storage provider has an enforceable obligation to preserve confidentiality and security.

♦ Ensure that the online storage provider will notify the lawyer if the cloud provider is requested to produce client information to a third party.

♦ Ensure that the online provider employs technology to guard against reasonably foreseeable attempts to infiltrate the data.

♦ Investigate the online providers' security measures, policies and recoverability methods.

In 2010, the Alabama Disciplinary Commission addressed cloud computing in the broader context of a comprehensive opinion on client files. Alabama Ethics Opinion 2010-02, "Retention, Storage, Ownership, Production and Destruction of Client Files." The opinion concludes that a "lawyer may use 'cloud computing' or third party providers to store client data provided that the attorney exercises reasonable care in doing so."

It explains the duties as follows:

> The duty of reasonable care requires the lawyer to become knowl-edgeable about how the provider will handle the storage and security of the data being stored and to reasonably ensure that the provider will abide by a confidentiality agreement in handling the data. Additionally, because technology is constantly evolving, the lawyer will have a continuing duty to stay abreast of appropriate security safeguards that should be employed by the lawyer and the third party provider. If there is a breach of confidentiality, the focus of any inquiry will be whether the lawyer acted reasonably in selecting the method of storage and/or the third party provider.

In November 2011, the Pennsylvania Bar Association issued an ethics opinion on cloud computing. Pennsylvania Bar Association, Committee on Legal Ethics and Professional Responsibility, Formal Opinion 2011-200, *"Ethical Obligations for Attorneys Using Cloud Computing/Software as a Service While Fulfilling the Duties of Confidentiality and Preservation of Client Property"* (November 2011) (see Appendix C). The opinion addresses cloud computing generally and answers the question, "[m]ay an attorney ethi-cally store confidential client material in 'the cloud'?" It concludes:

> Yes. An attorney may ethically allow client confidential material to be stored in "the cloud" provided the attorney takes reasonable care to assure that (1) all such materials remain confidential, and (2) reasonable safeguards are employed to ensure that the data is protected from breaches, data loss and other risks.

It notes that the duty is one of "reasonable care" and will vary depending on the specific technology:

> In the context of "cloud computing," an attorney must take rea-sonable care to make sure that the conduct of the cloud comput-ing service provider conforms to the rules to which the attorney himself is subject. Because the operation is outside of an attorney's direct control, some of the steps taken to ensure reasonable care are different from those applicable to traditional information storage.

> While the measures necessary to protect confidential information will vary based upon the technology and infrastructure of each office—and this Committee acknowledges that the advances in technology make it difficult, if not impossible to provide specific standards that will apply to every attorney—there are common procedures and safeguards that attorneys should employ.

The opinion includes a detailed listing of what reasonable care "may include":

♦ Backing up data to allow the firm to restore data that has been lost, corrupted or accidentally deleted;

♦ Installing a firewall to limit access to the firm's network;

♦ Limiting information that is provided to others to what is required, needed or requested;

♦ Avoiding inadvertent disclosure of information;

♦ Verifying the identity of individuals to whom the attorney provides confidential information;

♦ Refusing to disclose confidential information to unauthorized individuals (including family members and friends) without client permission;

♦ Protecting electronic records containing confidential data, including backups, by encrypting the confidential data;

♦ Implementing electronic audit trail procedures to monitor who is accessing the data;

♦ Creating plans to address security breaches, including the identification of persons to be notified about any known or suspected security breach involving confidential data;

♦ Ensuring the provider:

  ♦ explicitly agrees that it has no ownership or security interest in the data;

  ♦ has an enforceable obligation to preserve security;

  ♦ will notify the lawyer if requested to produce data to a third party and provide the lawyer with the ability to respond to the request before the provider produces the requested information;

  ♦ has technology built to withstand a reasonably foreseeable attempt to infiltrate data, including penetration testing;

  ♦ includes in its "Terms of Service" or "Service Level Agreement" an agreement about how confidential client information will be handled;

  ♦ provides the firm with the right to audit the provider's security procedures and to obtain copies of any security audits performed;

  ♦ will host the firm's data only within a specified geographic area. If by agreement, the data is hosted outside the United States, the law firm must determine that the hosting jurisdiction has privacy laws, data security laws and protections against unlawful search and seizure that are as rigorous as those of the United States and Pennsylvania;

+ provides a method of retrieving data if the lawyer terminates use of the SaaS product, the SaaS vendor goes out of business or the service otherwise has a break in continuity; and

+ provides the ability for the law firm to get data "off" of the vendor's or third-party data hosting company's servers for the firm's own use or in-house backup offline.

♦ Investigating the provider's:

+ security measures, policies and recovery methods;

+ system for backing up data;

+ security of data centers and whether the storage is in multiple centers;

+ safeguards against disasters, including different server locations;

+ history, including how long the provider has been in business;

+ funding and stability;

+ policies for data retrieval upon termination of the relationship and any related charges; and

+ process to comply with data that are subject to a litigation hold.

♦ Determining whether:

+ data is in nonproprietary format;

+ the service level agreement clearly states that the attorney owns the data;

+ there is a third-party audit of security; and

+ there is an uptime guarantee and whether failure results in service credits.

♦ Employees of the firm who use the SaaS must receive training on and are required to abide by all end-user security measures, including, but not limited to, the creation of strong passwords and the regular replacement of passwords.

♦ Protecting the ability to represent the client reliably by ensuring that a copy of digital data is stored onsite.

♦ Having an alternate way to connect to the Internet, since cloud service is accessed through the Internet.

The opinion notes that these safeguards also apply to traditional law offices. It points out that some service providers' "take it or leave it" approach to service level agreements may be obstacles to reasonable care efforts. It also approves the use of smartphones that are synchronized "in the cloud" if using "standard precautions to ensure the information transmitted over the smartphone is secure."

As cloud computing continues to emerge, new ethics questions are likely to develop. At this stage, it is clear that attorneys using cloud services have a duty to conduct appropriate due diligence, to take competent and reasonable measures to protect the confidentiality and availability of client data, to make sure there are appropriate, enforceable requirements for security, and to conduct appropriate supervision or monitoring. Duties beyond that will require a careful analysis of the specific cloud services involved in light of the ethics rules and opinions of the appropriate jurisdiction(s).

Developing Cloud Security Standards

Security of cloud services are continuing to evolve and consensus guidelines and standards are being developed. For example, the *NIST Guidelines on Security and Privacy in Public Cloud Computing*, SP 800-144 (December 2011) covers this area. The introduction includes:

> The emergence of cloud computing promises to have far-reaching effects on the systems and networks of federal agencies and other organizations. Many of the features that make cloud computing attractive, however, can also be at odds with traditional security models and controls. The primary purpose of this report is to provide an overview of public cloud computing and the security and privacy considerations involved. More specifically, this document describes the threats, technology risks, and safeguards surrounding public cloud environments, and their treatment.

Its guidelines include:

- Carefully plan the security and privacy aspects of cloud computing solutions before engaging them.
- Understand the public cloud computing environment offered by the cloud provider.
- Ensure that a cloud computing solution satisfies organizational security and privacy requirements.
- Ensure that the client-side computing environment meets organizational security and privacy requirements for cloud computing.
- Maintain accountability over the privacy and security of data and applications implemented and deployed in public cloud computing environments.

It includes details about implementation of these guidelines.

The federal government has adopted a strategy that encourages federal agencies to use appropriate cloud services. Service providers to federal agencies are required to comply with information security requirements in the Federal Information Processing Standard (FIPS) and applicable NIST standards. The government has established the Federal Risk and Authorization Management Program (FedRAMP, **www.fedramp.gov**), administered by the General Services Administration, which provides a centralized process for determining compliance by cloud services with these requirements. With this process, each agency does not have to make the determination on its own and duplicate what other agencies have done. It includes a process for accredited independent assessors to perform assessments of a service provider's compliance with FedRAMP requirements. The website lists compliant cloud service providers and ones that are in the process of achieving compliance.

When considering whether a cloud service provider is compliant with FedRAMP, it is important to focus on the specific services that are compliant. Service providers will often provide stronger security for services that they provide to government agencies than they generally provide to all customers. For example, some service providers will agree to host government data only on servers in the United States, but will not agree to this restriction for other customers.

For example, Box is listed as in process for compliance. It must be close to achieving it because it has recently been awarded a major contract for the U.S. Department of Justice.

The Cloud Security Alliance is an organization that works to promote best practices to provide security assurance for cloud computing. (**https://cloudsecurityalliance.org**) Its members include major tech companies like Amazon Web Services, Microsoft, Oracle, Rackspace and Salesforce. It has published the Cloud Control Matrix, currently v3.0.1, which describes over a dozen areas of cloud infrastructure including risk management and security. It includes an Excel spreadsheet for analyzing a vendor's or vendors' compliance with it. It does not define minimum security standards, but provides a comprehensive list and provides a common format in which subscribers can easily see which controls a provider has implemented and which it has not.

There are also consensus international standards in the area. There is a consensus standard for protecting personally identifiable information and a developing standard for cloud security. ISO/IEC 27018:2014 Information technology—Security techniques—Code of practice for protection of personally identifiable information (PII) in public clouds acting as PII processors focuses on protecting PII, including contractual protection, processes, and security controls. ISO/IEC 27017—Information technology—Security techniques—Code of practice for information security controls based on ISO/IEC 27002 for cloud services (FDIS) (under development) will coordinate the safeguards necessary for cloud services to coordinate with other ISO/IEC standards. They include security controls that coordinate with an ISO 27001 Information Security Management System.

The American Institute of Certified Public Accounts (AICPA) has published standards for auditors to use in assessments of service organizations like cloud service providers: (1) Statement on Standards for Attestation Engagements No. 16 (SSAE 16), Reporting on Controls at a Service Organization, for service auditors and (2) AT Section 101, *Attest Engagements*, using the trust services principles and criteria, for user auditors. Under these standards, cloud service providers are service organizations and their customers, like law firms, are users.

There are three types of Service Organization Controls (SOC) reports that may be issued under these standards. SOC 1 reports are based on assessing financial statement controls at service organizations. SOC 2 and SOC 3 reports both assess a service organization's controls relevant to the security, availability or processing integrity of a service organization's system, or the privacy or confidentiality of the information the system processes. SOC 3 reports cover the same subjects as SOC 2 reports, but are more general, with less detail. Distribution of SOC 2 reports is usually restricted because of the details that they include. Distribution of SOC 3 reports is generally not restricted and can go to potential customers and others who may not have confidentiality obligations.

Here are some examples of certifications and attestations of cloud service providers. Box reports that it is certified under ISO 27001, has SOC 1 and 2 attestations, and will sign a business associate agreement to comply with HIPAA. Dropbox reports that it is certified under ISO27001 and 27018, has SOC 2 and 3 attestations, and will sign a business associate agreement to comply with HIPAA. Google for Work reports that it is certified under ISO27001 and 27018, has SOC 2 and 3 attestations, and will sign a business associate agreement to comply with HIPAA. Microsoft, for Office 365, reports that it is certified under ISO27001 and 27018, has SOC 1 and 2 attestations, and will sign a business associate agreement to comply with HIPAA.

In considering these kinds of certifications and attestations, it is critical to be sure that they apply to the cloud services being considered. They are part of the due diligence process but only part. The ethics opinions discussed above provide good lists that include the highlights of the core requirements that are included in these more detailed standards.

Encryption in the Cloud

Confidential data should be encrypted when it is stored in the cloud. An important consideration for security of encrypted data in storage is who controls the decryption key. Encryption controlled by the end-user can protect the confidentiality of the data since the encryption key is only known to the end user or creator of the data. Figure 22-1 shows the difference with control of the key by the end-user and control by the service provider. If the end-user controls the key, the data is protected everywhere it resides away from the end-user. The cloud service provider does not have access to the encryption key, so confidentiality does not depend on the effectiveness of the security of the service provider.

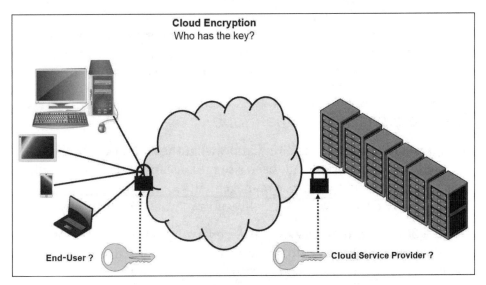

Figure 22-1

Consensus security standards for cloud services are still developing. There is not an absolute requirement that encryption must be controlled by the end-user, but it should be the default. End-user control of encryption should be required unless the end-user makes an informed decision that the data is not sensitive enough to require this level of protection or that the cloud service provider will implement and maintain sufficient security controls without end-user encryption. For attorneys, this requires the analysis required by the ethics rules and opinions discussed in Chapter

3. It requires competent and reasonable measures to safeguard information relating to clients, due diligence concerning service providers, and requiring service providers to safeguard data in accordance with attorneys' confidentiality obligations.

It is also important to make sure the data is transferred to and from the cloud provider over a secure encrypted connection such as https://, a dedicated circuit or a virtual private network, and that the cloud provider implements strong encryption for data at rest. Finally, no system is secure if you use weak login credentials. You should be using a strong password or passphrase (complexity and length) for authentication and enable two factor authentication if available. See Chapter 7 for recommendations on strong passwords and authentication.

As discussed below, some cloud service providers, like Box, provide for end-user controlled encryption. You can improve the security of cloud storage services that don't, like Dropbox, by encrypting the data prior to placing it in the cloud storage service. Products such as BoxCryptor, Dell Data Protection—Cloud Edition, Sookasa and Viivo encrypt the data prior to transferring it to the cloud provider. The end user controls encryption and decryption so it is not accessible to the service providers, its employees, any person or agency that is given access (or gets access) or hackers.

The Practical Side of the Cloud

Five years ago, many lawyers didn't know what the cloud was. Today, it's a very different story. There has been a sea change in cloud usage. Besides cloud storage solutions, practice management cloud solutions are increasingly being used by lawyers, especially solo and small firm attorneys.

The ABA 2015 Legal Technology Survey Report explores the numbers of attorneys (by firm size) using cloud services, the services they use, the functions for which they use them, their concerns, and plans for the future.

There was a day when many cloud providers were on shaky financial ground. Not so today. Cloud providers are here to stay and growing at a rapid pace. More and more applications are moving to the cloud as we become a more mobile society. After all, using cloud services means you have access to your data from any device, from any place at any time.

Over and over, we repeat the mantra "read the service level agreement and the terms of service." The Pennsylvania ethics opinion, discussed above, provides a good checklist of what to look for in due diligence investigation of a cloud service provider and in an SLA (Service Level Agreement) or TOS

(Terms of Service) from a prospective cloud provider. Someone who understands the legal and technical issues needs to determine what is reasonable and what complies with all applicable requirements.

Although Dropbox is a popular cloud tool for storing documents and accessing them from anywhere, it has had its share of security problems. Even though Dropbox encrypts data in transit and in storage, the privacy notice still allows Dropbox to decrypt your data and give it to law enforcement without telling you. This means that even though the data is encrypted, Dropbox has the decrypt keys. Does that sound like a good place for a lawyer to hold confidential data? Absolutely not.

But Dropbox is so easy to use—and free (for the consumer version), a lawyer's favorite price—that lawyers have glommed on to it in spite of the security problems. Other document storage clouds include Box, SugarSync, OneDrive, Google Drive, Amazon Cloud Drive and Apple iCloud. We've seen security issues with virtually all of these clouds, particularly in the terms of service, so read, read, read.

It should be noted that Dropbox does have a business offering, which has additional features for the enterprise environment. Audit logs, device management, two factor authentication, single sign-on, file recovery and remote wipe are just some of the additional features in the Dropbox for Business offering. As Dropbox continues to evolve its business offerings, it may reach the point where it is an option for confidential data.

The authors use Dropbox extensively, for materials relating to speaking and educational writing, like this book. They do not use it for confidential information or client data. Dropbox is reportedly the most blocked or one of the most blocked services in enterprise networks (where it is not used by the enterprise) because of security concerns.

Many lawyers use Gmail, especially the free version. Is that a good idea? Absolutely not. Why? Because the terms of service allow Google to do anything it wants with your data. Do most lawyers know this? Nope. Pay $50 to get a premium account (Google Apps for Work) and now your data is safer. Is your law license worth $50? We're pretty sure it is.

Will cloud providers often provide greater security than you can by yourself? Yes, especially the established cloud providers. Solo and small firms often do a mediocre job with information security, but seasoned cloud providers stay on top of it. As an example, we've seen many lawyers use cloud practice management systems like Clio and Rocket Matter without any problems. When investigating cloud providers, see if they comply with the various standards discussed above, like ISO 27018 for PII. Microsoft was the first cloud provider to achieve the standard in February of 2015. Dropbox is now compliant as well. It's part of the analysis—not the end. The appropriate range of the considerations discussed above also need to be factored into your analysis.

We were horrified to read a report from the Ponemon Institute in 2011 that found that 70% of the cloud service providers believe that their customers are responsible for data security, and only 30% thought it was a shared responsibility. Those percentages didn't improve much with the 2013 study with some organizations expecting their cloud service providers to ensure the security of SaaS (Software as a Service) and IaaS (Infrastructure as a Service) applications (36% and 22% respectively).

Be cognizant that security isn't the only issue. If your data is in the cloud, can you keep a copy locally? Even the big boys, such as Amazon and Google, have had their clouds go down. If you go with some "held together with a spit and a promise" cloud provider, you are likely to have even more mishaps. And remember that if your Internet is down (especially if you don't have a backup method of connecting to the Internet), you won't have access to your data unless it is stored locally. Lawyers tend to forget these things when they move to the cloud. Always remember that nothing is 100% reliable, and we've seen a lot of panic-stricken lawyers who were essentially out of business when they lost their connection to their data in the cloud.

Remember that even though your data is in the cloud, you may need to preserve it in the event of litigation since you will be found to have control over the data. This means there had better be a procedure in place to allow for the preservation of data. The preservation issue has really come to the forefront, especially following on the heels of the BYOD (Bring Your Own Device) movement. The latest challenge for law firms and businesses is the BYOC (Bring Your Own Cloud) issue. BYOC is defined as employees owning and controlling public or third-party cloud services for storage of data. This means that you really don't know all the places that data may reside. Having client data spread across multiple devices can be a good thing, but it can also create a huge risk for compromise. When data is spread across multiple devices using a cloud service, it makes it almost impossible to confirm that the data is destroyed once an employee leaves the firm. Do you have methods and policies in place to deal with the recent BYOC movement?

Another potential headache: Your data may well be stored on a server with other users' data. So, what if law enforcement shows up with a warrant to seize that server with the commingled data—what then? It has happened—taking away all users' data on the server or servers until a court sorts it out. One major impediment to cloud development, particularly with respect to the legal profession, is how easily the Feds can get to cloud data. Many commentators have said that Congress really needs to pass a law which preserves data confidentiality and privacy in the cloud, but so far, Congress has not done so.

Conclusion

Appropriate use of technology, including cloud computing, can be a great benefit for attorneys. However, before proceeding with new technologies, it is important for attorneys to understand and evaluate the technology and to comply with the various duties that apply in implementing and using it. Particularly critical are the ethical duties of competence and confidentiality. The minimum requirement is to comply with the appropriate state ethics rules and opinions and any other regulatory and contractual duties that may apply. Attorneys should strive for stronger safeguards. Themes are consistent through these opinions as to minimum requirements, including the core duties of conducting appropriate due diligence, taking competent and reasonable measures to protect the confidentiality and availability of client data, making sure there are appropriate, enforceable requirements for security, and conducting appropriate supervision or monitoring.

CHAPTER TWENTY-THREE

Social Media

Social media sites have become wonderful places for cybercriminals and hackers to set up shop. Even developers for social media sites have been found with their hands in the cookie jar. And yet, we find very few small to midsize firms with social media policies or training about the safe usage of social media or technology which might intercept malware spread by clicking on a social media link before it is installed on the network.

Employees love social media, especially Facebook, LinkedIn and Twitter—but there are many contenders for their attention. Pew Research Center reported in September of 2014 that 74% of adults use social media sites. Roughly the same percentage of your employees are likely to be users.

Social media sites, especially the major ones, tend to have some kind of real-time scanning to screen malware out, but they are not infallible. Cybercriminals and hackers keep finding new ways to compromise social media.

Manual sharing (that's what the experts call it) of phony posts (a free $250 Walmart gift card) are very likely to be redistributed (shared) with friends at the law firm. Clicking on the bogus offer downloads malware in the background, unknown to the user. Now you may have lots of breaches in a short time. Fake offerings arrive with something wonderful (if only you click)—and many do—another likely breach.

The bad guys can even create a "Like" button on Facebook featuring an alluring story (it may well be based on reality), perhaps about the triumph of a handicapped athlete who won a wounded veterans event, which then downloads malware when the "Like" button is clicked.

Employees, especially millennials, can increase security challenges to their employers as they mix personal and private lives. They often disregard privacy concerns and even polite behavior online. They tend to say that era of privacy is over—and they are unconcerned about the absence of privacy. Unfortunately, they often tend to treat a law firm's confidentiality with the same disregard. There have even been CLEs about this behavior entitled, "You're Not the Boss of Me"—and here you thought you were their boss.

One tip we saw recently advocated sending around news stories or blog posts where an employee's failure to be careful resulted in a data breach or other security incident. Not a bad idea—it serves as a constant reminder that there are real-life stories and that these breaches are not theoretical—they happen all the time when employees are careless.

Employees may talk about cases online, disparage opponents in cases—and the list goes on and on. Some employers ban social media, either by policy, by technology or both. But employees will end run anything they can in order to connect to their social media, oblivious to security risks.

While an employee may stupidly let law firm data be communicated via social media, it is also dangerous because social media sites are often a target for cybercriminals and hackers.

According to the Cisco *2013 Annual Security Report*, the highest concentration of online security threats are on mass audience sites, including social media. The report revealed that online advertisements are 182 times more likely to deliver malicious content than pornography sites, for example. That stopped us in our tracks—182 times? Wow.

Besides the possibility of employees spreading sensitive data, they can also, intentionally or not, spread false information. The rapid spread of false information through social media was among the emerging risks identified by the World Economic Forum in its *Global Risks 2013* report.

The report's authors draw the analogy of shouting "Fire" in a crowded cinema. People can be trampled quickly before any correction to the message can be made. Your firm's reputation may suffer the same fate.

Social media can present a risk even when it is properly used. Attackers can get a wealth of information about a law firm, attorneys, and firm employees from social media and use it to craft targeted phishing e-mails to launch an attack on the firm. Penetration testers often use social media research as intelligence for finding weaknesses in a firm's defenses.

How do you limit the risk of social media? Certainly, someone needs to have a Google alert on the law firm's name—this may quickly alert you to a problem. You may decide, via technology, to restrict access to social media only to the person responsible for managing the law firm's social media. But can your employees use their own devices to connect to your network? If they can, they will, and you are back looking at the same threats you were trying to avoid.

If you decide to manage social media with policies, be aware that the risk remains substantial. Unless you monitor and enforce the policy, it is probably not doing you a lot of good. Unfortunately, a lot of lawyers have a limited understanding of social media and its risks. You need to instruct employees to understand that that if they witness an absence of security (a shared password or a laptop left unlocked in a conference room with sensitive data visible) they need to adopt the "See something, say something" motto that the government uses to combat terrorism. This is sometimes called the "broken window" approach—perhaps because a broken window is a small offense but attention to petty infractions creates an atmosphere of security and may help to prevent behavior that constitutes a much greater threat.

Policies need to make clear the kind of information that may not be disseminated. Firms need to understand social media and its risks and benefit. They also need to accept that it is not going away. If they decide to allow it, they need to monitor for any immoral, illegal or offensive content on official firm sites and remove it (and maybe the person who put it there) promptly. Allowing one or more of your employees to run law firm social media pages is empowering to them and can do the law firm a lot of good—but it is fraught with danger, as many organizations have discovered when an employee decides to wage digital war with an unhappy customer/client online in a public forum.

Some experts advise that you should not block access to external social media because attempts to do so have proven ineffective and because they make employees so unhappy, even angry. And a strict policy impedes the development of enterprise social media initiatives. There is a lot of risk/benefit analysis to do—obviously.

Your employees aren't the only security threat. Your own law firm social media accounts can be hacked. In January of 2015, ISIS compromised the Twitter account and YouTube channel of U.S. Central Command (CENTCOM) which has responsibility for the Middle East, North Africa and Central Asia. The Twitter compromise lasted only 30 minutes during which the hackers posted a number of threats and renamed the Twitter Account CyberCaliphate and added the tagline "I love you isis." With the compromised YouTube account, ISIS was able to post two propaganda videos. The account was quickly suspended and was later restored to the original owner.

Perhaps the most important part of this chapter is to emphasize that you can and should train your employees annually on this aspect of security. We hear complaints constantly that these training sessions are boring and their attention drifts. So find good speakers—this is one case where hiring outsiders who are known to be good speakers and knowledgeable may be well advised. In our experience, employees take the dangers of the cyber-world more seriously from outsiders than from members of their own firm.

Be strict—no laptops, tablets or smartphones during training. They may suffer withdrawal symptoms, but they stand a much better chance of learning if they are not distracted.

Inject a bit of fun into the process (hand out security stress balls? Starbucks cards? Have a contest with a prize?) and keep the coffee and bagels coming—employees tend to be at their most alert in the morning. What you are trying to do is create a culture of cybersecurity throughout the law firm. It is one heck of a challenge, but an absolute necessity.

CHAPTER TWENTY-FOUR

Securing Documents

Most law firms use Word to create their documents and convert them to PDF as part of their normal workflow. It is a fairly simple task to secure your documents. It is important to understand how to properly secure your documents from unwanted eyes to protect the confidentiality of the information. Passwords are the simplest way to secure your documents.

As discussed in the duty to safeguard chapter, New Jersey Ethics Opinion 701, published in 2006, states that attorneys should password protect confidential documents sent over the Internet. File password protection in some software, like current versions of Microsoft Office, Adobe Acrobat, and WinZip uses encryption to protect security.

It should be noted that there are products available to crack passwords and enable brute force access to files. Depending on the strength of your password, this could take minutes or years. The more effective products cost thousands of dollars. The message is: don't consider your documents to be 100% secured even if strong passwords are used. However, for all practical purposes, a strong password is sufficient protection to restrict access to the data.

Word

Ever since Word XP (also known as Word 2002), applying a password to your document also encrypts it. There are two levels of security that can be set for the document. One level allows you to open the file, and the other level allows for editing of the document itself. We'll only discuss securing documents using Word 2007 and above. Office 2003 and earlier is out of support and no longer receiving any updates, including security updates. That means that you may be violating your ethical duties if you continue to use it since the software is vulnerable to attack and compromise of confidential client information.

The only real security password is the Open Password, which performs the document encryption. The other passwords (restrict editing, authorized access, etc.) can be removed by using many of the password recovery tools. Later versions of Word are clearer and explicitly state that you are protecting the document by encrypting it with a password.

The procedure for Word 2007 is a simple task. Click on the Office button and then put your mouse over the Prepare choice. This will open up additional selections to the right of Prepare. Select the Encrypt Document option to bring up a password dialog box. Make sure that you use a strong password as we've recommended throughout this book. Click on OK and you will be asked to confirm the password. This password encrypts the document and will be required to open the file in the future. Don't forget the password; if you do, you won't be able to recover it or the contents of the document.

Encrypting a Word 2010 document is a little easier, primarily since the Ribbon was redesigned with the removal of the Office button. Select File and then the Protect Document button in the Permissions section. Select Encrypt with Password to launch the password dialog box. Enter a strong password and click OK. You will be asked to confirm the password, which will encrypt the document.

The process for Word 2013 and Word 2016 is very similar to Word 2010. Select the File tab and the Info selection in the left hand menu structure. Click on the Protect Document button in the Securing Documents (figure 24-1) section. Word 2016 removed the "Securing Documents" and folder location above the Protect Document button. Once you click on the Protect Document button, select Encrypt with Password. Like Word 2010, you will be prompted to enter a password and to confirm the password that will be used to encrypt the document.

Adobe Acrobat

PDF is another common document format that may need to be secured. There are some open source products available to secure a PDF file, but we'll concentrate on using Adobe Acrobat because that's what most lawyers use for PDF generation.

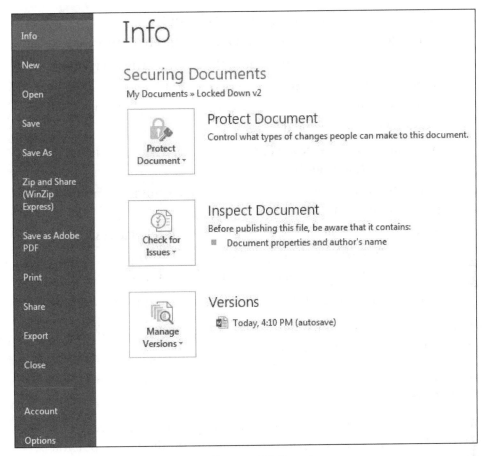

Figure 24-1

There are two types of passwords available for Acrobat. The first is the Document Open Password. This password must be entered just to open the document. The second one is the Permissions Password. This password is used to set or change features of the document. If both passwords are set (our recommendation), either one can be used to open the document, but the Permissions Password is the only one that can change the restricted features. It is important to note that you cannot set passwords for any document that has been signed or certified.

To set the security using Adobe Acrobat,

1. Select file -> Properties and then the Security tab
2. Select the security method: Pull down list and choose Password Security
3. A new dialog box will launch

4. Select the compatibility (e.g., Acrobat 7.0 or later)

    a. The compatibility level will determine the encryption level

    b. The higher the Acrobat version, the stronger the encryption

5. Select the document components to encrypt

    a. If you want the contents to be searched, you need to leave the metadata unencrypted

    b. If you want to create a security envelope, then select to encrypt only file attachments

6. Select the type of password (Open and/or Permissions) and type the password in the appropriate field

    a. For the Permissions Password, select the level of access

        i. Select whether printing is allowed and at what resolution

        ii. Select the type of changes that may be allowed

7. Click on OK and reenter the password in the appropriate dialog box

Don't forget to save the document after setting the security. The security is not set until the document is saved.

Document Management

You have even more flexibility if you have a document management system. The capabilities vary depending on the product used, but you can achieve a much higher level of security granularity by setting permissions. As an example, you can set permissions as read-only for certain individuals. Some may be allowed to change documents. Others may be totally restricted from accessing the document. The document management system can also enforce categorization and version control. Perhaps an associate is only allowed to create a single version of a document, and a reviewing attorney must approve it before it can be finalized. This type of security is used more frequently in larger firms, but we do see some rudimentary amount of document restriction used in small firms.

Compound Files

Finally, you may have multiple files contained within a single container. You probably recognize this as a ZIP file or some other common compressed file name. Not only can you individually protect each file within the compound file, but you can also protect the entire container. Just like a Word or Acrobat file, you apply a password to the compound file, which encrypts the contents. This is generally done when transmitting information to protect it in transit. The recipient then uses the password to open the container and decrypt the contents.

Metadata

You've probably heard horror stories about information being revealed via metadata. Metadata is of particular concern to attorneys since they could reveal such things as trial strategy and client information. Metadata is a double-edged sword, and a fundamental understanding of metadata is key for any practicing attorney.

So, what is metadata? Very often, you will hear that metadata is "data about data," which is not very helpful at all. Essentially, there are two types of metadata. The first type is operating system metadata. This is information about when the file was created at the particular location of the computer, when it was last accessed, when it was last modified and other such values that are assigned by the operating system of the computer. The second type is the application metadata and is the one most feared by attorneys. This is information that the application software embeds in the file to help it perform various tasks and display of the information.

As an example, Word files contain metadata about such items as the document author, when the document was last printed, what fonts are used, who last saved the document, and comments and changes to the document. Acrobat files contain such items as the creator of the file, the title of the file and what was used to create the PDF. Digital camera pictures contain values such as the camera model, serial number, aperture setting, pixel size and possibly the GPS coordinates for where the picture was taken.

You may or may not care about the application metadata, but a part of securing a document is knowing how to remove and/or view the metadata. For most applications, you can simply go to File and then Properties. There are several commercial products available to view and/or scrub the metadata from documents. One of the most widely used products among solo and small firm attorneys is Metadata Assistant by Payne-Group (**www.thepaynegroup.com**). Metadata Assistant integrates with Microsoft Office directly on the Ribbon interface. It also integrates with Outlook and will prompt you to scrub the metadata of any file attachments. This is particularly helpful when you send an attachment to opposing counsel and may have forgotten to clear the metadata from the file. There are other metadata products such as iScrub or Metadact-e. Metadact-e by Litera (**www.litera.com**) is a server-based product that scales better than Metadata Assistant and can be controlled to a more granular level using profiles. Metadact-e is the only product we are aware of that will scrub metadata from all devices, including mobile devices such as iPads, smartphones and tablets. It is able to accomplish this since all messages are processed by the Metadact-e server applying the settings as defined in the profile. Metadact-e tends to be used in mid to larger law firms and provides centralized management of metadata processing.

If you convert a Word document to PDF that will get rid of almost all the metadata and what remains is generally benign. Hence, Acrobat is sometimes referred to as the poor man's metadata scrubber.

Most states that have considered the ethical implications of metadata have said that attorneys have an affirmative duty to scrub metadata to avoid revealing client confidences. Of course, if you are collaborating with someone (e.g., using Track Changes in Word), you cannot scrub the metadata because that would remove the tracked changes. But any final documents you send as attachments should always be cleaned.

The ABA Legal Technology Resource Center maintains an excellent guide to metadata ethics opinions around the United States which may be found at **www.americanbar.org/groups/departments_offices/legal_technology_resources/resources/charts_fyis/metadatachart.html**.

It is important to note that e-discovery presents a different issue for metadata in attorney documents and communications. Metadata must generally be preserved and sometimes produced in e-discovery. In this context, failure to preserve metadata or wiping of metadata may be spoliation and lead to sanctions.

Final Thoughts

Securing documents is at the edge of lawyer consciousness these days, but it is not mainstream. It really isn't that hard, but lawyers seem to resist anything that adds even one extra step or perhaps a bit of complexity. As we've said over and over again, it really is time to step up your attention to security. Securing documents is typically as easy as defining a password for the document file.

CHAPTER TWENTY-FIVE

Cyberinsurance

Introduction

Do you know if you have cyberinsurance at your law firm? In the ABA's *2015 Legal Technology Resource Center Survey*, only 11% said yes. That's alarming when the same survey showed a marked increase in data breaches and security incidents.

The survey showed that many lawyers didn't know whether their law firms had cyberinsurance—in fact, in firms of more than 100 lawyers, 80% didn't know if the law firm carried such insurance. Now that the *ABA Model Rules of Professional Conduct* have required more technological competence of lawyers (Rules 1.1 and 1.6—thus far adopted by 20 states, and that number expected to grow), it may be an ethical violation if you don't inform yourself about the state of your information security—and of course one way you protect your clients is by managing risk through cyberinsurance.

Over and over again, we hear lawyers insist that their comprehensive general liability (CGL) policy will protect them. It almost never does. Sadly, that scenario has now been played out in courts—and almost without fail, the CGL is held not to cover data breaches. There used to be happy results in which insurers did cover breaches under the CGL policy, but most insurers have now riddled the CGL with exclusions to push clients into new specialized cybersecurity insurance policies. We've seen some try to make claims under the Errors and Omissions policy, generally with the same unhappy result. Those new exclusions have shown up there too. Cyberinsurance is its own beast—and a law firm without it, in today's world, may be foolish.

Cybersecurity insurance policies, generally regarded as having been first introduced in the 1990s, are now the fastest growing segment of the insurance industry—and as you have previously read, there are many good reasons why. As of 2015, according to a report from insurer Allianz Global Corporate and Specialty (AGCS) the cyberinsurance market is estimated to be worth around $2 billion in premiums, with U.S. businesses accounting for about 90% of the market. While fewer than 10% of companies in the U.S. purchase cyberinsurance today, the market is expected to grow by double-digit figures from year to year and could reach more than $20 billion in the next decade. And no wonder—a recent study by the Ponemon Institute estimates that more than one billion records of personally identifiable information have been stolen worldwide to date.

Palo Alto Networks published an infographic called *"The Year of Executive Accountability"* in 2015 that showed a 50% increase in the attention Boards of Directors are paying to cyberinsurance—the needle probably hasn't moved that far in the legal industry, but it is likely to in the future. You may want to take a look at the infographic to see how Boards are zeroing in on data about information security. You can find the infographic at **http://researchcenter.paloaltonetworks.com/2015/10/ governance-of-cybersecurity-report-infographic/**

As we've said many times, give up the notion that "it can't happen here." It is now widely accepted that most law firms have been breached, many more than once. Very simply, data that has value (and is usually sold on the Dark Web) is a magnet for the bad guys. While the largest victims of data breaches command the headlines, 30% of the victims are small businesses according to *Symantec's 2014 Internet Security Threat Report.*

Why is cyberinsurance such an important part of information security? The plain truth is that information security has no silver bullet. You can never secure your data 100% of the time. And there is always the unlucky chance that you will be the first kid on your block to get a zero day infection, one in which malware circulates in the wild for the very first time; there is no way to stop it because the enterprise security software you are using has not yet developed a signature or method to guard against this new form of malware.

Worse yet are the carbon-based units (your employees) who may steadfastly refuse to practice safe computing. According to *Verizon's 2015 Data Breach Investigations Report*, 23% of recipients open e-mails sent by scammers/hackers, and 11% download attachments from phishing emails. Results also showed that 50% of users click on phishing links within the first hour.

Given the depth and breadth of vulnerabilities, much of information security is about risk management. There is some point at which you've done all you can do, within your budget, to secure your data. Now you turn to managing the risk that, in spite of your best efforts, you'll be breached or your data will otherwise be compromised.

This is where cyberinsurance comes in. It "fills the gap" between all that you can reasonably do and the remaining risk your firm bears. Surprisingly, very few lawyers understand whether their insurance policy covers a data breach. The sad truth is that the average insurance policy does not. Most policies will replace computers that are damaged, stolen or lost, but they will not cover the consequences of the lost data or the remediation to repair an infected machine.

Given that, your first step is to review your current insurance policy and see what it does cover. If it is indeed the sort of standard policy described above, it is now time to talk to your insurance agent and explain the kind of coverage you want—and you should be sitting down when the costs are explained to you. Authors Simek and Nelson have keen and painful memories of the 25-page application that they filled out, and the sticker shock we experienced when we saw the price. That experience is forever etched in our minds.

Since the first edition of this book was published in 2012, there have certainly been changes in the cyberinsurance landscape. For one thing, many more insurance companies now offer cyberinsurance. Also, whereas many companies offer a cyberinsurance rider, sometimes cyberinsurance is part of the mainstream policies—but in our observation, not very often.

How Much Does It Cost?

Cyberinsurance is not cheap, so be a savvy shopper. The prices remain all over the map, so make sure your insurance agent looks around. There isn't yet a good model for measuring prices, risks and how to hedge the risks—hence the crazy variation in prices—one commentator remarked that some premiums are "stupid low" given the extent of the risk.

Some companies still do not offer cyberinsurance, although many have learned that there is gold in the cyberworld to be panned, particularly in a world where almost all states have data breach notifications laws.

As we go to press, forty-seven states, the District of Columbia, Guam, Puerto Rico and the Virgin Islands have enacted legislation requiring private or government entities to notify individuals of security breaches of information involving personally identifiable information. You can find the current list of states and territories (with links) at **http://www.ncsl.org/ research/telecommunications-and-information-technology/security- breach-notification-laws.aspx**. The federal Health Information Technology for Economic and Clinical Health Act (HITECH) already provides for data breach notification (and much more) when medical data is involved.

Insurance companies are still gathering actuarial data to help assist in setting prices, but as we are in the adolescence of cyberinsurance, pricing has not settled down. And because so many things are uncertain in the information security world, some insurers are capping their policies, often at $10-$100 million. Since the last edition of this book, we now have read that it is possible for a business to purchase up to $300 million in cyberin- surance from a single insurer but more likely that a business would have to obtain multiple policies to reach the $300 million mark.

Thank heavens solo and small firms are on the lower end of the spectrum, but it's still costly. In 2015, the cost is roughly $10,000 per $1,000,000 of coverage.

Just as we were going to press, Reuters reported that hacking has become such a problem that insurers are now in the process of massively increasing cyber premiums. Just your luck, right? Insurance companies are also rais- ing deductibles—in some cases by gargantuan amounts. The health indus- try has been hardest hit, with premiums tripling at renewal time. More typical are increases from 20-30%. The list of exclusions is growing too—so make sure you read that list carefully.

To minimize risk, insurance companies are submitting self-audits to prospective cyberinsurance customers. They are also taking more Draco- nian measures, sending in assessors to get an onsite picture of a law firm's security risks. The premium may be based on how closely the assessors' consequent recommendations are followed. If you do have a self-audit form you are filling out, don't be slipshod and do be candid—your false, misleading or vague answers will certainly be used against you in the event of a claim.

Consider being proactive—as an example, considering abiding by the National Institute of Standards Cybersecurity Framework (included in Appendix H). The more you can show that you are ahead of the curve in protecting confidential data, the better your negotiating posture with the insurance companies, which might earn you a preferred premium rate— not to mention the overall benefits of good risk management.

Very few things are as expensive as investigating a data breach, notifying everyone affected by the breach and otherwise complying with legal requirements through notification and the offer of credit monitoring, as well as remediating the problem that caused the breach. This often requires a full-scale security assessment followed by major expenditures to follow all of the recommendations.

If you're reaching for the Advil about now, you're not alone. The world of cyberinsurance is full of potholes and poorly understood by most lawyers.

Experts estimate that at least 50 (up from a dozen in 2012) companies now offer cyberinsurance specifically tailored for law firms, including AXIS Insurance, Travelers, Philadelphia Insurance Companies, Monitor Liability Managers, Ahern Insurance Brokerage, CAN and many others. As competition has increased, prices have come down, but don't look for Walmart prices.

Use a good insurance broker—one who is experienced in procuring cyberinsurance. It is amazing how few brokers have expertise in this area or know which companies to recommend. There are certainly companies who have a reputation for denying claims claiming that they fall under exclusion clauses and others who have a reputation for standing by their customers.

Firms are waking up to the potential cost of a data breach, especially if they are in a regulated industry such as finance or health care. The Ponemon Institute's 2015 Global Cost of Data Breach Study polled 350 companies in 11 countries and found that malicious attacks take an average of 256 days to discover while breaches caused by human error take an average of 158 days to identify. The median cost is $3.9 million a year (a 23% increase since 2013).

What Will a Prospective Insurer Ask You?

This varies widely. But be prepared to for questions regarding:

- An up-to-date network diagram
- Assets and revenues
- Number of employees
- Office locations
- Any plans for a merger or buy-out

- The kind of data you hold, including credit card data, personally identifiable information (PII), HIPAA data, classified data, etc.
- The nature and frequency of cybersecurity training given to employees
- Compliance with various information security standards
- Frequency of security assessments—are they conducted in-house or by an independent third party?
- Policies involving cybersecurity—and how often they are reevaluated, particularly your incident response plan
- Security currently in place, including firewalls, anti-malware software, data loss protection (DLP) hardware/software, intrusion detection systems (IDS) hardware/software
- Employment of people devoted to information security and with the appropriate certifications
- Report of previous data breaches, dates, vulnerabilities involved, length of breach, time to discover breach, number of records breached, etc.
- Any known current vulnerabilities or threats to your data
- Any known set of facts that might give rise to a claim under a prospective policy
- Security termination procedures upon an employee's departure
- Physical security of the office(s)
- How the backup is engineered, how often backups are made and where they are stored—and whether the backup is engineered so that that data compromised by ransomware can be reliably restored from an unaffected backup
- Prior cancellations or refusal of a cybersecurity policy
- Annual budget for cybersecurity and percentage of gross revenue
- Cybersecurity policies related to vendors and other third parties
- Do you allow BYOD (bring your own device) or BYON (bring your own network)? If so, how are they managed, by technology and policies?
- Password policies and how they are enforced
- Encryption policies and software/hardware employed
- Is two-factor authentication (2FA) available?
- How you ensure that all security patches are installed in a timely manner

- How you ensure that software that is no longer receiving security updates is replaced
- Remote access policies and any technology enforcement of those policies
- Social media policies and any technology enforcement of those policies
- Whether you conduct independent third-party audits of your network and how often
- Any penetration testing to simulate attacks

Coverage

Would-be purchasers of cyberinsurance are advised to read carefully and ask questions. There is no consistency between the coverage of the various insurance companies, and they all use different language. It is very hard to determine exactly what you're purchasing much less make an apples to apples comparison.

This makes it tough on the poor lawyer who finds that someone has invaded the law firm network and is now holding data hostage until a ransom is paid. You'd better make sure your policy covers that because it has happened—probably much more often than anyone knows. We are aware of four Northern Virginia law firms that got hit by ransomware within a two-week period in 2015.

What if data is somehow transported to a social media site? Are you covered there? And how about data breaches in the clouds? It is widely reported that cloud providers tend to have less coverage than might be prudent from the point of view of the law firm that engaged the cloud. And just read your cloud vendor's terms of service; we can guarantee that the provider will try to insulate itself from liability. With 50% or more of law firms storing data in the cloud, this is a threshold question to ask.

Not surprisingly, with all the confusion, battles over coverage have wound up in court. In *Zurich v. American Insurance Co. v. Sony Corp. of America,* Zurich was seeking to absolve itself of any responsibility to defend or indemnify Sony for claims asserted in class actions and other actions stemming from the 2011 hacking of Sony's PlayStation Network. Zurich maintained that the general liability policies it sold to Sony did not apply. Ultimately, the court agreed. Heck, if Sony's lawyers didn't know what their insurance covered, imagine the fog a solo or small firm attorney might be in.

One of the major developments of 2015 was that insurance companies were moving to offer "business interruption" coverage as part of their cyberinsurance policies. This is definitely something you want to inquire about.

Another major development of 2015 was the headline "We Don't Cover Stupid"—referring to an insurance company's position that it wasn't liable under a claim when a company that had been breached had not followed "minimum required practices" as spelled out in the policy. This story doesn't involve a law firm but it is instructive for law firms to read it— we've seen a number of insurance companies say there is no coverage where security of confidential data is sloppy—and they are putting "get out of jail free" clauses in their policies. So read on . . .

In 2013, California healthcare provider Cottage Health System discovered that security on one of its servers had been disabled, leaving tens of thousands of patients' files potentially open and exposed on the Internet. Those files included patients' names, addresses, dates of birth, and in a few cases, their diagnosis, lab results and procedures performed.

To no one's surprise, Cottage was sued, along with inSync, a company responsible for putting the records in a secure location online. As you might imagine, a lot of money was spent on a forensic investigation, security consultants to get rid of malware, patient notification, credit monitoring—and no doubt, attorney fees.

Cottage had cyberinsurance to cover the breach, and Columbia Casualty agreed to pay $4.2 million to settle a class action lawsuit but subsequently sued for reimbursement, pointing to a clause in the policy that effectively said it didn't have to cover the breach because Cottage hadn't followed "minimum required practices" as spelled out in the policy.

Specifically, Columbia claimed that Cottage "stored medical records on a system that was fully accessible to the Internet but failed to install encryption or take other security measures to protect patient information from becoming available to anyone who 'surfed' the Internet."

The patient data had been exposed (in clear text) for about two months, starting in October 2013. There was no cyberattack—the data was publicly available—you could just Google it. Pretty tough to know who accessed the data.

Besides the failure to encrypt, Columbia alleged the following security shortfalls.

Cottage and its third-party vendor, inSync, allegedly failed "to continuously implement the procedures and risk controls identified in its application" for the coverage, including configuration and change management for Cottage's IT systems as well as regular patch management. The insurer also alleged failure to regularly "re-assess its information security exposure and enhance risk controls" and to . . . "deploy a system to detect unauthorized access or attempts to access sensitive information stored on its servers."

An instructive example of how you can think you are covered—but maybe not . . .

While cyberinsurance is, in our judgment, mandatory these days, there are lots of possible ways to make a mistake in getting the right coverage.

Insurers can dodge covering data breaches for a host of reasons, including:

- **Not paying retroactively.** Given that breaches can be discovered months or even years after they begin or end, law firms should carefully consider when coverage starts.

- **Terrorism/act of foreign enemy exclusions.** Many cyberattacks originate from outside a country's borders, and many of them are believed to be state sponsored. Depending on the policy's wording, your firm could be left high and dry. Experts advise negotiating the removal of such exclusions.

- **Lack of coverage for negligence.** Insurers are starting to cover only data theft, not negligence. If an employee loses an unencrypted laptop with sensitive data, some policies won't cover the breach.

- **Failure to make a timely notification to the insurance company.** Make sure you know when you need to report an incident to your insurer. The clock may be ticking and you don't want to find that your delay means that there are costs you cannot recover—and remember that costs start to mount up quickly after a breach.

Amazingly, many folks enter into these policies without a full understanding of what is included and excluded.

Beyond making sure that you are providing adequate security, make sure you understand how an insurance company would expect you to prove a data breach. What documentation would you need? When would you receive the proceeds? You may have to cover a large portion of the investigative and remediation expenses before the insurer even acknowledge coverage.

Ask these questions of your current insurance representative:

- Does the current policy cover computer forensics or other investigative services in the event of a data breach?
- What about notifications to those affected and credit reports?
- Does it cover data and other nonphysical perils under the Property policies? Almost always, no.
- If an insider causes the breach, does this fall under the "intentional acts" exclusion? Probably, yes.
- What if bank credentials are compromised in the breach and monies are stolen from your bank account—are you covered? Several law firms have found, to their profound dismay that they were not.
- Is coverage unavailable for acts outside the provision of professional services?
- If you are liable for the destruction of electronic data, are you covered under the General Liability or Property policies? You're likely to hear, "No, you're not."
- Are direct losses caused by a vendor covered under crime policies?
- Crime policies usually cover theft of money, securities and other tangible property. Does yours cover the theft or destruction of electronic data?
- Are the services of a reputation management firm included?
- Are the costs of a data breach coach (usually an attorney specializing in data breaches) covered?
- Does the insurer provide a 7X24 data breach hotline?
- Does it have an incident response team to help manage the response to an incident?
- Are the expenses of responding to state Attorney General investigations or federal entity investigations covered?
- Are you covered for breaches at a third-party vendor such as a cloud service provider?
- Are you responsible for ensuring a third-party provider meets certain minimum security standards?
- Is business interruption protection offered as part of the policy? As noted above, this is a pretty recent development, so make sure you at least consider an insurer that offers this protection.

Chances are that you'll be appalled at how exposed you feel after a probing conversation with your insurance agent.

Too often, law firms believe they can self-insure, but that is a fallacy if any sort of major breach occurs. Consider all the possible exposures from a single incident:

- ◆ First party—direct losses, perhaps due to the need for data recovery or due to business interruption
- ◆ Third party—penalties, civil fines or claims from clients
- ◆ Network security—expenses due to security failures on the firm's part, perhaps involving the loss of client data or the transmission of computer malware
- ◆ Extortion—investigating or paying for the return of data
- ◆ Web liability—claims regarding information on your web site which might give rise to copyright/trademark actions or defamation, libel or advertising claims
- ◆ Computer crimes—damages caused by the destruction or manipulation of data or the posting of fraudulent data
- ◆ Incident management expenses—bringing in outside experts to investigate the incident and fix the problem; perhaps the need for a public relations firm to deal with the nightmare

If you decide to secure coverage, make sure it will cover all of the possibilities listed above and be aware that you may need more than one policy. There are umbrella policies which cover everything, but some insurers divide policies up into such things as privacy, technology security, business continuity, internal sabotage and theft, web services, breach notification and credit monitoring. Note that it costs $1–$3 to notify clients and approximately $165 for each record breached for data restoration and crisis management according to the Ponemon Institute's *2015 Global Cost of Data Breach Study*.

Is one kind of law firm more vulnerable than another? Yes, absolutely. Mergers and acquisitions firms are prime targets, as are firms that have litigation with China (the source of so many breaches). Firms that hold the intellectual property of clients are an appealing target. But even a small family law or real estate firm has a wealth of financial and other personal data on its clients—a perfect target for identity thieves. Remember what we said at the outset: Data that has value is a magnet for the bad guys.

In the end, you will have to balance the costs of making security improvements with the cost of cyberinsurance to determine where you are getting the maximum benefit and limiting your risks as much as possible. It is not an easy calculation.

CHAPTER TWENTY-SIX

The Future of Information Security

If anyone could accurately predict the future of information security, they would be wealthy beyond their dreams. The truth is that we can only speculate. Who would have predicted when we wrote our first edition that the Internet of Things would become a security nightmare of untold proportions?

Nonetheless, we'll give it our best shot based on what we know today.

Security Certifications and Security Audits

In 2015, *The American Lawyer* reported that 18 large law firms in the U.S. had received the ISO 27001 certification. This certification has become a way of assuring clients that law firms are indeed protecting their clients' data. The yearly audits to maintain the certification offer clients a lot of comfort and offer law firms the continuing opportunity to assess and respond to new risks.

We certainly predict that the number of law firms seeking that certification will grow—and that other certifications may be sought. You will likely see statements made that the law firm is compliant with some of the security standards referenced earlier in this book. Likewise, some clients are somewhat skeptical of law firms doing their own audits, even on the forms provided them by clients. There is a deeply human tendency to give the clients the answer they want. More and more frequently, clients are likely to be demanding an independent third party audit—or even sending in their own elite team of information security experts to make an assessment.

The bottom line is that clients who are unsatisfied with their law firm's security are going to require changes or take their business elsewhere. Some law firms are trying to get out ahead of the demands and are ramping up their security so they can point to it and use it as marketing leverage.

Policies and Plans

Expect more policies and plans as more security incidents take place in law firms. There is a great interest by clients in seeing a law firm's Incident Response Plan. Insurance companies want to see it as well—and information security policies generally. While all the large firms are likely to have Incident Response Plans, they are fairly rare in solo and small firms. As the authors have seen these firms become more and more interested in securing their data, their interest in policies and plans is bound to increase as well.

Clients are asking for stricter policies to be put into place, and that will likely continue. They may ask that no sensitive data be placed on a flash drive, or that only "clean devices" be taken to countries where state-sponsored hacking is common. They may forbid any linkage between a law firm's network and networks in another country, although there is the practical element since the majority of networks are connected to the Internet. All sorts of demands by clients are being made—and we predict that the initial trickle of demands will increase to a river. You may recall that, in 2012, information security company Mandiant (a division of Fire-Eye) put out a report estimating that 80% of the 100 largest American law firms had experienced some form of a data breach in 2011—is it any wonder that clients are so demanding in light of estimated numbers like those? We look for far tighter information security controls to be employed by law firms in response to client concerns.

Passwords and Multifactor Authentication

Passwords aren't dead yet and probably won't be for the foreseeable future. But they have to die ultimately because they offer such scant protection. The move to multifactor authentication is clearly mandated by its far greater ability to secure data. Solos and small firm lawyers may not move that way as fast, but clients are demanding tighter and tighter protection for their data and multifactor authentication is one robust and obvious solution.

Encryption

This train left the station very fast in 2015 as the word spread that clients were demanding encryption—and as products emerged that were very simple to use and didn't cost a lot of money either. No math skills are required and you don't have to understand encryption. You just have to point and click an "Encrypt and Send" button—or something similar. The most Luddite of American lawyers are beginning to understand this and we anticipate a widespread adoption of encryption everywhere before we "set pen to paper" for the next edition.

Social Media

The social media chapter of this book is brand new with this edition. Social media is now a mainstream form of communication for most people—and they spend a lot of time on social media. We expect to see more attack vectors using social media as a weapon for hackers. They are practicing what every fishing boat captains knows—they are fishing where the fish are. We expect our Social Media chapter to be very volatile in the next edition of this book.

Mobility

We expect an even greater increase of mobile access. Wireless connections are all the rage and we move towards an increased usage of tablets, smartphones and wearable technology. More and more of the younger generation will impose pressure for BYOD (Bring Your Own Device), BYON (Bring Your Own Network) and BYOC (Bring Your Own Cloud). The access to any data from any place using any device will create new challenges for information security. Detection tools will be needed to identify when a device is connected to the firm network. You can't protect it if you don't know it exists.

File-Syncing Software—Dropbox and its Brethren

Though there are many kinds of file syncing software, lawyers have glommed on to Dropbox in droves. The Washington Post reported that 33% of its users in Washington D.C. were sharing files. We are hearing repeatedly of e-discovery productions being made via Dropbox and similar services. We expect to see breaches via services like Dropbox—some users misunderstanding how to use these kinds of services securely and some keeping data (like those e-discovery productions) around as "dark data" that they don't remember they have which may be hacked, inadvertently shared, etc.

Drone Cyberattacks

Don't laugh. We predict that they are coming. Drones rigged with hacking tools can hover over a law firm's building and break into the firm's wireless network. Think of it as having an airborne Pineapple (see the Security Tools chapter). They are not breaking any new hacking ground (they are exploiting weaknesses in Wi-Fi and radio frequency security), but they provide a new method of transport. Drones can hack smartphones—and other drones. It has been seen in the wild now—to the point where drone detection systems are a hot commodity and an intrusion detection system for drones which are capable of cyberattacking is now being developed. We are sure we'll have much more about this in the next edition.

Information Rights Management

Though in its infancy, information rights management (IRM) will surely take off. Making a "reasonable effort" to protect confidentiality is being redefined by technology that features plug-in free information rights management (IRM). IRM provides the sender with control of electronic information by protecting each piece of content individually. It protects data at the file level, when it's at rest, in transit, on the recipient's computer, a flash drive—wherever it is located. Files are encrypted and require authentication each time they are opened. IRM "calls home" to ask for permission whenever an individual attempts to access a document. More sophisticated IRM technology can also prevent screen capture, copying text or printing.

In general, once you've sent someone an encrypted e-mail and they open it, the sender has no control over it. IRM can revoke access rights at any time, even after data has been downloaded. As one expert asked, "How many times do lawyers hand over documents to opposing counsel who promises to destroy them but never do? IRM makes these problems go away." We expect to explore that topic when we write this book again.

Changing Focus to Detection, Response and Recovery

As security expert Bruce Schneier noted of current day information security, "We aren't resilient. We can't recover. We can't adapt. We can't mitigate. We don't think in those ways. We think in terms of prevention instead of response and recovery."

While that has been true, that way of looking at things has markedly changed as we shift to detection, response and recovery. We now assume that a sophisticated hacker with sophisticated tools will succeed. We want to find the hack, respond to it and recover from it. We believe we will see a far greater emphasis on this approach in the future.

Who You Gonna Call? Information Security Experts

The 2015 Study of the Legal Industry's Information Security Assessment Practices was developed by Digital Defense Inc. (DDI), in collaboration with ILTA's LegalSEC Steering Committee. One of the key findings was that 66% of law firms surveyed had no staff devoted to Information Security. Many firms will not be able to afford to hire certified information security specialists, but we think you'll see a growing number of law firms employing the services of such specialists to periodically review their security and make recommendations to enhance it in light of new risks and new technologies. And they will have to budget for information security, an unhappy thought to those firms already bemoaning the monies they have to pay their IT consultants.

Final Words

You'll never be finished with information security; we're all stuck with it, and its morphing nature. But because lawyers have an ethical duty, we have no choice but to keep ourselves as well educated as we can and to hire expert help where needed. We hope this book has given you a good grasp of some of the essential issues in information security—and keep watching the horizon because the view changes daily in the InfoSec world.

CHAPTER TWENTY-SEVEN

Additional Information Resources

Here is a list of our very favorite resources. A number of folks contributed to the very long list of resources that follows, but if you are trying to stay up with the fundamentals of information security, our short list of favorites may be enough.

Short List of Favorite Information Sources

American Bar Association, Law Practice Division, **www.americanbar .org/groups/law_practice.html**, provides information on security geared to attorneys through CLE programs, the Legal Technology Resource Center, ABA TECHSHOW, *Law Practice Magazine* and *Law Practice Today* webzine

American Bar Association, Cybersecurity Resources, **www.american bar.org/groups/leadership/office_of_the_president/cybersecurity/ resources.html**, provides links to cybersecurity materials and publications by various ABA sections, divisions and committees

CERT Coordination Center, **www.cert.org** (Carnegie Mellon University), a leading information security research and training center, provides security information for both technical and nontechnical users

Computerworld Security Topic Center, **www.computerworld.com/ category/security**, an online news service, regularly addresses security and privacy issues

CSO Online, **www.csoonline.com**, a news site that covers security and risk management

Dark Reading, **www.darkreading.com**, a comprehensive security information and news site published by *InformationWeek*

ILTA LegalSEC, **http://connect.iltanet.org/resources/legalsec?ssopc=1** (International Legal Technology Association), provides the legal community with guidelines for risk-based information programs, including publications, peer group discussions, webinars, an annual LegalSEC SUMMIT conference and other live programs; some materials are publicly available while others are available only to members

KrebsonSecurity, **http://krebsonsecurity.com**, a blog that covers selected security and privacy developments, including current data breaches and threats

Microsoft, Safety & Security, **www.microsoft.com/security/default. aspx** (for nontechnical users) and **http://technet.microsoft.com/ en-us/security/bb291012** (for technical users)

Naked Security, **https://nakedsecurity.sophos.com**, security news site presented by Sophos, a leading security solution provider

SANS Institute, **www.sans.org**, a leading information security research, training and certification organization, provides security information for both technical and nontechnical users, including its extensive Reading Room, the Internet Storm Center and Security Awareness Tips of the Day

SC Magazine, **www.scmagazine.com**, a news site, electronic newsletter, and magazine that focuses on business and technical security topics

Schneier on Security, **www.schneier.com**, a blog by a highly respected security and cryptography professional; ranges from basic to highly technical; publishes *Cryptogram*, a monthly newsletter

SearchSecurity, **http://searchsecurity.techtarget.com** (a comprehensive security site by the publisher of *Information Security* magazine), includes SearchMidmarketSecurity, **http://searchmidmarketsecurity. techtarget.com** (targeted to small and midsize businesses)

US-CERT: United States Computer Readiness Team, **www.us-cert.gov** (part of the Department of Homeland Security), provides security information for both technical and nontechnical users; includes resources for implementing the NIST Framework (businesses **www.us-cert.gov/ ccubedvp/getting-started-business**) and (small and midsize businesses **https://www.us-cert.gov/ccubedvp/getting-started-smb**)

Threat Level Blog, **www.wired.com/category/security**, a part of *Wired* magazine's blog that covers privacy and security

Top 50 InfoSec Blogs

Last Updated: Monday September 28, 2015

Source: **https://digitalguardian.com/blog/top-50-infosec-blogs-you-should-be-reading**

1. Wired's Threat Level—**http://www.wired.com/category/threatlevel**
2. Roger's Information Security Blog—**http://www.infosecblog.org/**
3. Dark Reading—**http://www.darkreading.com/**
4. Krebs on Security—**http://krebsonsecurity.com/**
5. ThreatPost—**https://threatpost.com/**
6. IT Security Guru—**http://www.itsecurityguru.org/**
7. Dan Kaminsky's Blog—**http://dankaminsky.com/**
8. Security Weekly—**http://securityweekly.com/**
9. Kevin Townsend's IT Security—**http://itsecurity.co.uk/**
10. BH Consulting IT Security Watch—**http://bhconsulting.ie/security watch/**
11. Liquidmatrix Security Digest—**http://www.liquidmatrix.org/blog/**
12. Cryptogasm—**https://cryptogasm.com/**
13. Dr. Eric Cole—**http://drericcole.blogspot.com/**
14. Andrew Hay—**http://www.andrewhay.ca/**
15. McGrew Security—**http://mcgrewsecurity.com/**
16. Schneier on Security—**https://www.schneier.com/**
17. NoticeBored—**http://blog.noticebored.com/**
18. Emergent Chaos—**http://emergentchaos.com/**
19. flyingpenguin—**http://www.flyingpenguin.com/**
20. Elie Bursztein—**http://www.elie.net/blog**
21. Graham Cluley—**https://grahamcluley.com/**
22. Tony on Security—**http://perezbox.com/**

23. eLearn Security—**https://blog.elearnsecurity.com/**
24. Holistic InfoSec—**http://holisticinfosec.blogspot.com/**
25. Hacking Articles—**http://www.hackingarticles.in/**
26. SkullSecurity—**https://blog.skullsecurity.org/**
27. Security Through Education—**http://www.social-engineer.org/blog/**
28. The Harmony Guy—**http://theharmonyguy.com/blog/**
29. Jeff Soh on NetSec—**http://jeffsoh.blogspot.com/**
30. Lucius on Security—**http://luciusonsecurity.blogspot.com/**
31. Sophos Naked Security—**https://nakedsecurity.sophos.com/**
32. Matt Flynn's Identity Management Blog—**http://360tek.blogspot.com/**
33. Marco Ramilli's Blog—**http://marcoramilli.blogspot.com/**
34. WiKID Blog—**https://www.wikidsystems.com/WiKIDBlog/**
35. Rational Survivability—**http://www.rationalsurvivability.com/blog/**
36. Robert Penz Blog—**http://robert.penz.name/**
37. The Smoothwall Blog—**http://smoothwall.blogspot.com/**
38. The Security Ledger—**https://securityledger.com/**
39. Infosec Island—**http://infosecisland.com/blogs.html**
40. Lenny Zeltser on Information security—**https://zeltser.com/google-domains-registrar/**
41. DataLossDB—**http://datalossdb.org/**
42. WTFuzz—**http://wtfuzz.com/blog/**
43. Dr. InfoSec—**http://blog.drinfosec.com/**
44. Tech Wreck InfoSec Blog—**http://tech-wreckblog.blogspot.com/**
45. Uncommon Sense Security—**http://blog.uncommonsensesecurity.com/**
46. TaoSecurity—**http://taosecurity.blogspot.com/**
47. . . . And You Will Know Us by the Trail of Bits—**http://blog.trailofbits.com/**
48. The Veracode Blog—**https://www.veracode.com/blog/**
49. F-Secure Blog—**https://www.f-secure.com/weblog/**
50. Observations on InfoSec—**https://danielmiessler.com/blog/observations-infosec/**

We would (of course) add Ride the Lightning to the list! **http://ridethelightning.senseient.com/**

Further Resources

Thanks to Derek Milroy, a security specialist who was kind enough to share with our readers his personal list of security resources. He can be reached at *derekmilroy@yahoo.com*. There was very little point in reinventing the wheel, so with his gracious permission, we have simply placed additions at the end of the list below. We'd also like to thank Seth Wilson, Brian Honan, Aaron Turner, Anthony Freed, Sean Gajewski and Andrew Simmons, all of whom replied to a *Ride the Lightning* blog post asking for readers' favorite InfoSec resources. You can perform an Internet search for these resources.

Security Feeds

SANS Internet Storm Center, InfoCON: green

CNET **News.com**

SANS NewsBites

US-CERT Technical Cyber Security Alerts

CERT Advisories

CERT Announcements

SecurityFocus Vulnerabilities

DVLabs: Published Advisories

Bugtraq

Microsoft Security Content: Comprehensive Edition

Microsoft Security Advisories

Microsoft Sec Notification

Securosis Highlights

GFI Labs blog

ZeroDay Labs blog

Naked Security: Sophos

THN: The Hackers News

SecuriTeam

Packet Storm: News

Web App Security

Help Net Security: News

Full Disclosure

eWeek Security Watch

ZDnet Security: RSS Feed

Cisco Security Advisories

Verizon Business Security blog

SANS Computer Forensics and e-Discovery with Rob Lee

Common Exploits: Penetration Testing Information

FireEye Malware Intelligence Lab

TrendLabs: Malware blog by Trend Micro

AVG: Top Threats Malware Advisor Security Labs

SecurityNewsPortal.com Security Virus Alerts and News

Securelist: All Updates

Security Web Sites

Talisker Computer Network Defence Operational Picture

Talisker Network Security Tools provides salient details on every available network security product either commercial or freeware

National Vulnerability Database Home

Comprehensive CVE vulnerability database integrates all U.S. government publicly available vulnerability resources; repository of information technology security content automation

Exploits Database by Offensive Security

The Exploit Database: Exploits, Shellcode, vulnerability reports, remote exploits, local exploits, security articles, tutorials and more

Secunia Advisories: Community

SecurityTracker.com: Keep track of the latest vulnerabilities! Exhaustive Research on the Windows Security Log

Daily Dashboard, CSO Online: Security and Risk

Dark Reading, Security, Protect the Business—Enable Access: Dark Reading is the premier online resource helping information security professionals manage the balance between protection and access; it offers breaking news and analysis on attacks, breaches and vulnerabilities, as well as strategies for protecting enterprise data. It also offers guidance on setting risk management and compliance policies

Security Ninja, security research, news and guidance

Government information security news, regulations, white papers, webinars, and education: **GovInfoSecurity.com** is your source for government industry information security related news, articles, regulations, bulletins, white papers, webinars, education and events

Healthcare information security news, regulations, white papers, webinars and education: **HealthcareInfoSecurity.com**

BankInfoSecurity.com is your source for banking information security related news, articles, regulations, bulletins, white papers, webinars, education and events

InfraGard—Public Private Partnership—Federal Bureau of Investigation (FBI): Improving and extending information sharing between private industry and the government, particularly the FBI, when it comes to critical national infrastructures

International Legal Technical Standards Organization

HackerWatch.org

Hack In The Box: Keeping knowledge free

The Elite Hackers Site, by Schiz0id: Learn how to become an elite hacker today! This is the only site that will teach you the true ways of becoming a real hacker

ha.ckers.org web application security blog

InfoSec Daily: Your daily source of pwnage, policy and politics

Information security, information security positions, security training, diagrams, exploit, outerz0ne 2011, truecrypt android, isdpodcast, software engineer, infosec daily, infosec, infosec daily podcast, health information privacy and security, stuxnet, penetration, stuxnet code information, smartphone, rick hayes

Irongeek.com: Irongeek's Information Security site with tutorials, articles and other information

(IN)SECURE Magazine

Help Net Security is a daily updated information security news web site

SecurityTube

IT Security Magazine—Hakin9 **www.hakin9.org**: Hacking, IT security, covering techniques, breaking into computer systems, defense and protection methods. Hakin9 offers an in-depth look at both attack and defense, web site protection

Digital Forensics Magazine: supporting the professional computer security industry with news, views and information for the computer forensics specialist

Home Of PaulDotCom Security Podcast

HackerJournals: The premium security portal for ethical hackers

ShmooCon 2011: January 28–30

DEF CON-Hacking Conference: The Hacker Community's Foremost Social Network. Started in 1992 by the Dark Tangent, DEFCON is the world's longest running and largest underground hacking conference. Hackers, corporate IT professionals and three letter government agencies all converge on Las Vegas every summer to absorb cutting-edge hacking research from the most brilliant minds in the world and test their skills in contests of hacking might.

THOTCON: Chicago's Hacking Conference

GrrCON the premier Midwestern information security and hacking conference hosted in Grand Rapids, Mich. It features two tracks, food, and beverages for all attendees.

Black Hat-Technical Security Conference

Netcraft: Internet research, antiphishing and PCI security services: Netcraft provides monthly Internet research reports on the hosting industry and specializes in phishing detection and countermeasures.

SecLists.Org Security Mailing List Archive: Security mailing list archive for the Nmap lists, Bugtraq, full disclosure, security basics, pen-test, and dozens more. Search capabilities and RSS feeds with smart excerpts are available

RSS: Symantec Corp.

RSS List: *SC Magazine US*: Find the latest security news, SC Magazine online for products reviews, group tests, latest news and features, security news, portals, whitepapers, vulnerability alerts, jobs and events from SC magazine US.

Ziff Davis Enterprise RSS

CNET blogs: News and tech blogs; CNET blogs feature news and commentary from CNET editors and guest bloggers covering the latest news in technology, gadgets, business, Web 2.0 and much more

SANS RSS Feeds

SpiderLabs: Trustwave; SpiderLabs is an advanced security team within Trustwave focused on forensics, ethical hacking and application security testing for their premier clients; the team has performed hundreds of forensic investigations, thousands of ethical hacking exercises and hundreds application security tests globally

RSS—CSO Online: Security and risk

Security RSS feeds deliver the latest security news, critical alerts and expert opinion

ISACA RSS Feeds

ISSA: RSS Feeds

Cryptome

Digital Forensics: Computer forensic training, e-discovery; digital forensics training and computer forensics news at Forensic Focus; digital computer forensic analysis for computer forensics professionals

Shared Assessments: The Shared Assessments Program provides financial institutions and other organizations an efficient, cost-effective means of meeting internal and external compliance and audit requirements

Cloud Computing Vendors Taxonomy, OpenCrowd: Cloud Taxonomy provides information on cloud computing services and creates a dialog between cloud computing software and product vendors and consumers as well as developers to foster further understanding and adoption of cloud computing solutions

Cloutage: Tracking cloud incidents, security and outages Documents, CloudComputing, TWiki NIST Cloud

Symantec Global Threats

MessageLabs provides a range of managed services to protect, control, encrypt and archive electronic communications to more than 15,000 clients in more than 80 countries

The Research Daily (Post, Courier, Crier): A newspaper built from all the articles, blog posts, videos and photos shared by the people Sourcefire VRT follows on Twitter

incident response daily: A newspaper created by christopher ashby—built from articles, blog posts, videos and photos shared on Twitter

Common Event Expression: CEE, a standard log language for event interoperability in Electronic Systems

ActiveDirSec.Org is a dedicated global online community of IT professionals interested in active directory security

BurbSec: Chicago suburb security meet-ups

OS Feeds

WindowSecurity.com

Mark Minasi's web site

WServerNews.com

Win7news TechNet

blogs Windows

Security blog Microsoft

Security blog

People Feeds

Anton Chuvakin blog: "Security Warrior"

TaoSecurity

Branden R. Williams, business security specialist, blog

PaulDotCom

Irongeek's Security Site

Windows Incident Response

RFS blog

Ed Adams's blog

Mark Runals' blog

MadMark's blog

danielmiessler.com

Daily Dave

Jeremiah Grossman

Jesper's blog

Lenny Zeltser on Information Security

Jaime Blasco blog

Nicholas Bate

Zach's Posterous

The "RISKY BUSINESS" blog

Nigel Fenwick's blog

Mark's blog

I, Cringely

1 Raindrop

Jay Heiser

Security Nut

Following the White Rabbit: A Realistic Blog on Enterprise Security Articles Krypt3

ia RealGeneKim blog

Episteme: Belief. Knowledge. Wisdom

Dancho Danchev's blog: Mind Streams of Information Security Knowledge

Roger A. Grimes's blog

SecManiac.com

Krebs on Security

Forensic Incident Response

Inside Laura's Lab

Network Security blog

Command Line Kung Fu

Jeff Bardin's blog

Greg Martin's blog: InfoSecurity 2.0

CyberSpeak's Podcast

ShackF00

Ivan Risti?

Cloud

Cloutage.org: Latest News from the Cloud

Cloud Security Alliance blog

CSOONLINE.com: Cloud Security

EyeOnTheCloud

Cloud Security

Common Assurance Cloud blog

TWiki's CloudComputing web

Security News Feeds

CSOONLINE.com: News

CISO/CSO Security News

CSOONLINE.com Feed: Podcast

SearchSecurity: Security Wire Daily News

eWeek: RSS Feed

Info Security News

InfoWorld Tech Watch's blog

The Ethical Hacker Network RSS News Feed

CIO

Security: Infoworld

PCMag.com Security Coverage

SecurityNewsPortal.com: Computer security blogs; latest breaking computer security, antivirus and hacking news

General Feeds

BlogInfoSec.com

CSO's blog

Security Operations by Visible Risk

OSF Data Loss: Latest incidents

Data Loss

Insider Threat blog

Darknet: The Darkside

PCI DSS Compliance blog

CSOONLINE.com: PCI and compliance

eEye IT Security blog

(ISC)2 blog

Enterprise Risk Management Initiative (ERM), North Carolina State University

The H Security

SANS Institute Security Awareness Tip of the Day

US-CERT Cyber Security Tips

IT Security

securitymetrics.org:Welcome

Log Management Central

LogInspect

403 blogs Penetration

Testing WhiteHat

Security blog Think

Forward blog

NovaInfosecPortal.com

nukona's blog

Blog postings from **honeynet.org**

Perpetual Horizon

InfoSec Resources

Mandiant News

Question Defense

A Day in the Life of an Information Security Investigator

Digital Forensics Magazine blog

Forensic Focus blog

Forensic Focus

SecurityTube.Net

EFF.org Updates

Enclave Security blogs

JadedSecurity

Techworld.com Security

Infosec Island latest articles

CYBER ARMS: Computer Security

Secrecy News

Digital Threat

SANS Securing the Human

Tools

Social-Engineer.Org PodCast

Microsoft Solution Accelerators Security & Compliance

Nessus.org Plugins

Tenable Network Security

SecDocs Feed

BackTrack Linux: Penetration Testing Distribution

Penetration Testing and Security Auditing Linux Distribution

Samurai |: Download Samurai software for free at **SourceForge.net**; fast, secure and free downloads from the largest open source applications and software directory

SANS SIFT Kit/Workstation: Investigative Forensic Toolkit download; a free VMware appliance preconfigured with all the necessary tools to perform a detailed digital forensic examination

e-fense: Cybersecurity and computer forensics software; a global computer forensics and cybersecurity software company with software to assist with internal and criminal investigations

CAINE Computer Aided INvestigative Environment Live CD, computer forensics, digital forensics; NewLight computer forensics digital forensics

DFF: Open Source technology for computer forensics, data recovery, e-Discovery and incident response

Qualys BrowserCheck: A free tool that scans your browser and its plug-ins to find potential vulnerabilities and security holes and help you fix them.

IronBee: Open source web application firewall

Seccubus: Site of the open source program Seccubus, a program to easily automate vulnerability scanning with Nessus and OpenVAS; Seccubus reduces the time needed to analyze subsequent scans by delta reporting.

Spider for Windows

OSSEC: Open Source Security, Host-Based Intrusion Detection System—Top 10 free tools for IT professionals

NetWrix Corporation: Products for systems management, compliance, change management and active directory management

MD5: Command Line Message Digest Utility

Ophcrack is a Windows password cracker based on Rainbow Tables. Password Safe allows you to safely and easily create a secured and encrypted user name/password list. With Password Safe, all you have to do is create and remember a single master password of your choice to unlock and access your entire user name/password list.

FreeMind: Main page

Get Open Workbench at **SourceForge.net**; fast, secure and free downloads from the largest open source applications and software directory

PortableApps.com: Portable software for USB, portable and cloud drives

Eraser

WarVOX: Introduction

IMMUNITY: Knowing You're Secure

PacketFence: PacketFence is a free and open source network access control (NAC) system. It is actively maintained and has been deployed in numerous large-scale institutions over the past years; it can be used to effectively secure small to very large heterogeneous networks

Oxygen Forensic Suite 2011: Mobile forensic software for cell phones, smartphones and other mobile devices

default password database

default password

Microsoft Web Application Configuration Analyzer v2.0: Download the newest and most popular products and updates from Microsoft in dozens of languages

HBGary has a free tool aimed at eliminating Adobe Acrobat Reader security risks.

opendlp: Data loss prevention suite with centralized web front end to manage Windows agents and database scanners, which identifies sensitive data at rest; Google Project Hosting

Shrubbery Networks, Inc.: RANCID

hashbot

Cisco IOS Software

Checker Carbon Black Security Sensor

Wordle: Beautiful Word Clouds

Log Parser Lizard GUI: The free, powerful and versatile query software from Lizard Labs provides query access to all your text-based data

Index of computer-forensics-expert-florida-miami-palm-beach-lauderdale-dave-kleiman-forensic-training-files

Event Management Automation Protocol (EMAP): The Security Content Automation Protocol (SCAP); NIST

ToolsWatch: IT Vulnerability and ToolsWatch

Tools: Open Source Digital Forensics

Digital Forensics Magazine blog: The authoritative blog on all matters concerning cybersecurity; get the latest news and announcements from DFM and contribute to the site

Havij v1.14 Advanced SQL Injection

ShouldIChangeMyPassword.com has been created to help the average person check if their password(s) may have been compromised and need to be changed

GRC's, Password Haystacks: How Well Hidden Is Your Needle?

Security Tools: SecureState

Google Hacking Diggity Project: Stach and Liu

Live RFID Hacking System: OpenPCD

RawCap: a Free Tiny Command Line Sniffer; IT Vulnerability and ToolsWatch

AuditCasts

Security Tools Benchmarking

OWASP Zed Attack Proxy Project: OWASP

eventlog-to-syslog: Eventlog to Syslog Service for Windows (2k, XP, 2k3, 2k8+); Google Project Hosting

NumberInvestigator.com: The Comprehensive Reverse Phone Number Investigator Database

Snorby:—All About Simplicity

owade: Offline windows analysis and data extraction; Google Search

Information Sources: Professional Responsibility and Cloud Computing

American Bar Association, Commission on Ethics 20/20:

- ◆ "Issues Paper Concerning Client Confidentiality and Lawyers' Use of Technology" (September 20, 2010) (raises for discussion issues concerning confidentiality and technology and seeks comments on them, includes cloud computing), available at **www.american bar.org/content/dam/aba/migrated/ethics2020/pdfs/client**

confidentiality_issuespaper.authcheckdam.pdf or http://tinyurl
.com/3pa84hv

♦ September 2011 revised proposals for amendments to the Model
Rules concerning Outsourcing, Technology and Confidentiality, and
Technology and Client Development, available at **www.american
bar.org/groups/professional_responsibility/aba_commission_on_
ethics_20_20.html or http://tinyurl.com/3op6tx3**

R. Acello, "Get Your Head in the Cloud," *ABA Journal* (April 2010)

D. Bilinsky, blog post, "What if the Cloud Evaporates?" *Slaw*
(online magazine) (March 24, 2010), available at **http://www.slaw.
ca/2010/03/24/ what-if-the-cloud-evaporates/**

K. Brady, "Cloud Computing—Panacea or Ethical 'Black Hole' for Lawyers," *The Bencher* (November/December 2010)

Shannon Brown, "Navigating the Fog of Cloud Computing," *The Pennsylvania Lawyer* (September/October 2011)

B. Burney, S. Nelson and D. Siegel, "Flying Safely in the Clouds,"
course materials, ABA TECHSHOW 2011 (April 2011)

D. Caplan, "Lawyers in the Cloud—Cooling Shade or Impending
Thunderstorm?" course materials, ABA 2010 Annual Meeting (August
2010)

J. Dysart, "Online Applications Too Risky? One Firm Takes the
Plunge," *ABA Journal* (April 2011)

J. Feinberg and M. Grossman, "Introduction to Cloud Computing and
Its Ethical Implications—Is There a Silver Lining? (Part I of II)," *New
York Professional Responsibility Report* (May 2010)

T. Forsheit, blog post, "Legal Implications of Cloud Computing—Part
Five (Ethics or Why All Lawyers—Not Just Technogeek Lawyers Like
Me—Should Care About Data Security" (posted October 19, 2010),
available on the Info Law Group's web site, **www.infolawgroup.com** or
http://tinyurl.com/3qdt4wn

W. Hornsby and M. Lauritsen, "Going Virtual with Web Applications:
New Forms of Practice," course materials, ABA TECHSHOW 2010
(March 2010)

D. Kawairamani, "Cloud Computing: Ethical Shades of Gray," *New
York Law Journal* (March 22, 2011)

D. Kennedy, "Working in the Cloud," *ABA Journal* (August 2009)

Legalethics.com, blog post, "Google Docs: Unethical?" (March 7, 2011) (posting Google Docs' license terms), available at **www.legal ethics.com/?p=504**

J. McCauley, "Cloud Computing—A Silver Lining or Ethical Thunderstorm for Lawyers?" *Virginia Lawyer* (February 2011)

P. Mohan and S. Krause, "Up in the Cloud: Ethical Issues That Arise in the Age of Cloud Computing," *ABI Committee News*, American Bankruptcy Institute, Ethics & Professional Compensation Committee (February 2011)

C. Reach, "A Chance of Rain: Ethics and Cloud Computing," *Law Practice TODAY* (October 2010)

R. Trope and C. Ray, "The Real Realities of Cloud Computing: Ethical Issues for Lawyers, Law Firms and Judges," course materials, ABA 2010 Annual Meeting, excerpt from a book manuscript, *Head in the "Cloud"—Feet on the Ground: Understanding the Ethical Challenges of Web 2.0 for Lawyers, Law Firms and Judges* (2010)

Your ABA, "Cloud Caution: Look Before You Leap" (October 2010)

Your ABA, "Head in the Clouds Yet? Pitfalls and Benefits of Cloud Computing" (April 2010)

Mobile Security

Online Resources

CIO, Mobile Security website, **www.cio.com/category/mobile-security/**

CSO, Mobile Security website, **www.csoonline.com/category/ mobile-security/**

Federal Communications Commission, "FCC Smartphone Security Checker" (**www.fcc.gov/smartphone-security**)

InfoWorld, Mobile Security website, **http://www.infoworld.com/ category/mobile-security/**

National Institute of Standards and Technology (NIST), National Cybersecurity Center of Excellence (NCCoE), Mobile Device Security, (**https://nccoe.nist.gov/projects/building_blocks/ mobile_device_security**)

SANS Institute, a highly regarded information security research, education, and certification organization, that provides a broad range of information, both technical and basic. (**www.sans.org**) Publishes *OUCH*, a free monthly security awareness newsletter designed for common computer users. (**www.sans.org/newsletters/#ouch**) Examples of editions on mobile security topics include:

♦ "Losing Your Mobile Device" (October 2012)

♦ "Securing Your Mobile Device Apps" (February 2012)

♦ "Using Your Smartphone Securely" (February 2011)

SC Magazine, Mobile Security website, **www.scmagazine.com/mobile-security/topic/9541**

US-CERT—U.S. Computer Emergency Readiness Team, part of the U.S. Department of Homeland Security that provides both technical and basic security information. (**www.us-cert.gov**) Publishes Tips for nontechnical users. (**www.us-cert.gov/cas/tips**) Examples on mobile security include:

♦ Cyber Security Tip ST04-017 "Protecting Portable Devices: Physical Security" (last updated December 2011)

♦ Cyber Security Tip ST05-017 "Cybersecurity for Electronic Devices" (last updated December 2011)

♦ Cyber Security Tip ST05-03, "Securing Wireless Networks" (last updated March 2010)

♦ Cyber Security Tip ST04-020 "Protecting Portable Devices: Data Security" (last updated March 2010)

U.S. Department of Health and Human Services (**www.healthit.gov**)

♦ **HealthIT.gov**, Privacy & Security, "Your Mobile Device and Health Information Privacy and Security"

♦ **HealthIT.gov**, "How Can You Protect and Secure Health Information When Using a Mobile Device?

♦ **HealthIT.gov**, "You, Your Organization, and Mobile Devices"

♦ **HealthIT.gov**, "Mobile Device Privacy and Security"

♦ **HealthIT.gov**, Videos, "Securing Your Mobile Device Is Important"

Books

Rich Campagna, Subbu Iyer and Ashwin Krishin, *Mobile Security for Dummies* (John Wiley & Sons, Inc. 2011)

Stephen Fried, *Mobile Device Security* (CRC Press 2010)

John Sileo, *Smartphone Survival Guide* (Amazon Kindle Ed. 2011)

Robert Vamosi, *When Gadgets Betray Us, The Dark Side of Our Infatuation With New Technologies* (Basic Books 2011)

Stephen Wu, *A Legal Guide to Enterprise Mobile Device Management* (American Bar Association 2013) (includes a 15 page sample BYOD policy)

Reports and Papers*

CDW Reference Guide: "Securing BYOD" (March 2013)

Citrix White Paper, "BYOD and Information Security" (2013)

ComputerWorld, "Digital Spotlight: BYOD Invasion" (November 2013)

ComputerWorld, "Digital Spotlight: BYOD Morphs form Lockdown to True Mobility" (Summer 2014)

CSO, "CSO's 2015 Mobile Security Survival Guide" (January 2015)

CyLab and McAfee, Inc., "Mobility and Security: Dazzling Opportunity and Profound Challenge" (2011)

FireEye, "Out of Pocket: A Comprehensive Mobile Threat Assessment of 7 Million iOS and Android Apps" (February 2015)

Forrester Research, Inc., "The Mobile Security Playbook for 2015"

Gartner, "Critical Capabilities for Mobile Device Management" (May 2013)

Gartner, "Hype Cycle for Enterprise Mobile Security" (July 2015)

Gartner, "2015 Magic Quadrant for Enterprise Mobility Management Suites"

Gartner, "Magic Quadrant for Mobile Data Protection"

InformationWeek, "10 Things to Consider When Developing BYOD Security Policy" (September 2013)

InformationWeek, "Mobile Security" (December 2013)

InfoWorld, "Digital Spotlight: Mobile Enablement" (Winter 2014)

InfoWorld, "Mobile and BYOD" (February 2013)

InfoWorld, "Deep Dive Mobile Security" (2015)

ISACA, "Securing Mobile Devices" (2010)

Juniper Networks, "Juniper Mobile Security Report 2011" (February 2012)

Lookout Mobile Security, "Five Critical Security Steps in Three Minutes" (2012)

Lookout Mobile Security, "The State of Mobile Security 2012"

Murugiah Souppaya and Karen Scarfone, "Guidelines for Managing and Securing Mobile Devices in the Enterprise" NIST SP800-124, Rev. 1 (June 2013)

SC Magazine, "Shining a Spotlight on: Mobile Security" (May 2013)

Sophos Naked Security blog, "To encrypt or not to encrypt" (September 4, 2015)

"The Symantec Smartphone Honey Stick Project" (2012)

Trend Micro, "Enterprise Readiness of Consumer Mobile Platforms" (April 2012)

U.S. Government Accountability Office, "Information Security—Better Implementation of Controls for Mobile Devices Should Be Encouraged" (September 2012)

Articles*

Andrew Cunningham, "Phone and laptop encryption guide: Protect your stuff and yourself," *Arstechnica* (August 23, 2015)

Dionisio Zumerle, "Mobile Security Challenges in the Age of Digital Business," *Forbes* (June 10, 2015)

Orrie Dinstein, "Getting Through BYOD Without PTSD," *SciTech Lawyer* (Summer 2013)

ILTA *Peer to Peer*, cover story: "Communications Technology: Attack of the Consumer Products!" (March 2011) (includes articles on smartphone and mobile security)

Cade Metz, "Google's 'Android for Work' Gives Your Phone a Split Personality," *Wired* (February 2015)

Robert Thibadeau and Lucy Thomson, "Mobile Device Security," *SciTech Lawyer* (Summer 2013)

Malia Wollan, "Outsmarting Smartphone Thieves," *New York Times* (May 8, 2013)

*These materials are available on the Internet and can be located through online searches.

Other Resources

ENISA (The European Network and Information Security Agency): A body set up by the European Union to provide research and advice to the European Council on issues relating to information security; all their material is freely available. They have excellent resources:

Incident Response—**http://www.enisa.europa.eu/act/cert**

Security Awareness—**http://www.enisa.europa.eu/act/ar**

Risk Management—**http://www.enisa.europa.eu/act/rm**

All their publications are freely available at **http://www.enisa.europa.eu/publications**

The SANS Institute's reading room: **http://www.sans.org/reading_room/**

Blog and industry news site: **http://www.integricell.com/wordpress**

Infosec Island: **https://infosecisland.com**

Bruce Schneier's Crypto Gram: **http://www.schneier.com/crypto-gram.html**

SANS/ISC Handler's Diary: **http://isc.sans.edu/diary.html**

The Full Disclosure mailing list: **http://seclists.org/fulldisclosure/**

E-Discovery: Avoiding Disaster: **http://ediscovery.cdllpblogs.com/**

Ride the Lightning: **http://ridethelightning.senseient.com/**

APPENDIX A

Excerpts from ABA 2015 Legal Technology Survey Report

Security: Technology Policies

28. Which of the following policies governing technology use by employees does your law firm have?

		NUMBER OF LAWYERS AT ALL LOCATIONS					
	Total	Solo	2-9	10-49	50-99	100-499	500 or more
Document/records management and retention policy	54.8%	34.1%	50.4%	63.3%	70.6%	84.8%	88.5%
E-mail use policy	46.0%	22.4%	36.2%	56.7%	72.5%	86.4%	85.2%
Internet use policy	42.3%	18.1%	33.2%	52.5%	74.5%	81.8%	78.7%
Computer acceptable use policy	41.5%	19.0%	31.9%	52.5%	68.6%	78.8%	78.7%
E-mail retention policy	41.1%	21.6%	31.5%	45.0%	62.7%	84.8%	78.7%
Social media policy	33.6%	14.2%	24.1%	35.8%	54.9%	78.8%	70.5%
Employee privacy policy	31.3%	14.2%	23.3%	38.3%	47.1%	62.1%	67.2%
Don't know	10.2%	4.7%	12.5%	15.8%	13.7%	10.6%	6.6%
None	25.2%	53.9%	25.0%	6.7%	–	–	1.6%
One or more	74.8%	46.1%	75.0%	93.3%	100.0%	100.0%	98.4%
Count	766	232	232	120	51	66	61

Security: Technology Policies

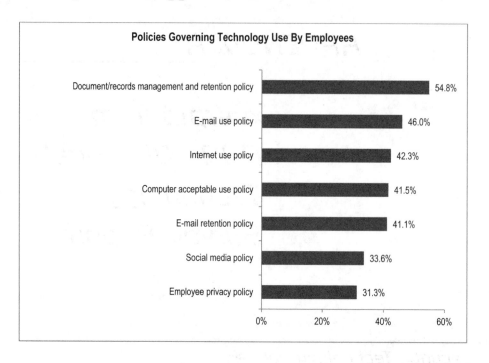

Policies Governing Technology Use By Employees

Policy	Percentage
Document/records management and retention policy	54.8%
E-mail use policy	46.0%
Internet use policy	42.3%
Computer acceptable use policy	41.5%
E-mail retention policy	41.1%
Social media policy	33.6%
Employee privacy policy	31.3%

Security: Technology Policies

29. Does your firm have a dedicated Chief Information Security Officer or other staff person charged with the firm's data security?

	Total	NUMBER OF LAWYERS AT ALL LOCATIONS					
		Solo	2-9	10-49	50-99	100-499	500 or more
Yes	34.1%	14.6%	20.9%	43.0%	55.8%	75.8%	77.0%
No	58.0%	84.5%	75.2%	41.3%	21.2%	12.1%	4.9%
Don't know	7.9%	.9%	3.8%	15.7%	23.1%	12.1%	18.0%
	100.0%	100.0%	100.0%	100.0%	100.0%	100.0%	100.0%
Count	771	233	234	121	52	66	61

Security: Technology Policies

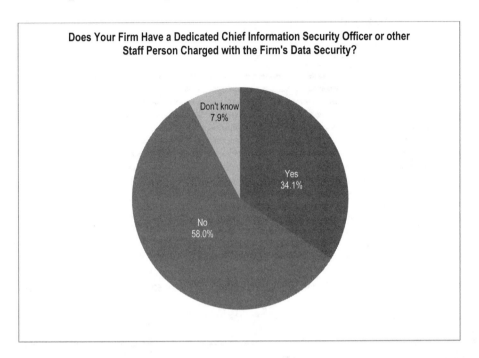

Does Your Firm Have a Dedicated Chief Information Security Officer or other Staff Person Charged with the Firm's Data Security?

Don't know 7.9%

Yes 34.1%

No 58.0%

Security: Security Tools

30. Does your firm have the following security tools?

		NUMBER OF LAWYERS AT ALL LOCATIONS					
	Total	Solo	2-9	10-49	50-99	100-499	500 or more
Spam filter	86.8%	87.6%	82.8%	86.0%	86.5%	93.9%	91.8%
Firewall (software)	79.1%	79.9%	80.3%	73.6%	73.1%	81.8%	83.6%
Anti-spyware	78.2%	82.9%	75.1%	70.2%	78.8%	83.3%	82.0%
Pop-up blocker	76.4%	82.1%	73.0%	65.3%	76.9%	80.3%	85.2%
Virus scanning (desktop/laptop)	70.0%	76.5%	67.0%	66.1%	57.7%	75.8%	68.9%
Virus scanning (email)	67.7%	68.4%	63.9%	64.5%	67.3%	80.3%	72.1%
Mandatory passwords	64.6%	53.0%	61.4%	70.2%	76.9%	80.3%	83.6%
Virus scanning (network)	60.8%	39.7%	67.0%	69.4%	67.3%	80.3%	75.4%
Firewall (hardware)	51.9%	32.9%	54.1%	59.5%	59.6%	75.8%	68.9%
Encryption (files)	41.4%	31.2%	32.6%	43.8%	51.9%	59.1%	78.7%
File access restrictions	40.5%	24.8%	30.5%	48.8%	61.5%	68.2%	73.8%
Encryption (email)	31.1%	23.5%	21.5%	33.1%	40.4%	50.0%	63.9%
Web filtering	26.3%	17.1%	13.3%	36.4%	48.1%	43.9%	54.1%
Intrusion prevention	22.4%	15.0%	14.2%	24.0%	44.2%	37.9%	44.3%
Employee monitoring	20.9%	9.0%	16.7%	28.1%	34.6%	31.8%	42.6%
Encryption (whole/full disk)	19.7%	13.7%	14.2%	15.7%	23.1%	30.3%	55.7%
Don't know	4.9%	2.1%	3.9%	8.3%	11.5%	6.1%	6.6%
Count	771	234	233	121	52	66	61

Security: Security Tools

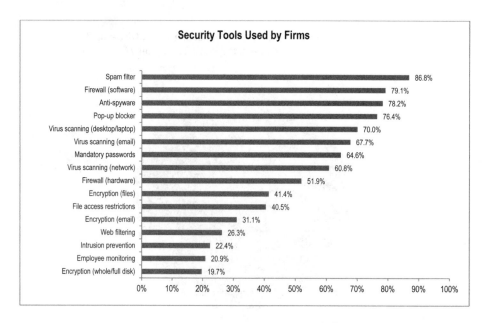

Security Tools Used by Firms

Security Tool	Percentage
Spam filter	86.8%
Firewall (software)	79.1%
Anti-spyware	78.2%
Pop-up blocker	76.4%
Virus scanning (desktop/laptop)	70.0%
Virus scanning (email)	67.7%
Mandatory passwords	64.6%
Virus scanning (network)	60.8%
Firewall (hardware)	51.9%
Encryption (files)	41.4%
File access restrictions	40.5%
Encryption (email)	31.1%
Web filtering	26.3%
Intrusion prevention	22.4%
Employee monitoring	20.9%
Encryption (whole/full disk)	19.7%

Security: Security Tools

31. Does your firm allow personal mobile devices (e.g., tablets, laptops, smartphones) to access the firm's network?

		NUMBER OF LAWYERS AT ALL LOCATIONS					
	Total	Solo	2-9	10-49	50-99	100-499	500 or more
Yes – without restriction	29.0%	34.3%	34.5%	28.1%	19.2%	19.7%	10.0%
Yes – with restrictions and/or pre-approval	51.5%	25.7%	47.8%	66.1%	76.9%	77.3%	83.3%
No	15.6%	33.9%	14.2%	2.5%	–	1.5%	5.0%
Don't know	2.2%	2.2%	2.2%	2.5%	3.8%	1.5%	1.7%
Other	1.7%	3.9%	1.3%	.8%	–	–	–
	100.0%	100.0%	100.0%	100.0%	100.0%	100.0%	100.0%
Count	765	230	232	121	52	66	60

Security: Security Tools

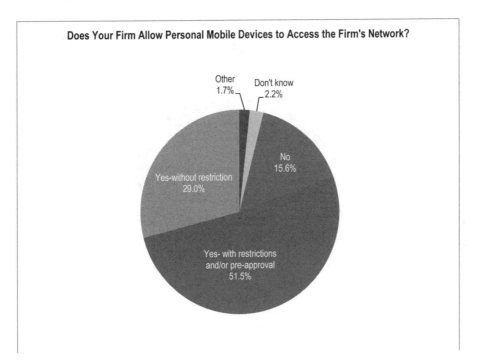

Does Your Firm Allow Personal Mobile Devices to Access the Firm's Network?

Other 1.7%

Don't know 2.2%

No 15.6%

Yes-without restriction 29.0%

Yes- with restrictions and/or pre-approval 51.5%

Security: Security Tools

32. Has your firm had a full security assessment conducted by an independent third party?

		NUMBER OF LAWYERS AT ALL LOCATIONS					
	Total	Solo	2-9	10-49	50-99	100-499	500 or more
Yes	20.2%	12.0%	20.9%	21.5%	33.3%	34.8%	21.3%
No	52.9%	87.1%	61.3%	34.7%	17.6%	7.6%	1.6%
Don't know	26.9%	.9%	17.8%	43.8%	49.0%	57.6%	77.0%
	100.0%	100.0%	100.0%	100.0%	100.0%	100.0%	100.0%
Count	766	233	230	121	51	66	61

Security: Security Tools

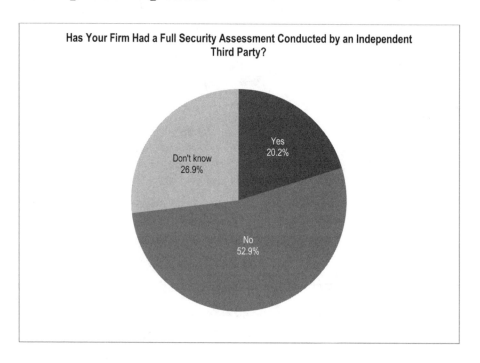

Has Your Firm Had a Full Security Assessment Conducted by an Independent Third Party?

Yes
20.2%

Don't know
26.9%

No
52.9%

Security: Security Tools

33. Has a client or potential client ever requested a security audit or otherwise asked you to verify your firm's security practices?

			NUMBER OF LAWYERS AT ALL LOCATIONS				
	Total	Solo	2-9	10-49	50-99	100-499	500 or more
Yes	12.1%	3.4%	7.3%	11.6%	21.6%	30.8%	37.7%
No	65.4%	95.3%	80.2%	52.1%	23.5%	16.9%	4.9%
Don't know	22.5%	1.3%	12.5%	36.4%	54.9%	52.3%	57.4%
	100.0%	100.0%	100.0%	100.0%	100.0%	100.0%	100.0%
Count	769	235	232	121	51	65	61

Security: Security Tools

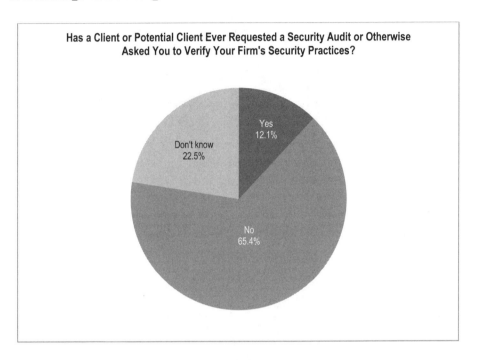

Has a Client or Potential Client Ever Requested a Security Audit or Otherwise Asked You to Verify Your Firm's Security Practices?

- Yes 12.1%
- Don't know 22.5%
- No 65.4%

Security: Security Tools

34. Does your firm have cyber liability insurance?

		NUMBER OF LAWYERS AT ALL LOCATIONS					
	Total	Solo	2-9	10-49	50-99	100-499	500 or more
Yes	11.4%	9.9%	11.3%	15.0%	7.8%	10.6%	14.8%
No	41.0%	70.4%	48.5%	21.7%	5.9%	6.1%	4.9%
Don't know	47.6%	19.7%	40.3%	63.3%	86.3%	83.3%	80.3%
	100.0%	100.0%	100.0%	100.0%	100.0%	100.0%	100.0%
Count	766	233	231	120	51	66	61

Security: Security Tools

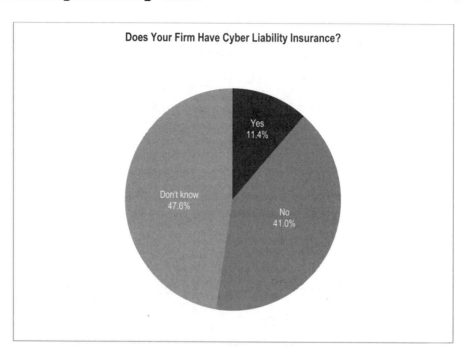

Does Your Firm Have Cyber Liability Insurance?

Yes
11.4%

Don't know
47.6%

No
41.0%

Security: Security Breaches

35. a. Has your firm ever experienced a security breach (e.g., lost/stolen computer or smartphone, hacker, break-in, website exploit)?

		NUMBER OF LAWYERS AT ALL LOCATIONS					
	Total	Solo	2-9	10-49	50-99	100-499	500 or more
Yes	15.3%	11.1%	16.0%	14.2%	15.7%	22.7%	23.0%
No	61.8%	84.2%	74.0%	55.8%	29.4%	18.2%	13.1%
Don't know	22.9%	4.7%	10.0%	30.0%	54.9%	59.1%	63.9%
	100.0%	100.0%	100.0%	100.0%	100.0%	100.0%	100.0%
Count	767	234	231	120	51	66	61

Security: Security Breaches

b. What was the result of the security breach?

		NUMBER OF LAWYERS AT ALL LOCATIONS					
	Total	Solo	2-9	10-49	50-99	100-499	500 or more
No significant business disruption or loss	60.3%	64.0%	45.9%	58.8%	87.5%	66.7%	71.4%
Downtime/loss of billable hours	30.2%	40.0%	45.9%	29.4%	25.0%	6.7%	–
Replace hardware/software	29.3%	28.0%	37.8%	29.4%	50.0%	20.0%	7.1%
Consulting fees for repair	22.4%	20.0%	40.5%	23.5%	25.0%	–	–
Destruction or loss of files	18.1%	28.0%	24.3%	23.5%	12.5%	–	–
Unauthorized access to other (non-client) sensitive data	6.9%	4.0%	10.8%	–	12.5%	13.3%	–
Notify client(s) of breach	5.2%	4.0%	10.8%	–	–	–	7.1%
Unauthorized access to sensitive client data	2.6%	–	5.4%	–	–	–	7.1%
Other	3.4%	4.0%	2.7%	5.9%	–	6.7%	–
Don't know	7.8%	–	2.7%	5.9%	–	20.0%	28.6%
Count	116	25	37	17	8	15	14

Security: Viruses/Spyware/Malware

36. a. Has your law firm technology ever been infected with a virus/spyware/malware?

		NUMBER OF LAWYERS AT ALL LOCATIONS					
	Total	Solo	2-9	10-49	50-99	100-499	500 or more
Yes	42.4%	43.7%	43.1%	51.7%	39.2%	25.8%	36.7%
No	34.9%	52.4%	43.1%	23.3%	15.7%	10.6%	3.3%
Don't know	22.7%	3.9%	13.8%	25.0%	45.1%	63.6%	60.0%
	100.0%	100.0%	100.0%	100.0%	100.0%	100.0%	100.0%
Count	754	229	225	120	51	66	60

b. What business losses/breaches resulted from the virus/spyware/malware attack?

		NUMBER OF LAWYERS AT ALL LOCATIONS					
	Total	Solo	2-9	10-49	50-99	100-499	500 or more
No significant business disruption or loss	56.5%	65.3%	52.6%	61.3%	36.8%	47.1%	40.9%
Downtime/loss of billable hours	37.5%	30.6%	46.4%	41.9%	42.1%	17.6%	22.7%
Consulting fees for repair	36.3%	36.7%	49.5%	37.1%	31.6%	–	4.5%
Temporary loss of network access	26.8%	15.3%	35.1%	27.4%	52.6%	23.5%	18.2%
Replace hardware/software	16.1%	16.3%	22.7%	12.9%	15.8%	–	9.1%
Temporary loss of web site access	13.9%	14.3%	20.6%	6.5%	31.6%	–	–
Destruction or loss of files	12.6%	16.3%	16.5%	4.8%	10.5%	5.9%	9.1%
Unauthorized access to other (non-client) sensitive data	.9%	–	2.1%	–	5.3%	–	–
Unauthorized access to sensitive client data	.9%	–	3.1%	–	–	–	–
Other	1.3%	1.0%	1.0%	3.2%	–	–	–
Don't know	9.8%	3.1%	2.1%	12.9%	26.3%	35.3%	31.8%
Count	317	98	97	62	19	17	22

Security: Disaster Recovery and Business Continuity

37. Does your firm have an incident response plan to address a security breach?

		NUMBER OF LAWYERS AT ALL LOCATIONS					
	Total	Solo	2-9	10-49	50-99	100-499	500 or more
Yes	27.9%	21.6%	19.7%	33.9%	36.0%	38.5%	55.0%
No	47.4%	76.6%	62.9%	23.7%	10.0%	3.1%	1.7%
Don't know	24.7%	1.7%	17.5%	42.4%	54.0%	58.5%	43.3%
	100.0%	100.0%	100.0%	100.0%	100.0%	100.0%	100.0%
Count	757	231	229	118	50	65	60

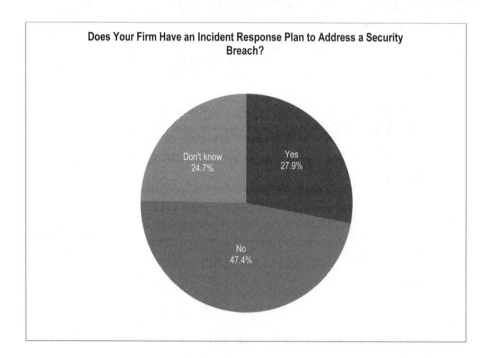

Does Your Firm Have an Incident Response Plan to Address a Security Breach?

Don't know 24.7%

Yes 27.9%

No 47.4%

Security: Disaster Recovery and Business Continuity

38. Does your firm have a disaster recovery/business continuity plan?

	Total	NUMBER OF LAWYERS AT ALL LOCATIONS					
		Solo	2-9	10-49	50-99	100-499	500 or more
Yes	48.8%	44.3%	40.3%	50.0%	60.0%	64.6%	71.7%
No	32.2%	54.8%	42.4%	13.6%	4.0%	1.5%	–
Don't know	19.0%	.9%	17.3%	36.4%	36.0%	33.8%	28.3%
	100.0%	100.0%	100.0%	100.0%	100.0%	100.0%	100.0%
Count	758	230	231	118	50	65	60

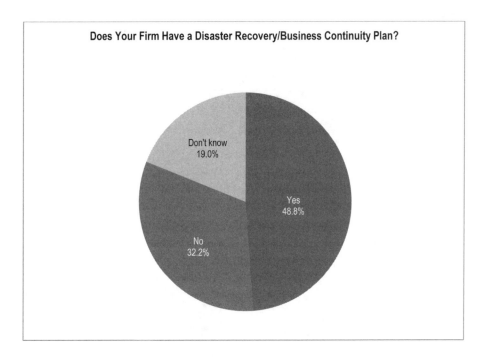

Does Your Firm Have a Disaster Recovery/Business Continuity Plan?

Security: Disaster Recovery and Business Continuity

39. Has your firm experienced a hard drive failure?

		NUMBER OF LAWYERS AT ALL LOCATIONS					
	Total	Solo	2-9	10-49	50-99	100-499	500 or more
Yes	37.4%	41.6%	42.4%	38.8%	31.4%	19.7%	18.6%
No	36.5%	57.5%	39.7%	27.6%	13.7%	12.1%	8.5%
Don't know	26.1%	.9%	17.9%	33.6%	54.9%	68.2%	72.9%
	100.0%	100.0%	100.0%	100.0%	100.0%	100.0%	100.0%
Count	758	233	229	116	51	66	59

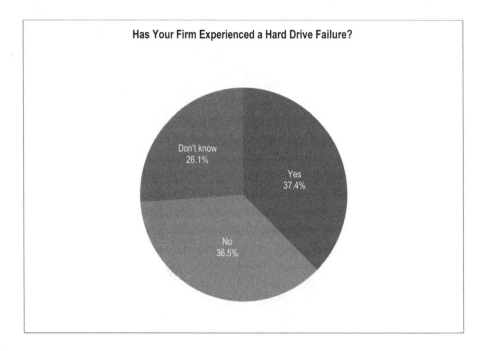

Has Your Firm Experienced a Hard Drive Failure?

Don't know 26.1%

Yes 37.4%

No 36.5%

Security: Disaster Recovery and Business Continuity

40. Has your firm experienced a natural or man-made disaster (e.g. fire, flood)?

	Total	NUMBER OF LAWYERS AT ALL LOCATIONS					
		Solo	2-9	10-49	50-99	100-499	500 or more
Yes	17.1%	9.5%	11.7%	21.8%	28.0%	25.8%	40.7%
No	69.9%	89.2%	82.7%	64.7%	42.0%	39.4%	11.9%
Don't know	13.0%	1.3%	5.6%	13.4%	30.0%	34.8%	47.5%
	100.0%	100.0%	100.0%	100.0%	100.0%	100.0%	100.0%
Count	760	231	231	119	50	66	59

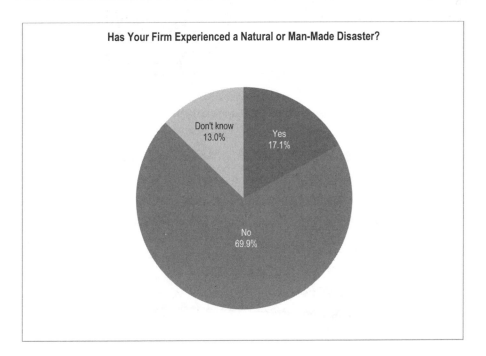

Has Your Firm Experienced a Natural or Man-Made Disaster?

Security: Backup

41. How does your firm back up its computer files?

		NUMBER OF LAWYERS AT ALL LOCATIONS					
	Total	Solo	2-9	10-49	50-99	100-499	500 or more
External hard drive	41.9%	67.0%	43.7%	35.6%	11.8%	15.2%	5.0%
Offsite (e.g., store backups at home, bank, other office)	31.2%	21.9%	33.3%	43.2%	37.3%	33.3%	28.3%
Online (e.g., Mozy, Carbonite)	25.8%	38.2%	32.9%	14.4%	13.7%	6.1%	5.0%
Network attached storage (NAS)	15.6%	11.2%	19.5%	20.3%	19.6%	10.6%	10.0%
USB	10.5%	23.2%	7.8%	3.4%	3.9%	–	1.7%
Tape	10.1%	1.3%	17.3%	13.6%	9.8%	13.6%	6.7%
CD	7.2%	13.3%	6.5%	5.1%	–	3.0%	–
RAID	6.6%	4.3%	10.8%	7.6%	2.0%	3.0%	1.7%
DVD	4.2%	6.9%	3.5%	5.9%	–	–	–
Other	3.4%	6.0%	3.0%	2.5%	4.0%	–	–
Don't back up	.7%	1.7%	.4%	–	–	–	–
Don't know	22.1%	2.6%	11.3%	30.5%	39.2%	60.6%	66.7%
Count	763	233	231	118	51	66	60

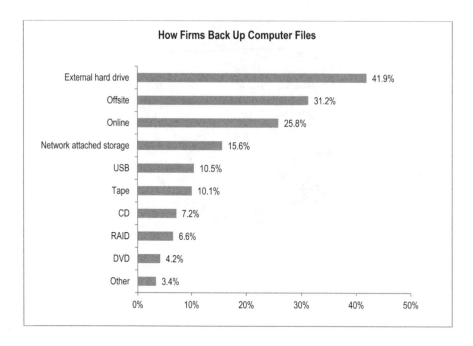

Security: Backup

(Question 42 is based on respondents who indicated that firms back up its computer files in Question 41)

42. At the minimum, how often does your firm back up its computer files?

		NUMBER OF LAWYERS AT ALL LOCATIONS					
	Total	Solo	2-9	10-49	50-99	100-499	500 or more
Once a day	48.8%	36.7%	60.1%	58.5%	50.0%	45.8%	31.6%
More than one time a day	19.4%	18.6%	16.7%	22.0%	16.7%	33.3%	31.6%
Weekly	13.4%	22.2%	11.8%	3.7%	6.7%	–	–
Monthly	4.6%	10.0%	2.0%	–	3.3%	–	–
Quarterly	2.1%	4.1%	1.0%	–	–	–	–
Other	2.9%	5.4%	2.0%	1.2%	–	–	–
Don't know	8.8%	3.2%	6.4%	14.6%	23.3%	20.8%	36.8%
	100.0%	100.0%	100.0%	100.0%	100.0%	100.0%	100.0%
Count	582	221	203	82	30	24	19

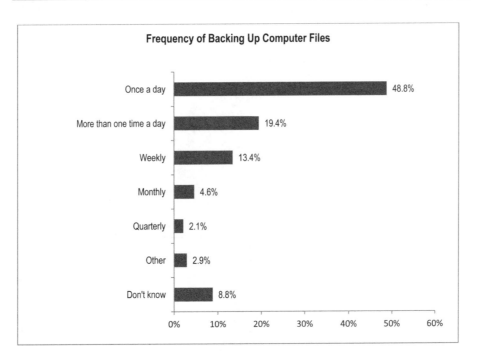

Frequency of Backing Up Computer Files

- Once a day — 48.8%
- More than one time a day — 19.4%
- Weekly — 13.4%
- Monthly — 4.6%
- Quarterly — 2.1%
- Other — 2.9%
- Don't know — 8.8%

APPENDIX B

Selected ABA Model Rules of Professional Conduct

Rule 1.1: Competence

Client-Lawyer Relationship
Rule 1.1 Competence

A lawyer shall provide competent representation to a client. Competent representation requires the legal knowledge, skill, thoroughness and preparation reasonably necessary for the representation.

Comment on Rule 1.1
Client-Lawyer Relationship
Rule 1.1 Competence—Comment

Legal Knowledge and Skill

[1] In determining whether a lawyer employs the requisite knowledge and skill in a particular matter, relevant factors include the relative complexity and specialized nature of the matter, the lawyer's general experience, the lawyer's training and experience in the field in question, the preparation and study the lawyer is able to give the matter and whether it is feasible to refer the matter to, or associate or consult with, a lawyer of established competence in the field in question. In many instances, the required proficiency is that of a general practitioner. Expertise in a particular field of law may be required in some circumstances.

[2] A lawyer need not necessarily have special training or prior experience to handle legal problems of a type with which the lawyer is unfamiliar. A newly admitted lawyer can be as competent as a practitioner with long experience. Some important legal skills, such as the analysis of precedent, the evaluation of evidence and legal drafting, are required in all legal problems. Perhaps the most fundamental legal skill consists of determining what kind of legal problems a situation may involve, a skill that necessarily transcends any particular specialized knowledge. A lawyer can provide adequate representation in a wholly novel field through necessary study. Competent representation can also be provided through the association of a lawyer of established competence in the field in question.

[3] In an emergency a lawyer may give advice or assistance in a matter in which the lawyer does not have the skill ordinarily required where referral to or consultation or association with another lawyer would be impractical. Even in an emergency, however, assistance should be limited to that reasonably necessary in the circumstances, for ill-considered action under emergency conditions can jeopardize the client's interest.

[4] A lawyer may accept representation where the requisite level of competence can be achieved by reasonable preparation. This applies as well to a lawyer who is appointed as counsel for an unrepresented person. See also Rule 6.2.

Thoroughness and Preparation
[5] Competent handling of a particular matter includes inquiry into and analysis of the factual and legal elements of the problem, and use of methods and procedures meeting the standards of competent practitioners. It also includes adequate preparation. The required attention and preparation are determined in part by what is at stake; major litigation and complex transactions ordinarily require more extensive treatment than matters of lesser complexity and consequence. An agreement between the lawyer and the client regarding the scope of the representation may limit the matters for which the lawyer is responsible. See Rule 1.2(c).

Retaining or Contracting With Other Lawyers
[6] Before a lawyer retains or contracts with other lawyers outside the lawyer's own firm to provide or assist in the provision of legal services to a client, the lawyer should ordinarily obtain informed consent from the client and must reasonably believe that the other lawyers' services will contribute to the competent and ethical representation of the client. See also Rules 1.2 (allocation of authority), 1.4 (communication with client), 1.5(e) (fee sharing), 1.6 (confidentiality), and 5.5(a) (unauthorized practice

of law). The reasonableness of the decision to retain or contract with other lawyers outside the lawyer's own firm will depend upon the circumstances, including the education, experience and reputation of the nonfirm lawyers; the nature of the services assigned to the nonfirm lawyers; and the legal protections, professional conduct rules, and ethical environments of the jurisdictions in which the services will be performed, particularly relating to confidential information.

[7] When lawyers from more than one law firm are providing legal services to the client on a particular matter, the lawyers ordinarily should consult with each other and the client about the scope of their respective representations and the allocation of responsibility among them. See Rule 1.2. When making allocations of responsibility in a matter pending before a tribunal, lawyers and parties may have additional obligations that are a matter of law beyond the scope of these Rules.

Maintaining Competence
[8] To maintain the requisite knowledge and skill, a lawyer should keep abreast of changes in the law and its practice, including the benefits and risks associated with relevant technology, engage in continuing study and education and comply with all continuing legal education requirements to which the lawyer is subject.

Rule 1.6: Confidentiality of Information

Client-Lawyer Relationship
Rule 1.6 Confidentiality Of Information
(a) A lawyer shall not reveal information relating to the representation of a client unless the client gives informed consent, the disclosure is impliedly authorized in order to carry out the representation or the disclosure is permitted by paragraph (b).

(b) A lawyer may reveal information relating to the representation of a client to the extent the lawyer reasonably believes necessary:

(1) to prevent reasonably certain death or substantial bodily harm;

(2) to prevent the client from committing a crime or fraud that is reasonably certain to result in substantial injury to the financial interests or property of another and in furtherance of which the client has used or is using the lawyer's services;

(3) to prevent, mitigate or rectify substantial injury to the financial interests or property of another that is reasonably certain to result or

has resulted from the client's commission of a crime or fraud in furtherance of which the client has used the lawyer's services;

(4) to secure legal advice about the lawyer's compliance with these Rules;

(5) to establish a claim or defense on behalf of the lawyer in a controversy between the lawyer and the client, to establish a defense to a criminal charge or civil claim against the lawyer based upon conduct in which the client was involved, or to respond to allegations in any proceeding concerning the lawyer's representation of the client;

(6) to comply with other law or a court order; or

(7) to detect and resolve conflicts of interest arising from the lawyer's change of employment or from changes in the composition or ownership of a firm, but only if the revealed information would not compromise the attorney-client privilege or otherwise prejudice the client.

(c) A lawyer shall make reasonable efforts to prevent the inadvertent or unauthorized disclosure of, or unauthorized access to, information relating to the representation of a client.

Comment on Rule 1.6
Client-Lawyer Relationship
Rule 1.6 Confidentiality of Information—Comment

[1] This Rule governs the disclosure by a lawyer of information relating to the representation of a client during the lawyer's representation of the client. See Rule 1.18 for the lawyer's duties with respect to information provided to the lawyer by a prospective client, Rule 1.9(c)(2) for the lawyer's duty not to reveal information relating to the lawyer's prior representation of a former client and Rules 1.8(b) and 1.9(c)(1) for the lawyer's duties with respect to the use of such information to the disadvantage of clients and former clients.

[2] A fundamental principle in the client-lawyer relationship is that, in the absence of the client's informed consent, the lawyer must not reveal information relating to the representation. See Rule 1.0(e) for the definition of informed consent. This contributes to the trust that is the hallmark of the client-lawyer relationship. The client is thereby encouraged to seek legal assistance and to communicate fully and frankly with the lawyer even as to embarrassing or legally damaging subject matter. The lawyer needs this information to represent the client effectively and, if necessary, to advise the client to refrain from wrongful conduct. Almost without exception, clients come to lawyers in order to determine their rights and what

is, in the complex of laws and regulations, deemed to be legal and correct. Based upon experience, lawyers know that almost all clients follow the advice given, and the law is upheld.

[3] The principle of client-lawyer confidentiality is given effect by related bodies of law: the attorney-client privilege, the work product doctrine and the rule of confidentiality established in professional ethics. The attorney-client privilege and work product doctrine apply in judicial and other proceedings in which a lawyer may be called as a witness or otherwise required to produce evidence concerning a client. The rule of client-lawyer confidentiality applies in situations other than those where evidence is sought from the lawyer through compulsion of law. The confidentiality rule, for example, applies not only to matters communicated in confidence by the client but also to all information relating to the representation, whatever its source. A lawyer may not disclose such information except as authorized or required by the Rules of Professional Conduct or other law. See also Scope.

[4] Paragraph (a) prohibits a lawyer from revealing information relating to the representation of a client. This prohibition also applies to disclosures by a lawyer that do not in themselves reveal protected information but could reasonably lead to the discovery of such information by a third person. A lawyer's use of a hypothetical to discuss issues relating to the representation is permissible so long as there is no reasonable likelihood that the listener will be able to ascertain the identity of the client or the situation involved.

Authorized Disclosure

[5] Except to the extent that the client's instructions or special circumstances limit that authority, a lawyer is impliedly authorized to make disclosures about a client when appropriate in carrying out the representation. In some situations, for example, a lawyer may be impliedly authorized to admit a fact that cannot properly be disputed or to make a disclosure that facilitates a satisfactory conclusion to a matter. Lawyers in a firm may, in the course of the firm's practice, disclose to each other information relating to a client of the firm, unless the client has instructed that particular information be confined to specified lawyers.

Disclosure Adverse to Client

[6] Although the public interest is usually best served by a strict rule requiring lawyers to preserve the confidentiality of information relating to the representation of their clients, the confidentiality rule is subject to limited exceptions. Paragraph (b)(1) recognizes the overriding value of life and

physical integrity and permits disclosure reasonably necessary to prevent reasonably certain death or substantial bodily harm. Such harm is reasonably certain to occur if it will be suffered imminently or if there is a present and substantial threat that a person will suffer such harm at a later date if the lawyer fails to take action necessary to eliminate the threat. Thus, a lawyer who knows that a client has accidentally discharged toxic waste into a town's water supply may reveal this information to the authorities if there is a present and substantial risk that a person who drinks the water will contract a life-threatening or debilitating disease and the lawyer's disclosure is necessary to eliminate the threat or reduce the number of victims.

[7] Paragraph (b)(2) is a limited exception to the rule of confidentiality that permits the lawyer to reveal information to the extent necessary to enable affected persons or appropriate authorities to prevent the client from committing a crime or fraud, as defined in Rule 1.0(d), that is reasonably certain to result in substantial injury to the financial or property interests of another and in furtherance of which the client has used or is using the lawyer's services. Such a serious abuse of the client-lawyer relationship by the client forfeits the protection of this Rule. The client can, of course, prevent such disclosure by refraining from the wrongful conduct. Although paragraph (b)(2) does not require the lawyer to reveal the client's misconduct, the lawyer may not counsel or assist the client in conduct the lawyer knows is criminal or fraudulent. See Rule 1.2(d). See also Rule 1.16 with respect to the lawyer's obligation or right to withdraw from the representation of the client in such circumstances, and Rule 1.13(c), which permits the lawyer, where the client is an organization, to reveal information relating to the representation in limited circumstances.

[8] Paragraph (b)(3) addresses the situation in which the lawyer does not learn of the client's crime or fraud until after it has been consummated. Although the client no longer has the option of preventing disclosure by refraining from the wrongful conduct, there will be situations in which the loss suffered by the affected person can be prevented, rectified or mitigated. In such situations, the lawyer may disclose information relating to the representation to the extent necessary to enable the affected persons to prevent or mitigate reasonably certain losses or to attempt to recoup their losses. Paragraph (b)(3) does not apply when a person who has committed a crime or fraud thereafter employs a lawyer for representation concerning that offense.

[9] A lawyer's confidentiality obligations do not preclude a lawyer from securing confidential legal advice about the lawyer's personal responsibility to comply with these Rules. In most situations, disclosing information

to secure such advice will be impliedly authorized for the lawyer to carry out the representation. Even when the disclosure is not impliedly authorized, paragraph (b)(4) permits such disclosure because of the importance of a lawyer's compliance with the Rules of Professional Conduct.

[10] Where a legal claim or disciplinary charge alleges complicity of the lawyer in a client's conduct or other misconduct of the lawyer involving representation of the client, the lawyer may respond to the extent the lawyer reasonably believes necessary to establish a defense. The same is true with respect to a claim involving the conduct or representation of a former client. Such a charge can arise in a civil, criminal, disciplinary or other proceeding and can be based on a wrong allegedly committed by the lawyer against the client or on a wrong alleged by a third person, for example, a person claiming to have been defrauded by the lawyer and client acting together. The lawyer's right to respond arises when an assertion of such complicity has been made. Paragraph (b)(5) does not require the lawyer to await the commencement of an action or proceeding that charges such complicity, so that the defense may be established by responding directly to a third party who has made such an assertion. The right to defend also applies, of course, where a proceeding has been commenced.

[11] A lawyer entitled to a fee is permitted by paragraph (b)(5) to prove the services rendered in an action to collect it. This aspect of the rule expresses the principle that the beneficiary of a fiduciary relationship may not exploit it to the detriment of the fiduciary.

[12] Other law may require that a lawyer disclose information about a client. Whether such a law supersedes Rule 1.6 is a question of law beyond the scope of these Rules. When disclosure of information relating to the representation appears to be required by other law, the lawyer must discuss the matter with the client to the extent required by Rule 1.4. If, however, the other law supersedes this Rule and requires disclosure, paragraph (b)(6) permits the lawyer to make such disclosures as are necessary to comply with the law.

Detection of Conflicts of Interest
[13] Paragraph (b)(7) recognizes that lawyers in different firms may need to disclose limited information to each other to detect and resolve conflicts of interest, such as when a lawyer is considering an association with another firm, two or more firms are considering a merger, or a lawyer is considering the purchase of a law practice. See Rule 1.17, Comment [7]. Under these circumstances, lawyers and law firms are permitted to disclose limited information, but only once substantive discussions regarding the new relationship have occurred. Any such disclosure should ordinarily include

no more than the identity of the persons and entities involved in a matter, a brief summary of the general issues involved, and information about whether the matter has terminated. Even this limited information, however, should be disclosed only to the extent reasonably necessary to detect and resolve conflicts of interest that might arise from the possible new relationship. Moreover, the disclosure of any information is prohibited if it would compromise the attorney-client privilege or otherwise prejudice the client (e.g., the fact that a corporate client is seeking advice on a corporate takeover that has not been publicly announced; that a person has consulted a lawyer about the possibility of divorce before the person's intentions are known to the person's spouse; or that a person has consulted a lawyer about a criminal investigation that has not led to a public charge). Under those circumstances, paragraph (a) prohibits disclosure unless the client or former client gives informed consent. A lawyer's fiduciary duty to the lawyer's firm may also govern a lawyer's conduct when exploring an association with another firm and is beyond the scope of these Rules.

[14] Any information disclosed pursuant to paragraph (b)(7) may be used or further disclosed only to the extent necessary to detect and resolve conflicts of interest. Paragraph (b)(7) does not restrict the use of information acquired by means independent of any disclosure pursuant to paragraph (b)(7). Paragraph (b)(7) also does not affect the disclosure of information within a law firm when the disclosure is otherwise authorized, see Comment [5], such as when a lawyer in a firm discloses information to another lawyer in the same firm to detect and resolve conflicts of interest that could arise in connection with undertaking a new representation.

[15] A lawyer may be ordered to reveal information relating to the representation of a client by a court or by another tribunal or governmental entity claiming authority pursuant to other law to compel the disclosure. Absent informed consent of the client to do otherwise, the lawyer should assert on behalf of the client all nonfrivolous claims that the order is not authorized by other law or that the information sought is protected against disclosure by the attorney-client privilege or other applicable law. In the event of an adverse ruling, the lawyer must consult with the client about the possibility of appeal to the extent required by Rule 1.4. Unless review is sought, however, paragraph (b)(6) permits the lawyer to comply with the court's order.

[16] Paragraph (b) permits disclosure only to the extent the lawyer reasonably believes the disclosure is necessary to accomplish one of the purposes specified. Where practicable, the lawyer should first seek to persuade the client to take suitable action to obviate the need for disclosure. In any case, a disclosure adverse to the client's interest should be no greater than the

lawyer reasonably believes necessary to accomplish the purpose. If the disclosure will be made in connection with a judicial proceeding, the disclosure should be made in a manner that limits access to the information to the tribunal or other persons having a need to know it and appropriate protective orders or other arrangements should be sought by the lawyer to the fullest extent practicable.

[17] Paragraph (b) permits but does not require the disclosure of information relating to a client's representation to accomplish the purposes specified in paragraphs (b)(1) through (b)(6). In exercising the discretion conferred by this Rule, the lawyer may consider such factors as the nature of the lawyer's relationship with the client and with those who might be injured by the client, the lawyer's own involvement in the transaction and factors that may extenuate the conduct in question. A lawyer's decision not to disclose as permitted by paragraph (b) does not violate this Rule. Disclosure may be required, however, by other Rules. Some Rules require disclosure only if such disclosure would be permitted by paragraph (b). See Rules 1.2(d), 4.1(b), 8.1 and 8.3. Rule 3.3, on the other hand, requires disclosure in some circumstances regardless of whether such disclosure is permitted by this Rule. See Rule 3.3(c).

Acting Competently to Preserve Confidentiality

[18] Paragraph (c) requires a lawyer to act competently to safeguard information relating to the representation of a client against unauthorized access by third parties and against inadvertent or unauthorized disclosure by the lawyer or other persons who are participating in the representation of the client or who are subject to the lawyer's supervision. See Rules 1.1, 5.1 and 5.3. The unauthorized access to, or the inadvertent or unauthorized disclosure of, information relating to the representation of a client does not constitute a violation of paragraph (c) if the lawyer has made reasonable efforts to prevent the access or disclosure. Factors to be considered in determining the reasonableness of the lawyer's efforts include, but are not limited to, the sensitivity of the information, the likelihood of disclosure if additional safeguards are not employed, the cost of employing additional safeguards, the difficulty of implementing the safeguards, and the extent to which the safeguards adversely affect the lawyer's ability to represent clients (e.g., by making a device or important piece of software excessively difficult to use). A client may require the lawyer to implement special security measures not required by this Rule or may give informed consent to forgo security measures that would otherwise be required by this Rule. Whether a lawyer may be required to take additional steps to safeguard a client's information in order to comply with other law, such as state and federal laws that govern data privacy or that impose notifica-

tion requirements upon the loss of, or unauthorized access to, electronic information, is beyond the scope of these Rules. For a lawyer's duties when sharing information with nonlawyers outside the lawyer's own firm, see Rule 5.3, Comments [3]-[4].

[19] When transmitting a communication that includes information relating to the representation of a client, the lawyer must take reasonable precautions to prevent the information from coming into the hands of unintended recipients. This duty, however, does not require that the lawyer use special security measures if the method of communication affords a reasonable expectation of privacy. Special circumstances, however, may warrant special precautions. Factors to be considered in determining the reasonableness of the lawyer's expectation of confidentiality include the sensitivity of the information and the extent to which the privacy of the communication is protected by law or by a confidentiality agreement. A client may require the lawyer to implement special security measures not required by this Rule or may give informed consent to the use of a means of communication that would otherwise be prohibited by this Rule. Whether a lawyer may be required to take additional steps in order to comply with other law, such as state and federal laws that govern data privacy, is beyond the scope of these Rules.

Former Client

[20] The duty of confidentiality continues after the client-lawyer relationship has terminated. See Rule 1.9(c)(2). See Rule 1.9(c)(1) for the prohibition against using such information to the disadvantage of the former client.

Rule 5.3: Responsibilities Regarding Nonlawyer Assistance

With respect to a nonlawyer employed or retained by or associated with a lawyer:

(a) a partner, and a lawyer who individually or together with other lawyers possesses comparable managerial authority in a law firm shall make reasonable efforts to ensure that the firm has in effect measures giving reasonable assurance that the person's conduct is compatible with the professional obligations of the lawyer;

(b) a lawyer having direct supervisory authority over the nonlawyer shall make reasonable efforts to ensure that the person's conduct is compatible with the professional obligations of the lawyer; and

(c) a lawyer shall be responsible for conduct of such a person that would be a violation of the Rules of Professional Conduct if engaged in by a lawyer if:

> (1) the lawyer orders or, with the knowledge of the specific conduct, ratifies the conduct involved; or

> (2) the lawyer is a partner or has comparable managerial authority in the law firm in which the person is employed, or has direct supervisory authority over the person, and knows of the conduct at a time when its consequences can be avoided or mitigated but fails to take reasonable remedial action.

Comment on Rule 5.3
Law Firms And Associations
Rule 5.3 Responsibilities Regarding Nonlawyer Assistance—Comment

[1] Paragraph (a) requires lawyers with managerial authority within a law firm to make reasonable efforts to ensure that the firm has in effect measures giving reasonable assurance that nonlawyers in the firm and nonlawyers outside the firm who work on firm matters act in a way compatible with the professional obligations of the lawyer. See Comment [6] to Rule 1.1 (retaining lawyers outside the firm) and Comment [1] to Rule 5.1 (responsibilities with respect to lawyers within a firm). Paragraph (b) applies to lawyers who have supervisory authority over such nonlawyers within or outside the firm. Paragraph (c) specifies the circumstances in which a lawyer is responsible for the conduct of such nonlawyers within or outside the firm that would be a violation of the Rules of Professional Conduct if engaged in by a lawyer.

Nonlawyers Within the Firm

[2] Lawyers generally employ assistants in their practice, including secretaries, investigators, law student interns, and paraprofessionals. Such assistants, whether employees or independent contractors, act for the lawyer in rendition of the lawyer's professional services. A lawyer must give such assistants appropriate instruction and supervision concerning the ethical aspects of their employment, particularly regarding the obligation not to disclose information relating to representation of the client, and should be responsible for their work product. The measures employed in supervising nonlawyers should take account of the fact that they do not have legal training and are not subject to professional discipline.

Nonlawyers Outside the Firm

[3] A lawyer may use nonlawyers outside the firm to assist the lawyer in rendering legal services to the client. Examples include the retention of an investigative or paraprofessional service, hiring a document management company to create and maintain a database for complex litigation, sending client documents to a third party for printing or scanning, and using an Internet-based service to store client information. When using such services outside the firm, a lawyer must make reasonable efforts to ensure that the services are provided in a manner that is compatible with the lawyer's professional obligations. The extent of this obligation will depend upon the circumstances, including the education, experience and reputation of the nonlawyer; the nature of the services involved; the terms of any arrangements concerning the protection of client information; and the legal and ethical environments of the jurisdictions in which the services will be performed, particularly with regard to confidentiality. See also Rules 1.1 (competence), 1.2 (allocation of authority), 1.4 (communication with client), 1.6 (confidentiality), 5.4(a) (professional independence of the lawyer), and 5.5(a) (unauthorized practice of law). When retaining or directing a nonlawyer outside the firm, a lawyer should communicate directions appropriate under the circumstances to give reasonable assurance that the nonlawyer's conduct is compatible with the professional obligations of the lawyer.

[4] Where the client directs the selection of a particular nonlawyer service provider outside the firm, the lawyer ordinarily should agree with the client concerning the allocation of responsibility for monitoring as between the client and the lawyer. See Rule 1.2. When making such an allocation in a matter pending before a tribunal, lawyers and parties may have additional obligations that are a matter of law beyond the scope of these Rules.

APPENDIX C

Pennsylvania Ethics Opinion— Cloud Computing

Your Other Partner

PENNSYLVANIA BAR ASSOCIATION COMMITTEE ON LEGAL ETHICS AND PROFESSIONAL RESPONSIBILITY

ETHICAL OBLIGATIONS FOR ATTORNEYS USING CLOUD COMPUTING/ SOFTWARE AS A SERVICE WHILE FULFILLING THE DUTIES OF CONFIDENTIALITY AND PRESERVATION OF CLIENT PROPERTY

FORMAL OPINION 2011-200

I.   Introduction and Summary

If an attorney uses a Smartphone or an iPhone, or uses web-based electronic mail (e-mail) such as Gmail, Yahoo!, Hotmail or AOL Mail, or uses products such as Google Docs, Microsoft Office 365 or Dropbox, the attorney is using "cloud computing." While there are many technical ways to describe cloud computing, perhaps the best description is that cloud computing is merely "a fancy way of saying stuff's not on your computer." [1]

From a more technical perspective, "cloud computing" encompasses several similar types of services under different names and brands, including: web-based e-mail, online data storage, software-as-a-service ("SaaS"), platform-as-a-service ("PaaS"), infrastructure-as-a-service ("IaaS"), Amazon Elastic Cloud Compute ("Amazon EC2"), and Google Docs.

This opinion places all such software and services under the "cloud computing" label, as each raises essentially the same ethical issues. In particular, the central question posed by "cloud computing" may be summarized as follows:

> May an attorney ethically store confidential client material in "the cloud"?

In response to this question, this Committee concludes:

> Yes. An attorney may ethically allow client confidential material to be stored in "the cloud" provided the attorney takes reasonable care to assure that (1) all such materials remain confidential, and (2) reasonable safeguards are employed to ensure that the data is protected from breaches, data loss and other risks.

****

In recent years, technological advances have occurred that have dramatically changed the way attorneys and law firms store, retrieve and access client information. Many law firms view these

---

[1] Quinn Norton, "Byte Rights," *Maximum PC*, September 2010, at 12.

technological advances as an opportunity to reduce costs, improve efficiency and provide better client service. Perhaps no area has seen greater changes than "cloud computing," which refers to software and related services that store information on a remote computer, *i.e.,* a computer or server that is not located at the law office's physical location. Rather, the information is stored on another company's server, or many servers, possibly all over the world, and the user's computer becomes just a way of accessing the information.[2]

The advent of "cloud computing," as well as the use of electronic devices such as cell phones that take advantage of cloud services, has raised serious questions concerning the manner in which lawyers and law firms handle client information, and has been the subject of numerous ethical inquiries in Pennsylvania and throughout the country. The American Bar Association Commission on Ethics 20/20 has suggested changes to the Model Rules of Professional Conduct designed to remind lawyers of the need to safeguard client confidentiality when engaging in "cloud computing."

Recent "cloud" data breaches from multiple companies, causing millions of dollars in penalties and consumer redress, have increased concerns about data security for cloud services. The Federal Trade Commission ("FTC") has received complaints that inadequate cloud security is placing consumer data at risk, and it is currently studying the security of "cloud computing" and the efficacy of increased regulation. Moreover, the Federal Bureau of Investigations ("FBI") warned law firms in 2010 that they were being specifically targeted by hackers who have designs on accessing the firms' databases.

This Committee has also considered the client confidentiality implications for electronic document transmission and storage in Formal Opinions 2009-100 ("Metadata") and 2010-200 ("Virtual Law Offices"), and an informal Opinion directly addressing "cloud computing." Because of the importance of "cloud computing" to attorneys – and the potential impact that this technological advance may have on the practice of law – this Committee believes that it is appropriate to issue this Formal Opinion to provide guidance to Pennsylvania attorneys concerning their ethical obligations when utilizing "cloud computing."

This Opinion also includes a section discussing the specific implications of web-based electronic mail (e-mail). With regard to web-based email, *i.e.,* products such as Gmail, AOL Mail, Yahoo! and Hotmail, the Committee concludes that attorneys may use e-mail but that, when circumstances require, attorneys must take additional precautions to assure the confidentiality of client information transmitted electronically.

II.   Background

For lawyers, "cloud computing" may be desirable because it can provide costs savings and increased efficiency in handling voluminous data. Better still, cloud service is elastic, and users can have as much or as little of a service as they want at any given time. The service is sold on demand, typically by the minute, hour or other increment. Thus, for example, with "cloud computing," an attorney can simplify document management and control costs.

---

[2] *Id.*

The benefits of using "cloud computing" may include:

- Reduced infrastructure and management;
- Cost identification and effectiveness;
- Improved work production;
- Quick, efficient communication;
- Reduction in routine tasks, enabling staff to elevate work level;
- Constant service;
- Ease of use;
- Mobility;
- Immediate access to updates; and
- Possible enhanced security.

Because "cloud computing" refers to "offsite" storage of client data, much of the control over that data and its security is left with the service provider. Further, data may be stored in other jurisdictions that have different laws and procedures concerning access to or destruction of electronic data. Lawyers using cloud services must therefore be aware of potential risks and take appropriate precautions to prevent compromising client confidentiality, *i.e.,* attorneys must take great care to assure that any data stored offsite remains confidential and not accessible to anyone other than those persons authorized by their firms. They must also assure that the jurisdictions in which the data are physical stored do not have laws or rules that would permit a breach of confidentiality in violation of the Rules of Professional Conduct.

III.   Discussion

A.   Prior Pennsylvania Opinions

In Formal Opinion 2009-100, this Committee concluded that a transmitting attorney has a duty of reasonable care to remove unwanted metadata from electronic documents before sending them to an adverse or third party. Metadata is hidden information contained in an electronic document that is not ordinarily visible to the reader. The Committee also concluded, *inter alia*, that a receiving lawyer has a duty pursuant to RPC 4.4(b) to notify the transmitting lawyer if an inadvertent metadata disclosure occurs.

Formal Opinion 2010-200 advised that an attorney with a virtual law office "is under the same obligation to maintain client confidentiality as is the attorney in a traditional physical office." Virtual law offices generally are law offices that do not have traditional brick and mortar facilities. Instead, client communications and file access exist entirely online. This Committee also concluded that attorneys practicing in a virtual law office need not take additional precautions beyond those utilized by traditional law offices to ensure confidentiality, because virtual law firms and many brick-and-mortar firms use electronic filing systems and incur the same or similar risks endemic to accessing electronic files remotely.

Informal Opinion 2010-060 on "cloud computing" stated that an attorney may ethically allow client confidential material to be stored in "the cloud" provided the attorney makes reasonable efforts to protect confidential electronic communications and information. Reasonable efforts discussed include regularly backing up data, installing firewalls, and avoiding inadvertent disclosures.

B.   Pennsylvania Rules of Professional Conduct

An attorney using "cloud computing" is under the same obligation to maintain client confidentiality as is the attorney who uses offline documents management. While no Pennsylvania Rule of Profession Conduct specifically addresses "cloud computing," the following rules, *inter alia,* are implicated:

> Rule 1.0 ("Terminology");
> Rule 1.1 ("Competence");
> Rule 1.4 ("Communication");
> Rule 1.6 ("Confidentiality of Information");
> Rule 1.15 ("Safekeeping Property"); and
> Rule 5.3 ("Responsibilities Regarding Nonlawyer Assistants").

Rule 1.1 ("Competence") states:

> A lawyer shall provide competent representation to a client. Competent representation requires the legal knowledge, skill, thoroughness and preparation reasonably necessary for the representation.

Comment [5] ("Thoroughness and Preparation") of Rule 1.1 provides further guidance about an attorney's obligations to clients that extend beyond legal skills:

> Competent handling of particular matter includes inquiry into and analysis of the factual and legal elements of the problem, and use of methods and procedures meeting the standards of competent practitioners. ...

Competency is affected by the manner in which an attorney chooses to represent his or her client, or, as Comment [5] to Rule 1.1 succinctly puts it, an attorney's "methods and procedures." Part of a lawyer's responsibility of competency is to take reasonable steps to ensure that client data and information is maintained, organized and kept confidential when required. A lawyer has latitude in choosing how or where to store files and use software that may best accomplish these goals. However, it is important that he or she is aware that some methods, like "cloud computing," require suitable measures to protect confidential electronic communications and information. The risk of security breaches and even the complete loss of data in "cloud computing" is magnified because the security of any stored data is with the service provider. For example, in 2011, the syndicated children's show "Zodiac Island" lost an entire season's worth of episodes when a fired employee for the show's data hosting service accessed the show's content without authorization and wiped it out.[3]

---

[3] Eriq Gardner, "Hacker Erased a Season's Worth of 'Zodiac Island'," *Yahoo! TV* (March 31, 2011), available at http://tv.yahoo.com/news/article/tv-news.en.reuters.com/tv-news.en.reuters.com-20110331-us_zodiac

Rule 1.15 ("Safekeeping Property") requires that client property should be "appropriately safeguarded."[4] Client property generally includes files, information and documents, including those existing electronically. Appropriate safeguards will vary depending on the nature and sensitivity of the property. Rule 1.15 provides in relevant part:

> (b)   A lawyer shall hold all Rule 1.15 Funds and property separate from the lawyer's own property. Such property shall be identified and appropriately safeguarded.

Rule 1.6 ("Confidentiality of Information") states in relevant part:

> (a)   A lawyer shall not reveal information relating to representation of a client unless the client gives informed consent, except for disclosures that are impliedly authorized in order to carry out the representation, and except as stated in paragraphs (b) and (c).
> (d)   The duty not to reveal information relating to representation of a client continues after the client-lawyer relationship has terminated.

Comment [2] of Rule 1.6 explains the importance and some of the foundation underlying the confidential relationship that lawyers must afford to a client. It is vital for the promotion of trust, justice and social welfare that a client can reasonably believe that his or her personal information or information related to a case is kept private and protected. Comment [2] explains the nature of the confidential attorney-client relationship:

> A fundamental principle in the client-lawyer relationship is that, in the absence of the client's informed consent, the lawyer must not reveal information relating to the representation. See Rule 1.0(e) for the definition of informed consent. This contributes to the trust that is the hallmark of the client-lawyer relationship. The client is thereby encouraged to seek legal assistance and to communicate fully and frankly with the lawyer even as to embarrassing or legally damaging subject matter. ...

Also relevant is Rule 1.0(e) defining the requisite "Informed Consent":

> "Informed consent" denotes the consent by a person to a proposed course of conduct after the lawyer has communicated adequate information and explanation about the material risks of and reasonably available alternatives to the proposed course of conduct.

Rule 1.4 directs a lawyer to promptly inform the client of any decision with respect to which the client's informed consent is required. While it is not necessary to communicate every minute

---

[4] In previous Opinions, this Committee has noted that the intent of Rule 1.15 does not extend to the entirety of client files, information and documents, including those existing electronically. In light of the expansion of technology as a basis for storing client data, it would appear that the strictures of diligence required of counsel under Rule 1.15 are, at a minimum, analogous to the "cloud."

detail of a client's representation, "adequate information" should be provided to the client so that the client understands the nature of the representation and "material risks" inherent in an attorney's methods. So for example, if an attorney intends to use "cloud computing" to manage a client's confidential information or data, it may be necessary, depending on the scope of representation and the sensitivity of the data involved, to inform the client of the nature of the attorney's use of "cloud computing" and the advantages as well as the risks endemic to online storage and transmission.

Absent a client's informed consent, as stated in Rule 1.6(a), confidential client information cannot be disclosed unless either it is "impliedly authorized" for the representation or enumerated among the limited exceptions in Rule 1.6(b) or Rule 1.6(c).[5] This may mean that a third party vendor, as with "cloud computing," could be "impliedly authorized" to handle client data provided that the information remains confidential, is kept secure, and any disclosure is confined only to necessary personnel. It also means that various safeguards should be in place so that an attorney can be reasonably certain to protect any information that is transmitted, stored, accessed, or otherwise processed through cloud services. Comment [24] to Rule 1.6(a) further clarifies an attorney's duties and obligations:

> When transmitting a communication that includes information relating to the representation of a client, the lawyer must take reasonable precautions to prevent the information from coming into the hands of unintended recipients. This duty, however, does not require that the lawyer use special security measures if the method of communication affords a reasonable expectation of privacy. Special circumstances, however, may warrant special precautions. Factors to be considered in determining the reasonableness of the lawyer's expectation of confidentiality include the sensitivity of the information and the extent to which the privacy of the communication is protected by law or by a confidentiality agreement. A client may require the lawyer to implement special security measures not required by this Rule or may give informed consent to the use of a means of communication that would otherwise be prohibited by this Rule.

An attorney utilizing "cloud computing" will likely encounter circumstances that require unique considerations to secure client confidentiality. For example, because a server used by a "cloud computing" provider may physically be kept in another country, an attorney must ensure that the data in the server is protected by privacy laws that reasonably mirror those of the United States. Also, there may be situations in which the provider's ability to protect the information is compromised, whether through hacking, internal impropriety, technical failures, bankruptcy, or other circumstances. While some of these situations may also affect attorneys who use offline

---

[5] The exceptions covered in Rule 1.6(b) and (c) are not implicated in "cloud computing." Generally, they cover compliance with Rule 3.3 ("Candor Toward the Tribunal"), the prevention of serious bodily harm, criminal and fraudulent acts, proceedings concerning the lawyer's representation of the client, legal advice sought for Rule compliance, and the sale of a law practice.

storage, an attorney using "cloud computing" services may need to take special steps to satisfy his or her obligation under Rules 1.0, 1.6 and 1.15.[6]

Rule 5.3 ("Responsibilities Regarding Nonlawyer Assistants") states:

> With respect to a nonlawyer employed or retained by or associated with a lawyer:
>
> (a)   A partner and a lawyer who individually or together with other lawyers possesses comparable managerial authority in a law firm shall make reasonable efforts to ensure that the firm has in effect measures giving reasonable assurance that the person's conduct is compatible with the professional obligations of the lawyer.
>
> (b)   A lawyer having direct supervisory authority over the nonlawyer shall make reasonable efforts to ensure that the person's conduct is compatible with the professional obligations of the lawyer; and
>
> (c)   A lawyer shall be responsible for conduct of such a person that would be a violation of the Rules of Professional Conduct if engaged in by a lawyer if:
>
> > (1)   the lawyer orders or, with the knowledge of the specific conduct, ratifies the conduct involved; or
> >
> > (2)   the lawyer is a partner or has comparable managerial authority in the law firm in which the person is employed, or has direct supervisory authority over the person, and in either case knows of the conduct at a time when its consequences can be avoided or mitigated but fails to take reasonable remedial action.

At its essence, "cloud computing" can be seen as an online form of outsourcing subject to Rule 5.1 and Rule 5.3 governing the supervision of those who are associated with an attorney. Therefore, a lawyer must ensure that tasks are delegated to competent people and organizations. This means that any service provider who handles client information needs to be able to limit authorized access to the data to only necessary personnel, ensure that the information is backed up, reasonably available to the attorney, and reasonably safe from unauthorized intrusion.

It is also important that the vendor understands, embraces, and is obligated to conform to the professional responsibilities required of lawyers, including a specific agreement to comply with all ethical guidelines, as outlined below. Attorneys may also need a written service agreement that can be enforced on the provider to protect the client's interests. In some circumstances, a client may need to be advised of the outsourcing or use of a service provider and the identification of the provider. A lawyer may also need an agreement or written disclosure with the client to outline the nature of the cloud services used, and its impact upon the client's matter.

C.   Obligations of Reasonable Care for Pennsylvania/Factors to Consider

---

[6] Advisable steps for an attorney to take reasonable care to meet his or her obligations for Professional Conduct are outlined below.

In the context of "cloud computing," an attorney must take reasonable care to make sure that the conduct of the cloud computing service provider conforms to the rules to which the attorney himself is subject. Because the operation is outside of an attorney's direct control, some of the steps taken to ensure reasonable care are different from those applicable to traditional information storage.

While the measures necessary to protect confidential information will vary based upon the technology and infrastructure of each office – and this Committee acknowledges that the advances in technology make it difficult, if not impossible to provide specific standards that will apply to every attorney – there are common procedures and safeguards that attorneys should employ.

These various safeguards also apply to traditional law offices. Competency extends beyond protecting client information and confidentiality; it also includes a lawyer's ability to reliably access and provide information relevant to a client's case when needed. This is essential for attorneys regardless of whether data is stored onsite or offsite with a cloud service provider. However, since cloud services are under the provider's control, using "the cloud" to store data electronically could have unwanted consequences, such as interruptions in service or data loss. There are numerous examples of these types of events. Amazon EC2 has experienced outages in the past few years, leaving a portion of users without service for hours at a time. Google has also had multiple service outages, as have other providers. Digital Railroad, a photo archiving service, collapsed financially and simply shut down. These types of risks should alert anyone contemplating using cloud services to select a suitable provider, take reasonable precautions to back up data and ensure its accessibility when the user needs it.

Thus, the standard of reasonable care for "cloud computing" may include:

- Backing up data to allow the firm to restore data that has been lost, corrupted, or accidentally deleted;

- Installing a firewall to limit access to the firm's network;

- Limiting information that is provided to others to what is required, needed, or requested;

- Avoiding inadvertent disclosure of information;

- Verifying the identity of individuals to whom the attorney provides confidential information;

- Refusing to disclose confidential information to unauthorized individuals (including family members and friends) without client permission;

- Protecting electronic records containing confidential data, including backups, by encrypting the confidential data;

- Implementing electronic audit trail procedures to monitor who is accessing the data;

- Creating plans to address security breaches, including the identification of persons to be notified about any known or suspected security breach involving confidential data;

- Ensuring the provider:
  o explicitly agrees that it has no ownership or security interest in the data;
  o has an enforceable obligation to preserve security;
  o will notify the lawyer if requested to produce data to a third party, and provide the lawyer with the ability to respond to the request before the provider produces the requested information;
  o has technology built to withstand a reasonably foreseeable attempt to infiltrate data, including penetration testing;
  o includes in its "Terms of Service" or "Service Level Agreement" an agreement about how confidential client information will be handled;
  o provides the firm with right to audit the provider's security procedures and to obtain copies of any security audits performed;
  o will host the firm's data only within a specified geographic area. If by agreement, the data are hosted outside of the United States, the law firm must determine that the hosting jurisdiction has privacy laws, data security laws, and protections against unlawful search and seizure that are as rigorous as those of the United States and Pennsylvania;
  o provides a method of retrieving data if the lawyer terminates use of the SaaS product, the SaaS vendor goes out of business, or the service otherwise has a break in continuity; and,
  o provides the ability for the law firm to get data "off" of the vendor's or third party data hosting company's servers for the firm's own use or in-house backup offline.

- Investigating the provider's:
  o security measures, policies and recovery methods;
  o system for backing up data;
  o security of data centers and whether the storage is in multiple centers;
  o safeguards against disasters, including different server locations;
  o history, including how long the provider has been in business;
  o funding and stability;
  o policies for data retrieval upon termination of the relationship and any related charges; and,
  o process to comply with data that is subject to a litigation hold.

- Determining whether:
  o data is in non-proprietary format;
  o the Service Level Agreement clearly states that the attorney owns the data;
  o there is a 3rd party audit of security; and,
  o there is an uptime guarantee and whether failure results in service credits.

- Employees of the firm who use the SaaS must receive training on and are required to abide by all end-user security measures, including, but not limited to, the creation of strong passwords and the regular replacement of passwords.

- Protecting the ability to represent the client reliably by ensuring that a copy of digital data is stored onsite.[7]

- Having an alternate way to connect to the internet, since cloud service is accessed through the internet.

The terms and conditions under which the "cloud computing" services are offered, *i.e.,* Service Level Agreements ("SLAs"), may also present obstacles to reasonable care efforts. Most SLAs are essentially "take it or leave it,"[8] and often users, including lawyers, do not read the terms closely or at all. As a result, compliance with ethical mandates can be difficult. However, new competition in the "cloud computing" field is now causing vendors to consider altering terms. This can help attorneys meet their ethical obligations by facilitating an agreement with a vendor that adequately safeguards security and reliability.[9]

Additional responsibilities flow from actual breaches of data. At least forty-five states, including Pennsylvania, currently have data breach notification laws and a federal law is expected. Pennsylvania's notification law, 73 P.S. § 2303 (2011) ("Notification of Breach"), states:

(a) GENERAL RULE. -- An entity that maintains, stores or manages computerized data that includes personal information shall provide notice of any breach of the security of the system following discovery of the breach of the security of the system to any resident of this Commonwealth whose unencrypted and unredacted personal information was or is reasonably believed to have been accessed and acquired by an unauthorized person. Except as provided in section 4 or in order to take any measures necessary to determine the scope of the breach and to restore the reasonable integrity of the data system, the notice shall be made without unreasonable delay. For the purpose of this section, a resident of this Commonwealth may be determined to be an individual whose principal mailing address, as reflected in the computerized data which is maintained, stored or managed by the entity, is in this Commonwealth.

(b) ENCRYPTED INFORMATION. -- An entity must provide notice of the breach if encrypted information is accessed and acquired in an unencrypted form, if the security breach is linked to a breach of the security of the encryption or if the security breach involves a person with access to the encryption key.

---

[7] This is recommended even though many vendors will claim that it is not necessary.
[8] Larger providers can be especially rigid with SLAs, since standardized agreements help providers to reduce costs.
[9] One caveat in an increasing field of vendors is that some upstart providers may not have staying power. Attorneys are well advised to consider the stability of any company that may handle sensitive information and the ramifications for the data in the event of bankruptcy, disruption in service or potential data breaches.

(c)   VENDOR NOTIFICATION. -- A vendor that maintains, stores or manages computerized data on behalf of another entity shall provide notice of any breach of the security system following discovery by the vendor to the entity on whose behalf the vendor maintains, stores or manages the data. The entity shall be responsible for making the determinations and discharging any remaining duties under this act.

A June, 2010, Pew survey highlighted concerns about security for "cloud computing." In the survey, a number of the nearly 900 internet experts surveyed agreed that it "presents security problems and further exposes private information," and some experts even predicted that "the cloud" will eventually have a massive breach from cyber-attacks.[10] Incident response plans should be in place before attorneys move to "the cloud", and the plans need to be reviewed annually. Lawyers may need to consider that at least some data may be too important to risk inclusion in cloud services.

One alternative to increase security measures against data breaches could be "private clouds." Private clouds are not hosted on the Internet, and give users completely internal security and control. Therefore, outsourcing rules do not apply to private clouds. Reasonable care standards still apply, however, as private clouds do not have impenetrable security. Another consideration might be hybrid clouds, which combine standard and private cloud functions.

D.   Web-based E-mail

Web-based email ("webmail") is a common way to communicate for individuals and businesses alike. Examples of webmail include AOL Mail, Hotmail, Gmail, and Yahoo! Mail. These services transmit and store e-mails and other files entirely online and, like other forms of "cloud computing," are accessed through an internet browser. While pervasive, webmail carries with it risks that attorneys should be aware of and mitigate in order to stay in compliance with their ethical obligations. As with all other cloud services, reasonable care in transmitting and storing client information through webmail is appropriate.

In 1999, The ABA Standing Commission on Ethics and Professional Responsibility issued Formal Opinion No. 99-413, discussed in further detail above, and concluded that using unencrypted email is permissible. Generally, concerns about e-mail security are increasing, particularly unencrypted e-mail. Whether an attorney's obligations should include the safeguard of encrypting emails is a matter of debate. An article entitled, "Legal Ethics in the Cloud: Avoiding the Storms," explains:

> Respected security professionals for years have compared e-mail to postcards or postcards written in pencil. Encryption is being increasingly required in areas like banking and health care. New laws in Nevada and Massachusetts (which apply to attorneys as well as others) require defined personal information to be encrypted when it is electronically transmitted. As the use of encryption grows in areas like

---

[10] Janna Quitney Anderson & Lee Rainie, The Future of Cloud Computing. Pew Internet & American Life Project, June 11, 2010, http://www.pewinternet.org/Reports/2010/The-future-of-cloud-computing/Main-Findings.aspx?view=all

these, it will become difficult for attorneys to demonstrate that confidential client data needs lesser protection.[11]

The article also provides a list of nine potential e-mail risk areas, including: confidentiality, authenticity, integrity, misdirection or forwarding, permanence (wanted e-mail may become lost and unwanted e-mail may remain accessible even if deleted), and malware. The article further provides guidance for protecting e-mail by stating:

> In addition to complying with any legal requirements that apply, the most prudent approach to the ethical duty of protecting confidentiality is to have an express understanding with clients about the nature of communications that will be (and will not be) sent by e-mail and whether or not encryption and other security measures will be utilized.
>
> It has now reached the point (or at least is reaching it) where most attorneys should have encryption available for use in appropriate circumstances.[12]

Compounding the general security concerns for e-mail is that users increasingly access webmail using unsecure or vulnerable methods such as cell phones or laptops with public wireless internet connections. Reasonable precautions are necessary to minimize the risk of unauthorized access to sensitive client information when using these devices and services, possibly including precautions such as encryption and strong password protection in the event of lost or stolen devices, or hacking.

The Committee further notes that this issue was addressed by the District of Columbia Bar in Opinion 281 (Feb. 18, 1998) ("Transmission of Confidential Information by Electronic Mail"), which concluded that, "In most circumstances, transmission of confidential information by unencrypted electronic mail does not per se violate the confidentiality rules of the legal profession. However, individual circumstances may require greater means of security."

The Committee concluded, and this Committee agrees, that the use of unencrypted electronic mail is not, by itself, a violation of the Rules of Professional Conduct, in particular Rule 1.6 ("Confidentiality of Information").

> Thus, we hold that the mere use of electronic communication is not a violation of Rule 1.6 absent special factors. We recognize that as to any confidential communication, the sensitivity of the contents of the communication and/or the circumstances of the transmission may, in specific instances, dictate higher levels of security. Thus, it may be necessary in certain circumstances to use extraordinary means to protect client confidences. To give an obvious example, a lawyer representing an associate in a dispute with the associate's law firm could very easily violate Rule 1.6 by sending a fax concerning the dispute to the law firm's mail room if that message contained client confidential

---

[11] David G. Ries, Esquire, "Legal Ethics in the Cloud: Avoiding the Storms," course handbook, *Cloud Computing 2011: Cut Through the Fluff & Tackle the Critical Stuff* (June 2011) (internal citations omitted).

[12] *Id.*

information. It is reasonable to suppose that employees of the firm, other lawyer employed at the firm, indeed firm management, could very well inadvertently see such a fax and learn of its contents concerning the associate's dispute with the law firm. Thus, what may ordinarily be permissible—the transmission of confidential information by facsimile—may not be permissible in a particularly factual context.

By the same analysis, what may ordinarily be permissible – the use of unencrypted electronic transmission – may not be acceptable in the context of a particularly heightened degree of concern or in a particular set of facts. But with that exception, we find that a lawyer takes reasonable steps to protect his client's confidence when he uses unencrypted electronically transmitted messages.

E.   Opinions From Other Ethics Committees

Other Ethics Committees have reached conclusions similar in substance to those in this Opinion. Generally, the consensus is that, while "cloud computing" is permissible, lawyers should proceed with caution because they have an ethical duty to protect sensitive client data. In service to that essential duty, and in order to meet the standard of reasonable care, other Committees have determined that attorneys must (1) include terms in any agreement with the provider that require the provider to preserve the confidentiality and security of the data, and (2) be knowledgeable about how providers will handle the data entrusted to them. Some Committees have also raised ethical concerns regarding confidentiality issues with third-party access or general electronic transmission (*e.g.,* web-based email) and these conclusions are consistent with opinions about emergent emergent "cloud computing" technologies.

The American Bar Association Standing Committee on Ethics and Professional Responsibility has not yet issued a formal opinion on "cloud computing." However, the ABA Commission on Ethics 20/20 Working Group on the Implications of New Technologies, published an "Issues Paper Concerning Client Confidentiality and Lawyers' Use of Technology" (Sept. 20, 2010) and considered some of the concerns and ethical implications of using "the cloud." The Working Group found that potential confidentiality problems involved with "cloud computing" include:

- Storage in countries with less legal protection for data;
- Unclear policies regarding data ownership;
- Failure to adequately back up data;
- Unclear policies for data breach notice;
- Insufficient encryption;
- Unclear data destruction policies;
- Bankruptcy;
- Protocol for a change of cloud providers;
- Disgruntled/dishonest insiders;
- Hackers;
- Technical failures;
- Server crashes;
- Viruses;

- Data corruption;
- Data destruction;
- Business interruption (*e.g.*, weather, accident, terrorism); and,
- Absolute loss (*i.e.*, natural or man-made disasters that destroy everything).

Id. The Working Group also stated, "[f]orms of technology other than 'cloud computing' can produce just as many confidentiality-related concerns, such as when laptops, flash drives, and smart phones are lost or stolen." *Id.* Among the precautions the Commission is considering recommending are:

- Physical protection for devices (*e.g.*, laptops) or methods for remotely deleting data from lost or stolen devices;
- Strong passwords;
- Purging data from replaced devices (*e.g.*, computers, smart phones, and copiers with scanners);
- Safeguards against malware (*e.g.*, virus and spyware protection);
- Firewalls to prevent unauthorized access;
- Frequent backups of data;
- Updating to operating systems with the latest security protections;
- Configuring software and network settings to minimize security risks;
- Encrypting sensitive information;
- Identifying or eliminating metadata from electronic documents; and
- Avoiding public Wi-Fi when transmitting confidential information (*e.g.*, sending an email to a client).

Id. Additionally, the ABA Commission on Ethics 20/20 has drafted a proposal to amend, *inter alia*, Model Rule 1.0 ("Terminology"), Model Rule 1.1 ("Competence"), and Model Rule 1.6 ("Duty of Confidentiality") to account for confidentiality concerns with the use of technology, in particular confidential information stored in an electronic format. Among the proposed amendments (insertions underlined, deletions ~~struck through~~):

> Rule 1.1 ("Competence") Comment [6] ("Maintaining Competence"): "To maintain the requisite knowledge and skill, a lawyer should keep abreast of changes in the law and its practice, including the benefits and risks associated with technology, engage in continuing study and education and comply with all continuing legal education requirements to which the lawyer is subject."

> Rule 1.6(c) ("Duty of Confidentiality"): "A lawyer shall make reasonable efforts to prevent the inadvertent disclosure of, or unauthorized access to, information relating to the representation of a client."

> Rule 1.6 ("Duty of Confidentiality") Comment [16] ("Acting Competently to Preserve Confidentiality"): "Paragraph (c) requires a ~~A~~ lawyer ~~must~~ to act competently to safeguard information relating to the representation of a client against inadvertent or unauthorized disclosure by the lawyer or other persons or entities who are participating in the representation of the client or who are subject to the lawyer's supervision or monitoring. See Rules 1.1, 5.1, and 5.3. Factors to

be considered in determining the reasonableness of the lawyer's efforts include the sensitivity of the information, the likelihood of disclosure if additional safeguards are not employed, and the cost of employing additional safeguards. Whether a lawyer may be required to take additional steps to safeguard a client's information in order to comply with other law, such as state and federal laws that govern data privacy or that impose notification requirements upon the loss of, or unauthorized access to, electronic information, is beyond the scope of these Rules.

In Formal Opinion No. 99-413 (March 10, 1999), the ABA Standing Committee on Ethics and Professional Responsibility determined that using e-mail for professional correspondence is acceptable. Ultimately, it concluded that unencrypted e-mail poses no greater risks than other communication modes commonly relied upon. As the Committee reasoned, "The risk of unauthorized interception and disclosure exists in every medium of communication, including e-mail. It is not, however, reasonable to require that a mode of communicating information must be avoided simply because interception is technologically possible, especially when unauthorized interception or dissemination of the information is a violation of the law." *Id.*

Also relevant is ABA Formal Opinion 08-451 (August 5, 2008), which concluded that the ABA Model Rules generally allow for outsourcing of legal and non-legal support services if the outsourcing attorney ensures compliance with competency, confidentiality, and supervision. The Committee stated that an attorney has a supervisory obligation to ensure compliance with professional ethics even if the attorney's affiliation with the other lawyer or nonlawyer is indirect. An attorney is therefore obligated to ensure that any service provider complies with confidentiality standards. The Committee advised attorneys to utilize written confidentiality agreements and to verify that the provider does not also work for an adversary.

The Alabama State Bar Office of General Council Disciplinary Commission issued Ethics Opinion 2010-02, concluding that an attorney must exercise reasonable care in storing client files, which includes becoming knowledgeable about a provider's storage and security and ensuring that the provider will abide by a confidentiality agreement. Lawyers should stay on top of emerging technology to ensure security is safeguarded. Attorneys may also need to back up electronic data to protect against technical or physical impairment, and install firewalls and intrusion detection software.

State Bar of Arizona Ethics Opinion 09-04 (Dec. 2009) stated that an attorney should take reasonable precautions to protect the security and confidentiality of data, precautions which are satisfied when data is accessible exclusively through a Secure Sockets Layer ("SSL") encrypted connection and at least one other password was used to protect each document on the system. The Opinion further stated, "It is important that lawyers recognize their own competence limitations regarding computer security measures and take the necessary time and energy to become competent or alternatively consult experts in the field." *Id.* Also, lawyers should ensure reasonable protection through a periodic review of security as new technologies emerge.

The California State Bar Standing Committee on Professional Responsibility and Conduct concluded in its Formal Opinion 2010-179 that an attorney using public wireless connections to conduct research and send e-mails should use precautions, such as personal firewalls and encrypting files and transmissions, or else risk violating his or her confidentiality and competence obligations. Some highly sensitive matters may necessitate discussing the use of public wireless connections with the client or in the alternative avoiding their use altogether. Appropriately secure personal connections meet a lawyer's professional obligations. Ultimately, the Committee found that attorneys should (1) use technology in conjunction with appropriate measures to protect client confidentiality, (2) tailor such measures to each unique type of technology, and (3) stay abreast of technological advances to ensure those measures remain sufficient.

The Florida Bar Standing Committee on Professional Ethics, in Opinion 06-1 (April 10, 2006), concluded that lawyers may utilize electronic filing provided that attorneys "take reasonable precautions to ensure confidentiality of client information, particularly if the lawyer relies on third parties to convert and store paper documents to electronic records." *Id.*

Illinois State Bar Association Ethics Opinion 10-01 (July 2009) stated that "[a] law firm's use of an off-site network administrator to assist in the operation of its law practice will not violate the Illinois Rules of Professional Conduct regarding the confidentiality of client information if the law firm makes reasonable efforts to ensure the protection of confidential client information."[13]

The Maine Board of Overseers of the Bar Professional Ethics Commission adopted Opinion 194 (June 30, 2008) in which it stated that attorneys may use third-party electronic back-up and transcription services so long as appropriate safeguards are taken, including "reasonable efforts to prevent the disclosure of confidential information," and at minimum an agreement with the vendor that contains "a legally enforceable obligation to maintain the confidentiality of the client data involved." *Id.*

Of note, the Maine Ethics Commission, in a footnote, suggests in Opinion 194 that the federal Health Insurance Portability and Accountability Act ("HIPAA") Privacy and Security Rule 45 C.F.R. Subpart 164.314(a)(2) provide a good medical field example of contract requirements between medical professionals and third party service providers ("business associates") that handle confidential patient information. SLAs that reflect these or similar requirements may be advisable for lawyers who use cloud services.

45 C.F.R. Subpart 164.314(a)(2)(i) states:

> The contract between a covered entity and a business associate must provide that the business associate will:
>
> (A)   Implement administrative, physical, and technical safeguards that reasonably and appropriately protect the confidentiality, integrity, and availability of the electronic protected health information that it creates, receives, maintains, or transmits on behalf of the covered entity as required by this subpart;

---

[13] Mark Mathewson, *New ISBA Ethics Opinion Re: Confidentiality and Third-Party Tech Vendors*, Illinois Lawyer Now, July 24, 2009, available at http://www.illinoislawyernow.com/2009/07/24/new-isba-ethics-opinion-re-confidentiality-and-third-party-tech-vendors/

(B)   Ensure that any agent, including a subcontractor, to whom it provides such information agrees to implement reasonable and appropriate safeguards to protect it;

(C)   Report to the covered entity any security incident of which it becomes aware;

(D)   Authorize termination of the contract by the covered entity, if the covered entity determines that the business associate has violated a material term of the contract.

Massachusetts Bar Association Ethics Opinion 05-04 (March 3, 2005) addressed ethical concerns surrounding a computer support vendor's access to a firm's computers containing confidential client information. The committee concluded that a lawyer may provide a third-party vendor with access to confidential client information to support and maintain a firm's software. Clients have "impliedly authorized" lawyers to make confidential information accessible to vendors "pursuant to Rule 1.6(a) in order to permit the firm to provide representation to its clients." *Id.* Lawyers must "make reasonable efforts to ensure" a vendor's conduct comports with professional obligations. *Id.*

The State Bar of Nevada Standing Committee on Ethics and Professional Responsibility issued Formal Opinion No. 33 (Feb. 9, 2006) in which it stated, "an attorney may use an outside agency to store confidential information in electronic form, and on hardware located outside an attorney's direct supervision and control, so long as the attorney observed the usual obligations applicable to such arrangements for third party storage services." *Id.* Providers should, as part of the service agreement, safeguard confidentiality and prevent unauthorized access to data. The Committee determined that an attorney does not violate ethical standards by using third-party storage, even if a breach occurs, so long as he or she acts competently and reasonably in protecting information.

The New Jersey State Bar Association Advisory Committee on Professional Ethics issued Opinion 701 (April 2006) in which it concluded that, when using electronic filing systems, attorneys must safeguard client confidentiality by exercising "sound professional judgment" and reasonable care against unauthorized access, employing reasonably available technology. *Id.* Attorneys should obligate outside vendors, through "contract, professional standards, or otherwise," to safeguard confidential information. *Id.* The Committee recognized that Internet service providers often have better security than a firm would, so information is not necessarily safer when it is stored on a firm's local server. The Committee also noted that a strict guarantee of invulnerability is impossible in any method of file maintenance, even in paper document filing, since a burglar could conceivably break into a file room or a thief could steal mail.

The New York State Bar Association Committee on Professional Ethics concluded in Opinion 842 (Sept. 10, 2010) that the reasonable care standard for confidentiality should be maintained for online data storage and a lawyer is required to stay abreast of technology advances to ensure protection. Reasonable care may include: (1) obligating the provider to preserve confidentiality and security and to notify the attorney if served with process to produce client information, (2) making sure the provider has adequate security measures, policies, and recoverability methods, and (3) guarding against "reasonably foreseeable" data infiltration by using available technology. *Id.*

The North Carolina State Bar Ethics Committee has addressed the issue of "cloud computing" directly, and this Opinion adopts in large part the recommendations of this Committee. Proposed Formal Opinion 6 (April 21, 2011) concluded that "a law firm may use SaaS[14] if reasonable care is taken effectively to minimize the risks to the disclosure of confidential information and to the security of client information and client files." *Id.* The Committee reasoned that North Carolina Rules of Professional Conduct do not require a specific mode of protection for client information or prohibit using vendors who may handle confidential information, but they do require reasonable care in determining the best method of representation while preserving client data integrity. Further, the Committee determined that lawyers "must protect against security weaknesses unique to the Internet, particularly 'end-user' vulnerabilities found in the lawyer's own law office." *Id.*

The Committee's minimum requirements for reasonable care in Proposed Formal Opinion 6 included:[15]

- An agreement on how confidential client information will be handled in keeping with the lawyer's professional responsibilities must be included in the SaaS vendor's Terms of Service or Service Level Agreement, or in a separate agreement that states that the employees at the vendor's data center are agents of the law firm and have a fiduciary responsibility to protect confidential client information and client property;

- The agreement with the vendor must specify that firm's data will be hosted only within a specified geographic area. If by agreement the data is hosted outside of the United States, the law firm must determine that the hosting jurisdiction has privacy laws, data security laws, and protections against unlawful search and seizure that are as rigorous as those of the United States and the state of North Carolina;

- If the lawyer terminates use of the SaaS product, the SaaS vendor goes out of business, or the service otherwise has a break in continuity, the law firm must have a method for retrieving the data, the data must be available in a non-proprietary format that is compatible with other firm software or the firm must have access to the vendor's software or source code, and data hosted by the vendor or third party data hosting company must be destroyed or returned promptly;

---

[14] SaaS, as stated above, stands for Software-as-a-Service and is a type of "cloud computing."

[15] The Committee emphasized that these are minimum requirements, and, because risks constantly evolve, "due diligence and perpetual education as to the security risks of SaaS are required." Consequently, lawyers may need security consultants to assess whether additional measures are necessary.

- The law firm must be able get data "off" the vendor's or third party data hosting company's servers for lawyers' own use or in-house backup offline; and,

- Employees of the firm who use SaaS should receive training on and be required to abide by end-user security measures including, but not limited to, the creation of strong passwords and the regular replacement of passwords.

In Opinion 99-03 (June 21, 1999), the **State Bar Association of North Dakota** Ethics Committee determined that attorneys are permitted to use online data backup services protected by confidential passwords. Two separate confidentiality issues that the Committee identified are, (1) transmission of data over the internet, and (2) the storage of electronic data. The Committee concluded that the transmission of data and the use of online data backup services are permissible provided that lawyers ensure adequate security, including limiting access only to authorized personnel and requiring passwords.

Vermont Bar Association Advisory Ethics Opinion 2003-03 concluded that lawyers can use third-party vendors as consultants for confidential client data-base recovery if the vendor fully understands and embraces the clearly communicated confidentiality rules. Lawyers should determine whether contractors have sufficient safety measures to protect information. A significant breach obligates a lawyer to disclose the breach to the client.

Virginia State Bar Ethics Counsel Legal Ethics Opinion 1818 (Sept. 30, 2005) stated that lawyers using third party technical assistance and support for electronic storage should adhere to Virginia Rule of Professional Conduct 1.6(b)(6)[16], requiring "due care" in selecting the service provider and keeping the information confidential. *Id.*

These opinions have offered compelling rationales for concluding that using vendors for software, service, and information transmission and storage is permissible so long as attorneys meet the existing reasonable care standard under the applicable Rules of Professional Conduct, and are flexible in contemplating the steps that are required for reasonable care as technology changes.

IV.   Conclusion

The use of "cloud computing," and electronic devices such as cell phones that take advantage of cloud services, is a growing trend in many industries, including law. Firms may be eager to capitalize on cloud services in an effort to promote mobility, flexibility, organization and efficiency, reduce costs, and enable lawyers to focus more on legal, rather than technical and

---

[16] Virginia Rule of Professional Conduct 1.6(b) states in relevant part:
  To the extent a lawyer reasonably believes necessary, the lawyer may reveal:
      (6) information to an outside agency necessary for statistical, bookkeeping, accounting, data processing, printing, or other similar office management purposes, provided the lawyer exercises due care in the selection of the agency, advises the agency that the information must be kept confidential and reasonably believes that the information will be kept confidential.

administrative, issues. However, lawyers must be conscientious about maintaining traditional confidentiality, competence, and supervisory standards.

This Committee concludes that the Pennsylvania Rules of Professional Conduct require attorneys to make reasonable efforts to meet their obligations to ensure client confidentiality, and confirm that any third-party service provider is likewise obligated.

Accordingly, as outlined above, this Committee concludes that, under the Pennsylvania Rules of Professional Conduct an attorney may store confidential material in "the cloud." Because the need to maintain confidentiality is crucial to the attorney-client relationship, attorneys using "cloud" software or services must take appropriate measures to protect confidential electronic communications and information. In addition, attorneys may use email but must, under appropriate circumstances, take additional precautions to assure client confidentiality.

CAVEAT: THE FOREGOING OPINION IS ADVISORY ONLY AND IS NOT BINDING ON THE DISCIPLINARY BOARD OF THE SUPREME COURT OF PENNSYLVANIA OR ANY COURT. THIS OPINION CARRIES ONLY SUCH WEIGHT AS AN APPROPRIATE REVIEWING AUTHORITY MAY CHOOSE TO GIVE IT.

APPENDIX D

California Ethics Opinion— Confidentiality and Technology

**THE STATE BAR OF CALIFORNIA
STANDING COMMITTEE ON
PROFESSIONAL RESPONSIBILITY AND CONDUCT
FORMAL OPINION NO. 2010-179**

ISSUE: Does an attorney violate the duties of confidentiality and competence he or she owes to a client by using technology to transmit or store confidential client information when the technology may be susceptible to unauthorized access by third parties?

DIGEST: Whether an attorney violates his or her duties of confidentiality and competence when using technology to transmit or store confidential client information will depend on the particular technology being used and the circumstances surrounding such use. Before using a particular technology in the course of representing a client, an attorney must take appropriate steps to evaluate: 1) the level of security attendant to the use of that technology, including whether reasonable precautions may be taken when using the technology to increase the level of security; 2) the legal ramifications to a third party who intercepts, accesses or exceeds authorized use of the electronic information; 3) the degree of sensitivity of the information; 4) the possible impact on the client of an inadvertent disclosure of privileged or confidential information or work product; 5) the urgency of the situation; and 6) the client's instructions and circumstances, such as access by others to the client's devices and communications.

**AUTHORITIES
INTERPRETED:** Rules 3-100 and 3-110 of the California Rules of Professional Conduct.

Business and Professions Code section 6068, subdivision (e)(1).

Evidence Code sections 917(a) and 952.

STATEMENT OF FACTS

Attorney is an associate at a law firm that provides a laptop computer for his use on client and firm matters and which includes software necessary to his practice. As the firm informed Attorney when it hired him, the computer is subject to the law firm's access as a matter of course for routine maintenance and also for monitoring to ensure that the computer and software are not used in violation of the law firm's computer and Internet-use policy. Unauthorized access by employees or unauthorized use of the data obtained during the course of such maintenance or monitoring is expressly prohibited. Attorney's supervisor is also permitted access to Attorney's computer to review the substance of his work and related communications.

Client has asked for Attorney's advice on a matter. Attorney takes his laptop computer to the local coffee shop and accesses a public wireless Internet connection to conduct legal research on the matter and email Client. He also takes the laptop computer home to conduct the research and email Client from his personal wireless system.

DISCUSSION

Due to the ever-evolving nature of technology and its integration in virtually every aspect our daily lives, attorneys are faced with an ongoing responsibility of evaluating the level of security of technology that has increasingly become an indispensable tool in the practice of law. The Committee's own research – including conferring with computer security experts – causes it to understand that, without appropriate safeguards (such as firewalls, secure username/password combinations, and encryption), data transmitted wirelessly can be intercepted and read with increasing ease. Unfortunately, guidance to attorneys in this area has not kept pace with technology. Rather than engage in a technology-by-technology analysis, which would likely become obsolete shortly, this opinion sets forth the general analysis that an attorney should undertake when considering use of a particular form of technology.

1

1.   The Duty of Confidentiality

In California, attorneys have an express duty "[t]o maintain inviolate the confidence, and at every peril to himself or herself to preserve the secrets, of his or her client."[1] (Bus. & Prof. Code, § 6068, subd. (e)(1).) This duty arises from the relationship of trust between an attorney and a client and, absent the informed consent of the client to reveal such information, the duty of confidentiality has very few exceptions. (Rules Prof. Conduct, rule 3-100 & discussion ["[A] member may not reveal such information except with the consent of the client or as authorized or required by the State Bar Act, these rules, or other law."].)[2]

Unlike Rule 1.6 of the Model Rules of Professional Conduct ("MRPC"), the exceptions to the duty of confidentiality under rule 3-100 do not expressly include disclosure "impliedly authorized in order to carry out the representation." (MRPC, Rule 1.6.) Nevertheless, the absence of such language in the California Rules of Professional Conduct does not prohibit an attorney from using postal or courier services, telephone lines, or other modes of communication beyond face-to-face meetings, in order to effectively carry out the representation. There is a distinction between actually disclosing confidential information to a third party for purposes ancillary to the representation,[3] on the one hand, and using appropriately secure technology provided by a third party as a method of communicating with the client or researching a client's matter,[4] on the other hand.

Section 952 of the California Evidence Code, defining "confidential communication between client and lawyer" for purposes of application of the attorney-client privilege, includes disclosure of information to third persons "to whom disclosure is reasonably necessary for the transmission of the information or the accomplishment of the purpose for which the lawyer is consulted." (Evid. Code, § 952.) While the duty to protect confidential client information is broader in scope than the attorney-client privilege (Discussion [2] to rule 3-100; *Goldstein v. Lees* (1975) 46 Cal.App.3d 614, 621, fn. 5 [120 Cal.Rptr. 253]), the underlying principle remains the same, namely, that transmission of information through a third party reasonably necessary for purposes of the representation should not be deemed to have destroyed the confidentiality of the information. (See Cal. State Bar Formal Opn. No. 2003-161 [repeating the Committee's prior observation "that the duty of confidentiality and the evidentiary privilege share the same basic policy foundation: to encourage clients to disclose all possibly pertinent information to their attorneys so that the attorneys may effectively represent the clients' interests."].) Pertinent here, the manner in which an attorney acts to safeguard confidential client information is governed by the duty of competence, and determining whether a third party has the ability to access and use confidential client information in a manner that is unauthorized by the client is a subject that must be considered in conjunction with that duty.

2.   The Duty of Competence

Rule 3-110(A) prohibits the intentional, reckless or repeated failure to perform legal services with competence. Pertinent here, "competence" may apply to an attorney's diligence and learning with respect to handling matters for clients. (Rules Prof. Conduct, rule 3-110(B).) The duty of competence also applies to an attorney's "duty to supervise the work of subordinate attorney and non-attorney employees or agents." (Discussion to rule 3-110.)

---

[1]   "Secrets" include "[a]ny 'information gained in the professional relationship that the client has requested be held inviolate or the disclosure of which would be embarrassing or would likely be detrimental to the client.'" (Cal. State Bar Formal Opn. No. 1981-58.)

[2]   Unless otherwise indicated, all future references to rules in this opinion will be to the Rules of Professional Conduct of the State Bar of California.

[3]   In this regard, compare Cal. State Bar Formal Opn. No. 1971-25 (use of an outside data processing center without the client's consent for bookkeeping, billing, accounting and statistical purposes, if such information includes client secrets and confidences, would violate section 6068, subdivision (e)), with Los Angeles County Bar Assn. Formal Opn. No. 374 (1978) (concluding that in most circumstances, if protective conditions are observed, disclosure of client's secrets and confidences to a central data processor would not violate section 6068(e) and would be the same as disclosures to non-lawyer office employees).

[4]   Cf. Evid. Code, § 917(b) ("A communication ... does not lose its privileged character for the sole reason that it is communicated by electronic means or because persons involved in the delivery, facilitation, or storage of electronic communication may have access to the content of the communication.").

With respect to acting competently to preserve confidential client information, the comments to Rule 1.6 of the MRPC[5/] provide:

> [16] A lawyer must act competently to safeguard information relating to the representation of a client against inadvertent or unauthorized disclosure by the lawyer or other persons who are participating in the representation of the client or who are subject to the lawyer's supervision. See Rules 1.1, 5.1 and 5.3.

> [17] When transmitting a communication that includes information relating to the representation of a client, the lawyer must take reasonable precautions to prevent the information from coming into the hands of unintended recipients. This duty, however, does not require that the lawyer use special security measures if the method of communication affords a reasonable expectation of privacy. Special circumstances, however, may warrant special precautions. Factors to be considered in determining the reasonableness of the lawyer's expectation of confidentiality include the sensitivity of the information and the extent to which the privacy of the communication is protected by law or by a confidentiality agreement. A client may require the lawyer to implement special security measures not required by this Rule or may give informed consent to the use of a means of communication that would otherwise be prohibited by this Rule.

(MRPC, cmts. 16 & 17 to Rule 1.6.) In this regard, the duty of competence includes taking appropriate steps to ensure both that secrets and privileged information of a client remain confidential and that the attorney's handling of such information does not result in a waiver of any privileges or protections.

3.   **Factors to Consider**

In accordance with the duties of confidentiality and competence, an attorney should consider the following before using a specific technology:[6/]

a) The attorney's ability to assess the level of security afforded by the technology, including without limitation:

    i) Consideration of how the particular technology differs from other media use. For example, while one court has stated that, "[u]nlike postal mail, simple e-mail generally is not 'sealed' or secure, and can be accessed or viewed on intermediate computers between the sender and recipient (unless the message is encrypted)" (*American Civil Liberties Union v. Reno* (E.D.Pa. 1996) 929 F.Supp. 824, 834, aff'd (1997) 521 U.S. 844 [117 S.Ct. 2329]), most bar associations have taken the position that the risks of a third party's unauthorized review of email (whether by interception or delivery to an unintended recipient) are similar to the risks that confidential client information transmitted by standard mail service will be opened by any of the many hands it passes through on the way to its recipient or will be misdirected[7/] (see, e.g., ABA Formal Opn. No. 99-413[8/] [concluding that attorneys have a reasonable expectation of privacy in email communications, even if unencrypted, "despite some risk of interception and disclosure"]; Los Angeles County Bar Assn. Formal Opn. No. 514 (2005) ["Lawyers are not required to encrypt e-mail containing confidential client communications because e-mail poses no greater risk

---

[5/]   In the absence of on-point California authority and conflicting state public policy, the MRPC may serve as guidelines. (*City & County of San Francisco v. Cobra Solutions, Inc.* (2006) 38 Cal. 4th 839, 852 [43 Cal.Rptr.3d 771].)

[6/]   These factors should be considered regardless of whether the attorney practices in a law firm, a governmental agency, a non-profit organization, a company, as a sole practitioner or otherwise.

[7/]   Rule 1-100(A) provides that "[e]thics opinions and rules and standards promulgated by other jurisdictions and bar associations may . . . be considered" for professional conduct guidance.

[8/]   In 1999, the ABA Committee on Ethics and Professional Responsibility reviewed state bar ethics opinions across the country and determined that, as attorneys' understanding of technology has improved, the opinions generally have transitioned from concluding that use of Internet email violates confidentiality obligations to concluding that use of unencrypted Internet email is permitted without express client consent. (ABA Formal Opn. No. 99-413 [detailing various positions taken in state ethics opinions from Alaska, Washington D.C., Kentucky, New York, Illinois, North Dakota, South Carolina, Vermont, Pennsylvania, Arizona, Iowa and North Carolina].)

of interception and disclosure than regular mail, phones or faxes."]; Orange County Bar Assn. Formal Opn. No. 97-0002 [concluding use of encrypted email is encouraged, but not required].) (See also *City of Reno v. Reno Police Protective Assn.* (2003) 118 Nev. 889, 897-898 [59 P.3d 1212] [referencing an earlier version of section 952 of the California Evidence Code and concluding "that a document transmitted by e-mail is protected by the attorney-client privilege as long as the requirements of the privilege are met."].)

ii) Whether reasonable precautions may be taken when using the technology to increase the level of security.[9] As with the above-referenced views expressed on email, the fact that opinions differ on whether a particular technology is secure suggests that attorneys should take reasonable steps as a precautionary measure to protect against disclosure.[10] For example, depositing confidential client mail in a secure postal box or handing it directly to the postal carrier or courier is a reasonable step for an attorney to take to protect the confidentiality of such mail, as opposed to leaving the mail unattended in an open basket outside of the office door for pick up by the postal service. Similarly, encrypting email may be a reasonable step for an attorney to take in an effort to ensure the confidentiality of such communications remain so when the circumstance calls for it, particularly if the information at issue is highly sensitive and the use of encryption is not onerous. To place the risks in perspective, it should not be overlooked that the very nature of digital technologies makes it easier for a third party to intercept a much greater amount of confidential information in a much shorter period of time than would be required to transfer the same amount of data in hard copy format. In this regard, if an attorney can readily employ encryption when using public wireless connections and has enabled his or her personal firewall, the risks of unauthorized access may be significantly reduced.[11] Both of these tools are readily available and relatively inexpensive, and may already be built into the operating system. Likewise, activating password protection features on mobile devices, such as laptops and PDAs, presently helps protect against access to confidential client information by a third party if the device is lost, stolen or left unattended. (See David Ries & Reid Trautz, *Law Practice Today*, "Securing Your Clients' Data While On the Road," October 2008 [noting reports that "as many as 10% of laptops used by American businesses are stolen during their useful lives and 97% of them are never recovered"].)

iii) Limitations on who is permitted to monitor the use of the technology, to what extent and on what grounds. For example, if a license to use certain software or a technology service imposes a requirement of third party access to information related to the attorney's use of the technology, the attorney may need to confirm that the terms of the requirement or authorization do not permit the third party to disclose confidential client information to others or use such information for any purpose other than to ensure the functionality of the software or that the technology is not being used for an improper purpose, particularly if the information at issue is highly sensitive.[12] "Under Rule 5.3 [of the MRPC], a lawyer retaining such an outside service provider is required to make reasonable efforts to ensure that the service provider will not make unauthorized disclosures of client information. Thus when a lawyer

---

[9] Attorneys also should employ precautions to protect confidential information when in public, such as ensuring that the person sitting in the adjacent seat on an airplane cannot see the computer screen or moving to a private location before discussing confidential information on a mobile phone.

[10] Section 60(1)(b) of the Restatement (Third) of The Law Governing Lawyers provides that "a lawyer must take steps reasonable in the circumstances to protect confidential client information against impermissible use or disclosure by the lawyer's associates or agents that may adversely affect a material interest of the client or otherwise than as instructed by the client."

[11] Similarly, this Committee has stated that if an attorney is going to maintain client documents in electronic form, he or she must take reasonable steps to strip any metadata containing confidential information of other clients before turning such materials over to a current or former client or his or her new attorney. (See Cal. State Bar Formal Opn. 2007-174.)

[12] A similar approach might be appropriate if the attorney is employed by a non-profit or governmental organization where information may be monitored by a person or entity with interests potentially or actually in conflict with the attorney's client. In such cases, the attorney should not use the technology for the representation, absent informed consent by the client or the ability to employ safeguards to prevent access to confidential client information. The attorney also may need to consider whether he or she can competently represent the client without the technology.

considers entering into a relationship with such a service provider he must ensure that the service provider has in place, or will establish, reasonable procedures to protect the confidentiality of information to which it gains access, and moreover, that it fully understands its obligations in this regard. [Citation.] In connection with this inquiry, a lawyer might be well-advised to secure from the service provider in writing, along with or apart from any written contract for services that might exist, a written statement of the service provider's assurance of confidentiality." (ABA Formal Opn. No. 95-398.)

Many attorneys, as with a large contingent of the general public, do not possess much, if any, technological savvy. Although the Committee does not believe that attorneys must develop a mastery of the security features and deficiencies of each technology available, the duties of confidentiality and competence that attorneys owe to their clients do require a basic understanding of the electronic protections afforded by the technology they use in their practice. If the attorney lacks the necessary competence to assess the security of the technology, he or she must seek additional information or consult with someone who possesses the necessary knowledge, such as an information technology consultant.[13] (Cf. Rules Prof. Conduct, rule 3-110(C) ["If a member does not have sufficient learning and skill when the legal service is undertaken, the member may nonetheless perform such services competently by 1) associating with or, where appropriate, professionally consulting another lawyer reasonably believed to be competent, or 2) by acquiring sufficient learning and skill before performance is required."].)

b) Legal ramifications to third parties of intercepting, accessing or exceeding authorized use of another person's electronic information. The fact that a third party could be subject to criminal charges or civil claims for intercepting, accessing or engaging in unauthorized use of confidential client information favors an expectation of privacy with respect to a particular technology. (See, e.g., 18 U.S.C. § 2510 et seq. [Electronic Communications Privacy Act of 1986]; 18 U.S.C. § 1030 et seq. [Computer Fraud and Abuse Act]; Pen. Code, § 502(c) [making certain unauthorized access to computers, computer systems and computer data a criminal offense]; Cal. Pen. Code, § 629.86 [providing a civil cause of action to "[a]ny person whose wire, electronic pager, or electronic cellular telephone communication is intercepted, disclosed, or used in violation of [Chapter 1.4 on Interception of Wire, Electronic Digital Pager, or Electronic Cellular Telephone Communications]."]; *eBay, Inc. v. Bidder's Edge, Inc.* (N.D.Cal. 2000) 100 F.Supp.2d 1058, 1070 [in case involving use of web crawlers that exceeded plaintiff's consent, court stated "[c]onduct that does not amount to a substantial interference with possession, but which consists of intermeddling with or use of another's personal property, is sufficient to establish a cause of action for trespass to chattel."].)[14]

c) The degree of sensitivity of the information. The greater the sensitivity of the information, the less risk an attorney should take with technology. If the information is of a highly sensitive nature and there is a risk of disclosure when using a particular technology, the attorney should consider alternatives unless the client provides informed consent.[15] As noted above, if another person may have access to the communications transmitted between the attorney and the client (or others necessary to the representation), and may have an interest in the information being disclosed that is in conflict with the client's interest, the attorney should take precautions to ensure that the person will not be able to access the information or should avoid using the technology. These types of situations increase the likelihood for intrusion.

---

[13] Some potential security issues may be more apparent than others. For example, users of unsecured public wireless connections may receive a warning when accessing the connection. However, in most instances, users must take affirmative steps to determine whether the technology is secure.

[14] Attorneys also have corresponding legal and ethical obligations not to invade the confidential and privileged information of others.

[15] For the client's consent to be informed, the attorney should fully advise the client about the nature of the information to be transmitted with the technology, the purpose of the transmission and use of the information, the benefits and detriments that may result from transmission (both legal and nonlegal), and any other facts that may be important to the client's decision. (Los Angeles County Bar Assn. Formal Opn. No. 456 (1989).) It is particularly important for an attorney to discuss the risks and potential harmful consequences of using the technology when seeking informed consent.

d) Possible impact on the client of an inadvertent disclosure of privileged or confidential information or work product, including possible waiver of the privileges.[16] Section 917(a) of the California Evidence Code provides that "a communication made in confidence in the course of the lawyer-client, physician-patient, psychotherapist-patient, clergy-penitent, husband-wife, sexual assault counselor-victim, or domestic violence counselor-victim relationship ... is presumed to have been made in confidence and the opponent of the claim of privilege has the burden of proof to establish that the communication was not confidential." (Evid. Code, § 917(a).) Significantly, subsection (b) of section 917 states that such a communication "does not lose its privileged character for the sole reason that it is communicated by electronic means or because persons involved in the delivery, facilitation, or storage of electronic communication may have access to the content of the communication." (Evid. Code, § 917(b). See also Penal Code, § 629.80 ["No otherwise privileged communication intercepted in accordance with, or in violation of, the provisions of [Chapter 1.4] shall lose its privileged character."]; 18 U.S.C. § 2517(4) ["No otherwise privileged wire, oral, or electronic communication intercepted in accordance with, or in violation of, the provisions of [18 U.S.C. § 2510 et seq.] shall lose its privileged character."].) While these provisions seem to provide a certain level of comfort in using technology for such communications, they are not a complete safeguard. For example, it is possible that, if a particular technology lacks essential security features, use of such a technology could be deemed to have waived these protections. Where the attorney-client privilege is at issue, failure to use sufficient precautions may be considered in determining waiver.[17] Further, the analysis differs with regard to an attorney's duty of confidentiality. Harm from waiver of attorney-client privilege is possible depending on if and how the information is used, but harm from disclosure of confidential client information may be immediate as it does not necessarily depend on use or admissibility of the information, including as it does matters which would be embarrassing or would likely be detrimental to the client if disclosed.

e) The urgency of the situation. If use of the technology is necessary to address an imminent situation or exigent circumstances and other alternatives are not reasonably available, it may be reasonable in limited cases for the attorney to do so without taking additional precautions.

f) Client instructions and circumstances. If a client has instructed an attorney not to use certain technology due to confidentiality or other concerns or an attorney is aware that others have access to the client's electronic devices or accounts and may intercept or be exposed to confidential client information, then such technology should not be used in the course of the representation.[18]

4.   **Application to Fact Pattern**[19]

In applying these factors to Attorney's situation, the Committee does not believe that Attorney would violate his duties of confidentiality or competence to Client by using the laptop computer because access is limited to authorized individuals to perform required tasks. However, Attorney should confirm that personnel have been appropriately instructed regarding client confidentiality and are supervised in accordance with rule 3-110. (See *Crane v. State Bar* (1981) 30 Cal.3d 117, 123 [177 Cal.Rptr. 670] ["An attorney is responsible for the work product of his employees which is performed pursuant to his direction and authority."]; *In re Complex Asbestos Litig.* (1991) 232 Cal.App.3d 572, 588 [283 Cal.Rptr. 732] [discussing law firm's ability to supervise employees and ensure they protect client confidences]; Cal. State Bar Formal Opn. No. 1979-50 [discussing lawyer's duty to explain to

---

[16] Consideration of evidentiary issues is beyond the scope of this opinion, which addresses only the ethical implications of using certain technologies.

[17] For example, with respect to the impact of inadvertent disclosure on the attorney-client privilege or work-product protection, rule 502(b) of the Federal Rules of Evidence states: "When made in a Federal proceeding or to a Federal office or agency, the disclosure does not operate as a waiver in a Federal or State proceeding if: 1. the disclosure is inadvertent; 2. the holder of the privilege or protection took reasonable steps to prevent disclosure; and 3. the holder promptly took reasonable steps to rectify the error, including (if applicable) following Federal Rule of Civil Procedure 26(b)(5)(B)." As a practical matter, attorneys also should use appropriate confidentiality labels and notices when transmitting confidential or privileged client information.

[18] In certain circumstances, it may be appropriate to obtain a client's informed consent to the use of a particular technology.

[19] In this opinion, we are applying the factors to the use of computers and wireless connections to assist the reader in understanding how such factors function in practice. Use of other electronic devices would require similar considerations.

employee what obligations exist with respect to confidentiality].) In addition, access to the laptop by Attorney's supervisor would be appropriate in light of her duty to supervise Attorney in accordance with rule 3-110 and her own fiduciary duty to Client to keep such information confidential.

With regard to the use of a public wireless connection, the Committee believes that, due to the lack of security features provided in most public wireless access locations, Attorney risks violating his duties of confidentiality and competence in using the wireless connection at the coffee shop to work on Client's matter unless he takes appropriate precautions, such as using a combination of file encryption, encryption of wireless transmissions and a personal firewall.[20] Depending on the sensitivity of the matter, Attorney may need to avoid using the public wireless connection entirely or notify Client of possible risks attendant to his use of the public wireless connection, including potential disclosure of confidential information and possible waiver of attorney-client privilege or work product protections, and seek her informed consent to do so.[21]

Finally, if Attorney's personal wireless system has been configured with appropriate security features,[22] the Committee does not believe that Attorney would violate his duties of confidentiality and competence by working on Client's matter at home. Otherwise, Attorney may need to notify Client of the risks and seek her informed consent, as with the public wireless connection.

CONCLUSION

An attorney's duties of confidentiality and competence require the attorney to take appropriate steps to ensure that his or her use of technology in conjunction with a client's representation does not subject confidential client information to an undue risk of unauthorized disclosure. Because of the evolving nature of technology and differences in security features that are available, the attorney must ensure the steps are sufficient for each form of technology being used and must continue to monitor the efficacy of such steps.

This opinion is issued by the Standing Committee on Professional Responsibility and Conduct of the State Bar of California. It is advisory only. It is not binding upon the courts, the State Bar of California, its Board of Governors, any persons, or tribunals charged with regulatory responsibilities, or any member of the State Bar.

---

[20] Local security features available for use on individual computers include operating system firewalls, antivirus and antispam software, secure username and password combinations, and file permissions, while network safeguards that may be employed include network firewalls, network access controls such as virtual private networks (VPNs), inspection and monitoring. This list is not intended to be exhaustive.

[21] Due to the possibility that files contained on a computer may be accessed by hackers while the computer is operating on an unsecure network connection and when appropriate local security features, such as firewalls, are not enabled, attorneys should be aware that *any* client's confidential information stored on the computer may be at risk regardless of whether the attorney has the file open at the time.

[22] Security features available on wireless access points will vary and should be evaluated on an individual basis.

APPENDIX E

New York Ethics Opinion—Remote Access

Reprinted with permission from the NYSBA Committee on Professional Ethics, New York State Bar Association, One Elk Street, Albany, New York 12207.

NEW YORK STATE BAR ASSOCIATION
Serving the legal profession and the community since 1876

ETHICS OPINION 1019

New York State Bar Association
Committee on Professional Ethics

Opinion 1019 (8/6/2014)

Topic: Confidentiality; Remote Access to Firm's Electronic Files

Digest: A law firm may give its lawyers remote access to client files, so that lawyers may work from home, as long as the firm determines that the particular technology used provides reasonable protection to client confidential information, or, in the absence of such reasonable protection, if the law firm obtains informed consent from the client, after informing the client of the risks.

Rules: 1.0(j), 1.5(a), 1.6, 1.6(a), 1.6(b), 1.6(c), 1.15(d).

QUESTION

1.   May a law firm provide its lawyers with remote access to its electronic files, so that they may work from home?

OPINION

2. Our committee has often been asked about the application of New York's ethical rules -- now the Rules of Professional Conduct -- to the use of modern technology. While some of our technology opinions involve the application of the advertising rules to advertising using electronic means, many involve other ethical issues. See, *e.g.*:

N.Y. State 680 (1996). Retaining records by electronic imaging during the period required by DR 9-102(D) [now Rule 1.15(d)].

N.Y. State 709 (1998). Operating a trademark law practice over the internet and using e-mail.

N.Y. State 782 (2004). Use of electronic documents that may contain "metadata".

N.Y. State 820 (2008). Use of an e-mail service provider that conducts computer scans of emails to generate computer advertising.

N.Y. State 833 (2009). Whether a lawyer must respond to unsolicited emails requesting representation.

N.Y. State 842 (2010). Use of a "cloud" data storage system to store and back up client confidential information.

N.Y. State 940 (2012). Storage of confidential information on off-site backup tapes.

N.Y. State 950 (2012). Storage of emails in electronic rather than paper form.

3.   Much of our advice in these opinions turns on whether the use of technology would violate the lawyer's duty to preserve the confidential information of the client. Rule 1.6(a) sets forth a simple prohibition against disclosure of such information, i.e. "A lawyer shall not knowingly reveal confidential information, as defined in this Rule . . . unless . . . the client gives informed consent, as defined in Rule 1.0(j)." In addition, Rule 1.6(c) provides that a lawyer must "exercise reasonable care to prevent . . . others whose services are utilized by the lawyer from disclosing or using confidential information of a client" except as provided in Rule 1.6(b).

4.   Comment 17 to Rule 1.6 provides some additional guidance that reflects the advent of the information age:

> [17] When transmitting a communication that includes information relating to the representation of a client, the lawyer must take reasonable precautions to prevent the information from coming into the hands of unintended recipients. The duty does not require that the lawyer use special security measures if the method of communication affords a reasonable expectation of privacy. Special circumstances, however, may warrant special precautions. Factors to be considered to determining the reasonableness of the lawyer's expectation of confidentiality include the sensitivity of the information and the extent to which the privacy of the communication is protected by law or by a confidentiality agreement. A client may require the lawyer to use a means of communication or security measures not required by this Rule, or may give informed consent (as in an engagement letter or similar document) to the use of means or measures that would otherwise be prohibited by this Rule.

5. As is clear from Comment 17, the key to whether a lawyer may use any particular technology is whether the lawyer has determined that the technology affords reasonable protection against disclosure and that the lawyer has taken reasonable precautions in the use of the technology.

6. In some of our early opinions, despite language indicating that the inquiring lawyer must make the reasonableness determination, this Committee had reached general conclusions. In N.Y. State 709, we concluded that there is a reasonable expectation that e-mails will be as private as other forms of telecommunication, such as telephone or fax machine, and that a lawyer ordinarily may utilize unencrypted e-mail to transmit confidential information, unless there is a heightened risk of interception. We also noted, however, that "when the confidential information is of such an extraordinarily sensitive nature that it is reasonable to use only a means of communication that is completely under the lawyer's control, the lawyer must select a more secure means of communication than unencrypted internet e-mail." Moreover, we said the lawyer was obligated to stay abreast of evolving technology to assess changes in the likelihood of interception, as well as the availability of improved technologies that might reduce the risks at a reasonable cost.

7. In N.Y. State 820, we approved the use of an internet service provider that scanned e-mails to assist in providing user-targeted advertising, in part based on the published privacy policies of the provider.

8. Our more recent opinions, however, put the determination of reasonableness squarely on the inquiring lawyer. See, e.g. N.Y. State 842, 940, 950. For example, in N.Y. State 842, involving the use of "cloud" data storage, we were told that the storage system was password protected and that data stored in the system was encrypted. We concluded that the lawyer could use such a system, but only if the lawyer took reasonable care to ensure that the system was secure and that client confidentiality would be maintained. We said that "reasonable care" to protect a client's confidential information against unauthorized disclosure may include consideration of the following steps:

(1) Ensuring that the online data storage provider has an enforceable obligation to preserve confidentiality and security, and that the provider will notify the lawyer if served with process requiring the production of client information;

(2) Investigating the online data storage provider's security measures, policies, recoverability methods, and other procedures to determine if they are adequate under the circumstances;

(3) Employing available technology to guard against reasonably foreseeable attempts to infiltrate the data that is stored; and/or

(4) Investigating the storage provider's ability to purge and wipe any copies of the data, and to move the data to a different host, if the lawyer becomes dissatisfied with the storage provider or for other reasons changes storage providers.

Moreover, in view of rapid changes in technology and the security of stored data, we suggested that the lawyer should periodically reconfirm that the provider's security measures remained effective in light of advances in technology. We also warned that, if the lawyer learned information suggesting that the security measures used by the online data storage provider were insufficient to adequately protect the confidentiality of client information, or if the lawyer learned of any breaches of confidentiality by the provider, then the lawyer must discontinue use of the service unless the lawyer received assurances that security issues had been sufficiently remediated.

9. Cyber-security issues have continued to be a major concern for lawyers, as cyber-criminals have begun to target lawyers to access client information, including trade secrets, business plans and personal data. Lawyers can no longer assume that their document systems are of no interest to cyber-crooks. That is particularly true where there is outside access to the internal system by third parties, including law firm employees working at other firm offices, at home or when traveling, or clients who have been given access to the firm's document system. See, e.g. Matthew Goldstein, "Law Firms Are Pressed on Security For Data," N.Y. Times (Mar. 22, 2014) at B1 (corporate clients are demanding that their law firms take more steps to guard against online intrusions that could compromise sensitive information as global concerns about hacker threats mount; companies are asking law firms to stop putting files on portable thumb drives, emailing them to non-secure iPads or working on computers linked to a shared network in countries like China or Russia where hacking is prevalent); Joe Dysart, "Moving Targets: New Hacker Technology Threatens Lawyers' Mobile Devices," ABA Journal 25 (September 2012); Rachel M. Zahorsky, "Being Insecure: Firms are at Risk Inside and Out," ABA Journal 32 (June 2013); Sharon D. Nelson, John W. Simek & David G. Ries, Locked Down: Information Security for Lawyers (ABA Section of Law Practice Management, 2012).

10. In light of these developments, it is even more important for a law firm to determine that the technology it will use to provide remote access (as well as the devices that firm lawyers will use to effect remote access), provides reasonable assurance that confidential client information will be protected. Because of the fact-specific and evolving nature of both technology and cyber risks, we cannot recommend particular steps that would constitute reasonable precautions to prevent confidential information from coming into the hands of unintended recipients, including the degree of password protection to ensure that persons who access the system are authorized, the degree of security of the devices that firm lawyers use to gain access, whether encryption is required, and the security measures the firm must use to determine whether there has been any unauthorized access to client confidential information. However, assuming that the law firm determines that its precautions are reasonable, we believe it may provide such remote access. When the law firm is able to make a determination of reasonableness, we do not believe that client consent is necessary.

11.   Where a law firm cannot conclude that its precautions would provide reasonable protection to client confidential information, Rule 1.6(a) allows the law firm to request the client's informed consent. See also Comment 17 to Rule 1.6, which provides that a client may give informed consent (as in an engagement letter or similar document) to the use of means that would otherwise be prohibited by the rule. In N.Y. State 842, however, we stated that the obligation to preserve client confidential information extends beyond merely prohibiting an attorney from revealing confidential information without client consent. A lawyer must take reasonable care to affirmatively protect a client's confidential information. Consequently, we believe that before requesting client consent to a technology system used by the law firm, the firm must disclose the risks that the system does not provide reasonable assurance of confidentiality, so that the consent is "informed" within the meaning of Rule 1.0(j), i.e. that the client has information adequate to make an informed decision.

CONCLUSION

12.   A law firm may use a system that allows its lawyers to access the firm's document system remotely, as long as it takes reasonable steps to ensure that confidentiality of information is maintained. Because of the fact-specific and evolving nature of both technology and cyber risks, this Committee cannot recommend particular steps that constitute reasonable precautions to prevent confidential information from coming into the hands of unintended recipients. If the firm cannot conclude that its security precautions are reasonable, then it may request the informed consent of the client to its security precautions, as long as the firm discloses the risks that the system does not provide reasonable assurance of confidentiality, so that the consent is "informed" within the meaning of Rule 1.0(j).

7-14

One Elk Street, Albany , NY 12207
Phone: 518-463-3200 Secure Fax: 518.463.5993

APPENDIX F

Massachusetts Regulations— Personal Information Protection

Massachusetts Regulations on Personal Information Protection

201 CMR 17.00: STANDARDS FOR THE PROTECTION OF PERSONAL INFORMATION OF RESIDENTS OF THE COMMONWEALTH

Section:

17.01: Purpose and Scope

17.02: Definitions

17.03: Duty to Protect and Standards for Protecting Personal Information

17.04: Computer System Security Requirements

17.05: Compliance Deadline

17.01 Purpose and Scope

(1) Purpose

This regulation implements the provisions of M.G.L. c. 93H relative to the standards to be met by persons who own or license personal information about a resident of the Commonwealth of Massachusetts. This regulation establishes minimum standards to be met in connection with the safeguarding of personal information contained in both paper and electronic records. The objectives of this regulation are to ensure the security and confidentiality of customer information in a manner fully consistent with industry standards; protect against anticipated threats or hazards to the security or integrity of such information; and protect against unauthorized access to or use of such information that may result in substantial harm or inconvenience to any consumer.

(2) Scope

The provisions of this regulation apply to all persons that own or license personal information about a resident of the Commonwealth.

17.02: Definitions

The following words as used herein shall, unless the context requires otherwise, have the following meanings:

Breach of security, the unauthorized acquisition or unauthorized use of unencrypted data or, encrypted electronic data and the confidential process or key that is capable of compromising the security, confidentiality, or integrity of personal information, maintained by a person or agency that creates a substantial risk of identity theft or fraud against a resident of the commonwealth. A good faith but unauthorized acquisition of personal information by a person or agency, or employee or agent thereof, for the lawful purposes of such person or agency, is not a breach of security unless the personal information is used in an unauthorized manner or subject to further unauthorized disclosure.

Electronic, relating to technology having electrical, digital, magnetic, wireless, optical, electromagnetic or similar capabilities.

Encrypted, the transformation of data into a form in which meaning cannot be assigned without the use of a confidential process or key.

Owns or licenses, receives, stores, maintains, processes, or otherwise has access to personal information in connection with the provision of goods or services or in connection with employment.

Person, a natural person, corporation, association, partnership or other legal entity, other than an agency, executive office, department, board, commission, bureau, division or authority of the Commonwealth, or any of its branches, or any political subdivision thereof.

Personal information, a Massachusetts resident's first name and last name or first initial and last name in combination with any one or more of the following data elements that relate to such resident: (a) Social Security number; (b) driver's license number or state-issued identification card number; or (c) financial account number, or credit or debit card number, with or without any required security code, access code, personal identification number or password, that would permit access to a resident's financial account; provided, however, that "Personal information" shall not include information that is lawfully obtained from publicly available information, or from federal, state or local government records lawfully made available to the general public.

Record or Records, any material upon which written, drawn, spoken, visual, or electromagnetic information or images are recorded or preserved, regardless of physical form or characteristics.

Service provider, any person that receives, stores, maintains, processes, or otherwise is permitted access to personal information through its provision of services directly to a person that is subject to this regulation.

17.03: Duty to Protect and Standards for Protecting Personal Information

(1) Every person that owns or licenses personal information about a resident of the Commonwealth shall develop, implement, and maintain a comprehensive information security program that is written in one or more readily accessible parts and contains administrative, technical, and physical safeguards that are appropriate to (a) the size, scope and type of business of the person obligated to safeguard the personal information under such comprehensive information security program; (b) the amount of resources available to such person; (c) the amount of stored data; and (d) the need for security and confidentiality of both consumer and employee information. The safeguards contained in such program must be consistent with the safeguards for protection of personal information and information of a similar character set forth in any state or federal regulations by which the person who owns or licenses such information may be regulated.

(2) Without limiting the generality of the foregoing, every comprehensive information security program shall include, but shall not be limited to:

(a) Designating one or more employees to maintain the comprehensive information security program;

(b) Identifying and assessing reasonably foreseeable internal and external risks to the security, confidentiality, and/or integrity of any electronic, paper or other records containing personal information, and evaluating and improving, where necessary, the effectiveness of the current safeguards for limiting such risks, including but not limited to:

1. ongoing employee (including temporary and contract employee) training;
2. employee compliance with policies and procedures; and
3. means for detecting and preventing security system failures.

(c) Developing security policies for employees relating to the storage, access and transportation of records containing personal information outside of business premises.

(d) Imposing disciplinary measures for violations of the comprehensive information security program rules.

(e) Preventing terminated employees from accessing records containing personal information.

(f) Oversee service providers, by:

1. Taking reasonable steps to select and retain third-party service providers that are capable of maintaining appropriate security measures to protect such personal information consistent with these regulations and any applicable federal regulations; and
2. Requiring such third-party service providers by contract to implement and maintain such appropriate security measures for personal information; provided, however, that until March 1, 2012, a contract a person has entered into with a third party service provider to perform services for said person or functions on said person's behalf satisfies the provisions of 17.03(2)(f)(2) even if the contract does not include a requirement that the third party service provider maintain such appropriate safeguards, as long as said person entered into the contract no later than March 1, 2010.

(g) Reasonable restrictions upon physical access to records containing personal information, and storage of such records and data in locked facilities, storage areas or containers.

(h) Regular monitoring to ensure that the comprehensive information security program is operating in a manner reasonably calculated to prevent unauthorized access to or unauthorized use of personal information; and upgrading information safeguards as necessary to limit risks.

(i) Reviewing the scope of the security measures at least annually or whenever there is a material change in business practices that may reasonably implicate the security or integrity of records containing personal information.

(j) Documenting responsive actions taken in connection with any incident involving a breach of security, and mandatory post-incident review of events and actions taken, if any, to make changes in business practices relating to protection of personal information.

17.04: Computer System Security Requirements

Every person that owns or licenses personal information about a resident of the Commonwealth and electronically stores or transmits such information shall include in its written, comprehensive information security program the establishment and maintenance of a security system covering its computers, including any wireless system, that, at a minimum, and to the extent technically feasible, shall have the following elements:

(1) Secure user authentication protocols including:

(a) control of user IDs and other identifiers;

(b) a reasonably secure method of assigning and selecting passwords, or use of unique identifier technologies, such as biometrics or token devices;

(c) control of data security passwords to ensure that such passwords are kept in a location and/or format that does not compromise the security of the data they protect;

(d) restricting access to active users and active user accounts only; and

(e) blocking access to user identification after multiple unsuccessful attempts to gain access or the limitation placed on access for the particular system;

(2) Secure access control measures that:

(a) restrict access to records and files containing personal information to those who need such information to perform their job duties; and

(b) assign unique identifications plus passwords, which are not vendor supplied default passwords, to each person with computer access, that are reasonably designed to maintain the integrity of the security of the access controls;

3) Encryption of all transmitted records and files containing personal information that will travel across public networks, and encryption of all data containing personal information to be transmitted wirelessly.

(4) Reasonable monitoring of systems, for unauthorized use of or access to personal information;

(5) Encryption of all personal information stored on laptops or other portable devices;

(6) For files containing personal information on a system that is connected to the Internet, there must be reasonably up-to-date firewall protection and operating system security patches, reasonably designed to maintain the integrity of the personal information.

(7) Reasonably up-to-date versions of system security agent software which must include malware protection and reasonably up-to-date patches and virus definitions, or a version of such software that can still be supported with up-to-date patches and virus definitions, and is set to receive the most current security updates on a regular basis.

(8) Education and training of employees on the proper use of the computer security system and the importance of personal information security.

17.05: Compliance Deadline
(1) Every person who owns or licenses personal information about a resident of the Commonwealth shall be in full compliance with 201 CMR 17.00 on or before March 1, 2010.

REGULATORY AUTHORITY

201 CMR 17.00: M.G.L. c. 93H

APPENDIX G

FTC Safeguards Rule

4. Description of the Projected Reporting, Recordkeeping and Other Compliance Requirements of the Rule, Including an Estimate of the Classes of Small Entities That Will Be Subject to the Requirement and the Type of Professional Skills Necessary for Preparation of the Report or Record

As explained in the Commission's IRFA and the Paperwork Reduction Act discussion that appears elsewhere in this document, the Safeguards Rule does not impose any specific reporting or recordkeeping requirements. Accordingly, compliance with the Rule does not entail expenditures for particular types of professional skills that might be needed for the preparation of such reports or records.

The Rule, however, requires each covered institution to develop a written information security program covering customer information that is appropriate to its size and complexity, the nature and scope of its activities, and the sensitivity of the customer information at issue. The institution must designate an employee or employees to coordinate its safeguards; identify reasonably foreseeable risks and assess the effectiveness of any existing safeguards for controlling these risks; design and implement a safeguards program and regularly monitor its effectiveness; require service providers (by contract) to implement appropriate safeguards for the customer information at issue; and evaluate and adjust its program to material changes that may affect its safeguards, such as new or emerging threats to information security. As discussed above, these requirements will apply to institutions of all sizes that are subject to the FTC's jurisdiction pursuant to the Rule, including small entities, although the Commission did not receive comments that would enable a reliable estimate of the number of such small entities.

In light of concerns that compliance with these requirements might require the use of professional consulting skills that could be costly, the Commission, as explained in its IRFA, fashioned the Rule's requirements to be as flexible as possible consistent with the purposes of the G–L–B Act, so that entities subject to the Rule, including small entities, could simplify their information security program to the same extent that their overall operations are simplified. Furthermore, the Commission invited comments on the costs of establishing and operating an information security program for such entities, particularly any costs stemming from the proposed requirements to: (1) Regularly test or otherwise monitor the effectiveness of

the safeguards' key controls, systems, and procedures, and (2) develop a comprehensive information security program in written form. In response to comments that raised concerns that many businesses would not possess the required resources or expertise to fulfill the Rule's requirements, the Commission notes that the Rule is not intended to require that entities hire outside experts or consultants in order to comply. Further, the Commission has noted that it intends to provide educational materials that will assist such entities in compliance. In addition, in response to concerns that the preparation of a written plan could be burdensome, the Commission amended this requirement slightly to emphasize the flexibility of the writing requirement and make clear that the writing need not be contained in a single document.

5. Description of the Steps the Agency Has Taken To Minimize the Significant Economic Impact on Small Entities, Consistent with the Stated Objectives of Applicable Statutes, Including a Statement of the Factual, Policy, and Legal Reasons for Selecting the Alternative Adopted in the Final Rule and Why Each of the Other Significant Alternatives to the Rule Considered by the Agency That Affect the Impact on Small Entities Was Rejected

The G–L–B Act requires the FTC to issue a rule that establishes standards for safeguarding customer information. The G–L–B Act requires that standards be developed for institutions of all sizes. Therefore, the Rule applies equally to entities with assets of $100 million or less, and not just to larger entities.

As previously noted, the Commission does not believe the Safeguards Rule imposes a significant economic impact on a substantial number of small entities. Nonetheless, to the extent that small entities are subject to the Rule, it imposes flexible standards that allow each institution to develop an information security program that is appropriate to its size and the nature of its operations. In this way, the impact of the Rule on small entities and any other entities subject to the Rule is no greater than necessary to effectuate the purposes and objectives of the G–L–B Act, which requires that the Commission adopt a rule specifying procedures sufficient to safeguard the privacy of customer information protected under the Act. To the extent that commenters suggested alternative regulatory approaches—such as that compliance with alternative standards be deemed compliance with the Rule— that could affect the Rule's impact on small entities, those comments and the

Commission's responses are discussed above in the statement of basis and purpose for the Final Rule.

List of Subjects for 16 CFR Part 314

Consumer protection, Credit, Data protection, Privacy, Trade practices.

Final Rule

For the reasons set forth in the preamble, the Federal Trade Commission amends 16 CFR chapter I, subchapter C, by adding a new part 314 to read as follows:

PART 314—STANDARDS FOR SAFEGUARDING CUSTOMER INFORMATION

Sec.
314.1 Purpose and scope.
314.2 Definitions.
314.3 Standards for safeguarding customer information.
314.4 Elements.
314.5 Effective date.

Authority: 15 U.S.C. 6801(b), 6805(b)(2).

§ 314.1 Purpose and scope.

(a) *Purpose.* This part, which implements sections 501 and 505(b)(2) of the Gramm-Leach-Bliley Act, sets forth standards for developing, implementing, and maintaining reasonable administrative, technical, and physical safeguards to protect the security, confidentiality, and integrity of customer information.

(b) *Scope.* This part applies to the handling of customer information by all financial institutions over which the Federal Trade Commission ("FTC" or "Commission") has jurisdiction. This part refers to such entities as "you." This part applies to all customer information in your possession, regardless of whether such information pertains to individuals with whom you have a customer relationship, or pertains to the customers of other financial institutions that have provided such information to you.

§ 314.2 Definitions.

(a) *In general.* Except as modified by this part or unless the context otherwise requires, the terms used in this part have the same meaning as set forth in the Commission's rule governing the Privacy of Consumer Financial Information, 16 CFR part 313.

(b) *Customer information* means any record containing nonpublic personal information as defined in 16 CFR 313.3(n), about a customer of a financial institution, whether in paper, electronic, or other form, that is handled or maintained by or on behalf of you or your affiliates.

(c) *Information security program* means the administrative, technical, or physical safeguards you use to access, collect, distribute, process, protect, store, use, transmit, dispose of, or otherwise handle customer information.

(d) *Service provider* means any person or entity that receives, maintains, processes, or otherwise is permitted access to customer information through its provision of services directly to a financial institution that is subject to this part.

§ 314.3   Standards for safeguarding customer information.

(a) *Information security program.* You shall develop, implement, and maintain a comprehensive information security program that is written in one or more readily accessible parts and contains administrative, technical, and physical safeguards that are appropriate to your size and complexity, the nature and scope of your activities, and the sensitivity of any customer information at issue. Such safeguards shall include the elements set forth in § 314.4 and shall be reasonably designed to achieve the objectives of this part, as set forth in paragraph (b) of this section.

(b) *Objectives.* The objectives of section 501(b) of the Act, and of this part, are to:

(1) Insure the security and confidentiality of customer information;

(2) Protect against any anticipated threats or hazards to the security or integrity of such information; and

(3) Protect against unauthorized access to or use of such information that could result in substantial harm or inconvenience to any customer.

§ 314.4   Elements.

In order to develop, implement, and maintain your information security program, you shall:

(a) Designate an employee or employees to coordinate your information security program.

(b) Identify reasonably foreseeable internal and external risks to the security, confidentiality, and integrity of customer information that could result in the unauthorized disclosure, misuse, alteration, destruction or other compromise of such information, and assess the sufficiency of any safeguards in place to control these risks. At a minimum, such a risk assessment should include consideration of risks in each relevant area of your operations, including:

(1) Employee training and management;

(2) Information systems, including network and software design, as well as information processing, storage, transmission and disposal; and

(3) Detecting, preventing and responding to attacks, intrusions, or other systems failures.

(c) Design and implement information safeguards to control the risks you identify through risk assessment, and regularly test or otherwise monitor the effectiveness of the safeguards' key controls, systems, and procedures.

(d) Oversee service providers, by:

(1) Taking reasonable steps to select and retain service providers that are capable of maintaining appropriate safeguards for the customer information at issue; and

(2) Requiring your service providers by contract to implement and maintain such safeguards.

(e) Evaluate and adjust your information security program in light of the results of the testing and monitoring required by paragraph (c) of this section; any material changes to your operations or business arrangements; or any other circumstances that you know or have reason to know may have a material impact on your information security program.

§ 314.5   Effective date.

(a) Each financial institution subject to the Commission's jurisdiction must implement an information security program pursuant to this part no later than May 23, 2003.

(b) Two-year grandfathering of service contracts. Until May 24, 2004, a contract you have entered into with a nonaffiliated third party to perform services for you or functions on your behalf satisfies the provisions of § 314.4(d), even if the contract does not include a requirement that the service provider maintain appropriate safeguards, as long as you entered into the contract not later than June 24, 2002.

By direction of the Commission.

Donald S. Clark,

Secretary.

[FR Doc. 02–12952 Filed 5–22–02; 8:45 am]

BILLING CODE 6750–01–P

APPENDIX H

NIST Cybersecurity Framework

Framework for Improving
Critical Infrastructure Cybersecurity

Version 1.0

National Institute of Standards and Technology

February 12, 2014

February 12, 2014   Cybersecurity Framework   Version 1.0

Table of Contents

List of Figures

List of Tables

February 12, 2014   Cybersecurity Framework   Version 1.0

Executive Summary

The national and economic security of the United States depends on the reliable functioning of critical infrastructure. Cybersecurity threats exploit the increased complexity and connectivity of critical infrastructure systems, placing the Nation's security, economy, and public safety and health at risk. Similar to financial and reputational risk, cybersecurity risk affects a company's bottom line. It can drive up costs and impact revenue. It can harm an organization's ability to innovate and to gain and maintain customers.

To better address these risks, the President issued Executive Order 13636, "Improving Critical Infrastructure Cybersecurity," on February 12, 2013, which established that "[i]t is the Policy of the United States to enhance the security and resilience of the Nation's critical infrastructure and to maintain a cyber environment that encourages efficiency, innovation, and economic prosperity while promoting safety, security, business confidentiality, privacy, and civil liberties." In enacting this policy, the Executive Order calls for the development of a voluntary risk-based Cybersecurity Framework – a set of industry standards and best practices to help organizations manage cybersecurity risks. The resulting Framework, created through collaboration between government and the private sector, uses a common language to address and manage cybersecurity risk in a cost-effective way based on business needs without placing additional regulatory requirements on businesses.

The Framework focuses on using business drivers to guide cybersecurity activities and considering cybersecurity risks as part of the organization's risk management processes. The Framework consists of three parts: the Framework Core, the Framework Profile, and the Framework Implementation Tiers. The Framework Core is a set of cybersecurity activities, outcomes, and informative references that are common across critical infrastructure sectors, providing the detailed guidance for developing individual organizational Profiles. Through use of the Profiles, the Framework will help the organization align its cybersecurity activities with its business requirements, risk tolerances, and resources. The Tiers provide a mechanism for organizations to view and understand the characteristics of their approach to managing cybersecurity risk.

The Executive Order also requires that the Framework include a methodology to protect individual privacy and civil liberties when critical infrastructure organizations conduct cybersecurity activities. While processes and existing needs will differ, the Framework can assist organizations in incorporating privacy and civil liberties as part of a comprehensive cybersecurity program.

The Framework enables organizations – regardless of size, degree of cybersecurity risk, or cybersecurity sophistication – to apply the principles and best practices of risk management to improving the security and resilience of critical infrastructure. The Framework provides organization and structure to today's multiple approaches to cybersecurity by assembling standards, guidelines, and practices that are working effectively in industry today. Moreover, because it references globally recognized standards for cybersecurity, the Framework can also be used by organizations located outside the United States and can serve as a model for international cooperation on strengthening critical infrastructure cybersecurity.

The Framework is not a one-size-fits-all approach to managing cybersecurity risk for critical infrastructure. Organizations will continue to have unique risks – different threats, different vulnerabilities, different risk tolerances – and how they implement the practices in the Framework will vary. Organizations can determine activities that are important to critical service delivery and can prioritize investments to maximize the impact of each dollar spent. Ultimately, the Framework is aimed at reducing and better managing cybersecurity risks.

The Framework is a living document and will continue to be updated and improved as industry provides feedback on implementation. As the Framework is put into practice, lessons learned will be integrated into future versions. This will ensure it is meeting the needs of critical infrastructure owners and operators in a dynamic and challenging environment of new threats, risks, and solutions.

Use of this voluntary Framework is the next step to improve the cybersecurity of our Nation's critical infrastructure – providing guidance for individual organizations, while increasing the cybersecurity posture of the Nation's critical infrastructure as a whole.

February 12, 2014   Cybersecurity Framework   Version 1.0

1.0 Framework Introduction

The national and economic security of the United States depends on the reliable functioning of critical infrastructure. To strengthen the resilience of this infrastructure, President Obama issued Executive Order 13636 (EO), "Improving Critical Infrastructure Cybersecurity," on February 12, 2013.[1] This Executive Order calls for the development of a voluntary Cybersecurity Framework ("Framework") that provides a "prioritized, flexible, repeatable, performance-based, and cost-effective approach" to manage cybersecurity risk for those processes, information, and systems directly involved in the delivery of critical infrastructure services. The Framework, developed in collaboration with industry, provides guidance to an organization on managing cybersecurity risk.

Critical infrastructure is defined in the EO as "systems and assets, whether physical or virtual, so vital to the United States that the incapacity or destruction of such systems and assets would have a debilitating impact on security, national economic security, national public health or safety, or any combination of those matters." Due to the increasing pressures from external and internal threats, organizations responsible for critical infrastructure need to have a consistent and iterative approach to identifying, assessing, and managing cybersecurity risk. This approach is necessary regardless of an organization's size, threat exposure, or cybersecurity sophistication today.

The critical infrastructure community includes public and private owners and operators, and other entities with a role in securing the Nation's infrastructure. Members of each critical infrastructure sector perform functions that are supported by information technology (IT) and industrial control systems (ICS).[2] This reliance on technology, communication, and the interconnectivity of IT and ICS has changed and expanded the potential vulnerabilities and increased potential risk to operations. For example, as ICS and the data produced in ICS operations are increasingly used to deliver critical services and support business decisions, the potential impacts of a cybersecurity incident on an organization's business, assets, health and safety of individuals, and the environment should be considered. To manage cybersecurity risks, a clear understanding of the organization's business drivers and security considerations specific to its use of IT and ICS is required. Because each organization's risk is unique, along with its use of IT and ICS, the tools and methods used to achieve the outcomes described by the Framework will vary.

Recognizing the role that the protection of privacy and civil liberties plays in creating greater public trust, the Executive Order requires that the Framework include a methodology to protect individual privacy and civil liberties when critical infrastructure organizations conduct cybersecurity activities. Many organizations already have processes for addressing privacy and civil liberties. The methodology is designed to complement such processes and provide guidance to facilitate privacy risk management consistent with an organization's approach to cybersecurity risk management. Integrating privacy and cybersecurity can benefit organizations by increasing customer confidence, enabling more standardized sharing of information, and simplifying operations across legal regimes.

---

[1]   Executive Order no. 13636, *Improving Critical Infrastructure Cybersecurity*, DCPD-201300091, February 12, 2013. http://www.gpo.gov/fdsys/pkg/FR-2013-02-19/pdf/2013-03915.pdf

[2]   The DHS Critical Infrastructure program provides a listing of the sectors and their associated critical functions and value chains. http://www.dhs.gov/critical-infrastructure-sectors

February 12, 2014   Cybersecurity Framework   Version 1.0

To ensure extensibility and enable technical innovation, the Framework is technology neutral. The Framework relies on a variety of existing standards, guidelines, and practices to enable critical infrastructure providers to achieve resilience. By relying on those global standards, guidelines, and practices developed, managed, and updated by industry, the tools and methods available to achieve the Framework outcomes will scale across borders, acknowledge the global nature of cybersecurity risks, and evolve with technological advances and business requirements. The use of existing and emerging standards will enable economies of scale and drive the development of effective products, services, and practices that meet identified market needs. Market competition also promotes faster diffusion of these technologies and practices and realization of many benefits by the stakeholders in these sectors.

Building from those standards, guidelines, and practices, the Framework provides a common taxonomy and mechanism for organizations to:

1) Describe their current cybersecurity posture;

2) Describe their target state for cybersecurity;

3) Identify and prioritize opportunities for improvement within the context of a continuous and repeatable process;

4) Assess progress toward the target state;

5) Communicate among internal and external stakeholders about cybersecurity risk.

The Framework complements, and does not replace, an organization's risk management process and cybersecurity program. The organization can use its current processes and leverage the Framework to identify opportunities to strengthen and communicate its management of cybersecurity risk while aligning with industry practices. Alternatively, an organization without an existing cybersecurity program can use the Framework as a reference to establish one.

Just as the Framework is not industry-specific, the common taxonomy of standards, guidelines, and practices that it provides also is not country-specific. Organizations outside the United States may also use the Framework to strengthen their own cybersecurity efforts, and the Framework can contribute to developing a common language for international cooperation on critical infrastructure cybersecurity.

1.1   Overview of the Framework

The Framework is a risk-based approach to managing cybersecurity risk, and is composed of three parts: the Framework Core, the Framework Implementation Tiers, and the Framework Profiles. Each Framework component reinforces the connection between business drivers and cybersecurity activities. These components are explained below.

- The *Framework Core* is a set of cybersecurity activities, desired outcomes, and applicable references that are common across critical infrastructure sectors. The Core presents industry standards, guidelines, and practices in a manner that allows for communication of cybersecurity activities and outcomes across the organization from the executive level to the implementation/operations level. The Framework Core consists of five concurrent and continuous Functions—Identify, Protect, Detect, Respond, Recover. When considered together, these Functions provide a high-level, strategic view of the lifecycle of an organization's management of cybersecurity risk. The Framework Core

February 12, 2014   Cybersecurity Framework   Version 1.0

then identifies underlying key Categories and Subcategories for each Function, and matches them with example Informative References such as existing standards, guidelines, and practices for each Subcategory.

- *Framework Implementation Tiers* ("Tiers") provide context on how an organization views cybersecurity risk and the processes in place to manage that risk. Tiers describe the degree to which an organization's cybersecurity risk management practices exhibit the characteristics defined in the Framework (e.g., risk and threat aware, repeatable, and adaptive). The Tiers characterize an organization's practices over a range, from Partial (Tier 1) to Adaptive (Tier 4). These Tiers reflect a progression from informal, reactive responses to approaches that are agile and risk-informed. During the Tier selection process, an organization should consider its current risk management practices, threat environment, legal and regulatory requirements, business/mission objectives, and organizational constraints.

- A *Framework Profile* ("Profile") represents the outcomes based on business needs that an organization has selected from the Framework Categories and Subcategories. The Profile can be characterized as the alignment of standards, guidelines, and practices to the Framework Core in a particular implementation scenario. Profiles can be used to identify opportunities for improving cybersecurity posture by comparing a "Current" Profile (the "as is" state) with a "Target" Profile (the "to be" state). To develop a Profile, an organization can review all of the Categories and Subcategories and, based on business drivers and a risk assessment, determine which are most important; they can add Categories and Subcategories as needed to address the organization's risks. The Current Profile can then be used to support prioritization and measurement of progress toward the Target Profile, while factoring in other business needs including cost-effectiveness and innovation. Profiles can be used to conduct self-assessments and communicate within an organization or between organizations.

1.2 Risk Management and the Cybersecurity Framework

Risk management is the ongoing process of identifying, assessing, and responding to risk. To manage risk, organizations should understand the likelihood that an event will occur and the resulting impact. With this information, organizations can determine the acceptable level of risk for delivery of services and can express this as their risk tolerance.

With an understanding of risk tolerance, organizations can prioritize cybersecurity activities, enabling organizations to make informed decisions about cybersecurity expenditures. Implementation of risk management programs offers organizations the ability to quantify and communicate adjustments to their cybersecurity programs. Organizations may choose to handle risk in different ways, including mitigating the risk, transferring the risk, avoiding the risk, or accepting the risk, depending on the potential impact to the delivery of critical services.

The Framework uses risk management processes to enable organizations to inform and prioritize decisions regarding cybersecurity. It supports recurring risk assessments and validation of business drivers to help organizations select target states for cybersecurity activities that reflect desired outcomes. Thus, the Framework gives organizations the ability to dynamically select and direct improvement in cybersecurity risk management for the IT and ICS environments.

February 12, 2014   Cybersecurity Framework   Version 1.0

The Framework is adaptive to provide a flexible and risk-based implementation that can be used with a broad array of cybersecurity risk management processes. Examples of cybersecurity risk management processes include International Organization for Standardization (ISO) 31000:2009[3], ISO/IEC 27005:2011[4], National Institute of Standards and Technology (NIST) Special Publication (SP) 800-39[5], and the *Electricity Subsector Cybersecurity Risk Management Process* (RMP) guideline[6].

1.3   Document Overview

The remainder of this document contains the following sections and appendices:

- Section 2 describes the Framework components: the Framework Core, the Tiers, and the Profiles.
- Section 3 presents examples of how the Framework can be used.
- Appendix A presents the Framework Core in a tabular format: the Functions, Categories, Subcategories, and Informative References.
- Appendix B contains a glossary of selected terms.
- Appendix C lists acronyms used in this document.

---

[3] International Organization for Standardization, *Risk management – Principles and guidelines*, ISO 31000:2009, 2009. http://www.iso.org/iso/home/standards/iso31000.htm

[4] International Organization for Standardization/International Electrotechnical Commission, *Information technology – Security techniques – Information security risk management*, ISO/IEC 27005:2011, 2011. http://www.iso.org/iso/catalogue_detail?csnumber=56742

[5] Joint Task Force Transformation Initiative, *Managing Information Security Risk: Organization, Mission, and Information System View*, NIST Special Publication 800-39, March 2011. http://csrc.nist.gov/publications/nistpubs/800-39/SP800-39-final.pdf

[6] U.S. Department of Energy, *Electricity Subsector Cybersecurity Risk Management Process*, DOE/OE-0003, May 2012. http://energy.gov/sites/prod/files/Cybersecurity%20Risk%20Management%20Process%20Guideline%20-%20Final%20-%20May%202012.pdf

February 12, 2014   Cybersecurity Framework   Version 1.0

2.0 Framework Basics

The Framework provides a common language for understanding, managing, and expressing cybersecurity risk both internally and externally. It can be used to help identify and prioritize actions for reducing cybersecurity risk, and it is a tool for aligning policy, business, and technological approaches to managing that risk. It can be used to manage cybersecurity risk across entire organizations or it can be focused on the delivery of critical services within an organization. Different types of entities – including sector coordinating structures, associations, and organizations – can use the Framework for different purposes, including the creation of common Profiles.

2.1 Framework Core

The *Framework Core* provides a set of activities to achieve specific cybersecurity outcomes, and references examples of guidance to achieve those outcomes. The Core is not a checklist of actions to perform. It presents key cybersecurity outcomes identified by industry as helpful in managing cybersecurity risk. The Core comprises four elements: Functions, Categories, Subcategories, and Informative References, depicted in **Figure 1**:

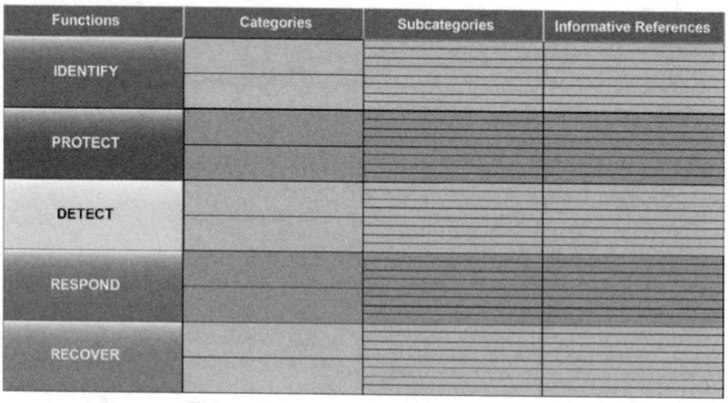

Figure 1: Framework Core Structure

The Framework Core elements work together as follows:

- **Functions** organize basic cybersecurity activities at their highest level. These Functions are Identify, Protect, Detect, Respond, and Recover. They aid an organization in expressing its management of cybersecurity risk by organizing information, enabling risk management decisions, addressing threats, and improving by learning from previous activities. The Functions also align with existing methodologies for incident management and help show the impact of investments in cybersecurity. For example, investments in planning and exercises support timely response and recovery actions, resulting in reduced impact to the delivery of services.

- **Categories** are the subdivisions of a Function into groups of cybersecurity outcomes closely tied to programmatic needs and particular activities. Examples of Categories include "Asset Management," "Access Control," and "Detection Processes."

February 12, 2014   Cybersecurity Framework   Version 1.0

- **Subcategories** further divide a Category into specific outcomes of technical and/or management activities. They provide a set of results that, while not exhaustive, help support achievement of the outcomes in each Category. Examples of Subcategories include "External information systems are catalogued," "Data-at-rest is protected," and "Notifications from detection systems are investigated."

- **Informative References** are specific sections of standards, guidelines, and practices common among critical infrastructure sectors that illustrate a method to achieve the outcomes associated with each Subcategory. The Informative References presented in the Framework Core are illustrative and not exhaustive. They are based upon cross-sector guidance most frequently referenced during the Framework development process.[7]

The five Framework Core Functions are defined below. These Functions are not intended to form a serial path, or lead to a static desired end state. Rather, the Functions can be performed concurrently and continuously to form an operational culture that addresses the dynamic cybersecurity risk. See Appendix A for the complete Framework Core listing.

- **Identify** – Develop the organizational understanding to manage cybersecurity risk to systems, assets, data, and capabilities.

  The activities in the Identify Function are foundational for effective use of the Framework. Understanding the business context, the resources that support critical functions, and the related cybersecurity risks enables an organization to focus and prioritize its efforts, consistent with its risk management strategy and business needs. Examples of outcome Categories within this Function include: Asset Management; Business Environment; Governance; Risk Assessment; and Risk Management Strategy.

- **Protect** – Develop and implement the appropriate safeguards to ensure delivery of critical infrastructure services.

  The Protect Function supports the ability to limit or contain the impact of a potential cybersecurity event. Examples of outcome Categories within this Function include: Access Control; Awareness and Training; Data Security; Information Protection Processes and Procedures; Maintenance; and Protective Technology.

- **Detect** – Develop and implement the appropriate activities to identify the occurrence of a cybersecurity event.

  The Detect Function enables timely discovery of cybersecurity events. Examples of outcome Categories within this Function include: Anomalies and Events; Security Continuous Monitoring; and Detection Processes.

- **Respond** – Develop and implement the appropriate activities to take action regarding a detected cybersecurity event.

---

[7] NIST developed a Compendium of informative references gathered from the Request for Information (RFI) input, Cybersecurity Framework workshops, and stakeholder engagement during the Framework development process. The Compendium includes standards, guidelines, and practices to assist with implementation. The Compendium is not intended to be an exhaustive list, but rather a starting point based on initial stakeholder input. The Compendium and other supporting material can be found at http://www.nist.gov/cyberframework/.

February 12, 2014   Cybersecurity Framework   Version 1.0

The Respond Function supports the ability to contain the impact of a potential cybersecurity event. Examples of outcome Categories within this Function include: Response Planning; Communications; Analysis; Mitigation; and Improvements.

*   **Recover** – Develop and implement the appropriate activities to maintain plans for resilience and to restore any capabilities or services that were impaired due to a cybersecurity event.

The Recover Function supports timely recovery to normal operations to reduce the impact from a cybersecurity event. Examples of outcome Categories within this Function include: Recovery Planning; Improvements; and Communications.

2.2   Framework Implementation Tiers

The Framework Implementation Tiers ("Tiers") provide context on how an organization views cybersecurity risk and the processes in place to manage that risk. The Tiers range from Partial (Tier 1) to Adaptive (Tier 4) and describe an increasing degree of rigor and sophistication in cybersecurity risk management practices and the extent to which cybersecurity risk management is informed by business needs and is integrated into an organization's overall risk management practices. Risk management considerations include many aspects of cybersecurity, including the degree to which privacy and civil liberties considerations are integrated into an organization's management of cybersecurity risk and potential risk responses.

The Tier selection process considers an organization's current risk management practices, threat environment, legal and regulatory requirements, business/mission objectives, and organizational constraints. Organizations should determine the desired Tier, ensuring that the selected level meets the organizational goals, is feasible to implement, and reduces cybersecurity risk to critical assets and resources to levels acceptable to the organization. Organizations should consider leveraging external guidance obtained from Federal government departments and agencies, Information Sharing and Analysis Centers (ISACs), existing maturity models, or other sources to assist in determining their desired tier.

While organizations identified as Tier 1 (Partial) are encouraged to consider moving toward Tier 2 or greater, Tiers do not represent maturity levels. Progression to higher Tiers is encouraged when such a change would reduce cybersecurity risk and be cost effective. Successful implementation of the Framework is based upon achievement of the outcomes described in the organization's Target Profile(s) and not upon Tier determination.

The Tier definitions are as follows:

Tier 1: Partial

- *Risk Management Process* – Organizational cybersecurity risk management practices are not formalized, and risk is managed in an *ad hoc* and sometimes reactive manner. Prioritization of cybersecurity activities may not be directly informed by organizational risk objectives, the threat environment, or business/mission requirements.

- *Integrated Risk Management Program* – There is limited awareness of cybersecurity risk at the organizational level and an organization-wide approach to managing cybersecurity risk has not been established. The organization implements cybersecurity risk management on an irregular, case-by-case basis due to varied experience or information gained from outside sources. The organization may not have processes that enable cybersecurity information to be shared within the organization.

- *External Participation* – An organization may not have the processes in place to participate in coordination or collaboration with other entities.

Tier 2: Risk Informed

- *Risk Management Process* – Risk management practices are approved by management but may not be established as organizational-wide policy. Prioritization of cybersecurity activities is directly informed by organizational risk objectives, the threat environment, or business/mission requirements.

- *Integrated Risk Management Program* – There is an awareness of cybersecurity risk at the organizational level but an organization-wide approach to managing cybersecurity risk has not been established. Risk-informed, management-approved processes and procedures are defined and implemented, and staff has adequate resources to perform their cybersecurity duties. Cybersecurity information is shared within the organization on an informal basis.

- *External Participation* – The organization knows its role in the larger ecosystem, but has not formalized its capabilities to interact and share information externally.

Tier 3: Repeatable

- *Risk Management Process* – The organization's risk management practices are formally approved and expressed as policy. Organizational cybersecurity practices are regularly updated based on the application of risk management processes to changes in business/mission requirements and a changing threat and technology landscape.

- *Integrated Risk Management Program* – There is an organization-wide approach to manage cybersecurity risk. Risk-informed policies, processes, and procedures are defined, implemented as intended, and reviewed. Consistent methods are in place to respond effectively to changes in risk. Personnel possess the knowledge and skills to perform their appointed roles and responsibilities.

- *External Participation* – The organization understands its dependencies and partners and receives information from these partners that enables collaboration and risk-based management decisions within the organization in response to events.

Tier 4: Adaptive

- *Risk Management Process* – The organization adapts its cybersecurity practices based on lessons learned and predictive indicators derived from previous and current cybersecurity activities. Through a process of continuous improvement incorporating advanced cybersecurity technologies and practices, the organization actively adapts to a changing cybersecurity landscape and responds to evolving and sophisticated threats in a timely manner.

- *Integrated Risk Management Program* – There is an organization-wide approach to managing cybersecurity risk that uses risk-informed policies, processes, and procedures to address potential cybersecurity events. Cybersecurity risk management is part of the organizational culture and evolves from an awareness of previous activities, information shared by other sources, and continuous awareness of activities on their systems and networks.

- *External Participation* – The organization manages risk and actively shares information with partners to ensure that accurate, current information is being distributed and consumed to improve cybersecurity before a cybersecurity event occurs.

2.3   Framework Profile

The Framework Profile ("Profile") is the alignment of the Functions, Categories, and Subcategories with the business requirements, risk tolerance, and resources of the organization. A Profile enables organizations to establish a roadmap for reducing cybersecurity risk that is well aligned with organizational and sector goals, considers legal/regulatory requirements and industry best practices, and reflects risk management priorities. Given the complexity of many organizations, they may choose to have multiple profiles, aligned with particular components and recognizing their individual needs.

Framework Profiles can be used to describe the current state or the desired target state of specific cybersecurity activities. The Current Profile indicates the cybersecurity outcomes that are currently being achieved. The Target Profile indicates the outcomes needed to achieve the desired cybersecurity risk management goals. Profiles support business/mission requirements and aid in the communication of risk within and between organizations. This Framework document does not prescribe Profile templates, allowing for flexibility in implementation.

Comparison of Profiles (e.g., the Current Profile and Target Profile) may reveal gaps to be addressed to meet cybersecurity risk management objectives. An action plan to address these gaps can contribute to the roadmap described above. Prioritization of gap mitigation is driven by the organization's business needs and risk management processes. This risk-based approach enables an organization to gauge resource estimates (e.g., staffing, funding) to achieve cybersecurity goals in a cost-effective, prioritized manner.

February 12, 2014   Cybersecurity Framework   Version 1.0

2.4   Coordination of Framework Implementation

Figure 2 describes a common flow of information and decisions at the following levels within an organization:

- Executive
- Business/Process
- Implementation/Operations

The executive level communicates the mission priorities, available resources, and overall risk tolerance to the business/process level. The business/process level uses the information as inputs into the risk management process, and then collaborates with the implementation/operations level to communicate business needs and create a Profile. The implementation/operations level communicates the Profile implementation progress to the business/process level. The business/process level uses this information to perform an impact assessment. Business/process level management reports the outcomes of that impact assessment to the executive level to inform the organization's overall risk management process and to the implementation/operations level for awareness of business impact.

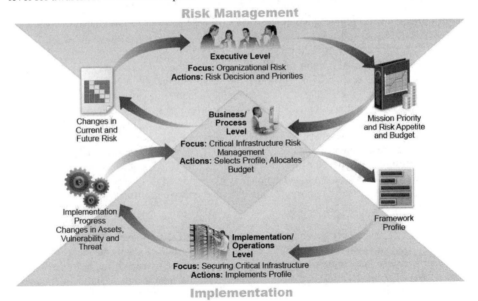

Figure 2: Notional Information and Decision Flows within an Organization

February 12, 2014   Cybersecurity Framework   Version 1.0

3.0   How to Use the Framework

An organization can use the Framework as a key part of its systematic process for identifying, assessing, and managing cybersecurity risk. The Framework is not designed to replace existing processes; an organization can use its current process and overlay it onto the Framework to determine gaps in its current cybersecurity risk approach and develop a roadmap to improvement. Utilizing the Framework as a cybersecurity risk management tool, an organization can determine activities that are most important to critical service delivery and prioritize expenditures to maximize the impact of the investment.

The Framework is designed to complement existing business and cybersecurity operations. It can serve as the foundation for a new cybersecurity program or a mechanism for improving an existing program. The Framework provides a means of expressing cybersecurity requirements to business partners and customers and can help identify gaps in an organization's cybersecurity practices. It also provides a general set of considerations and processes for considering privacy and civil liberties implications in the context of a cybersecurity program.

The following sections present different ways in which organizations can use the Framework.

3.1   Basic Review of Cybersecurity Practices

The Framework can be used to compare an organization's current cybersecurity activities with those outlined in the Framework Core. Through the creation of a Current Profile, organizations can examine the extent to which they are achieving the outcomes described in the Core Categories and Subcategories, aligned with the five high-level Functions: Identify, Protect, Detect, Respond, and Recover. An organization may find that it is already achieving the desired outcomes, thus managing cybersecurity commensurate with the known risk. Conversely, an organization may determine that it has opportunities to (or needs to) improve. The organization can use that information to develop an action plan to strengthen existing cybersecurity practices and reduce cybersecurity risk. An organization may also find that it is overinvesting to achieve certain outcomes. The organization can use this information to reprioritize resources to strengthen other cybersecurity practices.

While they do not replace a risk management process, these five high-level Functions will provide a concise way for senior executives and others to distill the fundamental concepts of cybersecurity risk so that they can assess how identified risks are managed, and how their organization stacks up at a high level against existing cybersecurity standards, guidelines, and practices. The Framework can also help an organization answer fundamental questions, including "How are we doing?" Then they can move in a more informed way to strengthen their cybersecurity practices where and when deemed necessary.

3.2   Establishing or Improving a Cybersecurity Program

The following steps illustrate how an organization could use the Framework to create a new cybersecurity program or improve an existing program. These steps should be repeated as necessary to continuously improve cybersecurity.

February 12, 2014   Cybersecurity Framework   Version 1.0

Step 1: Prioritize and Scope. The organization identifies its business/mission objectives and high-level organizational priorities. With this information, the organization makes strategic decisions regarding cybersecurity implementations and determines the scope of systems and assets that support the selected business line or process. The Framework can be adapted to support the different business lines or processes within an organization, which may have different business needs and associated risk tolerance.

Step 2: Orient. Once the scope of the cybersecurity program has been determined for the business line or process, the organization identifies related systems and assets, regulatory requirements, and overall risk approach. The organization then identifies threats to, and vulnerabilities of, those systems and assets.

Step 3: Create a Current Profile. The organization develops a Current Profile by indicating which Category and Subcategory outcomes from the Framework Core are currently being achieved.

Step 4: Conduct a Risk Assessment. This assessment could be guided by the organization's overall risk management process or previous risk assessment activities. The organization analyzes the operational environment in order to discern the likelihood of a cybersecurity event and the impact that the event could have on the organization. It is important that organizations seek to incorporate emerging risks and threat and vulnerability data to facilitate a robust understanding of the likelihood and impact of cybersecurity events.

Step 5: Create a Target Profile. The organization creates a Target Profile that focuses on the assessment of the Framework Categories and Subcategories describing the organization's desired cybersecurity outcomes. Organizations also may develop their own additional Categories and Subcategories to account for unique organizational risks. The organization may also consider influences and requirements of external stakeholders such as sector entities, customers, and business partners when creating a Target Profile.

Step 6: Determine, Analyze, and Prioritize Gaps. The organization compares the Current Profile and the Target Profile to determine gaps. Next it creates a prioritized action plan to address those gaps that draws upon mission drivers, a cost/benefit analysis, and understanding of risk to achieve the outcomes in the Target Profile. The organization then determines resources necessary to address the gaps. Using Profiles in this manner enables the organization to make informed decisions about cybersecurity activities, supports risk management, and enables the organization to perform cost-effective, targeted improvements.

Step 7: Implement Action Plan. The organization determines which actions to take in regards to the gaps, if any, identified in the previous step. It then monitors its current cybersecurity practices against the Target Profile. For further guidance, the Framework identifies example Informative References regarding the Categories and Subcategories, but organizations should determine which standards, guidelines, and practices, including those that are sector specific, work best for their needs.

An organization may repeat the steps as needed to continuously assess and improve its cybersecurity. For instance, organizations may find that more frequent repetition of the orient step improves the quality of risk assessments. Furthermore, organizations may monitor progress through iterative updates to the Current Profile, subsequently comparing the Current Profile to the Target Profile. Organizations may also utilize this process to align their cybersecurity program with their desired Framework Implementation Tier.

3.3 Communicating Cybersecurity Requirements with Stakeholders

The Framework provides a common language to communicate requirements among interdependent stakeholders responsible for the delivery of essential critical infrastructure services. Examples include:

- An organization may utilize a Target Profile to express cybersecurity risk management requirements to an external service provider (e.g., a cloud provider to which it is exporting data).
- An organization may express its cybersecurity state through a Current Profile to report results or to compare with acquisition requirements.
- A critical infrastructure owner/operator, having identified an external partner on whom that infrastructure depends, may use a Target Profile to convey required Categories and Subcategories.
- A critical infrastructure sector may establish a Target Profile that can be used among its constituents as an initial baseline Profile to build their tailored Target Profiles.

3.4 Identifying Opportunities for New or Revised Informative References

The Framework can be used to identify opportunities for new or revised standards, guidelines, or practices where additional Informative References would help organizations address emerging needs. An organization implementing a given Subcategory, or developing a new Subcategory, might discover that there are few Informative References, if any, for a related activity. To address that need, the organization might collaborate with technology leaders and/or standards bodies to draft, develop, and coordinate standards, guidelines, or practices.

3.5 Methodology to Protect Privacy and Civil Liberties

This section describes a methodology as required by the Executive Order to address individual privacy and civil liberties implications that may result from cybersecurity operations. This methodology is intended to be a general set of considerations and processes since privacy and civil liberties implications may differ by sector or over time and organizations may address these considerations and processes with a range of technical implementations. Nonetheless, not all activities in a cybersecurity program may give rise to these considerations. Consistent with Section 3.4, technical privacy standards, guidelines, and additional best practices may need to be developed to support improved technical implementations.

Privacy and civil liberties implications may arise when personal information is used, collected, processed, maintained, or disclosed in connection with an organization's cybersecurity activities. Some examples of activities that bear privacy or civil liberties considerations may include: cybersecurity activities that result in the over-collection or over-retention of personal information; disclosure or use of personal information unrelated to cybersecurity activities; cybersecurity mitigation activities that result in denial of service or other similar potentially adverse impacts, including activities such as some types of incident detection or monitoring that may impact freedom of expression or association.

The government and agents of the government have a direct responsibility to protect civil liberties arising from cybersecurity activities. As referenced in the methodology below, government or agents of the government that own or operate critical infrastructure should have a process in place to support compliance of cybersecurity activities with applicable privacy laws, regulations, and Constitutional requirements.

To address privacy implications, organizations may consider how, in circumstances where such measures are appropriate, their cybersecurity program might incorporate privacy principles such as: data minimization in the collection, disclosure, and retention of personal information material related to the cybersecurity incident; use limitations outside of cybersecurity activities on any information collected specifically for cybersecurity activities; transparency for certain cybersecurity activities; individual consent and redress for adverse impacts arising from use of personal information in cybersecurity activities; data quality, integrity, and security; and accountability and auditing.

As organizations assess the Framework Core in Appendix A, the following processes and activities may be considered as a means to address the above-referenced privacy and civil liberties implications:

Governance of cybersecurity risk

- An organization's assessment of cybersecurity risk and potential risk responses considers the privacy implications of its cybersecurity program
- Individuals with cybersecurity-related privacy responsibilities report to appropriate management and are appropriately trained
- Process is in place to support compliance of cybersecurity activities with applicable privacy laws, regulations, and Constitutional requirements
- Process is in place to assess implementation of the foregoing organizational measures and controls

Approaches to identifying and authorizing individuals to access organizational assets and systems

- Steps are taken to identify and address the privacy implications of access control measures to the extent that they involve collection, disclosure, or use of personal information

Awareness and training measures

- Applicable information from organizational privacy policies is included in cybersecurity workforce training and awareness activities
- Service providers that provide cybersecurity-related services for the organization are informed about the organization's applicable privacy policies

Anomalous activity detection and system and assets monitoring

- Process is in place to conduct a privacy review of an organization's anomalous activity detection and cybersecurity monitoring

Response activities, including information sharing or other mitigation efforts

- Process is in place to assess and address whether, when, how, and the extent to which personal information is shared outside the organization as part of cybersecurity information sharing activities
- Process is in place to conduct a privacy review of an organization's cybersecurity mitigation efforts

APPENDIX I

NIST Small
Business
Information
Security

DRAFT NISTIR 7621
Revision 1

Small Business Information Security: The Fundamentals

Richard Kissel
Hyunjeong Moon

This publication is available free of charge

**National Institute of
Standards and Technology**
U.S. Department of Commerce

DRAFT NISTIR 7621
Revision 1

Small Business Information Security: The Fundamentals

Richard Kissel
Hyunjeong Moon
Computer Security Division
Information Technology Laboratory

This publication is available free of charge

December 2014

U.S. Department of Commerce
Penny Pritzker, Secretary

National Institute of Standards and Technology
Willie May, Acting Under Secretary of Commerce for Standards and Technology and Acting Director

National Institute of Standards and Technology Interagency Report 7621 Revision 1
32 pages (December 2014)

This publication is available free of charge

Public comment period: *December 15, 2014* through *February 9, 2015*

National Institute of Standards and Technology
Attn: Computer Security Division, Information Technology Laboratory
100 Bureau Drive (Mail Stop 8930) Gaithersburg, MD 20899-8930
Email: smallbizsecurity@nist.gov

Reports on Computer Systems Technology

The Information Technology Laboratory (ITL) at the National Institute of Standards and Technology (NIST) promotes the U.S. economy and public welfare by providing technical leadership for the Nation's measurement and standards infrastructure. ITL develops tests, test methods, reference data, proof of concept implementations, and technical analyses to advance the development and productive use of information technology. ITL's responsibilities include the development of management, administrative, technical, and physical standards and guidelines for the cost-effective security and privacy of other than national security-related information in Federal information systems.

Abstract

NIST, as a partner with the Small Business Administration and the Federal Bureau of Investigation in an information security awareness outreach to the small business community, developed this NISTIR as a reference guideline for small businesses. This document is intended to present the fundamentals of a small business information security program in non-technical language.

Keywords

small business information security; cybersecurity fundamentals

Acknowledgements

The authors, Richard Kissel and Hyunjeong Moon, wish to thank their colleagues and reviewers who contributed greatly to the document's development.

NISTIR 7621 Rev. 1   Small Business Information Security: Fundamentals

Table of Contents

NISTIR 7621 Rev. 1   Small Business Information Security: Fundamentals

Overview

For some small businesses, the security of their information, systems, and networks might not be a high priority, but for their customers, employees, and trading partners it is very important. The term Small Enterprise (or Small Organization) is sometimes used for this same category of business or organization. A small enterprise/organization may also be a nonprofit organization. The size of a small business varies by type of business, but typically is a business or organization with up to 500 employees.[1]

In the United States, the number of small businesses totals to over 99 % of all businesses. The small business community produces around 46 % of our nation's private-sector output and creates around 63 % of all new jobs in our country.[2] Small businesses, therefore, are a very important part of our nation's economy. They are a significant part of our nation's critical economic and cyber infrastructure.

Larger businesses in the United States have been actively pursuing information security with significant resources including technology, people, and budgets for some years now. As a result, they have become a more difficult target for hackers and cyber criminals. What we are seeing is that the hackers and cyber criminals are now focusing more of their unwanted attention on less secure businesses.

Therefore, it is important that each small business improve the cybersecurity of its information, systems, and networks.

This NIST Interagency Report (NISTIR) will assist small business management in understanding how to provide basic security for their information, systems, and networks.

In addition to this NISTIR, NIST has fostered the creation of the *Framework for Improving Critical Infrastructure Cybersecurity*[3]. This Cybersecurity Framework, created through collaboration between government and the private sector, uses a common language to address and manage cybersecurity risk in a cost-effective way based on business needs without placing additional regulatory requirements on businesses. For more information, see Appendix D—.

Revision 1 of this publication reflects changes in technology and a reorganization of the information needed by small businesses to implement a reasonably effective cybersecurity program.

---

[1] U.S. Small Business Administration, *Table of Small Business Size Standards*, July 14, 2014.
   https://www.sba.gov/sites/default/files/Size_Standards_Table.pdf (accessed November 20, 2014).

[2] U.S. Small Business Administration, Office of Advocacy, *Frequently Asked Questions*, March 2014.
   https://www.sba.gov/sites/default/files/FAQ_March_2014_0.pdf (accessed November 20, 2014).

[3] National Institute of Standards and Technology, *Framework for Improving Critical Infrastructure Cybersecurity*, Version 1.0, February 12, 2014. http://www.nist.gov/cyberframework/upload/cybersecurity-framework-021214.pdf (accessed November 20, 2014).

1   Introduction

Why should a small business be interested in, or concerned with, information security?

The customers of small businesses have an expectation that their sensitive information will be respected and given adequate and appropriate protection. The employees of a small business also have an expectation that their sensitive personal information will be appropriately protected.

And, in addition to these two groups, current and/or potential business partners also have their expectations of the status of information security in a small business. These business partners want assurance that their information, systems, and networks are not put "at risk" when they connect to and do business with a small business. They expect an appropriate level of security in an actual or potential business partner—similar to the level of security that they have implemented in their own systems and networks.

Some of the information used in your business needs special protection for one or more of the following:

- **confidentiality**, to ensure that only those who need access to that information to do their jobs actually have access to it;
- **integrity**, to ensure that the information has not been tampered with or deleted by those who should not have had access to it; and
- **availability**, to ensure that the information is available when it is needed by those who conduct the organization's business.

Such information might be sensitive employee or customer information, confidential business research or plans, or financial information. Some of these information categories (e.g., health, privacy, and certain types of financial information) have special, more restrictive regulatory requirements for information security protection. Failure to properly protect such information, based on the required protections, can easily result in significant fines and penalties from the regulatory agencies involved.

Just as there is a cost involved in protecting information (for hardware, software, or management controls such as policies & procedures, etc), there is also a cost involved in not protecting information. Those engaged in risk management for a small business are also concerned with cost-avoidance—in this case, avoiding the costs of not protecting sensitive business information.

When we consider cost-avoidance, we need to be aware of those costs that aren't immediately obvious. Among such costs are the notification laws that many states have passed which require any business, including small businesses, to notify, in a specified manner, all persons whose data might have been exposed in a security breach (hacker incident, malicious code incident, an employee doing an unauthorized release of information, etc). The average estimated cost for these notifications and associated security breach costs is well over $130 per person. If you have 1000 customers whose data was/or *might have been* compromised in an incident, then your expected minimum cost would be $130,000, per incident. Prevention of identity theft is a goal of these laws and regulations. This should provide motivation to implement adequate security to

NISTIR 7621 Rev. 1   Small Business Information Security: Fundamentals

prevent such incidents. Of course, if there is such an incident then some customers will lose their trust in the affected business and take their business elsewhere. This is another cost that isn't immediately obvious, but which is included in the above per-person cost.

Considering viruses and other malicious code (programs), the severity and impact of current virus/Trojan/Malware attacks are becoming much greater. [4] It is unthinkable to operate a computer without protection from these harmful programs. Many, if not most, of these viruses or malicious code programs are used by organized crime to steal information from computers and make money by selling or illegally using that information for such purposes as identity theft.

It is not possible for any business to implement a perfect information security program, but it is possible (and reasonable) to implement sufficient security for information, systems, and networks that malicious individuals will go elsewhere to find an easier target. Additional information may be found on NIST's Computer Security Resource Center, http://csrc.nist.gov.

---

[4] Symantec Corporation, *Internet Security Threat Report 2014*, 2013 Trends vol. 19 (April 2014), p.24-40. http://www.symantec.com/security_response/publications/threatreport.jsp (accessed November 20, 2014).

2 The "absolutely necessary" cybersecurity actions that a small business should take to protect its information, systems, and networks.

These practices must be done to provide basic information security for your information, computers, and networks.

These practices will help your organization to **identify** and understand the value of your information and systems, **protect** those resources, **detect** possible incidents that could compromise them, and help your organization to **respond** to and **recover** from possible cybersecurity events. See Appendix D— for more detailed descriptions of these Cybersecurity Framework functions.

2.1 Manage Risk.

Cybersecurity Framework (CF) Function(s): ***Identify, Protect***

Risk Management is the process of identifying the risks that your business is exposed to and then managing that risk by implementing protective measures to limit the identified risks.

The action of Risk Assessment is engaged to identify the risks that your business is exposed to. Included in Risk Assessment is identifying the threats to your business and identifying the vulnerabilities that your business has to each of those threats.

Since most small business owners/managers are not cybersecurity professionals, this set of actions should be provided by a cybersecurity contracting firm (preferably one which specializes in small business risk assessment). It would be wise to have them conduct a penetration test of your systems and networks. This is a testing process which seeks out vulnerabilities in your hardware or software. Perhaps this could be arranged for through your local SCORE[5] chapter's cybersecurity professionals.

It is good risk management practice to arrange for an annual independent IT security review to verify the effectiveness of your IT security program. The annual IT security review should be done by an auditing business different from the business providing your cybersecurity services. In the event that you have a cybersecurity incident, this may support your due diligence in protecting your sensitive business information.

2.2 Protect information/systems/networks from damage by viruses, spyware, and other malicious code.

CF Function(s): ***Protect***

Malicious code is code (computer programs) written to do bad things to your data and/or computer (including smart phones, tablets, and other mobile devices). Bad things can be: "find and delete sensitive data;" "find and copy sensitive data – and send it to cyber criminals who

---

[5] Originally known as the Service Corps of Retired Executives, it is now simply referred to as SCORE.

will sell it or use it to make money; record all keystrokes made on the computer (including account numbers, passwords, answers to secret questions, etc) and report that information to a 'command center' somewhere on the Internet; encrypt your sensitive data and demand money for you to get it back; reformat your hard drive; and other actions that might significantly harm your business. There are a growing number of smartphone and tablet apps which contain malicious code.

Install, use (in "real-time" mode, if available), and regularly update anti-virus and anti-spyware software on every computer used in your business.

Many commercial software vendors provide adequate protection at a reasonable price or for free. An Internet search for anti-virus and anti-spyware products will show many of these organizations. Most vendors now offer subscriptions to "security service" applications, which provide multiple layers of protection (in addition to anti-virus and anti-spyware protection).

You should be able to set the anti-virus software to automatically check for updates at some scheduled time during the night (12:00 midnight, for example) and then set it to do a scan soon afterwards (12:30 am, for example). Schedule the anti-spyware software to check for updates at 2:30 am and to do a full system scan at 3:00 am. This assumes that you have an always-on, high-speed connection to the Internet. Regardless of the actual scheduled times for the above updates and scans, schedule them so that only one activity is taking place at any given time.

It is a good idea to obtain copies of your business anti-virus software for your and your employees' home computers. Most people do some business work at home, so it is important to protect their home systems, too.

For case studies of real small businesses that have been victims of cybercrime, go to: http://krebsonsecurity.com/category/smallbizvictims/

2.3   Protect your Internet connection.

CF Function(s): ***Protect***

Most businesses have broadband (high-speed) access to the Internet. It is important to keep in mind that this type of Internet access is always "on." Therefore, your computer—or any network your computer is attached to—is exposed to threats from the Internet on a 24 hours-a-day, 7 days-a-week basis.

For broadband Internet access, it is critical to install and keep operational a hardware firewall between your internal network and the Internet. This may be a function of a wireless access point/router, or it may be a function of a router provided by the Internet Service Provider (ISP) of the small business. There are many hardware vendors that provide firewall wireless access points/routers, firewall routers, and separate firewall devices.

Since employees will do some business work at home, ensure that all employees' home systems are protected by a hardware firewall between their system(s) and the Internet.

For these devices, the administrative password must be changed upon installation and regularly thereafter. It is a good idea to change the administrator's name as well. The default values are easily guessed, and, if not changed, may allow hackers to control your device and thus, to monitor or record your communications and data via the Internet.

2.4   Install and activate software firewalls on all your business systems.

CF Function(s): ***Protect, Detect***

Install, use, and regularly update a software firewall on each computer system used in your small business.

If you use the Microsoft Windows operating system, it probably has a firewall included.[6] You have to ensure that the firewall is operating.

It is important to note that you should only be using a current and vendor-supported version of whatever operating system you choose to use.

When using any commercial operating system, ensure that you review the operating manuals to discover if your system has a firewall included and how it is enabled and configured.

There are commercial software firewalls that you can purchase at a reasonable price or for free that you can use with your Windows systems or with other operating systems. Again, Internet searches and using online and trade magazine reviews and references can assist in selecting a good solution.

Again, since employees do some business work at home, ensure that employee's home systems have firewalls installed and operational on them, and that they are regularly updated.

It is necessary to have software firewalls on each computer even if you have a hardware firewall protecting your network. If your hardware firewall is compromised by a hacker or by malicious code of some kind, you don't want the intruder or malicious program to have unlimited access to your computers and the information on those computers.

2.5   Patch your operating systems and applications.

CF Function(s): ***Protect***

All operating system vendors provide patches and updates to their supported products to correct security problems and to improve functionality. Microsoft provides monthly patches on the second Tuesday of each month. From time to time, Microsoft will issue an "off schedule" patch to respond to a particularly serious threat. To update any supported version of Windows, go to "Start" and select "Windows Update" or "Microsoft Update." Follow the prompts to select and install the recommended patches. Other operating system vendors have similar functionality.

---

[6] See Microsoft's *Safety & Security Center* for more information and downloads: http://www.microsoft.com/security/default.aspx (accessed November 20, 2014).

NISTIR 7621 Rev. 1   Small Business Information Security: Fundamentals

Ensure that you know how to update and patch any operating system you select. When you purchase new computers, update them immediately. Do the same when installing new software.

To update Windows 7:

- click **Start**, then **All Programs**, then **Windows Update**;
- click **Change Settings** in the left pane;
- under **Important Settings**, select the option you want;
- under **Recommended Updates**, choose "Include recommended updates when downloading, installing, or notifying me about updates";
- click **OK**.

To update Windows 8:

- display the charms list by sliding across the top of the screen to the right edge;
- choose **Settings**, then **Control Panel**, then **System and Security**;
- in **Windows Update**, turn **Automatic Updating** "On" and select **Install Updates Automatically**;
- if you want to check for available updates, select **Check for Updates**;
- if you want to see what updates have been installed, select **Update History**.

It is important to note that you should only be using a current and vendor-supported version of whatever operating system you choose to use. Vendors **do not have to provide security updates** for unsupported products. For example, Microsoft ended support for Windows XP on April 8, 2014.[7]

Office productivity products such as Microsoft Office also need to be patched and updated on a regular basis. For Microsoft software, the patch/update process is similar to that of the Microsoft Windows operating systems. Other software products also need to be updated regularly.

2.6   Make backup copies of important business data/information.

*CF Function(s): **Respond, Recover***

Back up your data on each computer used in your business. Your data includes (but is not limited to) word processing documents, electronic spreadsheets, databases, financial files, human resources files, accounts receivable/payable files, and other information used in or generated by your business.

It is necessary to back up your data because computers die, hard disks fail, employees make mistakes, and malicious programs can destroy data on computers. Without data backups, you can

---

[7] Microsoft Corporation, *Windows lifecycle fact sheet* (April 2014), http://windows.microsoft.com/en-us/windows/lifecycle (accessed November 20, 2014).

easily get into a situation where you have to recreate your business data from paper copies and other manual files.

Do this automatically if possible. Many security software suites offer automated backup functions that will do this on a regular schedule for you. Back up only your data, not the applications themselves. **Automatic data backups should be done at least once a <u>week</u>,** and stored on a separate hard disk on your computer, on some form of removable media (e.g., external hard drive), or online storage (e.g., a cloud service provider). The storage device should have enough capacity to hold data for 52 weekly backups, so its size should be about 52 times the amount of data that you have, plus 30 % or so. Remember, this should be done on each of your business computers. It is important to periodically test your backed up data to ensure that you can read it reliably. There are "plug and play" products which, when connected to your computer, will automatically search for files and back them up to a removable media, such as an external USB hard disk.

It is important to **make a full backup of each computer once a <u>month</u>** and store it away from your office location in a protected place. If something happens to your office (fire, flood, tornado, theft, etc) then your data is safe in another location and you can restore your business operations using your backup data and replacement computers and other necessary hardware and software. As you test your individual computer backups to ensure they can be read, it is equally important that you test your monthly backups to ensure that you can read them. If you don't test your backups, you have no grounds for confidence that you will be able to use them in the event of a disaster or contingency.

If you choose to do this monthly backup manually, an easy way is to purchase a form of removable media, such as an external USB hard drive (at least 1 terabyte (TB) capacity). On the hard drive, create a separate folder for each of your computers, and create two folders in each computer folder—one for each odd numbered month and one for each even numbered month. Bring the external disk into your office on the day that you do your monthly backup. Then, complete the following steps: connect the external disk to your first computer and make your backup by copying your data into the appropriate designated folder; immediately do a test restore of a file or folder into a separate folder on your computer that has been set up for this test (to ensure that you can read the restored file or folder). Repeat this process for each of your business computers and, at the end of the process, disconnect the external drive. At the end of the day, take the backup hard drive to the location where you store your monthly backups. At the end of the year, label and store the hard disk in a safe place, and purchase another one for use in the next year.

It is very important to do a monthly backup for each computer used in your business.

Storing data in the "Cloud" is also a possibility. Do your due diligence when selecting a Cloud Service Provider. It is recommended that you encrypt all data prior to storing it in the Cloud. The

Cloud Security Alliance (CSA) provides information and guidance for using the Cloud safely. See Domain 11 "Encryption and Key Management" for additional advice on encryption.[8]

2.7   Control physical access to your computers and network components.

CF Function(s): ***Protect, Detect***

Do not allow unauthorized persons to have physical access to or to use of any of your business computers. This includes locking up laptops when they are not in use. It is a good idea to position each computer's display (or use a privacy screen) so that people walking by cannot see the information on the screen.

Controlling access to your systems and networks also involves being fully aware of anyone who has access to the systems or networks. This includes cleaning crews who come into the office space at night to clean the trash and office space. Criminals often attempt to get jobs on cleaning crews for the purpose of breaking into computers for the sensitive information that they expect to find there. Controlling access also includes being careful about having computer or network repair personnel working unsupervised on systems or devices. It is easy for them to steal privacy/sensitive information and walk out the door with it without anyone noticing anything unusual.

No one should be able to walk into your office space without being challenged by an employee. This can be done in a pleasant, cordial manner, but it must be done to identify those who do not have a legitimate reason for being in your offices. "How may I help you?" is a pleasant way to challenge an unknown individual.

2.8   Secure your wireless access point and networks.

CF Function(s): ***Protect***

If you use wireless networking, it is a good idea to set the wireless access point so that it does not broadcast its Service Set Identifier (SSID). Also, it is critical to change the administrative password that was on the device when you received it. It is important to use strong encryption so that your data being transmitted between your computers and the wireless access point cannot be easily intercepted and read by electronic eavesdroppers. The current recommended encryption is WiFi Protected Access 2 (WPA-2), using the Advanced Encryption Standard (AES) for secure encryption. See your owner's manual for directions on how to make the above changes. Note that WEP (Wired-Equivalent Privacy) is not considered secure; **do not use WEP for encrypting your wireless traffic**.

2.9   Train your employees in basic security principles.

CF Function(s): ***Protect***

---

[8] Cloud Security Alliance, *Security Guidance for Critical Areas of Focus in Cloud Computing v3.0* (2011), p.129. https://cloudsecurityalliance.org/download/security-guidance-for-critical-areas-of-focus-in-cloud-computing-v3/ (accessed November 20, 2014).

Employees who use any computer programs containing sensitive information should be told about that information and must be taught how to properly use and protect that information. On the first day that your new employees start work, they need to be taught what your information security policies are and what they are expected to do to protect your sensitive business information. They need to be taught what your policies require for their use of your computers, networks, and Internet connections.

In addition, teach them your expectations concerning limited personal use of telephones, printers, and any other business owned or provided resources. After this training, they should be requested to sign a statement that they understand these business policies, that they will follow your policies, and that they understand the penalties for not following your policies. (You will need clearly spelled-out penalties for violation of business policies.)

Set up and teach "rules of behavior" which describe how to handle and protect customer data and other business data. This may include not taking business data home or rules about doing business work on home computers.

Having your employees trained in the fundamentals of information, system, and network security is one of the most effective investments you can make to better secure your business information, systems, and networks. You want to develop a "culture of security" in your employees and in your business.

It would be helpful to make your employees aware of the cybersecurity issues arising from allowing children or grandchildren to use their home computers. This is especially true if children or grandchildren are using the computers unsupervised.

Typical providers of such security training could be your local Small Business Development Center (SBDC), SCORE Chapter, community college, technical college, or commercial training vendors.

2.10 Require all individual user accounts for each employee on business computers and for business applications.

*CF Function(s): **Protect***

Set up a separate account for each individual and require that good passwords be used for each account. Good passwords consist of a random sequence of letters (upper case and lower case), numbers, and special characters—and are at least 12 characters long.

To better protect systems and information, ensure that all employees use computer accounts which do not have administrative privileges. This will hinder any attempt—automated or not—to install unauthorized software. If an employee uses a computer with an administrative user account, then any malicious code that they activate (deliberately or by deception) will be able to install itself on their computer—since the malicious code will have the same administrative rights as the user account has.

Without individual accounts for each user, you may find it difficult to hold anyone accountable for data loss or unauthorized data manipulation.

Passwords that stay the same, will, over time, be shared and become common knowledge to an individual user's coworkers. Therefore, **passwords should be changed at least every 3 months**.

2.11 Limit employee access to data and information, and limit authority to install software.

*CF Function(s): **Protect***

Use good business practices to protect your information. Do not provide access to all data to any single employee. Do not provide access to all systems (financial, personnel, inventory, manufacturing, etc) to any single employee. For all employees, provide access to only those systems and only to the specific information that they need to do their jobs.

Do not allow a single individual to both initiate and approve a transaction (financial or otherwise).

The unfortunate truth is that insiders—those who work in a business—are the source of most security incidents in the business. The reason is that they are already known, trusted, and have been given access to important business information and systems. So, when they perform harmful actions (deliberately or otherwise), the business information, systems, and networks—and the business itself—suffer harm.

3   Highly Recommended Cybersecurity Practices

These practices are very important and should be completed immediately after those in Section 2.

3.1   Be careful with email attachments and emails requesting sensitive information.

CF Function(s): ***Protect, Detect***

For business or personal email, do not open email attachments unless you are expecting the email with the attachment and you trust the sender.

One of the more common means of distributing spyware or malicious code is via email attachments. Usually these threats are attached to emails that pretend to be from someone you know, but the "from" address has been altered and it only appears to be a legitimate message from a person you know.

It is always a good idea to call the individual who "sent" the email and ask them if they sent it and ask them what the attachment is about. Sometimes, a person's computer is compromised and malicious code becomes installed on it. Then, the malicious code uses the computer to send emails in the name of the owner of the computer to everyone in the computer owner's email address book. The emails appear to be from the person, but instead are sent by the computer when activated by the malicious code. Those emails typically have copies of the malicious code (with a deceptive file name) as attachments to the email and will attempt to install the malicious code on the computer of anyone who receives the email and opens the attachment.

Beware of emails which ask for sensitive personal or financial information—regardless of who the email appears to be from. No responsible business will ask for sensitive information to be provided in an email.

3.2   Be careful with web links in email, instant messages, social media, or other means.

CF Function(s): ***Protect, Detect***

For business or personal email, do not click on links in email messages. Some scams are in the form of embedded links in emails. Once a recipient clicks on the link, malicious software (e.g., viruses or key stroke logging software) is installed on the user's computer. It is not a good idea to click on links in a Facebook or other social media page.

Don't do it unless you know what the web link connects to and you trust the person who sent the email to you. It is a good idea to call the individual prior to clicking on a link and ask if they sent the email and what the link is for. Always hold the mouse pointer over the link and look at the bottom of the browser window to ensure that the actual link (displayed there) matches the link description in the message (the mouse pointer changes from an arrow to a tiny hand when placed over an active link).

3.3   Watch for harmful popup windows and other hacker tricks.

*CF Function(s): **Protect, Detect***

When connected to and using the Internet, do not respond to popup windows requesting that you to click "ok" for anything.

If a window pops up on your screen informing you that you have a virus or spyware and suggesting that you download an anti-virus or anti-spyware program to take care of it, close the popup window by selecting the X in the upper right corner of the popup window. Do not respond to popup windows informing you that you have to have a new codec, driver, or special program for something in the web page you are visiting. Close the popup window by selecting the X in the upper right corner of the popup window.

Some of these popup windows are actually trying to trick you into clicking on "OK" to download and install spyware or other malicious code onto your computer. Be aware that some of these popup windows are programmed to interpret any mouse click anywhere on the window as an "OK" and act accordingly. For such unexpected popup windows, a safe way to close the window is to reboot your computer. (first close any open applications, documents, etc)

Hackers are known to scatter infected USB drives with provocative labels in public places where their target business's employees hang out, knowing that curious individuals will pick them up and take them back to their office system to "see what's on them." What is on them is generally malicious code which attempts to install a spy program or remote control program on the computer. Teach your employees to not bring USB drives into the office and plug them into your business computers (or to take them home and plug into their home systems). It is a good idea to disable the "AutoRun" feature for the USB ports (and optical drives like CD and DVD drives) on your business computers to help prevent such malicious programs from installing on your systems.

3.4   Do online business or banking more securely.

*CF Function(s): **Protect***

Online business/commerce/banking should only be done using a secure browser connection. This will normally be indicated by a small lock visible in the lower right corner of your web browser window.

After any online commerce or banking session, erase your web browser cache, temporary internet files, cookies, and history so that if your system is compromised, that information will not be on your system to be stolen by the individual hacker or malware program. The steps for erasing this data in Microsoft Internet Explorer and Mozilla Firefox are described below.

For Microsoft Internet Explorer, version 10.0 (steps for other versions may vary slightly):

- select **Tools**, then **Safety**, and click **Delete Browsing History**;
- select those items you want to erase (e.g., temporary files, history, cookies, saved passwords and web form information) and click **Go** to erase them.

For Mozilla Firefox, version 32.0 (steps for other versions may vary slightly):

- select **Tools**, then near the bottom of the popup window click **Options**;
- select the **Privacy** tab, select **Remove Individual Cookies**, then select **Remove All Cookies** to erase your session information;
- it is a good idea to check the box **Tell Sites that I don't want to be tracked;**
- under **History**, select **Never remember history**.

If you do online business banking, the safest way to do this is to have a dedicated computer which is used ONLY for online banking. Do not use it for Internet searches. Do not use it for email. Use it only for online banking for the business.

3.5   Exercise due diligence in hiring employees.

CF Function(s): **Protect**

When hiring a new employee, conduct a comprehensive background check before making a job offer.

You should consider doing criminal background checks on all prospective new employees. Online background checks are quick and relatively inexpensive. Do a full, nationwide, background check. This should also include a sexual offender check. In some areas, the local police department provides a computer for requesting a background check. In some areas, this service is free to you. If possible, it is a good idea to do a credit check on prospective employees. This is especially true if they will be handling your business funds. And, do the rest of your homework—call their references and former employers.

If there are specific educational requirements for the job that they have applied for, call the schools they attended and verify their actual degree(s), date(s) of graduation, and GPA(s).

In considering doing background checks of potential employees, it is also an excellent idea for you to do a background check of yourself. Many people become aware that they are victims of identity theft only after they do a background check on themselves and find arrest records and unusual previous addresses where they never lived (some people become aware only after they are pulled over for a routine traffic stop and then arrested because the officer is notified of an outstanding arrest warrant for them).

3.6   Be careful when surfing the Web.

CF Function(s): **Protect**

No one should surf the Web using a user account with administrative privileges.

If you do surf the Web using an administrative user account, then any malicious code that you happen across on the Internet may be able to install itself on your computer–since the malicious code will have the same administrative rights as your user account. It is best to set up a special account with "guest" (limited) privileges to avoid this vulnerability.

3.7   Be concerned when downloading software from the Internet.

*CF Function(s): **Protect***

Do not download software from any unknown web page.

Only those web pages belonging to businesses with which you have a trusted business relationship should be considered reasonably safe for downloading software. Such trusted sites would include the Microsoft Update web page where you would get patches and updates for various versions of the Windows operating system and Microsoft Office or other similar software. Most other web pages should be viewed with suspicion.

Be very careful if you decide to use freeware or shareware from a source on the Web. Most of these do not come with technical support and some are deliberately crippled so that you do not have the full functionality you might be led to believe will be provided.

3.8   Get help with information security when you need it.

*CF Function(s): **Identify, Protect, Detect, Respond, Recover***

No one is an expert in every business and technical area. Therefore, when you need specialized expertise in information/computer/network security, get help. Ask your SBDC or SCORE Office–often co-located with your local Small Business Administration (SBA) office–for advice and recommendations. You might also consider your local Chamber of Commerce, Better Business Bureau, community college, and/or technical college as a source of referrals for potential providers. For information on identity theft, visit the Federal Trade Commission's (FTC) site on this topic: http://www.ftc.gov/bcp/edu/microsites/idtheft/.

When you get a list of service providers, prepare a request for quotes and send it out as a set of actions or outcomes that you want to receive. Carefully examine and review the quote from each firm responding to your request. Research each firm's past performance and check its references carefully. Request a list of past customers and contact each one to see if the customer was satisfied with the firm's performance and would hire the firm again for future work. Find out who (on the firm's professional staff) will be doing your work. Ask for their professional qualifications for doing your work. Find out how long the firm has been in business.

3.9   Dispose those old computers and media safely.

*CF Function(s): **Identify, Protect***

When disposing of old business computers, remove the hard disks and destroy them. The destruction can be done by taking apart the disk and beating the hard disk platters with a hammer. You could also use a drill with a long drill bit and drill several holes through the hard disk and through the recording platters. Remember to destroy the hard drive electronics and connectors as part of this project. You can also take your hard disks to companies who specialize in destroying storage devices such as hard disks.

When disposing of old media (CDs, floppy disks, USB drives, etc), destroy any containing sensitive business or personal data. Media also includes paper. When disposing of paper containing sensitive information, destroy it by using a crosscut shredder. Incinerate paper containing very sensitive information.

It is very common for small businesses to discard old computers and media without destroying the computers' hard disks or the media. Sensitive business and personal information is regularly found on computers purchased on eBay, thrift shops, Goodwill, etc, much to the embarrassment of the small businesses involved (and much to the annoyance of customers or employees whose sensitive data is compromised). This is a practice which can result in identity theft for the individuals whose information is retrieved from those systems. Destroy hard disks and media and recycle everything else.

3.10 Protect against Social Engineering.

CF Function(s): ***Protect, Detect***

Social engineering is a personal or electronic attempt to obtain unauthorized information or access to systems/facilities or sensitive areas by manipulating people.

The social engineer researches the organization to learn names, titles, responsibilities, and publicly available personal identification information. Then the social engineer usually calls the organization's receptionist or help desk with a believable, but made-up story designed to convince the person that the social engineer is someone in, or associated with, the organization and needs information or system access which the organization's employee can provide and will feel obligated to provide.

To protect against social engineering techniques, employees must be taught to be helpful, but vigilant when someone calls in for help and asks for information or special system access. The employee must first authenticate the caller by asking for identification information that only the person who is in or associated with the organization would know. If the individual is not able to provide such information, then the employee should politely, but firmly refuse to provide what has been requested by the social engineer.

The employee should then notify management of the attempt to obtain information or system access.

3.11 Perform An Asset Inventory (and identify sensitive business information).

CF Function(s): ***Identify***

Do an inventory of all of your hardware and software assets. This should include identifying all of your important business data that you use to run your business/organization. See Appendix A— for details about inventorying your business information. When you are done, you will have a list of hardware assets (e.g., computers, mobile devices, wireless routers, etc.), software assets (programs for word processing, accounting, etc), and information assets (e.g.,proprietary information, employee information, customer information, etc). The inventory should be kept updated by repeating it at least annually. See Section 4.1 for additional information.

3.12 Implement Encryption To Protect Your Business Information.

CF Function(s): **Protect**

Encryption is a process of protecting your sensitive business information by using an encryption program to make the information unreadable to anyone not having the encryption key. In several editions of Microsoft Windows 7 and Windows 8, the encryption function is called BitLocker. It is good practice to use full-disk encryption—which encrypts all information on the storage media—with BitLocker or another full-disk encryption product. Some other encryption programs for the Windows operating system include: Symantec Drive Encryption (Symantec Corporation); CheckPoint Full Disk Encryption and McAfee Endpoint Encryption (SafeBoot). For computers using the Apple OS X operating system (versions 10.3 and later), FileVault disk encryption is provided with the operating system. CheckPoint Full Disk Encryption and McAfee Endpoint Encryption also work with Apple OS X and Linux operating systems. For other operating systems, see the manufacturer's manual for information on full-disk encryption capabilities.

When implementing any full-disk encryption function, **do not forget your encryption key**— write it down and lock up the information in a safe place.

It is important to consider all computing and communications devices when considering encryption. For example, most businesses are using smartphones to help run the business. When smartphones have business information on them, it is important to encrypt those devices to help protect that business information from being stolen, modified or deleted. Most smartphone manufacturers are now providing encryption capabilities with their smartphones. This also applies to tablet devices used in the business.

4   More Advanced Cybersecurity Practices.

In addition to the operational guidelines provided above, there are other considerations that a small business needs to understand and address.

4.1   Plan for Contingency and Disaster Recovery.

*CF Function(s): **Identify, Protect, Detect, Respond, Recover***

What happens if there is a disaster (flood, fire, tornado, etc.) or a contingency (power outage, sewer backup, accidental sprinkler activation, etc.)? Do you have a plan for restoring business operations during or after a disaster or a contingency? Since we all experience power outages or brownouts from time to time, do you have Uninterruptible Power Supplies (UPS) on each of your computers and critical network components? They allow you to work through short power outages and provide enough time to save your data when the electricity goes off.

Have you done an inventory of all information used in running your business? Do you know where each type of information is located (on which computer or server)? Have you prioritized your business information so that you know which type of information is most critical to the operation of your business–and, therefore, which type of information must be restored first in order to run your most critical operations? If you have never (or not recently) done a full inventory of your important business information, now is the time. For a very small business, this shouldn't take longer than a few hours. For a larger small business, this might take from a day to a week or so (see Appendix A— for a worksheet template for such an inventory).

After you complete this inventory, ensure that the information is prioritized relative to its importance for the *entire* business, not necessarily for a single part of the business. When you have your prioritized information inventory (on an electronic spreadsheet), add three columns to address the kind of protection that each type of information needs. Some information will need protection for confidentiality, some for integrity, and some for availability. Some might need all three types of protection (see Appendix B— for a worksheet template for this information).

This list will be very handy when you start to decide how to implement security for your important information and where to spend your limited resources to protect your important information. No one has enough resources to protect every type of information in the best possible way, so you start with the highest priority information, protecting each successive priority level until you run out of resources. Using this method, you will get the most "bang for your buck" for protecting your important information.

In the event of a security incident which results in "lost" data because of malicious code, hackers, or employee misconduct, establish procedures to report incidents to employees and/or customers. Most states have notification laws requiring specific notifications to affected customers.

Insurance companies are offering various cybersecurity policies to cover all or part of the cost of a cybersecurity incident. Ask your business insurance agent for information on how this might work for your business–including coverage, cost, and exclusions. As part of the application process for such insurance, you will be required to implement a basic-level cybersecurity program for your business.

4.2   Identify Cost-Avoidance considerations in information security.

CF Function(s): **Protect**

In Section 1 we discussed cost avoidance factors. It is important to have an idea of how much loss exposure that your business has if something bad happens to your information.

Something "bad" might involve a loss of confidentiality. Perhaps a virus or other malicious program compromises one of your computers and steals a copy of your business' sensitive information (e.g., employee health information, employee personally identifiable information, customer financial information, etc.). Such a loss could easily result in identity theft for employees or customers. It's not unusual for business owners or managers to be unaware of the financial risk to the business in such situations.

Appendix C— contains a worksheet template to generate financial exposure amounts for different scenarios of data and information incidents. This worksheet should be filled out for each data type used in your business, from the highest priority to the lowest priority.

It is important to understand that there is a real cost associated with not providing adequate protection of sensitive business information and that this cost is usually invisible until something bad happens. Then it becomes all too real (and all too expensive) and visible to current and potential customers.

4.3   Create Business policies related to information security.

CF Function(s): **Identify, Protect, Detect, Respond, Recover**

Every business needs written policies to identify acceptable practices and expectations for business operations.

Some policies will be related to human resources, others will relate to expected employee practices for using business resources, such as telephones, computers, printers, fax machines, and Internet access. This is not an exhaustive list and the range of potential policies is largely determined by the type of business and the degree of control and accountability desired by management. Legal and regulatory requirements may also require certain policies to be put in place and enforced.

Policies for information, computer, network, and Internet security, should communicate clearly to employees the expectations that the business management has for appropriate use. These policies should identify the information and other resources that are important to management and should clearly describe how management expects those resources to be used and protected by all employees.

For example, for sensitive employee information a typical policy statement might say, "All employee personnel data shall be protected from viewing or changing by unauthorized persons."

This policy statement identifies a particular type of information and then describes the protection expected to be provided for that information.

Policies should be communicated clearly to each employee, and all employees should sign a statement agreeing that they have read the policies, that they will follow the policies, and that they understand the possible penalties for violating those policies. This will help management to hold employees accountable for violations of the business' policies. As noted, there should be penalties for disregarding business policies. And, those penalties should be enforced fairly and consistently for everyone in the business who violates the policies of the business.

Appendix A—Identifying and prioritizing your organization's information types

1. Think about the information used in/by your organization. Make a list of all the information types used in your organization. (define "information type" in any useful way that makes sense to your business)

2. Then list and prioritize the 5 most important types of information used in your organization. Enter them into the table below.

3. Identify the system on which each information type is located.

4. Identify who has access to each information type.

5. Finally, create a complete table for all your business information types – in priority order.

Table 1: The 5 Highest Priority Information Types In My Organization

Priority	Type of Information	Stored On Which System?	Who has access to this information?
1			
2			
3			
4			
5			

Use this area as your "scratch pad"
(Once you finish this exercise, fill out a full table for all your important business information)

Appendix B—Identifying the protection needed by your organization's priority information types

1. Think about the information used in/by your organization.

2. Enter the 5 highest priority information types in your organization into the table below.

3. Enter the protection required for each information type in the columns to the right. (C – Confidentiality; I – Integrity; A - Availability) <"Y"-needed; "N"-not needed>

4. Finally, finish a complete table for all your business information types.

(Note: this would usually be done by adding three columns to Table 1)

Table 2: The Protection Needed by the 5 Highest Priority Information Types in My Organization

Priority	Type of Information	C	I	A
1				
2				
3				
4				
5				

Appendix C—Estimated costs from bad things happening to your important business information

1. Think about the information used in/by your organization.

2. Enter into the table below your highest priority information type.

3. Enter *estimated* costs for each of the categories on the left.
   If it isn't applicable, please enter NA. Total the costs in each column in the bottom cell.

4. After doing the above three steps, finish a complete table for all your information types.

(Note: this would usually be done by adding three columns to Table 1)

Table 3: The Highest Priority Information Type in My Organization
and an estimated cost associated with specified bad things happening to it.

	<data type name> **Issue: Data Released**	<data type name> **Issue: Data Modified**	<data type name> **Issue: Data Missing**
Cost of Revelation			
Cost to Verify Information			
Cost of Lost Availability			
Cost of Lost Work			
Legal Costs			
Loss of Confidence Costs			
Cost to Repair Problem			
Fines & Penalties			
Other costs— Notification, etc.			
Total Cost Exposure for this data type & issue			

Appendix D—NIST Framework for Improving Critical Infrastructure Cybersecurity

The *Framework for Improving Critical Infrastructure Cybersecurity* includes the five Framework Core Functions defined below. These Functions are not intended to form a serial path, or lead to a static desired end state. Rather, the Functions can be performed concurrently and continuously to form an operational culture that addresses the dynamic cybersecurity risk.

- **Identify** – Develop the organizational understanding to manage cybersecurity risk to systems, assets, data, and capabilities.

  The activities in the Identify Function are foundational for effective use of the Framework. Understanding the business context, the resources that support critical functions, and the related cybersecurity risks enables an organization to focus and prioritize its efforts, consistent with its risk management strategy and business needs. Examples of outcome Categories within this Function include: Asset Management; Business Environment; Governance; Risk Assessment; and Risk Management Strategy.

- **Protect** – Develop and implement the appropriate safeguards to ensure delivery of critical infrastructure services.

  The Protect Function supports the ability to limit or contain the impact of a potential cybersecurity event. Examples of outcome Categories within this Function include: Access Control; Awareness and Training; Data Security; Information Protection Processes and Procedures; Maintenance; and Protective Technology.

- **Detect** – Develop and implement the appropriate activities to identify the occurrence of a cybersecurity event.

  The Detect Function enables timely discovery of cybersecurity events. Examples of outcome Categories within this Function include: Anomalies and Events; Security Continuous Monitoring; and Detection Processes.

- **Respond** – Develop and implement the appropriate activities to take action regarding a detected cybersecurity event.

  The Respond Function supports the ability to contain the impact of a potential cybersecurity event. Examples of outcome Categories within this Function include: Response Planning; Communications; Analysis; Mitigation; and Improvements.

- **Recover** – Develop and implement the appropriate activities to maintain plans for resilience and to restore any capabilities or services that were impaired due to a cybersecurity event.

  The Recover Function supports timely recovery to normal operations to reduce the impact from a cybersecurity event. Examples of outcome Categories within this Function include: Recovery Planning; Improvements; and Communications.

For additional information, see NIST's Cybersecurity Framework homepage: http://www.nist.gov/cyberframework/index.cfm.

APPENDIX J

Lockdown: Information Security Program Checklist

Risk Assessment
- ❑ Inventory of information assets
- ❑ Identify duties to safeguard (ethics, common law, contracts, statutes/regulations)
- ❑ Evaluate need for outside security resources
- ❑ Identify internal and external threats
- ❑ Identify and evaluate current safeguards
- ❑ Identify reasonable safeguards to address identified risks

Develop, Implement and Maintain a Comprehensive Information Security Program
- ❑ Reasonable safeguards (or stronger): appropriate to size of firm, sensitivity of the information, and types of data and systems to be protected
- ❑ Based on appropriate framework(s) and standard(s)
- ❑ Address **Identify, Protect, Detect, Respond and Recover**
- ❑ Cover people, policies and procedures, and technology

People

- ❑ Assign responsibility for security program
  - ❑ Person(s) in charge
  - ❑ Management
  - ❑ Responsibilities of all users
- ❑ Training
  - ❑ Initial, including new employees
  - ❑ Periodic
  - ❑ Promote constant security awareness
- ❑ Monitor compliance
- ❑ Enforcement

Policies and Procedures

- ❑ Comprehensive written program/policy
- ❑ Background checks for new employees
- ❑ Blocking terminated/resigned employees
- ❑ Design and follow an Employee Departure Checklist
- ❑ Management for third-parties given access to confidential information
- ❑ Limit access to confidential data to those with need to access
- ❑ Secure disposal—paper and electronic
- ❑ Training on a regular basis
- ❑ Supervision and monitoring
- ❑ Incident response, investigation, documentation and notification
- ❑ Review safeguards periodically and with changes in risk, threats and technology
- ❑ Periodically evaluate need for outside security resources (including security audits and penetration testing)

Technology

- ❑ Physical security of confidential information and network resources
- ❑ Secure configuration (network and endpoints)
- ❑ Firewall and network appliances
- ❑ Security software: current version + update
- ❑ Patch management (network and endpoints)

- ❑ Authentication and access control
  - ❑ Manage password/passphrase age and complexity
  - ❑ Change all default passwords
  - ❑ Block access after multiple failed attempts
  - ❑ Timeout after inactivity (automatic logoff or screensaver requiring password)
  - ❑ Strong authentication for remote access (two factor best)
- ❑ Encryption of confidential data on laptops and portable media
- ❑ Encryption of confidential data transmitted over the Internet or wireless networks
- ❑ Monitoring and logging
- ❑ Equipment or vendor for secure disposal

APPENDIX K

Federal Trade Commission: "Start With Security"

START
WITH SECURITY

A GUIDE FOR BUSINESS

LESSONS LEARNED FROM FTC CASES

FEDERAL TRADE COMMISSION

START WITH SECURITY

1. Start with security.

2. Control access to data sensibly.

3. Require secure passwords and authentication.

4. Store sensitive personal information securely and protect it during transmission.

5. Segment your network and monitor who's trying to get in and out.

6. Secure remote access to your network.

7. Apply sound security practices when developing new products.

8. Make sure your service providers implement reasonable security measures.

9. Put procedures in place to keep your security current and address vulnerabilities that may arise.

10. Secure paper, physical media, and devices.

When managing your network, developing an app, or even organizing paper files, sound security is no accident. Companies that consider security from the start assess their options and make reasonable choices based on the nature of their business and the sensitivity of the information involved. Threats to data may transform over time, but the fundamentals of sound security remain constant. As the Federal Trade Commission outlined in *Protecting Personal Information: A Guide for Business,* you should know what personal information you have in your files and on your computers, and keep only what you need for your business. You should protect the information that you keep, and properly dispose of what you no longer need. And, of course, you should create a plan to respond to security incidents.

In addition to *Protecting Personal Information*, the FTC has resources to help you think through how those principles apply to your business. There's an online tutorial to help train your employees; publications to address particular data security challenges; and news releases, blog posts, and guidance to help you identify – and possibly prevent – pitfalls.

There's another source of information about keeping sensitive data secure: the lessons learned from the more than 50 law enforcement actions the FTC has announced so far. These are settlements – no findings have been made by a court – and the specifics of the orders apply just to those companies, of course. But learning about alleged lapses that led to law enforcement can help your company improve its practices. And most of these alleged practices involve basic, fundamental security missteps. Distilling the facts of those cases down to their essence, here are ten lessons to learn that touch on vulnerabilities that could affect your company, along with practical guidance on how to reduce the risks they pose.

1 Start with security.

From personal data on employment applications to network files with customers' credit card numbers, sensitive information pervades every part of many companies. Business executives often ask how to manage confidential information. Experts agree on the key first step: Start with security. Factor it into the decisionmaking in every department of your business – personnel, sales, accounting, information technology, etc. Collecting and maintaining information "just because" is no longer a sound business strategy. Savvy companies think through the implication of their data decisions. By making conscious choices about the kind of information you collect, how long you keep it, and who can access it, you can reduce the risk of a data compromise down the road. Of course, all of those decisions will depend on the nature of your business. Lessons from FTC cases illustrate the benefits of building security in from the start by going lean and mean in your data collection, retention, and use policies.

Don't collect personal information you don't need.

Here's a foundational principle to inform your initial decision-making: No one can steal what you don't have. When does your company ask people for sensitive information? Perhaps when they're registering online or setting up a new account. When was the last time you looked at that process to make sure you really need everything you ask for? That's the lesson to learn from a number of FTC cases. For example, the FTC's complaint against *RockYou* charged that the company collected lots of information during the site registration process, including the user's email address and email password. By collecting email passwords – not something the business needed – and then storing them in clear text, the FTC said the company created an unnecessary risk to people's email accounts. The business could have avoided that risk simply by not collecting sensitive information in the first place.

Hold on to information only as long as you have a legitimate business need.

Sometimes it's necessary to collect personal data as part of a transaction. But once the deal is done, it may be unwise to keep it. In the FTC's *BJ's Wholesale Club* case, the company collected customers' credit and debit card information to process transactions in its retail stores. But according to the complaint, it continued to store that data for up to 30 days – long after the sale was complete. Not only did that violate bank rules, but by holding on to the information without a legitimate business need, the FTC said BJ's Wholesale Club created an unreasonable risk. By exploiting other weaknesses in the company's security practices, hackers stole the account data and used it to make counterfeit credit and debit cards. The business could have limited its risk by securely disposing of the financial information once it no longer had a legitimate need for it.

Don't use personal information when it's not necessary.

You wouldn't juggle with a Ming vase. Nor should businesses use personal information in contexts that create unnecessary risks. In the *Accretive* case, the FTC alleged that the company used real people's personal information in employee training sessions, and then failed to remove the information from employees' computers after the sessions were over. Similarly, in *foru International*, the FTC charged that the company gave access to sensitive consumer data to service providers who were developing applications for the company. In both cases, the risk could have been avoided by using fictitious information for training or development purposes.

2 ▶ Control access to data sensibly.

Once you've decided you have a legitimate business need to hold on to sensitive data, take reasonable steps to keep it secure. You'll want to keep it from the prying eyes of outsiders, of course, but what about your own employees? Not everyone on your staff needs unrestricted access to your network and the information stored on it. Put controls in place to make sure employees have access only on a "need to know" basis. For your network, consider steps such as separate user accounts to limit access to the places where personal data is stored or to control who can use particular databases. For paper files, external drives, disks, etc., an access control could be as simple as a locked file cabinet. When thinking about how to control access to sensitive information in your possession, consider these lessons from FTC cases.

Restrict access to sensitive data.

If employees don't have to use personal information as part of their job, there's no need for them to have access to it. For example, in *Goal Financial*, the FTC alleged that the company failed to restrict employee access to personal information stored in paper files and on its network. As a result, a group of employees transferred more than 7,000 consumer files containing sensitive information to third parties without authorization. The company could have prevented that misstep by implementing proper controls and ensuring that only authorized employees with a business need had access to people's personal information.

Limit administrative access.

Administrative access, which allows a user to make system-wide changes to your system, should be limited to the employees tasked to do that job. In its action against *Twitter*, for example, the FTC alleged that the company granted almost all of its employees administrative control over Twitter's system, including the ability to reset user account passwords, view users' nonpublic tweets, and send tweets on users' behalf. According to the complaint, by providing administrative access to just about everybody in-house, Twitter increased the risk that a compromise of any of its employees' credentials could result in a serious breach. How could the company have reduced that risk? By ensuring that employees' access to the system's administrative controls was tailored to their job needs.

3 ▶ Require secure passwords and authentication.

If you have personal information stored on your network, strong authentication procedures – including sensible password "hygiene" – can help ensure that only authorized individuals can access the data. When developing your company's policies, here are tips to take from FTC cases.

Insist on complex and unique passwords.

"Passwords" like 121212 or qwerty aren't much better than no passwords at all. That's why it's wise to give some thought to the password standards you implement. In the *Twitter* case, for example, the company let employees use common dictionary words as administrative passwords, as well as passwords they were already using for other accounts. According to the FTC, those lax practices left Twitter's system vulnerable to hackers who used password-guessing tools, or tried passwords stolen from other services in the hope that Twitter employees used the same password to access the company's system. Twitter could have limited those risks by implementing a more secure password system – for example, by requiring employees to choose complex passwords and training them not to use the same or similar passwords for both business and personal accounts.

Store passwords securely.

Don't make it easy for interlopers to access passwords. In *Guidance Software*, the FTC alleged that the company stored network user credentials in clear, readable text that helped a hacker access customer credit card information on the network. Similarly, in *Reed Elsevier*, the FTC charged that the business allowed customers to store user credentials in a vulnerable format in cookies on their computers. In *Twitter*, too, the FTC said the company failed to establish policies that prohibited employees from storing administrative passwords in plain text in personal email accounts. In each of those cases, the risks could have been reduced if the companies had policies and procedures in place to store credentials securely. Businesses also may want to consider other protections – two-factor authentication, for example – that can help protect against password compromises.

Guard against brute force attacks.

Remember that adage about an infinite number of monkeys at an infinite number of typewriters? Hackers use automated programs that perform a similar function. These brute force attacks work by typing endless combinations of characters until hackers luck into someone's password. In the *Lookout Services*, *Twitter*, and *Reed Elsevier* cases, the FTC alleged that the businesses didn't suspend or disable user credentials after a certain number of unsuccessful login attempts. By not adequately restricting the number of tries, the companies placed their networks at risk. Implementing a policy to suspend or disable accounts after repeated login attempts would have helped to eliminate that risk.

Protect against authentication bypass.

Locking the front door doesn't offer much protection if the back door is left open. In *Lookout Services*, the FTC charged that the company failed to adequately test its web application for widely-known security flaws, including one called "predictable resource location." As a result, a hacker could easily predict patterns and manipulate URLs to bypass the web app's authentication screen and gain unauthorized access to the company's databases. The company could have improved the security of its authentication mechanism by testing for common vulnerabilities.

Store sensitive personal information securely and protect it during transmission.

For many companies, storing sensitive data is a business necessity. And even if you take appropriate steps to secure your network, sometimes you have to send that data elsewhere. Use strong cryptography to secure confidential material during storage and transmission. The method will depend on the types of information your business collects, how you collect it, and how you process it. Given the nature of your business, some possibilities may include Transport Layer Security/Secure Sockets Layer (TLS/SSL) encryption, data-at-rest encryption, or an iterative cryptographic hash. But regardless of the method, it's only as good as the personnel who implement it. Make sure the people you designate to do that job understand how your company uses sensitive data and have the know-how to determine what's appropriate for each situation. With that in mind, here are a few lessons from FTC cases to consider when securing sensitive information during storage and transmission.

Keep sensitive information secure throughout its lifecycle.

Data doesn't stay in one place. That's why it's important to consider security at all stages, if transmitting information is a necessity for your business. In *Superior Mortgage Corporation*, for example, the FTC alleged that the company used SSL encryption to secure the transmission of sensitive personal information between the customer's web browser and the business's website server. But once the information reached the server, the company's service provider decrypted it and emailed it in clear, readable text to the company's headquarters and branch offices. That risk could have been prevented by ensuring the data was secure throughout its lifecycle, and not just during the initial transmission.

Use industry-tested and accepted methods.

When considering what technical standards to follow, keep in mind that experts already may have developed effective standards that can apply to your business. Savvy companies don't start from scratch when it isn't necessary. Instead, they take advantage of that collected wisdom. The *ValueClick* case illustrates that principle. According to the FTC, the company stored sensitive customer information collected through its e-commerce sites in a database that used a non-standard, proprietary form of encryption. Unlike widely-accepted encryption algorithms that are extensively tested, the complaint charged that ValueClick's method used a simple alphabetic substitution system subject to significant vulnerabilities. The company could have avoided those weaknesses by using tried-and-true industry-tested and accepted methods for securing data.

Ensure proper configuration.

Encryption – even strong methods – won't protect your users if you don't configure it properly. That's one message businesses can take from the FTC's actions against *Fandango* and *Credit Karma*. In those cases, the FTC alleged that the companies used SSL encryption in their mobile apps, but turned off a critical process known as SSL certificate validation without implementing other compensating security measures. That made the apps vulnerable to man-in-the-middle attacks, which could allow hackers to decrypt sensitive information the apps transmitted. Those risks could have been prevented if the companies' implementations of SSL had been properly configured.

5 ▶ Segment your network and monitor who's trying to get in and out.

When designing your network, consider using tools like firewalls to segment your network, thereby limiting access between computers on your network and between your computers and the internet. Another useful safeguard: intrusion detection and prevention tools to monitor your network for malicious activity. Here are some lessons from FTC cases to consider when designing your network.

Segment your network.

Not every computer in your system needs to be able to communicate with every other one. You can help protect particularly sensitive data by housing it in a separate secure place on your network. That's a lesson from the *DSW* case. The FTC alleged that the company didn't sufficiently limit computers from one in-store network from connecting to computers on other in-store and corporate networks. As a result, hackers could use one in-store network to connect to, and access personal information on, other in-store and corporate networks. The company could have reduced that risk by sufficiently segmenting its network.

Monitor activity on your network.

"Who's that knocking on my door?" That's what an effective intrusion detection tool asks when it detects unauthorized activity on your network. In the *Dave & Buster's* case, the FTC alleged that the company didn't use an intrusion detection system and didn't monitor system logs for suspicious activity. The FTC says something similar happened in *Cardsystem Solutions*. The business didn't use sufficient measures to detect unauthorized access to its network. Hackers exploited weaknesses, installing programs on the company's network that collected stored sensitive data and sent it outside the network every four days. In each of these cases, the businesses could have reduced the risk of a data compromise or its breadth by using tools to monitor activity on their networks.

6 ▶ Secure remote access to your network.

Business doesn't just happen in the office. While a mobile workforce can increase productivity, it also can pose new security challenges. If you give employees, clients, or service providers remote access to your network, have you taken steps to secure those access points? FTC cases suggest some factors to consider when developing your remote access policies.

Ensure endpoint security.

Just as a chain is only as strong as its weakest link, your network security is only as strong as the weakest security on a computer with remote access to it. That's the message of FTC cases in which companies failed to ensure that computers with remote access to their networks had appropriate endpoint security. For example, in *Premier Capital Lending*, the company allegedly activated a remote login account for a business client to obtain consumer reports, without first assessing the business's security. When hackers accessed the client's system, they stole its remote login credentials and used them to grab consumers' personal information. According to the complaint in *Settlement One*, the business allowed clients that didn't have basic security measures, like firewalls and updated antivirus software, to access consumer reports through its online portal. And in *Lifelock*, the FTC charged that the company failed to install antivirus programs on the computers that employees used to remotely access its network. These businesses could have reduced those risks by securing computers that had remote access to their networks.

Put sensible access limits in place.

Not everyone who might occasionally need to get on your network should have an all-access, backstage pass. That's why it's wise to limit access to what's needed to get the job done. In the *Dave & Buster's* case, for example, the FTC charged that the company failed to adequately restrict third-party access to its network. By exploiting security weaknesses in the third-party company's system, an intruder allegedly connected to the network numerous times and intercepted personal information. What could the company have done to reduce that risk? It could have placed limits on third-party access to its network – for example, by restricting connections to specified IP addresses or granting temporary, limited access.

 Apply sound security practices when developing new products.

So you have a great new app or innovative software on the drawing board. Early in the development process, think through how customers will likely use the product. If they'll be storing or sending sensitive information, is your product up to the task of handling that data securely? Before going to market, consider the lessons from FTC cases involving product development, design, testing, and roll-out.

Train your engineers in secure coding.

Have you explained to your developers the need to keep security at the forefront? In cases like *MTS*, *HTC America*, and *TRENDnet*, the FTC alleged that the companies failed to train their employees in secure coding practices. The upshot: questionable design decisions, including the introduction of vulnerabilities into the software. For example, according to the complaint in *HTC America*, the company failed to implement readily available secure communications mechanisms in the logging applications it pre-installed on its mobile devices. As a result, malicious third-party apps could communicate with the logging applications, placing consumers' text messages, location data, and other sensitive information at risk. The company could have reduced the risk of vulnerabilities like that by adequately training its engineers in secure coding practices.

Follow platform guidelines for security.

When it comes to security, there may not be a need to reinvent the wheel. Sometimes the wisest course is to listen to the experts. In actions against *HTC America*, *Fandango*, and *Credit Karma*, the FTC alleged that the companies failed to follow explicit platform guidelines about secure development practices. For example, Fandango and Credit Karma turned off a critical process known as SSL certificate validation in their mobile apps, leaving the sensitive information consumers transmitted through those apps open to interception through man-in-the-middle attacks. The companies could have prevented this vulnerability by following the iOS and Android guidelines for developers, which explicitly warn against turning off SSL certificate validation.

Verify that privacy and security features work.

If your software offers a privacy or security feature, verify that the feature works as advertised. In *TRENDnet*, for example, the FTC charged that the company failed to test that an option to make a consumer's camera feed private would, in fact, restrict access to that feed. As a result, hundreds of "private" camera feeds were publicly available. Similarly, in *Snapchat*, the company advertised that messages would "disappear forever," but the FTC says it failed to ensure the accuracy of that claim. Among other things, the app saved video files to a location outside of the app's sandbox, making it easy to recover the video files with common file browsing tools. The lesson for other companies: When offering privacy and security features, ensure that your product lives up to your advertising claims.

Test for common vulnerabilities.

There is no way to anticipate every threat, but some vulnerabilities are commonly known and reasonably foreseeable. In more than a dozen FTC cases, businesses failed to adequately assess their applications for well-known vulnerabilities. For example, in the *Guess?* case, the FTC alleged that the business failed to assess whether its web application was vulnerable to Structured Query Language (SQL) injection attacks. As a result, hackers were able to use SQL attacks to gain access to databases with consumers' credit card information. That's a risk that could have been avoided by testing for commonly-known vulnerabilities, like those identified by the Open Web Application Security Project (OWASP).

8 ▶ Make sure your service providers implement reasonable security measures.

When it comes to security, keep a watchful eye on your service providers – for example, companies you hire to process personal information collected from customers or to develop apps. Before hiring someone, be candid about your security expectations. Take reasonable steps to select providers able to implement appropriate security measures and monitor that they're meeting your requirements. FTC cases offer advice on what to consider when hiring and overseeing service providers.

Put it in writing.

Insist that appropriate security standards are part of your contracts. In *GMR Transcription*, for example, the FTC alleged that the company hired service providers to transcribe sensitive audio files, but failed to require the service provider to take reasonable security measures. As a result, the files – many containing highly confidential health-related information – were widely exposed on the internet. For starters, the business could have included contract provisions that required service providers to adopt reasonable security precautions – for example, encryption.

Verify compliance.

Security can't be a "take our word for it" thing. Including security expectations in contracts with service providers is an important first step, but it's also important to build oversight into the process. The *Upromise* case illustrates that point. There, the company hired a service provider to develop a browser toolbar. Upromise claimed that the toolbar, which collected consumers' browsing information to provide personalized offers, would use a filter to "remove any personally identifiable information" before transmission. But, according to the FTC, Upromise failed to verify that the service provider had implemented the information collection program in a manner consistent with Upromise's privacy and security policies and the terms in the contract designed to protect consumer information. As a result, the toolbar collected sensitive personal information – including financial account numbers and security codes from secure web pages – and transmitted it in clear text. How could the company have reduced that risk? By asking questions and following up with the service provider during the development process.

Put procedures in place to keep your security current and address vulnerabilities that may arise.

Securing your software and networks isn't a one-and-done deal. It's an ongoing process that requires you to keep your guard up. If you use third-party software on your networks, or you include third-party software libraries in your applications, apply updates as they're issued. If you develop your own software, how will people let you know if they spot a vulnerability, and how will you make things right? FTC cases offer points to consider in thinking through vulnerability management.

Update and patch third-party software.

Outdated software undermines security. The solution is to update it regularly and implement third-party patches. In the *TJX Companies* case, for example, the FTC alleged that the company didn't update its anti-virus software, increasing the risk that hackers could exploit known vulnerabilities or overcome the business's defenses. Depending on the complexity of your network or software, you may need to prioritize patches by severity; nonetheless, having a reasonable process in place to update and patch third-party software is an important step to reducing the risk of a compromise.

Heed credible security warnings and move quickly to fix them.

When vulnerabilities come to your attention, listen carefully and then get a move on. In the *HTC America* case, the FTC charged that the company didn't have a process for receiving and addressing reports about security vulnerabilities. HTC's alleged delay in responding to warnings meant that the vulnerabilities found their way onto even more devices across multiple operating system versions. Sometimes, companies receive security alerts, but they get lost in the shuffle. In *Fandango*, for example, the company relied on its general customer service system to respond to warnings about security risks. According to the complaint, when a researcher contacted the business about a vulnerability, the system incorrectly categorized the report as a password reset request, sent an automated response, and marked the message as "resolved" without flagging it for further review. As a result, Fandango didn't learn about the vulnerability until FTC staff contacted the company. The lesson for other businesses? Have an effective process in place to receive and address security vulnerability reports. Consider a clearly publicized and effective channel (for example, a dedicated email address like security@yourcompany.com) for receiving reports and flagging them for your security staff.

10 ❯ Secure paper, physical media, and devices.

Network security is a critical consideration, but many of the same lessons apply to paperwork and physical media like hard drives, laptops, flash drives, and disks. FTC cases offer some things to consider when evaluating physical security at your business.

Securely store sensitive files.

If it's necessary to retain important paperwork, take steps to keep it secure. In the *Gregory Navone* case, the FTC alleged that the defendant maintained sensitive consumer information, collected by his former businesses, in boxes in his garage. In *Lifelock*, the complaint charged that the company left faxed documents that included consumers' personal information in an open and easily accessible area. In each case, the business could have reduced the risk to their customers by implementing policies to store documents securely.

Protect devices that process personal information.

Securing information stored on your network won't protect your customers if the data has already been stolen through the device that collects it. In the 2007 *Dollar Tree* investigation, FTC staff said that the business's PIN entry devices were vulnerable to tampering and theft. As a result, unauthorized persons could capture consumer's payment card data, including the magnetic stripe data and PIN, through an attack known as "PED skimming." Given the novelty of this type of attack at the time, and a number of other factors, staff closed the investigation. However, attacks targeting point-of-sale devices are now common and well-known, and businesses should take reasonable steps to protect such devices from compromise.

Keep safety standards in place when data is en route.

Savvy businesses understand the importance of securing sensitive information when it's outside the office. In *Accretive*, for example, the FTC alleged that an employee left a laptop containing more than 600 files, with 20 million pieces of information related to 23,000 patients, in the locked passenger compartment of a car, which was then stolen. The *CBR Systems* case concerned alleged unencrypted backup tapes, a laptop, and an external hard drive – all of which contained sensitive information – that were lifted from an employee's car. In each case, the business could have reduced the risk to consumers' personal information by implementing reasonable security policies when data is en route. For example, when sending files, drives, disks, etc., use a mailing method that lets you track where the package is. Limit the instances when employees need to be out and about with sensitive data in their possession. But when there's a legitimate business need to travel with confidential information, employees should keep it out of sight and under lock and key whenever possible.

Dispose of sensitive data securely.

Paperwork or equipment you no longer need may look like trash, but it's treasure to identity thieves if it includes personal information about consumers or employees. For example, according to the FTC complaints in *Rite Aid* and *CVS Caremark*, the companies tossed sensitive personal information – like prescriptions – in dumpsters. In *Goal Financial*, the FTC alleged that an employee sold surplus hard drives that contained the sensitive personal information of approximately 34,000 customers in clear text. The companies could have prevented the risk to consumers' personal information by shredding, burning, or pulverizing documents to make them unreadable and by using available technology to wipe devices that aren't in use.

Looking for more information?

The FTC's Business Center (**business.ftc.gov**) has a Data Security section with an up-to-date listing of relevant cases and other free resources.

About the FTC

The FTC works for the consumer to prevent fraudulent, deceptive, and unfair practices in the marketplace. The Business Center gives you and your business tools to understand and comply with the law. Regardless of the size of your organization or the industry you're in, knowing – and fulfilling – your compliance responsibilities is smart, sound business. Visit the Business Center at **business.ftc.gov**.

Your Opportunity to Comment

The National Small Business Ombudsman and 10 Regional Fairness Boards collect comments from small businesses about federal compliance and enforcement activities. Each year, the Ombudsman evaluates the conduct of these activities and rates each agency's responsiveness to small businesses. Small businesses can comment to the Ombudsman without fear of reprisal. To comment, call toll-free 1-888-REGFAIR (1-888-734-3247) or go to **sba.gov/ombudsman**.

APPENDIX L

Sensei Employee Out-Process Checklist

Wednesday, December 23, 2015

Employee Name: _____

Please check all items that apply.

___ Time entry completed to-date

___ Phone(s) received

___ Phone accessories

Please note which items received:

___ Computer(s) received

___ Received any power on or encryption passwords

___ Computer accessories received (docking station, USB drives, etc)

Please note which items received:

___ Computer/Laptop bag received

___ Other HW received

Please note which items received:

___ Sensei keys/security cards received

___ Client keys/security cards received

___ Documentation received

___ Software/Licenses received

Please note which items received:

____ Sensei data

Please note what data has been received:

I hereby acknowledge verification or receipt of the above items from above named employee.

_____   _____
Name   Title

_____
Date

Former Employee hereby states that he/she has no Sensei data in his/her possession, that all billable time has been entered, that he/she has no Sensei physical property in his/her possession, and that the Former Employee will not attempt to access the computer network of any current or former client, or Sensei Enterprises' own network, through any means.

_____
Name

_____
Date

APPENDIX M

Sample Security
Policies for
Smaller Firms

Confidentiality Policy

Confidentiality Agreement

The undersigned understands that _____
frequently represents clients who are of interest to the press and whose
interests are the subject of investigation and litigation. The undersigned
agrees that disclosure of any client information would irreparably harm
_____ and agrees not to disclose such informa-
tion to anyone outside the firm without the express consent of _____
_____'s (insert name of position). It is understood that
breach of this agreement will result in the immediate termination of the
undersigned's employment with _____. This
agreement will survive the undersigned's termination.

Employee's signature:

_____

Date:

_____

Personal Device Policy

FORM: Request to Connect a Personal Portable Computing
Device to _____'s System

This is a request to use a personal portable computing device for the
purpose of connecting the device to _____'s
computer network and system.

> Employee Name _____

Before connecting your computer or other device to _____
_____'s computer network, below are some basic security
recommendations to implement when operating your personal computing device.

Recommendations:

- Maintain an antivirus or security protection program and regularly
  scan your system for viruses, malware and other threats.
- Periodically delete unnecessary data and e-mail.
- Maintain strong password security, including the usage of 12 or
  more alphanumeric and special characters.
- If available, the device should employ a data delete function to wipe
  information from the device after multiple incorrect passwords/PINs
  have been entered.
- If available, enable device encryption functionality to encrypt local
  storage.
- Turn off Bluetooth and Wi-Fi connectivity when not in use.
- Limit the use of 3rd party device applications. Unsigned third-party
  applications pose a significant risk to information contained on the
  device.
- Store devices in a secure location or keep them in your physical possession at all times.
- Carry devices in hand luggage when traveling.
- Remote tracking capabilities should be enabled on devices.
- Approved wireless transmission protocols and encryption must
  be used when transmitting *sensitive* information. *Sensitive* data
  traveling to and from the device must also be encrypted during
  transmission.

As a reminder: all employees are obligated to protect the firm data they have access to. The use of the device must conform to all firm policies.

Violations of this policy can result in disciplinary action, up to and including termination.

Individual Justification

The undersigned employee is requesting to use a personal device for the purpose of accessing and/or storing data belonging to _____ _____ and includes the following as supporting justification: _____

_____

_____

Device Information	Notes
Type of Device:	
Make:	
Model:	
Serial Number:	
Operating System:	
Antivirus/Security Suite Program:	
Other:	

I understand that in the event of litigation, or potential litigation, my personal device may be subject to discovery requirements up to and including impoundment of the device.

_____   _____

Employee   Date

_____   _____

Management   Date

_____ Approved   _____ Denied

_____

_____   _____

                                                Date

Information Security Policy

Information Security Policy of _____

It is the policy of _____ to protect the confidentiality of any sensitive information, including Social Security numbers, credit card numbers, medical information, and any other records that may contain personal information and/or are deemed sensitive and confidential. We make reasonable efforts to restrict and limit access to this type of information to those persons who require access through both physical and electronic means.

Introduction

This policy covers the security of firm information and must be distributed to all company employees. Management will review and update this information security policy at least once a year to incorporate relevant security needs in light of changing circumstances and cyber threats. Each employee must read and sign a form verifying they have read, understand and will abide by this policy.

Ethics and Acceptable Use Policies

The firm expects that all employees will conduct themselves in a professional and ethical manner. An employee should not conduct business that is unethical or illegal in any way, nor should an employee influence other employees to act unethically or illegally. Furthermore, an employee should report any dishonest activities or damaging conduct immediately to management.

Importance of Security of Firm Information

We are trusted by our clients to protect sensitive information that may be supplied while conducting business. "Sensitive information" is defined as any personal information (i.e.—name, address, phone number, e-mail, Social Security number, driver's license number, bank account, credit card numbers, etc.) or company information not publicly available (i.e.—clients, financial information, employee information, schedules, technology, etc.).

It is critically important that employees not reveal sensitive information about our company and/or our clients to outside resources that do not have a need to know such information.

Disciplinary Action

An employee's failure to comply with the standards and policies set forth in this document may result in disciplinary action up to and including termination of employment.

Protect Stored Data

Protection of sensitive information stored or handled by the company and its employees must be a primary concern. All sensitive information must be stored securely and disposed of in a secure manner when no longer needed for business reasons. Any media (e.g.—paper, disk, backup tape, computer hard drive, flash drive, etc.) that contains sensitive information must be protected against unauthorized access. Media no longer needed must be destroyed in a manner that will render sensitive data irrecoverable (e.g.—shredding, wiping, physical destruction, etc.).

Credit Card Information Handling Specifics

Credit card numbers or information should be handled only by employees authorized to submit and process credit cards.

If an employee is provided with a credit card number to be processed, they should immediately contact the Office Manager for instructions and processing.

At no time should an employee send a credit card number by e-mail.

All employees must destroy cardholder information in a secure method when no longer needed. Media containing card information must be destroyed by shredding or other means of physical destruction that would render the data irrecoverable.

It is prohibited to maintain and store the contents of the credit card magnetic stripe (track data) on any media whatsoever. After the credit card has been processed, the cardholder information must be securely and properly disposed of.

It is prohibited to maintain and store the card-validation code (3 or 4 digit value printed on the signature panel of the card) on any media whatsoever. After the credit card has been processed, the cardholder information must be securely and properly disposed of. All but the last 4 numbers of the credit card account number must be masked (i.e.—x's or *'s) when the number is displayed electronically or on paper.

Protect Data in Transit

If sensitive Information needs to be transported physically or electronically, it must be encrypted while in transit (e.g.—to a secure storage facility or via the Internet).

Media containing sensitive information and credit card account numbers must be given only to trusted persons for transport to off-site locations. Restrict access to sensitive information (business data and personal information) to those that have a need-to-know. No employees should have access to credit card account numbers unless they have a specific job function that requires such access.

Physical Security

Physical access to sensitive information or systems that store that information (such as computers or filing cabinets storing cardholder data) will be restricted to protect it from those who do not have a need to access that information.

Media containing sensitive information must be securely handled and distributed. If an employee has a question as to whether or not they should be handling sensitive information, they should immediately contact management for guidance.

Media containing stored sensitive information (especially credit card account numbers and social security numbers) should be properly inventoried and disposed of when no longer needed for business by wiping before disposal.

Visitors should always be escorted and monitored when in areas that may contain sensitive information.

Log-in and screen saver passwords are required on all firm computers. Passwords must be alphanumeric and contain at least 12 characters, including special characters, and are required to be changed every 30 days.

Firm provided smartphones will provide encryption of the stored data and be protected with an enforced PIN/Unlock Code. Written management approval must be obtained prior to installing any software or application on a company provided phone.

All firm issued laptops used to access _____'s network must have full disk encryption. Non–firm provided computer systems, media players, etc. must be approved by management in writing **before** connecting them to _____'s internal computer network, including the usage of the private wireless network. There must be a clear business need to approve the request.

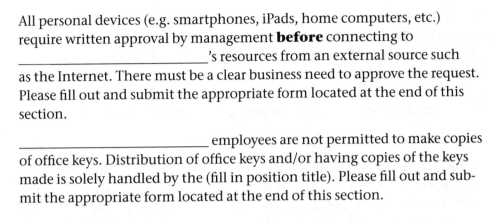

All personal devices (e.g. smartphones, iPads, home computers, etc.) require written approval by management **before** connecting to _____'s resources from an external source such as the Internet. There must be a clear business need to approve the request. Please fill out and submit the appropriate form located at the end of this section.

_____ employees are not permitted to make copies of office keys. Distribution of office keys and/or having copies of the keys made is solely handled by the (fill in position title). Please fill out and submit the appropriate form located at the end of this section.

Security Awareness and Procedures

Keeping sensitive information secure requires periodic training of employees to keep security awareness levels high. The following firm policies and procedures address this issue.

Employees are required to read this security policy and verify that they understand it by signing the acknowledgement form that follows. As changes are made to the Information Security Policy, employees will be notified of such changes.

Background checks (such as credit and criminal record checks, within the limits of local law) will be conducted for all employees.

All third parties with access to credit card account numbers are contractually obligated to comply with the Payment Card Industry Data Security Standard (PCI/DSS).

Company information security policies will be reviewed annually and updated as needed. This was stated previously.

Security Management/Incident Response Plan

If an employee suspects that a compromise of any information, sensitive or not, has taken place, the employee must immediately alert management.

Management will conduct an initial investigation of the suspected compromise.

If a compromise of sensitive information is confirmed, management may consult with a data breach attorney for guidance on how to proceed and to determine the best course of action. If the compromise involves sensitive information, management may take whatever steps are necessary to contain and limit the extent of the exposure by shutting down any systems or processes involved in the compromise.

If credit card numbers have been exposed, Management will alert necessary parties (Merchant Bank, Visa Fraud Control, law enforcement) and provide compromised or potentially compromised card numbers to a Fraud Control agent within 24 hours of being identified.

Agreement to Comply with Information Security Policies

Employee Name _____

I agree to take all reasonable precautions to assure that firm internal information, or information that has been entrusted to the firm by third parties such as clients, will not be disclosed to unauthorized persons. At the end of my employment or contract with the firm, I agree to return all information to which I have had access as a result of my position. I understand that I am not authorized to use sensitive information for my own purposes, nor am I at liberty to provide this information to third parties without the express written consent of management.

I have access to a copy of the Information Security Policy, I have read and understand this policy, and I understand how it impacts my job. As a condition of continued employment, I agree to abide by the policy. I understand that non-compliance will be cause for disciplinary action up to and including dismissal, and perhaps criminal and/or civil penalties.

I also agree to promptly report all violations or suspected violations of the policy to management.

Employee Signature _____

Date _____

Online Activity Policy

Online Activity Policy

Introduction

_____ encourages development of business and personal relationships, including through social networks and other online activities.

While this commitment to online activities is important, we also have substantial legal and ethical responsibilities that must be observed when posting online. These responsibilities include obligations to protect the privacy, confidentiality, and legal interests of _____ _____ and its clients. This Policy applies to any _____-related online activity.

Even when engaging in activities not related to _____ _____ or clients, you are encouraged to recognize that these guidelines may suggest best practices and, when possible, to observe these guidelines even in purely personal activities.

Risk of Online Activity

Both you and _____ owe very significant legal and ethical obligations to our clients. These obligations include duties to keep clients' confidences and to pursue the client's interests first and foremost, even before our own interests. Also, you have obligations not to endanger unnecessarily _____ _____'s interests or its clients' interests.

In light of these obligations, we ask you to be mindful that any online post should be presumed public and permanent. Presume that our client, any relevant court, opposing counsel, disciplinary counsel, and anyone hoping to sue _____ may have access to and use of your online statements. If you place it on the Internet, it can be copied, forwarded, or subpoenaed. You have no control over a post's ultimate use or dissemination.

Scope

This policy governs all _____-related online and Internet activities. Online activity is _____ _____-related if a post (1) contains our company's name, address, contact information, or _____'s e-mail suffix or links to _____'s website, or images of persons working at _____ or attending an event related to _____ business activities or (2) is created or maintained at _____ or using _____'s computers or other equipment.

Questions about Policy

If you have any questions about this Policy or its application, or believe application of the policy to certain circumstances is not appropriate, please contact management to discuss such issues.

Responsibility for Online Activities

The firm considers you personally responsible for any online activity that is linked to or may be traced back to _____ _____. This includes any use of the company name, Internet domain, or property including computers. When you use (a) _____ _____'s name, domain name, e-mail address, or other

contact information, or (b) images of _____
_____'s property, whether physical or electronic, or (c) _____
_____'s computers and other resources, this may
imply that you are acting on _____'s
behalf.

Respect Clients and Colleagues

You should respect the privacy, opinions, and interests of clients, colleagues and others online. Also, you should respect everyone else online.
While a rude response may seem witty at the moment, it may be damaging
to both _____ and you. Thus, we
advise you to avoid such circumstances. If you realize that you have made
a mistake in an online post, apologize and/or take the steps necessary to
correct the mistake.

Do not post anything embarrassing to _____,
colleagues, or clients, or others associated with _____
_____. Obtain permission before posting information from or
about others at or associated with _____.

Protect Client and _____ Confidences

We have a broad obligation to protect client confidences. Under no circumstances should you use or disclose, directly or indirectly, client-related
information—including that _____
represents a client. Exceptions would include cases in which documents
containing the client information are public, where the client has authorized us to release the information or where we are legally compelled to
do so.

Protect Contact Information

Contact information of our clients and business associates is important,
often confidential, information. Under no circumstances should you post
or share such information online. This means that you should not upload
your _____ contact list to a social
network site, because this may expose your contacts to outside review.

Think Before Connecting

Often you will receive requests to friend, connect or link to other social
network users. When considering including clients, referral sources and
others you deal with professionally in your network, please be aware
that you may be opening that information up to others accepted in your
network.

Run a Conflict Check Before Discussing Real Matters

Before discussing any specific matter online, you should determine whether _____ has any involvement in that matter. This includes running a conflict check before posting comments on stories or posts others have authored. If _____ _____ does have some involvement, post nothing without management's consent.

Honest Communications

You should avoid dishonest behavior and misrepresentations online. This includes engaging in online activity, such as communicating electronically or creating websites, while employing a misleading alias or suggesting that you are someone else.

Link to Firm Profile

To help monitor its online profile, _____ has a profile on the following social networks: LinkedIn, Facebook, Twitter and Google+. If you are creating a profile on these networks, we kindly request, but will not force you, to connect to or friend the _____ _____ user and ensure that you allow that user to observe information on your site that is viewable by other network participants.

Obedience to Applicable Rules

You should obey the law and the rules of the website or social network site in which you participate. Further, even if not explicitly directed by this Policy, you should obey other applicable legal and ethical rules. You should not send mass e-mails or other communications to persons whom you do not know to advertise services or solicit potential clients.

Right to Discipline

_____ reserves the right to take disciplinary action against, including to terminate employment of, any person who engages in any online activity that violates the law or otherwise reflects poorly upon or damages _____ or its clients.

_____

Employee signature

_____

Date

APPENDIX N

FTC Disposal Rules

Federal Trade Commission   **§ 682.2**

17. Personal identifying information provided is not consistent with personal identifying information that is on file with the financial institution or creditor.

18. For financial institutions and creditors that use challenge questions, the person opening the covered account or the customer cannot provide authenticating information beyond that which generally would be available from a wallet or consumer report.

Unusual Use of, or Suspicious Activity Related to, the Covered Account

19. Shortly following the notice of a change of address for a covered account, the institution or creditor receives a request for a new, additional, or replacement card or a cell phone, or for the addition of authorized users on the account.

20. A new revolving credit account is used in a manner commonly associated with known patterns of fraud. For example:

a. The majority of available credit is used for cash advances or merchandise that is easily convertible to cash (e.g., electronics equipment or jewelry); or

b. The customer fails to make the first payment or makes an initial payment but no subsequent payments.

21. A covered account is used in a manner that is not consistent with established patterns of activity on the account. There is, for example:

a. Nonpayment when there is no history of late or missed payments;

b. A material increase in the use of available credit;

c. A material change in purchasing or spending patterns;

d. A material change in electronic fund transfer patterns in connection with a deposit account; or

e. A material change in telephone call patterns in connection with a cellular phone account.

22. A covered account that has been inactive for a reasonably lengthy period of time is used (taking into consideration the type of account, the expected pattern of usage and other relevant factors).

23. Mail sent to the customer is returned repeatedly as undeliverable although transactions continue to be conducted in connection with the customer's covered account.

24. The financial institution or creditor is notified that the customer is not receiving paper account statements.

25. The financial institution or creditor is notified of unauthorized charges or transactions in connection with a customer's covered account.

Notice from Customers, Victims of Identity Theft, Law Enforcement Authorities, or Other Persons Regarding Possible Identity Theft in Connection With Covered Accounts Held by the Financial Institution or Creditor

26. The financial institution or creditor is notified by a customer, a victim of identity theft, a law enforcement authority, or any other person that it has opened a fraudulent account for a person engaged in identity theft.

[72 FR 63771, Nov. 9, 2007, as amended at 74 FR 22646, May 14, 2009]

PART 682—DISPOSAL OF CONSUMER REPORT INFORMATION AND RECORDS

Sec.
682.1 Definitions.
682.2 Purpose and scope.
682.3 Proper disposal of consumer information.
682.4 Relation to other laws.
682.5 Effective date.

AUTHORITY: Pub. L. 108–159, sec. 216.

SOURCE: 69 FR 68697, Nov. 24, 2004, unless otherwise noted

§ 682.1 Definitions.

(a) *In general.* Except as modified by this part or unless the context otherwise requires, the terms used in this part have the same meaning as set forth in the Fair Credit Reporting Act, 15 U.S.C. 1681 et seq.

(b) *"Consumer information"* means any record about an individual, whether in paper, electronic, or other form, that is a consumer report or is derived from a consumer report. Consumer information also means a compilation of such records. Consumer information does not include information that does not identify individuals, such as aggregate information or blind data.

(c) *"Dispose," "disposing,"* or *"disposal"* means:

(1) The discarding or abandonment of consumer information, or

(2) The sale, donation, or transfer of any medium, including computer equipment, upon which consumer information is stored.

§ 682.2 Purpose and scope.

(a) *Purpose.* This part ("rule") implements section 216 of the Fair and Accurate Credit Transactions Act of 2003, which is designed to reduce the risk of consumer fraud and related harms, including identity theft, created by improper disposal of consumer information.

(b) *Scope.* This rule applies to any person over which the Federal Trade Commission has jurisdiction, that, for a business purpose, maintains or otherwise possesses consumer information.

§ 682.3 Proper disposal of consumer information.

(a) *Standard.* Any person who maintains or otherwise possesses consumer information for a business purpose must properly dispose of such information by taking reasonable measures to protect against unauthorized access to or use of the information in connection with its disposal.

(b) *Examples.* Reasonable measures to protect against unauthorized access to or use of consumer information in connection with its disposal include the following examples. These examples are illustrative only and are not exclusive or exhaustive methods for complying with the rule in this part.

(1) Implementing and monitoring compliance with policies and procedures that require the burning, pulverizing, or shredding of papers containing consumer information so that the information cannot practicably be read or reconstructed.

(2) Implementing and monitoring compliance with policies and procedures that require the destruction or erasure of electronic media containing consumer information so that the information cannot practicably be read or reconstructed.

(3) After due diligence, entering into and monitoring compliance with a contract with another party engaged in the business of record destruction to dispose of material, specifically identified as consumer information, in a manner consistent with this rule. In this context, due diligence could include reviewing an independent audit of the disposal company's operations and/or its compliance with this rule, obtaining information about the disposal company from several references or other reliable sources, requiring that the disposal company be certified by a recognized trade association or similar third party, reviewing and evaluating the disposal company's information security policies or procedures, or taking other appropriate measures to determine the competency and integrity of the potential disposal company.

(4) For persons or entities who maintain or otherwise possess consumer information through their provision of services directly to a person subject to this part, implementing and monitoring compliance with policies and procedures that protect against unauthorized or unintentional disposal of consumer information, and disposing of such information in accordance with examples (b)(1) and (2) of this section.

(5) For persons subject to the Gramm-Leach-Bliley Act, 15 U.S.C. 6081 et seq., and the Federal Trade Commission's Standards for Safeguarding Customer Information, 16 CFR part 314 ("Safeguards Rule"), incorporating the proper disposal of consumer information as required by this rule into the information security program required by the Safeguards Rule.

§ 682.4 Relation to other laws.

Nothing in the rule in this part shall be construed:

(a) To require a person to maintain or destroy any record pertaining to a consumer that is not imposed under other law; or

(b) To alter or affect any requirement imposed under any other provision of law to maintain or destroy such a record.

§ 682.5 Effective date.

The rule in this part is effective on June 1, 2005.

PART 698—MODEL FORMS AND DISCLOSURES

APPENDIX O

SANS Institute Glossary of Security Terms

The authors are grateful to SANS Institute for allowing us to include this glossary in our book. You can visit the SANS Institute at **www.sans.org**

Access Control—Control that ensures resources are only granted to users who are entitled to them.

Access Control List (ACL)—A mechanism that implements access control for a system resource by listing the identities of the system entities that are permitted to access the resource.

Access Control Service—A security service that provides protection of system resources against unauthorized access. The two basic mechanisms for implementing this service are ACLs and tickets.

Access Management Access—Management is the maintenance of access information which consists of four tasks: account administration, maintenance, monitoring and revocation.

Access Matrix—A matrix that uses rows to represent subjects and columns to represent objects with privileges listed in each cell.

Account Harvesting—The process of collecting all the legitimate account names on a system.

ACK Piggybacking—The practice of sending an ACK inside another packet going to the same destination.

Active Content—Program code embedded in the contents of a web page. When the page is accessed by a web browser, the embedded code is automatically downloaded and executed on the user's workstation. Ex. Java, ActiveX (MS).

Activity Monitors—Monitors that aim to prevent virus infection by monitoring for malicious activity on a system and blocking that activity when possible.

Address Resolution Protocol (ARP)—A protocol for mapping an Internet Protocol address to a physical machine address that is recognized in the local network. A table, usually called the ARP cache, is used to maintain a correlation between each MAC address and its corresponding IP address. ARP provides the protocol rules for making this correlation and providing address conversion in both directions.

Advanced Encryption Standard (AES)—An encryption standard being developed by NIST. Intended to specify an unclassified, publicly disclosed, symmetric encryption algorithm.

Advanced Research Projects Agency Network (ARPANET)—A pioneer packet-switched network that was built in the early 1970s under contract to the U.S. government. It led to the development of today's Internet and was decommissioned in June 1990.

Algorithm—A finite set of step-by-step instructions for a problem-solving or computation procedure, especially one that can be implemented by a computer.

Applet—Java programs; an application program that uses the client's web browser to provide a user interface.

Asymmetric Cryptography—Public key cryptography; a modern branch of cryptography in which the algorithms employ a pair of keys (a public key and a private key) and use a different component of the pair for different steps of the algorithm.

Asymmetric Warfare—The fact that a small investment, properly leveraged, can yield incredible results.

Auditing—The information gathering and analysis of assets to ensure such things as policy compliance and security from vulnerabilities.

Authentication—The process of confirming the correctness of the claimed identity.

Authenticity—The validity and conformance of the original information.

Authorization—The approval, permission or empowerment for someone or something to do something.

Autonomous System—One network or series of networks that are all under one administrative control. An autonomous system is also sometimes referred to as a routing domain. It is assigned a globally unique number, sometimes called an Autonomous System Number (ASN).

Availability—The need to ensure that the business purpose of the system can be met and that it is accessible to those who need to use it.

Backdoor—A tool installed after a compromise to give an attacker easier access to the compromised system around any security mechanisms that are in place.

Bandwidth—Commonly used to mean the capacity of a communication channel to pass data through the channel in a given amount of time. Usually expressed in bits per second.

Banner—The information that is displayed to a remote user trying to connect to a service. This may include version information, system information or a warning about authorized use.

Basic Authentication—The simplest web-based authentication scheme that works by sending the username and password with each request.

Bastion Host—A host that has been hardened in anticipation of vulnerabilities that have not been discovered yet.

Berkeley Internet Name Domain (BIND)—An implementation of DNS; DNS is used for domain name to IP address resolution.

Biometrics—Metrics that use physical characteristics of the users to determine access.

Bit—The smallest unit of information storage; a contraction of the term binary digit; one of two symbols—"0" (zero) and "1" (one)—that are used to represent binary numbers.

Block Cipher—A cipher that encrypts one block of data at a time.

Boot Record Infector—A piece of malware that inserts malicious code into the boot sector of a disk.

Border Gateway Protocol (BGP)—An interautonomous system routing protocol. BGP is used to exchange routing information for the Internet and is the protocol used between Internet service providers (ISPs).

Botnet—A large number of compromised computers that are used to create and send spam or viruses or flood a network with messages as a denial of service attack.

Bridge—A product that connects a local area network (LAN) to another local area network that uses the same protocol (e.g., Ethernet or token ring).

British Standard 7799—A standard code of practice that provides guidance on how to secure an information system. It includes the management framework, objectives and control requirements for information security management systems.

Broadcast—To simultaneously send the same message to multiple recipients. One host to all hosts on network.

Broadcast Address—An address used to broadcast a datagram to all hosts on a given network using UDP or ICMP protocol.

Browser—A client computer program that can retrieve and display information from servers on the World Wide Web.

Brute Force—A cryptanalysis technique or other kind of attack method involving an exhaustive procedure that tries all possibilities one by one.

Buffer Overflow—An overflow that occurs when a program or process tries to store more data in a buffer (temporary data storage area) than it was intended to hold. Since buffers are created to contain a finite amount of data, the extra information—which has to go somewhere—can overflow into adjacent buffers, corrupting or overwriting the valid data held in them.

Business Continuity Plan (BCP)—The plan for emergency response, backup operations and post disaster recovery steps that will ensure the availability of critical resources and facilitate the continuity of operations in an emergency situation.

Business Impact Analysis (BIA)—An analysis that determines what levels of impact to a system are tolerable.

Byte—A fundamental unit of computer storage; the smallest addressable unit in a computer's architecture. Usually holds one character of information and usually means eight bits.

Cache—A special high-speed storage mechanism. It can be either a reserved section of main memory or an independent high-speed storage device. Two types of caching are commonly used in personal computers: memory caching and disk caching. Pronounced cash.

Cache Cramming—The technique of tricking a browser to run cached Java code from the local disk, instead of the Internet zone, so it runs with less restrictive permissions.

Cache Poisoning—Malicious or misleading data from a remote name server are saved (cached) by another name server. Typically used with DNS cache poisoning attacks.

Call Admission Control (CAC)—The inspection and control of all inbound and outbound voice network activity by a voice firewall based on user-defined policies.

Cell—A unit of data transmitted over an ATM network.

Certificate-Based Authentication—The use of SSL and certificates to authenticate and encrypt HTTP traffic.

CGI (Common Gateway Interface)—This mechanism is used by HTTP servers (web servers) to pass parameters to executable scripts to generate responses dynamically.

Chain of Custody—The important application of the federal rules of evidence and its handling.

Challenge-Handshake Authentication Protocol (CHAP)—A protocol that uses a challenge/response authentication mechanism where the response varies every challenge to prevent replay attacks.

Checksum—A value that is computed by a function that is dependent on the contents of a data object and is stored or transmitted together with the object for the purpose of detecting changes in the data.

Cipher—A cryptographic algorithm for encryption and decryption.

Cipher Text—The encrypted form of the message being sent.

Circuit Switched Network—A circuit switched network is where a single continuous physical circuit connected two endpoints where the route was immutable once set up.

Client—A system entity that requests and uses a service provided by another system entity, called a server. In some cases, the server may itself be a client of some other server.

Cold/Warm/Hot Disaster Recovery Site—Hot site: It contains fully redundant hardware and software, with telecommunications, telephone and utility connectivity to continue all primary site operations. Failover occurs within minutes or hours following a disaster. Daily data synchronization usually occurs between the primary and hot site, resulting in minimum or no data loss. Offsite data backup tapes might be obtained and delivered to the hot site to help restore operations. Backup tapes should be regularly tested to detect data corruption, malicious code and environmental damage. A hot site is the most expensive option. Warm site: It contains partially redundant hardware and software, with telecommunications, telephone and utility connectivity to continue some, but not all, primary site operations. Failover occurs within hours or days following a disaster. Daily or weekly data synchronization usually occurs between the primary and warm site, resulting in minimum data loss. Off-site data backup tapes must be obtained and delivered to the warm site to restore operations. A warm site is the second most expensive option. Cold site: Hardware is ordered, shipped and installed, and software is loaded. Basic telecommunications, telephone and utility connectivity might need turning on to continue some, but not all, primary site operations. Relocation occurs within weeks or longer depending on hardware arrival time following a disaster. No data synchronization occurs between the primary and cold site, which could result in significant data loss. Offsite data backup tapes must be obtained and delivered to the cold site to restore operations. A cold site is the least expensive option.

Collision—A collision occurs when multiple systems transmit simultaneously on the same wire.

Competitive Intelligence—Espionage using legal, or at least not obviously illegal, means.

Computer Emergency Response Team (CERT)—An organization that studies computer and network InfoSec to provide incident response services to victims of attacks, publish alerts concerning vulnerabilities and threats and offer other information to help improve computer and network security.

Computer Network—A collection of host computers together with the subnetwork or internetwork through which they can exchange data.

Confidentiality—The need to ensure that information is disclosed only to those who are authorized to view it.

Configuration Management—Establish a known baseline condition and manage it.

Cookie—Data exchanged between an http server and a browser (a client of the server) to store state information on the client side and retrieve it later for server use. An http server, when sending data to a client, may send along a cookie, which the client retains after the http connection closes. A server can use this mechanism to maintain persistent client-side state information for http-based applications, retrieving the state information in later connections.

Corruption—A threat action that undesirably alters system operation by adversely modifying system functions or data.

Cost-Benefit Analysis—An analysis that compares the cost of implementing countermeasures with the value of the reduced risk.

Countermeasure—Reactive methods used to prevent an exploit from successfully occurring once a threat has been detected. Intrusion prevention systems (IPSs) commonly employ countermeasures to prevent intruders from gaining further access to a computer network. Other countermeasures are patches, access control lists and malware filters.

Covert Channels—The means by which information can be communicated between two parties in a covert fashion using normal system operations. For example, changing the amount of hard drive space that is available on a file server can be used to communicate information.

Cron—A UNIX application that runs jobs for users and administrators at scheduled times of the day.

Crossover Cable—A cable that reverses the pairs of cables at the other end and can be used to connect devices directly together.

Cryptanalysis—The mathematical science that deals with analysis of a cryptographic system to gain knowledge needed to break or circumvent the protection that the system is designed to provide. In other words, convert the cipher text to plaintext without knowing the key.

Cryptographic Algorithm (or Hash)—An algorithm that employs the science of cryptography, including encryption algorithms, cryptographic hash algorithms, digital signature algorithms and key agreement algorithms.

Cut-Through—A method of switching where only the header of a packet is read before it is forwarded to its destination.

Cyclic Redundancy Check (CRC)—A type of checksum algorithm that is not a cryptographic hash but is used to implement data integrity service where accidental changes to data are expected. Sometimes called cyclic redundancy code.

Daemon—A program which is often started at the time the system boots and runs continuously without intervention from any of the users on the system. The daemon program forwards the requests to other programs (or processes) as appropriate. The term daemon is a UNIX term, but many other operating systems provide support for daemons, though they're sometimes called other names. Windows, for example, refers to daemons and system agents as services.

Data Aggregation—The ability to get a more complete picture of the information by analyzing several different types of records at once.

Data Custodian—The entity currently using or manipulating the data and, therefore, temporarily taking responsibility for the data.

Data Encryption Standard (DES)—A widely used method of data encryption using a private (secret) key. There are 72,000,000,000,000,000 (72 quadrillion) or more possible encryption keys that can be used. For each given message, the key is chosen at random from among this enormous number of keys. Like other private key cryptographic methods, both the sender and the receiver must know and use the same private key.

Data Mining—A technique used to analyze existing information, usually with the intention of pursuing new avenues to pursue business.

Data Owner—The entity having responsibility and authority for the data.

Data Warehousing—The consolidation of several previously independent databases into one location.

Datagram—Request for Comment 1594 says, "a self-contained, independent entity of data carrying sufficient information to be routed from the source to the destination computer without reliance on earlier exchanges between this source and destination computer and the transporting network." The term has been generally replaced by the term packet. Datagrams, or packets, are the message units that the Internet Protocol deals with and that the Internet transports. A datagram, or packet, needs to be self-contained without reliance on earlier exchanges because there is no connection of fixed duration between the two communicating points as there is, for example, in most voice telephone conversations. (This kind of protocol is referred to as connectionless.)

Day Zero—The day a new vulnerability is made known. In some cases, a day zero (or zero day) exploit is referred to as an exploit for which no patch is available yet (day one is the day at which the patch is made available).

Decapsulation—The process of stripping off one layer's headers and passing the rest of the packet up to the next higher layer on the protocol stack.

Decryption—The process of transforming an encrypted message into its original plaintext.

Defacement—The method of modifying the content of a web site in such a way that it becomes "vandalized" or embarrassing to the web site owner.

Defense in Depth—The approach of using multiple layers of security to guard against failure of a single security component.

Demilitarized Zone (DMZ)—In computer security in general, a demilitarized zone (DMZ) or perimeter network is a network area (a subnetwork) that sits between an organization's internal network and an external network, usually the Internet. DMZs help to enable the layered security model in that they provide subnetwork segmentation based on security requirements or policy. DMZs provide either a transit mechanism from a secure source to an insecure destination or from an insecure source to a more secure destination. In some cases, a screened subnet which is used for servers accessible from the outside is referred to as a DMZ.

Denial of Service—The prevention of authorized access to a system resource or the delaying of system operations and functions.

Dictionary Attack—An attack that tries all of the phrases or words in a dictionary, trying to crack a password or key. A dictionary attack uses a pre-defined list of words compared to a brute force attack that tries all possible combinations.

Diffie-Hellman—A key agreement algorithm published in 1976 by Whitfield Diffie and Martin Hellman. Diffie-Hellman does key establishment, not encryption. However, the key that it produces may be used for encryption, for further key management operations or for any other cryptography.

Digest Authentication—Authentication that allows a web client to compute MD5 hashes of the password to prove it has the password.

Digital Certificate—An electronic "credit card" that establishes your credentials when doing business or other transactions on the web. It is issued by a certification authority. It contains your name, a serial number, expiration dates, a copy of the certificate holder's public key (used for encrypting messages and digital signatures) and the digital signature of the certificate-issuing authority so that a recipient can verify that the certificate is real.

Digital Envelope—An encrypted message with the encrypted session key.

Digital Signature—A hash of a message that uniquely identifies the sender of the message and proves the message hasn't changed since transmission.

Digital Signature Algorithm (DSA)—An asymmetric cryptographic algorithm that produces a digital signature in the form of a pair of large numbers. The signature is computed using rules and parameters such that the identity of the signer, and the integrity of the signed data can be verified.

Digital Signature Standard (DSS)—The U.S. government standard that specifies the Digital Signature Algorithm (DSA), which involves asymmetric cryptography.

Disassembly—The process of taking a binary program and deriving the source code from it.

Disaster Recovery Plan (DRP)—The process of recovery of IT systems in the event of a disruption or disaster.

Discretionary Access Control (DAC)—Control that consists of something the user can manage, such as a document password.

Disruption—A circumstance or event that interrupts or prevents the correct operation of system services and functions.

Distance Vector—Vectors that measure the cost of routes to determine the best route to all known networks.

Distributed Scans—Scans that use multiple source addresses to gather information.

Domain—A sphere of knowledge, or a collection of facts about some program entities or a number of network points or addresses, identified by a name. On the Internet, a domain consists of a set of network addresses. In the Internet's domain name system, a domain is a name with which name server records are associated that describe subdomains or host. In Windows NT and Windows 2000, a domain is a set of network resources (applications, printers etc.) for a group of users. The user only needs to log in to the domain to gain access to the resources, which may be located on a number of different servers in the network.

Domain Hijacking—An attack by which an attacker takes over a domain by first blocking access to the domain's DNS server and then putting his or her own server up in its place.

Domain Name—A name that locates an organization or other entity on the Internet. For example, the domain name "www.sans.org" locates an Internet address for "sans.org" at Internet point 199.0.0.2 and a particular host server named "www." The "org" part of the domain name reflects the purpose of the organization or entity (in this example, "organization") and is called the top-level domain name. The "sans" part of the domain name defines the organization or entity and together with the top-level is called the second-level domain name.

Domain Name System (DNS)—The way that Internet domain names are located and translated into Internet Protocol addresses. A domain name is a meaningful and easy-to-remember "handle" for an Internet address.

Due Care—Care that ensures a minimal level of protection is in place in accordance with the best practice in the industry.

Due Diligence—The requirement that organizations must develop and deploy a protection plan to prevent fraud, abuse and, in addition, deploy a means to detect them if they occur.

DumpSec—A security tool that dumps a variety of information about a system's users, file system, registry, permissions, password policy and services.

Dumpster Diving—Obtaining passwords and corporate directories by searching through discarded media.

Dynamic Link Library—A collection of small programs, any of which can be called when needed by a larger program that is running in the computer. The small program that lets the larger program communicate with a specific device such as a printer or scanner is often packaged as a DLL program (usually referred to as a DLL file).

Dynamic Routing Protocol—Allows network devices to learn routes. Ex. RIP, EIGRP Dynamic routing occurs when routers talk to adjacent routers, informing each other of what networks each router is currently connected to. The routers must communicate using a routing protocol, of which there are many to choose from. The process on the router that is running the routing protocol, communicating with its neighbor routers, is usually called a routing daemon. The routing daemon updates the kernel's routing table with information it receives from neighbor routers.

Eavesdropping—Listening to a private conversation which may reveal information that can provide access to a facility or network.

Echo Reply—The response a machine that has received an echo request sends over ICMP.

Echo Request—An ICMP message sent to a machine to determine if it is online and how long traffic takes to get to it.

Egress Filtering—Filtering outbound traffic.

Emanations Analysis—Gaining direct knowledge of communicated data by monitoring and resolving a signal that is emitted by a system and that contains the data but is not intended to communicate the data.

Encapsulation—The inclusion of one data structure within another structure so that the first data structure is hidden for the time being.

Encryption—Cryptographic transformation of data (called plaintext) into a form (called cipher text) that conceals the data's original meaning to prevent them from being known or used.

Ephemeral Port—Usually is on the client side. It is set up when a client application wants to connect to a server and is destroyed when the client application terminates. It has a number chosen at random that is greater than 1023. Also called a transient port or a temporary port.

Escrow Passwords—Passwords that are written down and stored in a secure location (e.g., a safe) that are used by emergency personnel when privileged personnel are unavailable.

Ethernet—The most widely installed LAN technology. Specified in a standard IEEE 802.3, an Ethernet LAN typically uses coaxial cable or special grades of twisted pair wires. Devices are connected to the cable and compete for access using a CSMA/CD protocol.

Event—An observable occurrence in a system or network.

Exponential Backoff Algorithm—An algorithm used to adjust TCP timeout values on the fly so that network devices don't continue to time-out sending data over saturated links.

Exposure—A threat action whereby sensitive data are directly released to an unauthorized entity.

Extended ACLs (Cisco)—A more powerful form of Standard ACLs on Cisco routers. They can make filtering decisions based on IP addresses (source or destination), ports (source or destination), protocols and whether a session is established.

Extensible Authentication Protocol (EAP)—A framework that supports multiple, optional authentication mechanisms for PPP, including clear-text passwords, challenge-response and arbitrary dialog sequences.

Exterior Gateway Protocol (EGP)—A protocol that distributes routing information to the routers which connect autonomous systems.

False Rejects—When an authentication system fails to recognize a valid user.

Fast File System—The first major revision to the UNIX file system, providing faster read access and faster (delayed, asynchronous) write access through a disk cache and better file system layout on disk. It uses inodes (pointers) and data blocks.

Fast Flux—Protection method used by botnets consisting of a continuous and fast change of the DNS records for a domain name through different IP addresses.

Fault Line Attacks—Attacks that use weaknesses between interfaces of systems to exploit gaps in coverage.

File Transfer Protocol (FTP)—A TCP/IP protocol specifying the transfer of text or binary files across the network.

Filter—Specifies which packets will or will not be used. It can be used in sniffers to determine which packets get displayed or by firewalls to determine which packets get blocked.

Filtering Router—An internetwork router that selectively prevents the passage of data packets according to a security policy. A filtering router may be used as a firewall or part of a firewall. A router usually receives a packet from a network and decides where to forward it on a second network. A filtering router does the same but first decides whether the packet should be forwarded at all according to some security policy. The policy is implemented by rules (packet filters) loaded into the router.

Finger—A protocol to look up user information on a given host. A UNIX program that takes an e-mail address as input and returns information about the user who owns that e-mail address. On some systems, finger only reports whether the user is currently logged on. Other systems return additional information, such as the user's full name, address and telephone number. Of course, the user must first enter this information into the system. Many e-mail programs now have a finger utility built into them.

Fingerprinting—Sending strange packets to a system to gauge how it responds to determine the operating system.

Firewall—A logical or physical discontinuity in a network to prevent unauthorized access to data or resources.

Flooding—An attack that attempts to cause a failure in (especially, in the security of) a computer system or other data processing entity by providing more input than the entity can process properly.

Forest—A set of active directory domains that replicate their databases with each other.

Fork Bomb—A bomb that works by using the fork() call to create a new process which is a copy of the original. By doing this repeatedly, all available processes on the machine can be taken up.

Form-Based Authentication—Authentication that uses forms on a web page to ask a user to input username and password information.

Forward Lookup—Lookup that uses an Internet domain name to find an IP address.

Forward Proxy—Proxies that are designed to be the server through which all requests are made.

Fragment Offset—The field that tells the sender where a particular fragment falls in relation to other fragments in the original larger packet.

Fragment Overlap Attack—A TCP/IP fragmentation attack that is possible because IP allows packets to be broken down into fragments for more efficient transport across various media. The TCP packet (and its header) are carried in the IP packet. In this attack, the second fragment contains incorrect offset. When the packet is reconstructed, the port number will be overwritten.

Fragmentation—The process of storing a data file in several "chunks" or fragments rather than in a single contiguous sequence of bits in one place on the storage medium.

Frames—Data that is transmitted between network points as a unit complete with addressing and necessary protocol control information. A frame is usually transmitted serial bit by bit and contains a header field and a trailer field that "frame" the data. (Some control frames contain no data.)

Full Duplex—A type of duplex communications channel which carries data in both directions at once. Refers to the transmission of data in two directions simultaneously. Communications in which both sender and receiver can send at the same time.

Fully Qualified Domain Name—A server name with a host name followed by the full domain name.

Fuzzing—The use of special regression testing tools to generate out-of-spec input for an application to find security vulnerabilities. Also see Regression Testing.

Gateway—A network point that acts as an entrance to another network.

Gethostbyaddr—The DNS query that is used when the address of a machine is known and the name is needed.

Gethostbyname—The DNS query that is used when the name of a machine is known and the address is needed.

GNU—A UNIX-like operating system that comes with source code that can be copied, modified and redistributed. The GNU project was started in 1983 by Richard Stallman and others, who formed the Free Software Foundation.

Gnutella—An Internet file sharing utility. Gnutella acts as a server for sharing files while simultaneously acting as a client that searches for and downloads files from other users.

Hardening—The process of identifying and fixing vulnerabilities on a system.

Hash Function—An algorithm that computes a value based on a data object thereby mapping the data object to a smaller data object.

Hash Functions—(Cryptographic) hash functions are used to generate a one way "checksum" for a larger text, which is not trivially reversed. The result of this hash function can be used to validate if a larger file has been altered without having to compare the larger files to each other. Frequently used hash functions are MD5 and SHA1.

Header—The extra information in a packet that is needed for the protocol stack to process the packet.

Hijack Attack—A form of active wiretapping in which the attacker seizes control of a previously established communication association.

Honey Client—See Honeymonkey.

Honey Pot—Programs that simulate one or more network services that you designate on your computer's ports. An attacker assumes you're running vulnerable services that can be used to break into the machine. A honey pot can be used to log access attempts to those ports including the attacker's keystrokes. This could give you advanced warning of a more concerted attack.

Honeymonkey—Automated system simulating a user browsing web sites. The system is typically configured to detect web sites which exploit vulnerabilities in the browser. Also known as Honey Client.

Hops—Each exchange with a gateway a packet takes on its way to the destination.

Host—Any computer that has full two-way access to other computers on the Internet. Or a computer with a web server that serves the pages for one or more web sites.

Host-Based ID—Intrusion detection systems that use information from the operating system audit records to watch all operations occurring on the host that the intrusion detection software has been installed upon. These operations are then compared with a predefined security policy. This analysis of the audit trail imposes potentially significant overhead requirements on the system because of the increased amount of processing power which must be utilized by the intrusion detection system. Depending on the size of the audit trail and the processing ability of the system, the review of audit data could result in the loss of a real-time analysis capability.

HTTP Proxy—A server that acts as an intermediary in the communication between HTTP clients and servers.

HTTPS—When used in the first part of a URL (the part that precedes the colon and specifies an access scheme or protocol), this term specifies the use of HTTP enhanced by a security mechanism, which is usually SSL.

Hub—A network device that operates by repeating data that it receives on one port to all the other ports. As a result, data transmitted by one host are retransmitted to all other hosts on the hub.

Hybrid Attack—An attack that builds on the dictionary attack method by adding numerals and symbols to dictionary words.

Hybrid Encryption—An application of cryptography that combines two or more encryption algorithms, particularly a combination of symmetric and asymmetric encryption.

Hyperlink—In hypertext or hypermedia, an information object (e.g., a word, a phrase or an image; usually highlighted by color or underscoring) that points (indicates how to connect) to related information that is located elsewhere and can be retrieved by activating the link.

Hypertext Markup Language (HTML)—The set of markup symbols or codes inserted in a file intended for display on a World Wide Web browser page.

Hypertext Transfer Protocol (HTTP)—The protocol in the Internet Protocol (IP) family used to transport hypertext documents across an Internet.

Identity—Who someone is or what something is; for example, the name by which something is known.

Incident—An adverse network event in an information system or network or the threat of the occurrence of such an event.

Incident Handling—An action plan for dealing with intrusions, cyber theft, denial of service, fire, floods and other security-related events. It is comprised of a six-step process: preparation, identification, containment, eradication, recovery and lessons learned.

Incremental Backups—Backups that only back up the files that have been modified since the last backup. If dump levels are used, incremental backups only back up files changed since the last backup of a lower dump level.

Inetd (xinetd)—Inetd (or Internet Daemon) is an application that controls smaller Internet services like Telnet, ftp and POP.

Inference Attack—Attacks that rely on the user to make logical connections between seemingly unrelated pieces of information.

Information Warfare—The competition between offensive and defensive players over information resources.

Ingress Filtering—Filtering inbound traffic.

Input Validation Attacks—When an attacker intentionally sends unusual input in the hopes of confusing an application.

Integrity—The need to ensure that information has not been changed accidentally or deliberately and that it is accurate and complete.

Integrity Star Property—When users cannot read data of a lower integrity level than their own.

International Organization for Standardization (ISO)—a voluntary, nontreaty, nongovernment organization, established in 1947, with voting members that are designated standards bodies of participating nations and nonvoting observer organizations.

International Telecommunications Union, Telecommunication Standardization Sector (ITU-T)—A United Nations treaty organization that is composed mainly of postal, telephone and telegraph authorities of the member countries and that publishes standards called "Recommendations"; formerly CCITT.

Internet—A term to describe connecting multiple separate networks together.

Internet Control Message Protocol (ICMP)—An Internet Standard protocol that is used to report error conditions during IP datagram processing and to exchange other information concerning the state of the IP network.

Internet Engineering Task Force (IETF)—The body that defines standard Internet operating protocols such as TCP/IP. The IETF is supervised by the Internet Society Internet Architecture Board (IAB). IETF members are drawn from the Internet Society's individual and organization membership.

Internet Message Access Protocol (IMAP)—A protocol that defines how a client should fetch mail from and return mail to a mail server. IMAP is intended as a replacement for or extension to the Post Office Protocol (POP). It is defined in RFC 1203 (v3) and RFC 2060 (v4).

Internet Protocol (IP)—The method or protocol by which data is sent from one computer to another on the Internet.

Internet Protocol Security (IPsec)—A developing standard for security at the network or packet-processing layer of network communication.

Internet Standard—A specification, approved by the IESG and published as an RFC, that is stable and well understood, is technically competent, has multiple, independent, and interoperable implementations with substantial operational experience, enjoys significant public support and is recognizably useful in some or all parts of the Internet.

Interrupt—A signal that informs the OS that something has occurred.

Intranet—A computer network, especially one based on Internet technology, that an organization uses for its own internal, and usually private, purposes and that is closed to outsiders.

Intrusion Detection—A security management system for computers and networks. An IDS gathers and analyzes information from various areas within a computer or a network to identify possible security breaches, which include both intrusions (attacks from outside the organization) and misuse (attacks from within the organization).

IP Address—A computer's internetwork address that is assigned for use by the Internet Protocol and other protocols. An IP version 4 address is written as a series of four 8-bit numbers separated by periods.

IP Flood—A denial of service attack that sends a host more echo request ("ping") packets than the protocol implementation can handle.

IP Forwarding—An operating system option that allows a host to act as a router. A system that has more than one network interface card must have IP forwarding turned on for the system to be able to act as a router.

IP Spoofing—The technique of supplying a false IP address.

Issue-Specific Policy—A policy that is intended to address specific needs within an organization, such as a password policy.

Jitter—The modification of fields in a database while preserving the aggregate characteristics that make the database useful in the first place; also called noise.

Jump Bag—A container that has all the items necessary to respond to an incident inside to help mitigate the effects of delayed reactions.

Kerberos—A system developed at the Massachusetts Institute of Technology that depends on passwords and symmetric cryptography (DES) to implement ticket-based, peer entity authentication service and access control service distributed in a client-server network environment.

Kernel—The essential center of a computer operating system; the core that provides basic services for all other parts of the operating system. A synonym is nucleus. A kernel can be contrasted with a shell, the outermost part of an operating system that interacts with user commands. Kernel and shell are terms used more frequently in UNIX and some other operating systems than in IBM mainframe systems.

Lattice Techniques—Techniques that use security designations to determine access to information.

Layer 2 Forwarding Protocol (L2F)—An Internet protocol (originally developed by Cisco Corporation) that uses tunneling of PPP over IP to create a virtual extension of a dial-up link across a network, initiated by the dial-up server and transparent to the dial-up user.

Layer 2 Tunneling Protocol (L2TP)—An extension of the Point-to-Point Tunneling Protocol used by an Internet service provider to enable the operation of a virtual private network over the Internet.

Least Privilege—The principle of allowing users or applications the least amount of permissions necessary to perform their intended function.

Legion—Software to detect unprotected shares.

Lightweight Directory Access Protocol (LDAP)—A software protocol for enabling anyone to locate organizations, individuals and other resources such as files and devices in a network, whether on the public Internet or on a corporate intranet.

Link State—With link state, routes maintain information about all routers and router-to-router links within a geographic area and create a table of best routes with that information.

List-Based Access Control—Access control that associates a list of users and their privileges with each object.

Loadable Kernel Modules (LKM)—Modules that allow for the adding of functionality directly into the kernel while the system is running.

Log Clipping—The selective removal of log entries from a system log to hide a compromise.

Logic Bombs—Programs or snippets of code that execute when a certain predefined event occurs. Logic bombs may also be set to go off on a certain date or when a specified set of circumstances occurs.

Logic Gate—An elementary building block of a digital circuit. Most logic gates have two inputs and one output. As digital circuits can only understand binary, inputs and outputs can assume only one of two states, 0 or 1.

Loopback Address—The loopback address (127.0.0.1) is a pseudo IP address that always refers back to the local host and is never sent out onto a network.

MAC Address—A physical address; a numeric value that uniquely identifies that network device from every other device on the planet.

Malicious Code—Software (e.g., Trojan horse) that appears to perform a useful or desirable function but actually gains unauthorized access to system resources or tricks a user into executing other malicious logic.

Malware—A generic term for a number of different types of malicious code.

Mandatory Access Control (MAC)—Where the system controls access to resources based on classification levels assigned to both the objects and the users. These controls cannot be changed by anyone.

Masquerade Attack—A type of attack in which one system entity illegitimately poses as (assumes the identity of) another entity.

md5—A one-way cryptographic hash function. Also see Hash Functions and Sha1.

Measures of Effectiveness (MOE)—A probability model based on engineering concepts that allows one to approximate the impact a given action will have on an environment. In information warfare, it is the ability to attack or defend within an Internet environment.

Monoculture—The case where a large number of users run the same software and are vulnerable to the same attacks.

Morris Worm—A worm program written by Robert T. Morris Jr. that flooded the ARPANET in November 1988, causing problems for thousands of hosts.

Multicast—Broadcasting from one host to a given set of hosts.

Multihomed—When your network is directly connected to two or more ISPs.

Multiplexing—To combine multiple signals from possibly disparate sources to transmit them over a single path.

NAT—Network Address Translation. It is used to share one or a small number of publicly routable IP addresses among a larger number of hosts. The hosts are assigned private IP addresses, which are then "translated" into one of the publicly routed IP addresses. Typically home or small business networks use NAT to share a single DLS or cable modem IP address. However, in some cases, NAT is used for servers as an additional layer of protection.

National Institute of Standards and Technology (NIST)—A unit of the U.S. Commerce Department. Formerly known as the National Bureau of Standards, NIST promotes and maintains measurement standards. It also has active programs for encouraging and assisting industry and science to develop and use these standards.

Natural Disaster—Any "act of God" (e.g., fire, flood, earthquake, lightning or wind) that disables a system component.

Netmask—A 32-bit number indicating the range of IP addresses residing on a single IP network/subnet/supernet. This specification displays network masks as hexadecimal numbers. For example, the network mask for a class C IP network is displayed as 0xffffff00. Such a mask is often displayed elsewhere in the literature as 255.255.255.0.

Network Address Translation—The translation of an Internet Protocol address used within one network to a different IP address known within another network. One network is designated the inside network, and the other is the outside.

Network Mapping—To compile an electronic inventory of the systems and the services on your network.

Network Taps—Hardware devices that hook directly onto the network cable and send a copy of the traffic that passes through it to one or more other networked devices.

Network-Based IDS—An intrusion detection system that monitors the traffic on its network segment as a data source. This is generally accomplished by placing the network interface card in promiscuous mode to capture all network traffic that crosses its network segment. Network traffic on other segments and traffic on other means of communication (e.g., phone lines) can't be monitored. Network-based IDS involves looking at the packets on the network as they pass by some sensor. The sensor can only see the packets that happen to be carried on the network segment it's attached to. Packets are considered of interest if they match a signature. Network-based intrusion detection passively monitors network activity for indications of attacks. Network monitoring offers several advantages over traditional host-based intrusion detection systems. Because many intrusions occur over networks at some point, and because networks are increasingly becoming the targets of attack, these techniques are an excellent method of detecting many attacks which may be missed by host-based intrusion detection mechanisms.

Nonprintable Character—A character that doesn't have a corresponding character letter to its corresponding ASCII code. Examples would be the linefeed, which is ASCII character code 10 decimal, the carriage return, which is 13 decimal, or the bell sound, which is 7 decimal. On a PC, you can often add nonprintable characters by holding down the Alt key and typing in the decimal value (i.e., Alt-007 gets you a bell). There are other character encoding schemes, but ASCII is the most prevalent.

Nonrepudiation—The ability for a system to prove that a specific user and only that specific user sent a message and that it hasn't been modified.

Null Session—Known as anonymous log on, it is a way of letting an anonymous user retrieve information such as usernames and shares over the network or connect without authentication. It is used by applications such as explorer.exe to enumerate shares on remote servers.

Octet—A sequence of eight bits. An octet is an eight-bit byte.

One-Way Encryption—Irreversible transformation of plaintext to cipher text, such that the plaintext cannot be recovered from the cipher text by other than exhaustive procedures even if the cryptographic key is known.

One-Way Function—A (mathematical) function, f, which makes it easy to compute the output based on a given input. However, given only the output value, it is impossible (except for a brute force attack) to figure out what the input value is.

Open Shortest Path First (OSPF)—A link state routing algorithm used in interior gateway routing. Routers maintain a database of all routers in the autonomous system with links between the routers, link costs, and link states (up and down).

Open Systems Interconnection (OSI)—A standard description or "reference model" for how messages should be transmitted between any two points in a telecommunication network. Its purpose is to guide product implementers so that their products will consistently work with other products. The reference model defines seven layers of functions that take place at each end of a communication. Although OSI is not always strictly adhered to in terms of keeping related functions together in a well-defined layer, many if not most products involved in telecommunication make an attempt to describe themselves in relation to the OSI model. It is also valuable as a single reference view of communication that furnishes everyone a common ground for education and discussion.

OSI Layers—The main idea in OSI is that the process of communication between two endpoints in a telecommunication network can be divided into layers, with each layer adding its own set of special, related functions. Each communicating user or program is at a computer equipped with these seven layers of function. So, in a given message between users, there will be a flow of data through each layer at one end down through the layers in that computer and, at the other end, when the message arrives, another flow of data up through the layers in the receiving computer and ultimately to the end-user or program. The actual programming and hardware that furnishes these seven layers of function are usually a combination of the computer operating system, applications (e.g., your web browser), TCP/IP or alternative transport and network protocols and the software and hardware that enable you to put a signal on one of the lines attached to your computer. OSI divides telecommunication into seven layers. The layers are in two groups. The upper four layers are used whenever a message passes from or to a user. The lower three layers (up to the network layer) are used when any message passes through the host computer or router. Messages intended for this computer pass to the upper layers. Messages destined for some other host are not passed up to the upper layers but are forwarded to another host. The seven layers are: Layer 7: The application layer. This is the layer at which communication partners are identified, quality of service is identified, user authentication and privacy are considered and any constraints on data syntax are identified. (This layer is not the application itself, although some applications may perform application layer functions.) Layer 6: The presentation layer. This is a layer, usually part of an operating system, that converts incoming and outgoing data from one presentation format to another (e.g., from a text stream into a popup window with the newly arrived text). Sometimes called the syntax layer. Layer 5: The session layer. This layer sets up, coordinates and terminates conversations, exchanges and dialogs between the applications at each end. It deals with session and connection coordination. Layer 4: The transport layer. This layer manages the end-to-end control (e.g., determining whether all packets have arrived) and error checking. It ensures complete data transfer. Layer 3: The network layer. This layer handles the routing of the data (sending them in the right direction to the right destination on outgoing transmissions and receiving incoming transmissions at the packet level). The network layer does routing and forwarding. Layer 2: The data-link layer. This layer provides synchronization for the physical level and does bit-stuffing for strings of 1s in excess of five. It furnishes transmission protocol knowledge and management. Layer 1: The physical layer. This layer conveys the bitstream through the network at the electrical and mechanical level. It provides the hardware means of sending and receiving data on a carrier.

Overload—Hindrance of system operation by placing excess burden on the performance capabilities of a system component.

Packet—A piece of a message transmitted over a packet-switching network. One of the key features of a packet is that it contains the destination address in addition to the data. In IP networks, packets are often called datagrams.

Packet-Switched Network—A network where individual packets each follow their own paths through the network from one endpoint to another.

Partitions—Major divisions of the total physical hard disk space.

Password Authentication Protocol (PAP)—A simple, weak authentication mechanism where a user enters the password and it is then sent across the network, usually in the clear.

Password Cracking—The process of attempting to guess passwords, given the password file information.

Password Sniffing—Passive wiretapping, usually on a local area network, to gain knowledge of passwords.

Patch—A small update released by a software manufacturer to fix bugs in existing programs.

Patching—The process of updating software to a different version.

Payload—The actual application data a packet contains.

Penetration—Gaining unauthorized logical access to sensitive data by circumventing a system's protections.

Penetration Testing—Testing that is used to test the external perimeter security of a network or facility.

Permutation—Keeping the same letters but changing the position within a text to scramble the message.

Personal Firewalls—Firewalls that are installed and run on individual PCs.

Pharming—This is a more sophisticated form of MITM attack. A user's session is redirected to a masquerading web site. This can be achieved by corrupting a DNS server on the Internet and pointing a URL to the masquerading web site's IP. Almost all users use a URL like www.worldbank.com instead of the real IP (192.86.99.140) of the web site. Changing the pointers on a DNS server, the URL can be redirected to send traffic to the IP of the pseudo web site. At the pseudo web site, transactions can be mimicked and information like log in credentials can be gathered. With this, the attacker can access the real www.worldbank.com site and conduct transactions using the credentials of a valid user on that web site.

Phishing—The use of e-mails that appear to originate from a trusted source to trick a user into entering valid credentials at a fake web site. Typically, the e-mail and the web site look like they are part of a bank the user is doing business with.

Ping of Death—An attack that sends an improperly large ICMP echo request packet (a "ping") with the intent of overflowing the input buffers of the destination machine and causing it to crash.

Ping Scan—A scan that looks for machines that are responding to ICMP echo requests.

Ping Sweep—An attack that sends ICMP echo requests ("pings") to a range of IP addresses with the goal of finding hosts that can be probed for vulnerabilities.

Plaintext—Ordinary readable text before being encrypted into cipher text or after being decrypted.

Point-to-Point Protocol (PPP)—A protocol for communication between two computers using a serial interface, typically a personal computer connected by phone line to a server. It packages your computer's TCP/IP packets and forwards them to the server where they can be put on the Internet.

Point-to-Point Tunneling Protocol (PPTP)—A protocol (set of communication rules) that allows corporations to extend their own corporate network through private "tunnels" over the public Internet.

Poison Reverse—Split horizon with poisoned reverse (more simply, poison reverse) does include such routes in updates but sets their metrics to infinity. In effect, advertising the fact that their routes are not reachable.

Polyinstantiation—The ability of a database to maintain multiple records with the same key. It is used to prevent inference attacks.

Polymorphism—The process by which malicious software changes its underlying code to avoid detection.

Port—An integer that uniquely identifies an endpoint of a communication stream. Only one process per machine can listen on the same port number.

Port Scan—A series of messages sent by someone attempting to break into a computer to learn which computer network services, each associated with a "well-known" port number, the computer provides. Port scanning, a favorite approach of computer crackers, gives the assailant an idea where to probe for weaknesses. Essentially, a port scan consists of sending a message to each port one at a time. The kind of response received indicates whether the port is used and can therefore be probed for weakness.

Possession—The holding, control and ability to use information.

Post Office Protocol, Version 3 (POP3)—An Internet Standard protocol by which a client workstation can dynamically access a mailbox on a server host to retrieve mail messages that the server has received and is holding for the client.

Practical Extraction and Reporting Language (Perl)—A script programming language that is similar in syntax to the C language and includes a number of popular UNIX facilities such as sed, awk and tr.

Preamble—A signal used in network communications to synchronize the transmission timing between two or more systems. Proper timing ensures that all systems are interpreting the start of the information transfer correctly. A preamble defines a specific series of transmission pulses that is understood by communicating systems to mean "someone is about to transmit data." This ensures that systems receiving the information correctly interpret when the data transmission starts. The actual pulses used as a preamble vary depending on the network communication technology in use.

Pretty Good Privacy (PGP)™—Trademark of Network Associates, Inc., referring to a computer program (and related protocols) that uses cryptography to provide data security for electronic mail and other applications on the Internet.

Private Addressing—IANA has set aside three address ranges for use by private or non-Internet connected networks. This is referred to as Private Address Space and is defined in RFC 1918. The reserved address blocks are: 10.0.0.0 to 10.255.255.255 (10/8 prefix) 172.16.0.0 to 172.31.255.255 (172.16/12 prefix) 192.168.0.0 to 192.168.255.255 (192.168/16 prefix).

Program Infector—A piece of malware that attaches itself to existing program files.

Program Policy—A high-level policy that sets the overall tone of an organization's security approach.

Promiscuous Mode—When a machine reads all packets off the network regardless of whom they are addressed to. This is used by network administrators to diagnose network problems but also by unsavory characters who are trying to eavesdrop on network traffic (which might contain passwords or other information).

Proprietary Information—Information that is unique to a company and its ability to compete, such as customer lists, technical data, product costs and trade secrets.

Protocol—A formal specification for communicating; an IP address the special set of rules that endpoints in a telecommunication connection use when they communicate. Protocols exist at several levels in a telecommunication connection.

Protocol Stacks (OSI)—A set of network protocol layers that work together.

Proxy Server—A server that acts as an intermediary between a workstation user and the Internet so that the enterprise can ensure security, administrative control and caching service. A proxy server is associated with or part of a gateway server that separates the enterprise network from the outside network and a firewall server that protects the enterprise network from outside intrusion.

Public Key—The publicly disclosed component of a pair of cryptographic keys used for asymmetric cryptography.

Public Key Encryption—The popular synonym for asymmetric cryptography.

Public Key Forward Secrecy (PFS)—For a key agreement protocol based on asymmetric cryptography, the property that ensures that a session key derived from a set of long-term public and private keys will not be compromised if one of the private keys is compromised in the future.

Public Key Infrastructure (PKI)—An infrastructure that enables users of a basically unsecured public network such as the Internet to securely and privately exchange data and money through the use of a public and a private cryptographic key pair that is obtained and shared through a trusted authority. The public key infrastructure provides for a digital certificate that can identify an individual or an organization and directory services that can store and, when necessary, revoke the certificates.

QAZ—A network worm.

Race Condition—A condition that exploits the small window of time between a security control being applied and when the service is used.

Radiation Monitoring—The process of receiving images, data or audio from an unprotected source by listening to radiation signals.

Reconnaissance—The phase of an attack where an attacker finds new systems, maps out networks and probes for specific, exploitable vulnerabilities.

Reflexive ACLs (Cisco)—For Cisco routers, a step toward making the router act like a stateful firewall. The router will make filtering decisions based on whether connections are a part of established traffic or not.

Registry—In Windows operating systems, the central set of settings and information required to run the Windows computer.

Regression Analysis—The use of scripted tests which are used to test software for all possible input it should expect. Typically, developers will create a set of regression tests that are executed before a new version of software is released. Also see Fuzzing.

Request for Comment (RFC)—A series of notes about the Internet started in 1969 (when the Internet was the ARPANET). An Internet document can be submitted to the IETF by anyone, but the IETF decides if the document becomes an RFC. Eventually, if it gains enough interest, it may evolve into an Internet standard.

Resource Exhaustion—Attacks that involve tying up finite resources on a system, making them unavailable to others.

Response—Information sent in reply to some stimulus.

Reverse Address Resolution Protocol (RARP)—A protocol by which a physical machine in a local area network can request to learn its IP address from a gateway server's Address Resolution Protocol table or cache. A network administrator creates a table in a local area network's gateway router that maps the physical machine (or Media Access Control—MAC address) addresses to corresponding Internet Protocol addresses. When a new machine is set up, its RARP client program requests from the RARP server on the router to be sent its IP address. Assuming that an entry has been set up in the router table, the RARP server will return the IP address to the machine which can store it for future use.

Reverse Engineering—Acquiring sensitive data by disassembling and analyzing the design of a system component.

Reverse Lookup—Find out the host name that corresponds to a particular IP address. Reverse lookup uses an IP address to find a domain name.

Reverse Proxy—Proxies that take public HTTP requests and pass them to back-end web servers to send the content to it, so the proxy can then send the content to the end-user.

Risk—The product of the level of threat with the level of vulnerability. It establishes the likelihood of a successful attack.

Risk Assessment—The process by which risks are identified and the impact of those risks determined.

Risk Averse—Avoiding risk even if this leads to the loss of opportunity. For example, using a (more expensive) phone call versus sending an e-mail to avoid risks associated with e-mail may be considered risk averse.

Rivest-Shamir-Adleman (RSA)—An algorithm for asymmetric cryptography, invented in 1977 by Ron Rivest, Adi Shamir and Leonard Adleman.

Role-Based Access Control—Access control that assigns users to roles based on their organizational functions and determines authorization based on those roles.

Root—The name of the administrator account in UNIX systems.

Rootkit—A collection of tools (programs) that a hacker uses to mask intrusion and obtain administrator-level access to a computer or computer network.

Router—Routers interconnect logical networks by forwarding information to other networks based upon IP addresses.

Routing Information Protocol (RIP)—A distance vector protocol used for interior gateway routing which uses hop count as the sole metric of a path's cost.

Routing Loop—Where two or more poorly configured routers repeatedly exchange the same packet over and over.

RPC Scans—Scans that determine which RPC services are running on a machine.

Rule-Set-Based Access Control (RSBAC)—Access control that targets actions based on rules for entities operating on objects.

S/Key—A security mechanism that uses a cryptographic hash function to generate a sequence of 64-bit, one-time passwords for remote user log in. The client generates a one-time password by applying the MD4 cryptographic hash function multiple times to the user's secret key. For each successive authentication of the user, the number of hash applications is reduced by one.

Safety—The need to ensure that the people involved with the company, including employees, customers and visitors, are protected from harm.

Scavenging—Searching through data residue in a system to gain unauthorized knowledge of sensitive data.

Secure Electronic Transactions (SET)—A protocol developed for credit card transactions in which all parties (customers, merchant and bank) are authenticated using digital signatures; encryption protects the message, provides integrity and provides end-to-end security for credit card transactions online.

Secure Shell (SSH)—A program to log in to another computer over a network, to execute commands in a remote machine and to move files from one machine to another.

Secure Sockets Layer (SSL)—A protocol developed by Netscape for transmitting private documents via the Internet. SSL works by using a public key to encrypt data that is transferred over the SSL connection.

Security Policy—A set of rules and practices that specify or regulate how a system or organization provides security services to protect sensitive and critical system resources.

Segment—Another name for TCP packets.

Sensitive Information—As defined by the federal government, any unclassified information that, if compromised, could adversely affect the national interest or conduct of federal initiatives.

Separation of Duties—The principle of splitting privileges among multiple individuals or systems.

Server—A system entity that provides a service in response to requests from other system entities called clients.

Session—A virtual connection between two hosts by which network traffic is passed.

Session Hijacking—Taking over a session that someone else has established.

Session Key—In the context of symmetric encryption, a key that is temporary or is used for a relatively short period of time. Usually, a session key is used for a defined period of communication between two computers, such as for the duration of a single connection or transaction set, or the key is used in an application that protects relatively large amounts of data and, therefore, needs to be rekeyed frequently.

SHA1—A one-way cryptographic hash function. Also see MD5.

Shadow Password Files—A system file in which encryption user passwords are stored so that they aren't available to people who try to break into the system.

Share—A resource made public on a machine, such as a directory (file share) or printer (printer share).

Shell—A UNIX term for the interactive user interface with an operating system. The shell is the layer of programming that understands and executes the commands a user enters. In some systems, the shell is called a command interpreter. A shell usually implies an interface with a command syntax (think of the DOS operating system and its "C:>" prompts and user commands such as "dir" and "edit").

Signals Analysis—Gaining indirect knowledge of communicated data by monitoring and analyzing a signal that is emitted by a system and that contains the data but is not intended to communicate the data.

Signature—A distinct pattern in network traffic that can be identified to a specific tool or exploit.

Simple Integrity Property—In simple integrity property, users cannot write data to a higher integrity level than their own.

Simple Network Management Protocol (SNMP)—The protocol governing network management and the monitoring of network devices and their functions. A set of protocols for managing complex networks.

Simple Security Property—In simple security property, users cannot read data of a higher classification than their own.

Smartcard—An electronic badge that includes a magnetic strip or chip that can record and replay a set key.

Smurf—The smurf attack works by spoofing the target address and sending a ping to the broadcast address for a remote network, which results in a large amount of ping replies being sent to the target.

Sniffer—A tool that monitors network traffic as it is received in a network interface.

Sniffing—A synonym for passive wiretapping.

Social Engineering—A euphemism for nontechnical or low-technology means—such as lies, impersonation, tricks, bribes, blackmail and threats—used to attack information systems.

Socket—The socket tells a host's IP stack where to plug in a data stream so that it connects to the right application.

Socket Pair—A way to uniquely specify a connection (i.e., source IP address, source port, destination IP address, destination port).

SOCKS—A protocol that a proxy server can use to accept requests from client users in a company's network so that it can forward them across the Internet. SOCKS uses sockets to represent and keep track of individual connections. The client side of SOCKS is built into certain web browsers, and the server side can be added to a proxy server.

Software—Computer programs (which are stored in and executed by computer hardware) and associated data (which also are stored in the hardware) that may be dynamically written or modified during execution.

Source Port—The port that a host uses to connect to a server. It is usually a number greater than or equal to 1024. It is randomly generated and is different each time a connection is made.

Spam—Electronic junk mail or junk newsgroup postings.

Spanning Port—Configures the switch to behave like a hub for a specific port.

Split Horizon—An algorithm for avoiding problems caused by including routes in updates sent to the gateway from which they were learned.

Split Key—A cryptographic key that is divided into two or more separate data items that individually convey no knowledge of the whole key that results from combining the items.

Spoof—Attempt by an unauthorized entity to gain access to a system by posing as an authorized user.

SQL Injection—A type of input validation attack specific to database-driven applications where SQL code is inserted into application queries to manipulate the database.

Stack Mashing—The technique of using a buffer overflow to trick a computer into executing arbitrary code.

Standard ACLs (Cisco)—On Cisco, routers that make packet filtering decisions based on Source IP address only.

Star Property—In star property, a user cannot write data to a lower classification level without logging in at that lower classification level.

State Machine—A system that moves through a series of progressive conditions.

Stateful Inspection—A firewall architecture that works at the network layer. Unlike static packet filtering, which examines a packet based on the information in its header, stateful inspection examines not just the header information but also the contents of the packet up through the application layer to determine more about the packet than just information about its source and destination. Also referred to as dynamic packet filtering.

Static Host Tables—Text files that contain host name and address mapping.

Static Routing—Routing table entries that contain information that does not change.

Stealthing—Approaches used by malicious code to conceal its presence on the infected system.

Steganalysis—The process of detecting and defeating the use of steganography.

Steganography—Methods of hiding the existence of a message or other data. This is different from cryptography, which hides the meaning of a message but does not hide the message itself. An example of a steganographic method is "invisible" ink.

Stimulus—Network traffic that initiates a connection or solicits a response.

Store-and-Forward—A method of switching where the entire packet is read by a switch to determine if it is intact before forwarding it.

Straight-Through Cable—A cable where the pins on one side of the connector are wired to the same pins on the other end. It is used for inter-connecting nodes on the network.

Stream Cipher—A cipher that works by encryption of a message a single bit, byte or computer word at a time.

Strong Star Property—In strong star property, users cannot write data to higher or lower classification level than their own.

Subnet Mask—A mask (or number) that is used to determine the number of bits used for the subnet and host portions of the address. The mask is a 32-bit value that uses one-bits for the network and subnet portions and zero-bits for the host portion.

Subnetwork—A separately identifiable part of a larger network that typically represents a certain limited number of host computers, the hosts in a building or geographic area or the hosts on an individual local area network.

Switch—A networking device that keeps track of MAC addresses attached to each of its ports so that data is only transmitted on the ports that are the intended recipients of the data.

Switched Network—A communications network, such as the public switched telephone network, in which any user may be connected to any other user through the use of message, circuit or packet switching and control devices. Any network providing switched communications service.

Symbolic Links—Special files which point at another file.

Symmetric Cryptography—A branch of cryptography involving algorithms that use the same key for two different steps of the algorithm (e.g., encryption and decryption or signature creation and signature verification). Symmetric cryptography is sometimes called secret key cryptography (vs. public key cryptography) because of the entities that share the key.

Symmetric Key—A cryptographic key that is used in a symmetric cryptographic algorithm.

SYN Flood—A denial of service attack that sends a host more TCP SYN packets (request to synchronize sequence numbers, used when opening a connection) than the protocol implementation can handle.

Synchronization—The signal made up of a distinctive pattern of bits that network hardware looks for to signal that start of a frame.

Syslog—The system-logging facility for UNIX systems.

System Security Officer (SSO)—A person responsible for enforcement or administration of the security policy that applies to the system.

System-Specific Policy—A policy written for a specific system or device.

T1, T3—A digital circuit using time-division multiplexing (TDM).

Tamper—To deliberately alter a system's logic, data or control information to cause the system to perform unauthorized functions or services.

TCP Fingerprinting—The use of odd packet header combinations to determine a remote operating system.

TCP Full Open Scan—Scans that check each port by performing a full three-way handshake on each port to determine if it was open.

TCP Half Open Scan—Scans that work by performing the first half of a three-way handshake to determine if a port is open.

TCP Wrapper—A software package which can be used to restrict access to certain network services based on the source of the connection; a simple tool to monitor and control incoming network traffic.

TCP/IP—A synonym for Internet Protocol Suite, in which the Transmission Control Protocol and the Internet Protocol are important parts. TCP/IP is the basic communication language or protocol of the Internet. It can also be used as a communications protocol in a private network (either an intranet or an extranet).

TCPDump—A freeware protocol analyzer for UNIX that can monitor network traffic on a wire.

Telnet—A TCP-based, application-layer, Internet Standard protocol for remote login from one host to another.

Threat—A potential for violation of security, which exists when there is a circumstance, capability, action or event that could breach security and cause harm.

Threat Assessment—The identification of types of threats that an organization might be exposed to.

Threat Model—A model that is used to describe a given threat and the harm it could do to a system if it has a vulnerability.

Threat Vector—The method a threat used to get to the target.

Time to Live—A value in an Internet Protocol packet that tells a network router whether or not the packet has been in the network too long and should be discarded.

Tiny Fragment Attack—With many IP implementations, it is possible to impose an unusually small fragment size on outgoing packets. If the fragment size is made small enough to force some of a TCP packet's TCP header fields into the second fragment, filter rules that specify patterns for those fields will not match. If the filtering implementation does not enforce a minimum fragment size, a disallowed packet might be passed because it didn't hit a match in the filter. STD 5, RFC 791 states: Every Internet module must be able to forward a datagram of 68 octets without further fragmentation. This is because an Internet header may be up to 60 octets, and the minimum fragment is 8 octets.

Token Ring—A local area network in which all computers are connected in a ring or star topology, and a binary digit or token-passing scheme is used to prevent the collision of data between two computers that want to send messages at the same time.

Token-Based Access Control—Access control that associates a list of objects and their privileges with each user. (The opposite of list based.)

Token-Based Devices—A device that is triggered by the time of day, so every minute the password changes, requiring users to have the token with them when they log in.

Topology—The geometric arrangement of a computer system. Common topologies include a bus, star and ring. The specific physical (i.e., real) or logical (i.e., virtual) arrangement of the elements of a network. Note 1: Two networks have the same topology if the connection configuration is the same, although the networks may differ in physical interconnections, distances between nodes, transmission rates and/or signal types. Note 2: The common types of network topology are illustrated.

Traceroute (tracert.exe)—A tool that maps the route a packet takes from the local machine to a remote destination.

Transmission Control Protocol (TCP)—A set of rules (protocol) used along with the Internet Protocol to send data in the form of message units between computers over the Internet. While IP takes care of handling the actual delivery of the data, TCP takes care of keeping track of the individual units of data (called packets) that a message is divided into for efficient routing through the Internet. Whereas the IP protocol deals only with packets, TCP enables two hosts to establish a connection and exchange streams of data. TCP guarantees delivery of data and also guarantees that packets will be delivered in the same order in which they were sent.

Transport Layer Security (TLS)—A protocol that ensures privacy between communicating applications and their users on the Internet.

When a server and client communicate, TLS ensures that no third party may eavesdrop or tamper with any message. TLS is the successor to the Secure Sockets Layer.

Triple DES—A block cipher, based on DES, that transforms each 64-bit plaintext block by applying the Data Encryption Algorithm three successive times, using either two or three different keys, for an effective key length of 112 or 168 bits.

Triple-Wrapped—S/MIME usage: data that have been signed with a digital signature, then encrypted and then signed again.

Trojan Horse—A computer program that appears to have a useful function but also has a hidden and potentially malicious function that evades security mechanisms, sometimes by exploiting legitimate authorizations of a system entity that invokes the program.

Trunking—Connecting switches together so that they can share VLAN information between them.

Trust—A determination of which permissions and what actions other systems or users can perform on remote machines.

Trusted Ports—Ports below number 1024, usually allowed to be opened by the root user.

Tunnel—A communication channel created in a computer network by encapsulating a communication protocol's data packets in (on top of) a second protocol that normally would be carried above, or at the same layer as, the first one. Most often, a tunnel is a logical point-to-point link (i.e., an OSI layer 2 connection) created by encapsulating the layer 2 protocol in a transport protocol (e.g., TCP), in a network or internetwork layer protocol (e.g., IP) or in another link layer protocol. Tunneling can move data between computers that use a protocol not supported by the network connecting them.

UDP Scan—Scans that determine which UDP ports are open.

Unicast—Broadcasting from host to host.

Uniform Resource Identifier (URI)—The generic term for all types of names and addresses that refer to objects on the World Wide Web.

Uniform Resource Locator (URL)—The global address of documents and other resources on the World Wide Web. The first part of the address indicates what protocol to use, and the second part specifies the IP address or the domain name where the resource is located. For example, **http:// www.pcwebopedia.com/index.html**.

UNIX—A popular multiuser, multitasking operating system developed at Bell Labs in the early 1970s. Created by just a handful of programmers, UNIX was designed to be a small, flexible system used exclusively by programmers.

Unprotected Share—In Windows terminology, a share is a mechanism that allows a user to connect to file systems and printers on other systems. An unprotected share is one that allows anyone to connect to it.

User—A person, organization entity or automated process that accesses a system, whether authorized to do so or not.

User Contingency Plan—The alternative methods of continuing business operations if IT systems are unavailable.

User Datagram Protocol (UDP)—A communications protocol that, like TCP, runs on top of IP networks. Unlike TCP/IP, UDP/IP provides very few error recovery services, offering instead a direct way to send and receive datagrams over an IP network. It's used primarily for broadcasting messages over a network. UDP uses the Internet Protocol to get a datagram from one computer to another but does not divide a message into packets (datagrams) and reassemble it at the other end. Specifically, UDP doesn't provide sequencing of the packets that the data arrive in.

Virtual Private Network (VPN)—A restricted-use, logical (i.e., artificial or simulated) computer network that is constructed from the system resources of a relatively public, physical (i.e., real) network (e.g., the Internet), often by using encryption (located at hosts or gateways), and often by tunneling links of the virtual network across the real network. For example, if a corporation has LANs at several different sites, each connected to the Internet by a firewall, the corporation could create a VPN by (1) using encrypted tunnels to connect from firewall to firewall across the Internet and (2) not allowing any other traffic through the firewalls. A VPN is generally less expensive to build and operate than a dedicated real network because the virtual network shares the cost of system resources with other users of the real network.

Virus—A hidden, self-replicating section of computer software, usually malicious logic, that propagates by infecting (i.e., inserting a copy of itself into and becoming part of) another program. A virus cannot run by itself; it requires that its host program be run to make the virus active.

Voice Firewall—A physical discontinuity in a voice network that monitors, alerts and controls inbound and outbound voice network activity based on user-defined call admission control (CAC) policies, voice application layer security threats or unauthorized service use violations.

Voice Intrusion Prevention System (IPS)—Voice IPS is a security management system for voice networks which monitors voice traffic for multiple calling patterns or attack/abuse signatures to proactively detect and prevent toll fraud, denial of service, telecom attacks, service abuse and other anomalous activity.

War Chalking—Marking areas, usually on sidewalks with chalk, that receive wireless signals that can be accessed.

War Dialer—A computer program that automatically dials a series of telephone numbers to find lines connected to computer systems and catalogs those numbers so that a cracker can try to break into the systems.

War Dialing—A simple means of trying to identify modems in a telephone exchange that may be susceptible to compromise in an attempt to circumvent perimeter security.

War Driving—The process of traveling around looking for wireless access point signals that can be used to get network access.

Web of Trust—The trust that naturally evolves as a user starts to trust other's signatures and the signatures that they trust.

Web Server—A software process that runs on a host computer connected to the Internet to respond to HTTP requests for documents from client web browsers.

WHOIS—An IP for finding information about resources on networks.

Windowing—A system for sharing a computer's graphical display presentation resources among multiple applications at the same time. In a computer that has a graphical user interface (GUI), you may want to use a number of applications at the same time (this is called task). Using a separate window for each application, you can interact with each application and go from one application to another without having to reinitiate it. Having different information or activities in multiple windows may also make it easier for you to do your work. A windowing system uses a window manager to keep track of where each window is located on the display screen and its size and status. A windowing system doesn't manage only the windows but also other forms of graphical user interface entities.

Windump—A freeware tool for Windows that is a protocol analyzer that can monitor network traffic on a wire.

Wired Equivalent Privacy (WEP)—A security protocol for wireless local area networks defined in the standard IEEE 802.11b.

Wireless Application Protocol—A specification for a set of communication protocols to standardize the way that wireless devices, such as cellular telephones and radio transceivers, can be used for Internet access, including e-mail, the World Wide Web, newsgroups and Internet Relay Chat.

Wiretapping—Monitoring and recording data that is flowing between two points in a communication system.

World Wide Web (the Web, WWW, W3)—The global, hypermedia-based collection of information and services that is available on Internet servers and is accessed by browsers using Hypertext Transfer Protocol and other information retrieval mechanisms.

Worm—A computer program that can run independently, can propagate a complete working version of itself onto other hosts on a network and may consume computer resources destructively.

Zero Day (Zero Hour or Day Zero) Attack—A computer attack or threat that tries to exploit computer application vulnerabilities that are unknown to others or undisclosed to the software developer. Zero day exploits (actual code that can use a security hole to carry out an attack) are used or shared by attackers before the software developer knows about the vulnerability.

Zombies—A zombie computer (often shortened as zombie) is a computer connected to the Internet that has been compromised by a hacker, a computer virus or a Trojan horse. Generally, a compromised machine is only one of many in a botnet and will be used to perform malicious tasks of one sort or another under remote direction. Most owners of zombie computers are unaware that their system is being used in this way. Because the owner tends to be unaware, these computers are metaphorically compared to zombies.

APPENDIX P

Updates

The manuscript for this book was completed in November of 2015. Any print materials on information security cannot be completely up to date because threats and safeguards change over weeks and months—sometimes over hours. This appendix covers some key developments from November 2015 through mid-January 2016. Be sure to consult online resources like those listed in Chapter 27 for updated information.

The Cybersecurity Information Sharing Act (CISA). The omnibus government funding bill, passed in December 2015, included CISA as an add-on. The law is designed to "improve cybersecurity in the United States through enhanced sharing of information about cybersecurity threats, and for other purposes." It allows businesses and enterprises to share threat indicators, like malware and suspicious network activities, with each other and with the U.S. government and provides immunity for sharing covered information, including antitrust immunity. Sharing is voluntary. The law facilitates security information sharing, which is being increasingly recognized as a critical process in security, as discussed in Chapter 5. Privacy advocates have strongly opposed CISA because of privacy concerns, one calling it a "surveillance bill masquerading as a cybersecurity bill." The concern is that companies can provide information about individuals to the government, with immunity. Earlier versions of the bill included measures to protect privacy, but they were not included in the final law. (**www.americanbar.org/publications/governmental_affairs_periodicals/ washingtonletter/2015/december/cybersecurity.html**)

Chinese Economic Espionage. In January 2016, CBS's *60 Minutes* presented "The Great Brain Robbery," which reported on economic espionage sponsored by the Chinese government of U.S. companies. It noted that this espionage is costing U.S. companies billions of dollars and more than two million jobs. It reported that litigation strategy is one of the targeted areas. (**www.cbsnews.com/news/60-minutes-great-brain-robbery-china-cyber-espionage**)

Naked Security Tips. *Naked Security* News (one of our favorites) published a series of advent security tips in its daily posts at the end of last year. Tip #24, on December 24, was a collection of all of the tips in one post. The tips include a number of security measures that we have discussed in this book—both for law firms and individuals. They include subjects like passwords, defense against ransomware, software updates, phishing, and more. It's a good approach to promoting security awareness. (**https://nakedsecurity.sophos.com/2015/12/24/advent-tip-24-the-big-one**)

To start the New Year, *Naked Security* published a list of New Year's security resolutions of various members of its staff. A great example:

> *Mark Stockley*
>
> *In 2016 I will stop treating my Mac's offer to postpone software updates like the snooze button on my alarm clock.*
>
> *If my laptop is open then it means I'm working and I don't want to down tools for a software update. When I'm asked if I want to install software updates now or in one hour I choose one hour.*
>
> *I tell myself that one more hour won't hurt. I tell myself that what I'm doing is terribly important, that I'll have finished in an hour, and I'll do the update then.*
>
> *I tell myself this every hour, over and over for ~~days~~ weeks.*
>
> *In fact I have an update pending now . . .*

As we have discussed multiple times, prompt application of security updates to the operating system and all applications (including browser plug-ins) is a critical security measure. Like the tips, these resolutions are a good way to provide reminders and promote security awareness. (**https://nakedsecurity.sophos.com/2015/12/31/these-are-our-new-years-security-resolutions-tell-us-yours**)

SANS OUCH! While we're updating information on security tips and awareness, here are some examples from the SANS Institute (included in our Short List of Favorite Information Sources in Chapter 27). SANS publishes *OUCH!*, a monthly security newsletter for end users, as part of its Securing the Human training initiative. It is free and may be used by businesses and law firms to educate their employees. For example, the January 2016 edition covers "Securing Your New Tablet" and the December 2015 edition is on "Phishing." (**http://securingthehuman.sans.org/resources/ newsletters/ouch/2016#january2016**) and (**http://securingthehuman. sans.org/newsletters/ouch/issues/OUCH-201512_en.pdf**)

Authentication. As discussed in Chapter 7, Google is already offering two-step verification that sends a one-time password to a phone for a user logging on to a Google account on another device. The user enters this password on the other device to log in. Google is now experimenting with a method of multifactor authentication that is even easier to use—the user will not have to enter a one-time password. The user first enters his or her e-mail address on the other device. A notification then shows up on the phone asking if it is the user who is trying to log in. If the user presses "yes" on the phone, the log on is allowed. It provides a second authentication factor but eliminates the step of entering the one-time password. It is similar to one of the options offered by Duo Security that is discussed in Chapter 7. (**www.androidpolice.com/2015/12/22/google-appears-to-be-testing-a-new-way-to-log-into-your-account-on-other-devices-with-just-your-phone-no-password-needed**)

Amazon has now joined the growing number of online services that offer multifactor authentication to consumers. The user can receive a one-time code by text, automated phone call, or a third-party authentication app like Google Authenticator. Amazon already offered it for services like Amazon Web Services and is now offering it to consumers. (**http://krebson security.com/2015/11/how-to-enable-multifactor-security-on-amazon**)

Microsoft Ends Support for Internet Explorer 8, 9, and 10. Microsoft has announced that it will officially stop supporting Internet Explorer 8, 9, and 10 on January 12, 2016. This means that users will have to upgrade to IE 11, move to Windows 10 and the Edge browser, or move to an alternate browser like Chrome or Firefox. The problem is that a lot of vendors have software configuration applications that are coded for specific versions of the Internet Explorer browser. These applications just won't work with Chrome or Firefox, and some will not work with the later versions of Internet Explorer. Using a version of an operating system (like Windows XP), an Internet browser (like these), or other software is dangerous because security updates are no longer provided. If you're faced with this situation, check for solutions with the provider of the app or online forums that discuss it or look for another application. (**https://bgr. com/2016/01/06/internet-explorer-end-of-life-update**)

2015 Year End Statistics. The headlines during 2015 continued to be filled with reports of high-profile data breaches, including the federal Office of Personnel Management, Anthem, the Pentagon, Ashley Madison, and many more. The Privacy Rights Clearinghouse reports that there were 4,727 reported data breaches from 2005 through January 8, 2016, exposing 895,585,365 consumer records, with 209 data breaches during 2015, exposing 159,427,815 consumer records (**www.privacyrights.org/data-breach**). Watch for more detailed analyses as the various security reports are released later in the year. Some of our favorites are the Verizon *Data Breach Investigation Report*, Mandiant's *M-Trends*, and Symantec's *Internet Threat Report*.

Vulnerabilities in 2015. *VentureBeat* reported on the top-50 software products in order of distinct vulnerabilities in 2015. The "winner" was Apple for both Mac OS X and iOS. OS X was first in vulnerabilities, iOS was second, and Adobe Flash was third. For the Internet browsers (included in the same list), Internet Explorer was seventh, Chrome was eighth, Firefox ninth, and Safari twentieth. To be fair, it's partly how they group the data. The results come from CVE Details, which organize data provided by the National Vulnerability Database. The Common Vulnerabilities and Exposures (CVE) system keeps track of publicly known information security vulnerabilities and exposures.

The different versions of Apple's operating systems are all grouped together, whereas Windows is broken down by version. *SC Magazine* approached the data in a different fashion and reported some additional insights. No matter how you analyze the data for the mobile operating systems, Android (twentieth) had lower reported vulnerabilities compared to iOS (second). (**http://venturebeat.com/2015/12/31/software-with-the-most-vulnerabilities-in-2015-mac-os-x-ios-and-flash**) and (**www.scmagazine.com/researchers-at-malwarebytes-challenge-claims-of-os-x-frailty/article/464402**)

2016 Threat Predictions. Security service providers have been publishing their threat predictions for 2016, exploring what we should expect in the coming year. For example, the *Sophos Blog* has published the following cybersecurity predictions for 2016:

1. Android threats will become more than just headline-grabbers.
2. Will 2016 be the year iOS malware goes mainstream?
3. IoT platforms—not yet the weapon of choice for commercial malware authors—but businesses beware.
4. SMBs will become a bigger target for cybercriminals.

5. Data protection legislation changes will lead to increased fines for the unprepared.

6. VIP Spoofware is here to stay.

7. Ransomware momentum.

8. Social engineering is on the up.

9. Both bad and good guys will be more coordinated.

10. Commercial malware authors will continue to invest heavily.

11. Exploit kits will continue to dominate on the web.

These predictions, if they happen, will impact businesses and enterprises (including law firms and their clients) and individuals (including attorneys, law firm staff, individual clients, and employees and customers of clients). (**https://blogs.sophos.com/2015/12/11/our-cybersecurity-predictions-for-2016/#tip11**)

Intel Security (formerly McAfee) has published *Intel Security: A Five-Year Look Ahead* that includes its predictions for 2016 and beyond. It includes the following observations about the growing cyberattack surface:

> Five years ago, we thought that more users, more data, more devices, and more clouds were creating a perfect security storm of threats and vulnerabilities. Many of those predictions came true, but they were only the leading indicators of a much bigger storm, the acceleration of "more."

> On the work side, a dynamic workplace environment, highly mobile workforce, and rapidly changing workers' expectations have blurred the concept of a network perimeter. Workers no longer stay within the confines of a trusted network, or the restrictions of a specific device, making them more productive, but security more difficult. Over time, what we call perimeter inversion or outside-in happens: Applications and devices that were once directed primarily to the corporate network and data center are now directed primarily to the Internet and cloud, with the data center hosting limited processing and storage only for core intellectual property. The release and adoption of Microsoft Office 365 may be the tipping point that reorients the majority of us from PC-centric to cloud-centric storage. Security vendors will have to develop better protections for the growing variety of endpoint devices, the cloud storage and processing environments, and the communication channels that connect them all.

These observations indicate a continuation of trends that we have discussed and the continued growth of related threats. The report also discusses predictions in a number of specific areas, like hardware, ransomware, vulnerabilities, cloud services, cyber espionage, and hactivism. Attorneys and law firms are experiencing the "more" and should understand and address the related security threats. **(www.mcafee.com/us/ resources/reports/rp-threats-predictions-2016.pdf)**

Trend Micro has published *The Fine Line: 2016 Trend Micro Security Predictions*, which includes the following:

1. 2016 will be the Year of Online Extortion.
2. At least one consumer-grade smart device failure will be lethal in 2016.
3. China will drive mobile malware growth to 20M by the end of 2016; globally, mobile payment methods will be attacked.
4. Data breaches will be used to systematically destroy hacktivists' targets.
5. Despite the need for Data Protection Officers, less than 50% of organizations will have them by end of 2016.
6. Ad-blocking will shake up the advertising business model and kill malvertisements.
7. Cybercrime legislation will take a significant step towards becoming a truly global movement.

These predictions, if they occur, would impact both enterprises, including law firms, and consumers. They should be considered and appropriately addressed in updating information security programs.

As a final example, Symantec has published the following security predictions for the New Year:

1. The need for improved security on IoT cevices will become more pressing.
2. Opportunities for cybercriminals to compromise Apple devices will grow.
3. The battle between ransomware gangs and malware distribution networks will heat up.
4. Cyber attacks and data breaches will drive the need for cyber insurance.
5. Risk of serious attacks to critical infrastructure will increase.

6. The need for encryption escalates.

7. The tipping point for biometric security is approaching.

8. Security gamification and simulation will tackle the security aware-ness challenge.

As with the other predictions, these are potential developments that attorneys and law firms should consider and address to protect themselves and their clients. (**www.symantec.com/connect/blogs/ symantec-predictions-2016-looking-ahead**)

These are examples of threat predictions. Others are also available, with differing levels of detail.

Index